The Riddles of the Fourth Gospel

The Riddles of the Fourth Gospel

AN INTRODUCTION TO JOHN

Paul N. Anderson

Fortress Press
Minneapolis

THE RIDDLES OF THE FOURTH GOSPEL
An Introduction to John

Cover image: Henry Ossawa Tanner (1859–1937), *Nicodemus Visiting Christ*, 1899. Photo courtesy of the Pennsylvania Academy of Fine Arts, Philadelphia. Joseph E. Temple Fund.
Cover design: Paul Boehnke
Book design: PerfecType, Nashville, TN

Library of Congress Cataloging-in-Publication Data
Anderson, Paul N., 1956-
  The riddles of the fourth gospel : an introduction to John / Paul N. Anderson.
    p. cm.
  Includes bibliographical references and indexes.
  ISBN 978-0-8006-0427-1 (alk. paper)
  1. Bible. N.T. John—Criticism, interpretation, etc. 2. Riddles in the Bible. I. Title.
BS2615.52.A65 2011
226.5'06—dc22
                              2010049013

The paper used in this publication meets the minimum requirements of American National Standard for Information Sciences—Permanence of Paper for Printed Library Materials, ANSI Z329.48-1984.

Manufactured in the U.S.A.

To Dwight Moody Smith

Contents

Preface and Acknowledgments

This book is written for students of the Fourth Gospel—students on several levels. For those coming to the text for the first time, it is designed to pick up on things one notices in a first reading or two, but also the sorts of things one is forced to confront as familiarity grows. In that sense, it is also written for more seasoned students of the Fourth Gospel who have been seeking to understand and address its perplexing riddles for some time. Therefore, I am not content simply to list an overview of scholarly opinion without evaluating different approaches and arguing a thesis that poses a serviceable way forward. Rather, in this book I introduce a new set of paradigms in accessible ways, hoping to create conversations as well as report them.[1] Of course, very little in scholarship is new, although new configurations of compelling approaches sometimes come across as innovations.

No book is written in a vacuum, and I am greatly appreciative of the larger "Johannine Community" of scholars internationally, to whose work I am deeply indebted and for whose support I am deeply grateful. In particular, I am grateful to other scholars who have addressed the Johannine riddles before this work: in Britain to C. K. Barrett, Barnabas Lindars, and John Ashton, whose commentaries and other works on John provide helpful windows into the understanding and interpretation of the Fourth Gospel; in Germany, to Rudolf Bultmann, Rudolf Schnackenburg, and Martin Hengel, whose commentaries and other works engage the Johannine riddles and questions with unsurpassed intensity and acuity; in America, to Raymond Brown, Robert Kysar, and Alan Culpepper, whose commentaries and other works provide windows into the Johannine situation and its literary developments in genuinely serviceable ways. I build on the good work of others as well, but this book is a way of saying thank you to so many to whom my inquiry is deeply indebted.

I must also express my gratitude to the over five hundred colleagues from around the world who have attended or shown interest in the John, Jesus, and History Project at the annual meetings of the national Society of Biblical Literature, which I serve as a founding co-chair. The project is now in its ninth year, and in oral and written form, I think it is fair to say this is the most sustained and extensive collective investigation into the historical riddles of the Fourth Gospel in recent years, which may even have implications for the historical quest for Jesus in future years. To my fellow members on the steering committee, Tom Thatcher, Jaime Clark-Soles, Felix Just, SJ, Mary Coloe, PBVM, Alan Culpepper, Moody Smith, Catrin Williams, and Craig Koester, a big thank you is personally extended.

I also want to say thanks to the students we serve as teachers; it is often students' questions that force the scholar to dig deeper or to come at an issue again from a fresh angle. To my students at George Fox University (since 1989), at Yale Divinity School (1998–1999), and at the University of Mainz (2010) where I finished this book, I express my gratitude for the privilege of seeking the truth together along the lines of biblical inquiry. Students are often our best teachers! During my stay at Mainz, I had the opportunity to speak at several other universities, and the openness among students and colleagues alike to a new set of paradigms was most encouraging!

I must say a big thanks to Ruben Zimmermann, my gracious host at Mainz through the Deutscher Akademischer Austausch Dienst, and to Jan van der Watt at Nijmegen, Friedrich Avemarie at Marburg, and Folker Siegert at Münster, whose hospitality was greatly appreciated. Especially memorable was my visit to Marburg, where the students had been working all semester on various approaches to the Johannine riddles, culminating with Bultmann's paradigm and my engagements with it. To be able to have an informed and evaluative analysis of alternative ways of addressing the Johannine riddles by means of a Bi-Optic Hypothesis was a rare privilege indeed!

As I was conducting a bit of library sleuthing in the Mainz library a few days before my departure, I stumbled upon nearly thirty of Rudolf Bultmann's own books on John that had been donated to the Mainz library in 1950—the last year or two that Ernst Käsemann taught at Mainz. My guess is that he had something to do with their being given to Mainz just prior to Professor Bultmann's retirement in 1951. As I browsed through his books on John, I was impressed with how closely Bultmann had read the secondary literature of his day, as well as the biblical text! Many pages had underlining and notes in the margins—sometimes punctuating the page with a question mark or an exclamation point. At times, the master from Marburg would correct a grammatical error or a text citation (he was reading *very* closely), and he sometimes augmented a point with his own details. At other times, he would register his strong disagreement by writing in the margin, "*Falsch!*" What struck me is that he was also engaging the works of others, who had also been addressing the Johannine riddles before him, and in that sense, his work reflects a masterful synthesis of the intensive work that had been done a half-century or so before he produced his voluminous commentary in 1941. Because that's what other interpreters have also done, the present work is in good company.

This book builds upon my own books, *The Christology of the Fourth Gospel* (Anderson 1996) and *The Fourth Gospel and the Quest for Jesus* (Anderson 2006), as well as other works listed in the bibliography and appendix. My various theories and analytical treatments can be found elsewhere in further detail, but I want to acknowledge the use of several charts and outlines in the second book especially.[2]

In describing the "riddles" of the Fourth Gospel, however, let me first clarify that I am not describing what Tom Thatcher refers to as the provocative teachings of "Jesus the riddler," although such an analysis might also apply to John's Jesus (Thatcher 2006). Nor am I addressing Johannine rhetorical devices, which may include riddles, double entendres, parabolic speech, and other literary devices (see especially David Wead 1970). Those features are important, but they are not the central subject of this book. Rather, my focus is on the perplexing literary, histori-cal, and theological issues one runs into when taking the Gospel of John seriously. In that sense this book follows on the closing words of D. Moody Smith's foreword to *The Christology of the Fourth Gospel,* first published in 1996: "By putting old and important issues in a fresh perspective and attempting to apply new methods, Anderson stimulates us to reappraise our own solutions to the Johannine riddles. In doing so, he will have also set an agenda for his own career, if he undertakes to address all the counterquestions his proposals will doubtless engender" (Anderson 1996, x).

So, once again Moody Smith was right! Addressing the Johannine riddles has become something of a lifetime endeavor, and this book reflects a sustained effort to make sense of John's theological, historical, and literary perplexities within a larger new approach based upon the dialogical autonomy of the Fourth Gospel. In appreciation for his friendship and good work over the years as "the dean of American Johannine scholarship," this volume is dedicated to D. Moody Smith. Thanks, Moody, for your contributions and inspiration; let's keep thinking about those Johannine questions and counterquestions, and how to address them well.

Introduction

Navigating a Stream in which a Child Can Wade and an Elephant Can Swim

The Gospel according to John has been described as a stream in which a child can wade and an elephant can swim.[1] This imagery highlights an impressive fact: while the Fourth Gospel is widely considered the most reader friendly and accessible of nearly all biblical writings, it also continues to be one of the most perplexing of texts among serious interpreters. Why is that so?

Consider this: We see Christians flash "John 3:16" ("For God so loved the world . . .") at baseball games and on highway billboards, in a sincere effort to share the gospel. Mystics, within Christianity and beyond, have cited other Johannine (meaning "pertaining to John") passages as descriptive of people who have been drawn into a relationship with the divine in life-changing ways. The Gospel of John is often given to new Christians at evangelistic crusades and is used for discipleship training around the world. John is often called the "Gospel of Belief," the "Gospel of Life," and the "Gospel of Love." All of these are fitting titles to describe John's purpose and operation.[2]

On the other hand, there are few biblical subjects on which top scholars around the world disagree with each other more sharply, often diametrically, than those regarding matters Johannine. While the Fourth Gospel is the only Gospel claiming direct eyewitness origins, most scholars assume it is primarily theological rather than historical in its character. Given that scholars continue to debate John's origin and composition, its relation to the Synoptic Gospels (Matthew, Mark, and Luke, so called because they are similar to one another in ways they all differ from John), proximity to Jesus, historical setting, and theological meanings, these controversies make it hard to imagine any sort of scholarly consensus emerging about what is also called the "Enigmatic Gospel," the "Maverick Gospel," and the "Spiritual Gospel" (in contrast to the Synoptics).[3]

But *why* do different readers of John hold such differing perspectives about its origin and meaning? Is it like a Rorschach test, revealing more about the observer than the subject? I suppose any piece of classic literature can function that way—especially a religious one. A text becomes a classic because it speaks on many levels and in many directions. Then again, if the merits of any particular approach to John can be assessed, some agreement may yet be found—even among the experts. The goal of this book is thus to help both waders and swimmers navigate the living waters of this lively text more adequately.

Some readers of this book will know the Fourth Gospel well; others will be coming to the text for the first time. Whatever the case, I want to help all readers come to grips with some of John's enduring riddles, aided by understanding some of the most compelling ways of making sense of its glories and foibles. While the reader will be spared detailed bibliographic analyses of scholarly opinion on particular issues, some scholarly views must be noted in order to engage well the topic at hand. References to relevant passages in biblical texts, however, will be laid out clearly and generously so that readers can look things up for themselves and come to their own conclusions on important subjects.[4] Therefore, the reader is *encouraged actually to read the texts under discussion*; stimulating personal engagement with the Fourth Gospel is the most important purpose this book can serve.

We are not the first, however, to read the Gospel of John; others have found it meaningful and provocative for the last nineteen centuries as well. In the early church, the most enduring of theological debates over three centuries or more were largely caused by John's distinctive material—focusing in particular on John's Christology (theology about the person, nature, and role of Christ) and the relationships between the Father, the Son, and the Holy Spirit (the Trinity). In the modern era, some of the most pressing of historical-critical and literary-critical debates have focused upon John's origin, development, and relation to the Jesus of history. How, then, does one navigate such a stream, filled with many more rivulets and currents than are first noticed? This book suggests a variety of ways in which learning to swim and remembering how to wade might be linked—for novices and experts alike!

▓ On Wading with Children: The Gospel of John as an Entrée to Faith

Most readers approach a text interested in how it might speak to them. "Does the writer understand me and my situation?" the reader might ask. If so, the next question might be, "Does the content speak to my situation?" These questions are asked of editorials, technical manuals, philosophic treatises, and even poetry, but they are especially asked of narratives and stories. The Gospel of John is first and foremost a story, but it is a story with a set of theological claims. This means that the reader is drawn into the theological world of the writer and that the reader is invited to respond in faith to claims about Jesus within the text (see John 20:30-31). Put bluntly, the reader is invited into the realm of experience. As Robert Kysar has put so well, most religions emphasize seeking to replicate the experience of the founder, but not the Fourth Gospel; it advocates *experiencing the founder*!

Might this explain why the Johannine Gospel has had such a personal impact upon so many readers over the years? Rather than simply making claims *about* Jesus as the Jewish Messiah (anointed savior or deliverer), it invites people into a transformative encounter *with* the love of God as revealed in the mission and message of the prophet from Nazareth. The narrative begins, though, not just with a story set in history; it sets the stage within the cosmic origin of the universe. Even before time began, says the Prologue (1:1-18), God's creating-enlightening and saving-revealing actions were at work in the *Logos* (the divine Word; *logos* also has connotations of principle, thought, act), who became flesh in the ministry of Jesus. While some rejected him from the beginning—even his own—any who receive him, including, the Gospel suggests, present readers, receive the power to become the children of God, not born of creaturely origins, but born of God. Now *that* invitation is a powerfully inclusive one! It is also highly personal. It engages readers on the level of experience, and it invites them into a relationship with the divine, leading to transformative encounter and the promise of eternal life. In John's perspective, however, this life does not simply begin after we die; it involves abundant life, in the present, as well. The reader is not left on her own, however, as an individual in isolation. She is also drawn into community along with others who "have beheld his glory" (1:14). The characters in the story become exemplary patterns for later readers—showing the way forward, as well as exposing dead ends. Their positive responses to God's agents and witnesses (Moses, the Scriptures, John the Baptist, Jesus, the disciples) show readers the right ways to act and to be. Their negative responses, or lack of understanding, however, become warnings of pitfalls to avoid. In that sense, the narrative challenges readers not simply to come to faith for the first time, but also to abide in the faith and to remain in community instead of breaking fellowship with other believers. (As we shall see, different readings of John 20:31 in the earliest manuscripts allow both purposes.) Of course, matters of literary analysis move us already from wading with children to swimming with elephants.

▦ On Swimming with Elephants: The Fourth Gospel as a Puzzlement to Scholars

If scholars seek elaborate theories to explain the Fourth Gospel, it is because the Gospel confronts us with puzzles. Who wrote John, and what was he trying to accomplish? (Throughout the book, I will refer to the Fourth Gospel as "John," without presuming to identify its author or the author of the related Epistles of John. Issues of authorship will be addressed below.) Did the author have one goal only, or did he have multiple purposes? Why is John so different from the other Gospels? What do we do with the fact that the Gospel claims explicitly to have been authored by an eyewitness (21:23-24), while that claim appears to be made by another person apparently after the purported author's death? Further, the claim is that "*we* know his testimony is true," so who are "we"? Was John written by a committee? If the earliest manuscripts of John do not contain 7:53—8:11 (the woman caught in adultery), have other passages also been added to an earlier text?

How about questions of sequence? Mary is identified in John 11:2 as "the one who *anointed* the Lord with perfume and *wiped* his feet with her hair" (in the past tense), but that anointing does not take place until 12:1-8. In 16:5, Jesus claims that none of his disciples had been asking where he was going, but Peter had just asked a similar question in 13:36, echoed by Thomas in 14:5. Why does Jesus say "let us depart" in 14:31 and then continue speaking for three chapters before arriving at the garden in 18:1? Was this a sermon "in the alley" or a portrayal of Jesus giving one encore speech after another, with his hand fixed on the doorknob, delivering one lecture after another until his disciples could bear it no longer (16:12)? While John's text is largely a stylistic unity, these *aporias* (perplexities) weigh more heavily the more one reads it. These are just a few of John's *literary riddles*.

How about John's *historical riddles*? If the Jesus of history really spoke in parables, why is John the only Gospel without them? Likewise, if Jesus of Nazareth was involved in the casting out of demons, why does John's Jesus perform no exorcisms? If John's long I-am sayings were really spoken by Jesus, and if such miracles as the water-into-wine wonder and the raising of Lazarus from the dead really happened, why are they *not* included in the other Gospels?

Again, did Jesus minister for only a part of one year, or did his ministry span two or three years? John alone presents a multiyear ministry of Jesus in mentioning three Passovers (2:13; 6:4; 11:55). Did Jesus visit Jerusalem only once during his ministry (as portrayed in all three Synoptic Gospels), or do the four visits presented in John seem more plausible historically? John has more topographical detail and archaeologically attested data than all the Synoptic Gospels combined. Further, how should we adjudicate differences between John and the other Gospels? Is it really a matter of a three-against-one majority? Or if, as most biblical scholars rightly assume, Matthew and Luke built their texts upon Mark, is it largely a John-versus-Mark contest?

What about John's *theological riddles*? How could the eternal *Logos*, who was in the beginning with God and who was God, become flesh, weep at Lazarus's tomb, groan on the cross, and finally die a brutal physical death? John's presentation of Jesus as the Christ is both the most human and the most divine of any presentations in the entire Bible. What of the Son's relation to the Father? In John, Jesus declares, "I and the Father are one" (10:30), but he also declares that "the Father is greater than I" (14:28). Was Jesus equal to the Father or subordinate to him? Was the Holy Spirit sent by the Father (14:26) or the Son (15:26)? What should we make of the valuation of miracles in John? Jesus performs signs leading to belief (2:11; 20:31), but then he criticizes people for depending upon signs and for failing to see the "sign"-ificance of a miracle (4:48; 6:26). Jesus invites Thomas to touch his wounds, and then he declares the blessedness of those who have *not seen* and yet believe (20:27-29). Making sense of John's theological content has been a perennial challenge, but how should we approach that formidable task?

Simply pondering these and other issues forces the wader to become a swimmer! In truth, the issues scholars seek to address are most often the very things that waders also notice; they just seek to provide a fuller explanation for how the tensions came into being, laying out a road map for how to cover the territory. However, the road map is not the territory. Therefore, the best way forward is to move back and forth, between wading and swimming, grasping fuller understandings while returning to familiar meanings with fresh awareness and deeper levels of insight. If this book helps the reader to do that, it will have been well worth writing, and reading. At the outset, however, the reader is forewarned that a good deal of repetition will be employed with intentionality in this book (after all, it is *the Gospel of John* we're considering), hopefully without being redundant. Therefore, the above issues and others will be laid out several times within this book, attempting to bring new discussions to bear on familiar ground introduced earlier. The goal is serving the reader in a growing understanding of the issues, even if a bit of repetition is involved.

■ ■ ■

The outline of the book is as follows. Part 1 introduces the reader to the most perplexing of the Johannine riddles: theological, historical, and literary. Specific biblical texts are grouped together within each section, and the reader is invited to look up the texts in order to get a firsthand sense of the issues at stake and why differing approaches to John operate as they do. Part 2 engages approaches to the Johannine riddles, analyzing the strengths and weaknesses of traditional and critical approaches alike, finally suggesting a plausible way forward in navigating these issues. Part 3 leads the reader into an interpretation of John's content and theology, seeking to explore meanings that are both biblically sound and experientially adequate. Each chapter will conclude with a review of findings, leading into the next inquiry.

Questions at the end of each chapter help the reader go deeper into the material covered. New terms are defined briefly in the glossary at the end of the book. A select annotated bibliography is also included, suggesting the particular value of these works for those interested in further reading. A listing of my own relevant works points the reader to places where I develop more fully the components of the larger set of my theories that are presented more briefly or only summarized here. I have intended this book to operate on several levels, as an accessible introduction for the student while also proving instructive to the scholar. That may be an impossible task, but I have considered it worth the attempt.

Before continuing with Part 1, the reader is encouraged to read the entire Gospel of John in a translation that serves well the meaning of the Greek text (I will be quoting throughout from the New Revised Standard Version).[5] Whether a wader or a swimmer, the first task is to *jump in*!

Outlining the Johannine Riddles

The cover of this book features an artist's depiction of the conversation between Jesus and Nicodemus, a religious expert and a leader among the Jews. He declares what he knows: Jesus could not perform the signs he does unless he were sent from God (John 3:2). And yet he fails to understand what it means to be born "from above." The ways of the Spirit are like the uncontrollable wind—neither seen nor heard, but its effects are indeed felt (3:8). So it is with the mysterious ways of God, and those who claim to see often get it wrong (9:41). Did Nicodemus come around, though, later in the story? While he came to Jesus "by night" and initially failed to understand, he eventually stood up for Jesus in the face of opposition (7:50-51) and supplied the spices for Jesus' burial at the end of the story (19:39). Maybe he caught on after all; and, so might readers of the Fourth Gospel who may initially fail to understand its riddles. After all, the Gospel holds out the promise of being guided "into all the truth" (16:12) and holds that the truth is *always* liberating (8:32).

If you've now read John, either again or for the first time, you may wish to list or discuss the sorts of things you noticed. How did it speak to you personally—or did it? How did you feel? What did you think? In responding to these questions you are already becoming an interpreter.

Let's take these impressions further by raising more specific questions. How might this Gospel have spoken to its first audiences, individually and corporately, and how might they have responded to its message? Was it aimed primarily at Jewish audiences, or might Gentiles have also felt included in its address? What sort of literature is the Fourth Gospel, and does it have a plot? If so, how would one discern it? Or is John primarily a theological treatise upon which a narrative outline has been imposed? If it is historical, on the other hand, why is John so different from the Gospels of Matthew, Mark, and Luke?

What is the Johannine Gospel's relation to the three Johannine epistles? Were they written by the same author and in the same setting, or should they be kept apart for purposes of interpretation? Do you note any connections between the Fourth Gospel and the Acts of the Apostles, the writings of Paul, the letter to the Hebrews, or the book of Revelation? If any of these questions seem interesting to you, or if you've begun to raise a few of your own, you've already started to engage the riddles of the Fourth Gospel, and that's what Part 1 of this book does in greater detail.

In outlining the riddles of the Fourth Gospel, it is important to consider them together, including all three categories instead of only one or two of them. If one looks only at the theological riddles without taking literary and compositional matters into account, the contexts behind theological meanings will be missed. If one works on historical issues alone without appreciating the theological interests of the Gospel writer—often called the Evangelist—and his targeted audience, understanding the reasons for the Gospel of John's distinctive presentations of Jesus as the Christ will be lost in the analysis. Further, to really appreciate *why* traditional and critical scholars have approached John in the ways that they have, a basic appreciation of the issues they have sought to address is essential. Only after the theological, historical, and literary riddles of the Fourth Gospel are outlined can they be engaged, addressed, and interpreted meaningfully. So, that is the goal of Part 1.

The four chapters of Part 1 begin with an overview of the Gospel of John, advancing then with a chapter each on John's theological, historical, and literary riddles. Nicodemus apparently grew in his understanding as a result of his dialogue with Jesus; perhaps the same will happen for thoughtful readers of the Johannine text and their in-depth consideration of its riddles. So, let's begin with an overview of John's distinctive presentation of Jesus and his ministry.

An Overview of the Fourth Gospel

I n posing an overview of the Fourth Gospel, discerning the lay of the land will help. As the most distinctive among the four canonical Gospels, noting John's particular characteristics helps us focus on its contents in their own right. Therefore, the outline and flow of John's narrative, its material's distinctive features, and its intended purpose provides a fitting place to begin.

▧ Outlining John's Narrative

John's Gospel may be divided into four unequal parts: a shorter Prologue (1:1-18) and an Epilogue (21:1-25) and, between them, a more substantive "Book of Signs" (chaps. 1–12) and "Book of Glory" (chaps. 13–20). (These terms will be explained below.)

In contrast to the Gospel of Mark, which begins with the ministry of John the Baptist, or to Matthew and Luke, which begin with different wondrous birth narratives, John's Prologue features a worship hymn to the cosmic Word of God made flesh. Similar to other christological hymns (Phil. 2:5-11; Col. 1:15-20; Heb. 1:1-4), the Prologue of the Fourth Gospel exalts Jesus as the preexistent *Logos*, who was with God and was God from the beginning of time. God has now spoken through God's Son Jesus Christ, and the narrative tells how that came about.

The "Book of Signs," so called because it features the seven signs of Jesus,[1] then leads off with the witness of John the Baptist to Jesus and the calling of four disciples and Nathanael (1:19-51). The next eleven chapters (2–12) feature seven signs of Jesus (see Box 1.2, below), only two of which are also found in the Synoptics.

John's Jesus travels to and from Jerusalem at least four times. His prophetic sign in the Temple is presented at the beginning of his ministry, not at the end (as in the Synoptics), and he becomes involved in long, drawn-out debates with Jerusalem leaders in chapters 5 and 7–10. His culminative sign, the raising of Lazarus from the dead, becomes the occasion for Jewish leaders to seek to put him to death and to do away with Lazarus as well. The public ministry of Jesus closes with his prophecy-fulfilling entry to Jerusalem on a donkey's colt, Greeks coming to see Jesus, an affirming voice from heaven, Jesus' prediction about his death, and a final summary of his mission (12:12-50).

The "Book of Glory" (13:1—20:31), so called because it features the glorification of Jesus during the last week of his ministry (Brown 1970, 541–42), begins with the fulfillment of Jesus' "hour" and his imparting his last will and testament to his followers. In this section, the focus of the book changes radically from an apologetic endeavor to convince audiences to believe that Jesus is the Messiah/Christ to affirming their solidarity within community. Jesus washes his disciples' feet, beginning with Peter, and calls for them to follow his example and to serve one another. Jesus predicts both his denial by Peter and his betrayal by Judas. By contrast, "the disciple whom Jesus loved" is presented as leaning against the breast of Jesus, modeling the ideal relationship to the Lord (13:23-24). Jesus' commandment to love one another becomes the measure by which his followers will be known in the world, and his promise to send the Holy Spirit to be with and in his followers is declared with emphasis. The striking I-am sayings featured in the Book of Signs continue in the Book of Glory, as Jesus presents himself as the Way, the Truth, and the Life (14:6) and invites his followers to abide in him as the living branch abides in the true Vine (15:1-8). After his programmatic prayer, Jesus is arrested, tried, and crucified (chaps. 18–19). On the first day of the week, he appears to Mary Magdalene and other disciples (20:1-25). Jesus then appears to Thomas, who, despite not believing earlier, now climactically believes, confessing Jesus as "My Lord and my God!" (20:28). The closing words of this section actually seem like the closing words of the Gospel narrative, and they may originally have played such a role:

> Now Jesus did many other signs in the presence of his disciples, which are not written in this book. But these are written so that you may come to believe that Jesus is the Messiah, the Son of God, and that through believing you may have life in his name. (20:30-31)

Chapter 21 serves as an Epilogue, showing the disciples back at home in Galilee, having gone back to the familiar: fishing. They had not caught anything all night, but Jesus appears and instructs them to cast their net on the right side of the boat. When they haul it in, the great catch of fish numbers 153, counting only the big ones (21:1-11). There they enjoy breakfast with Jesus on the seashore, and Peter is interrogated by Jesus. Upon his threefold questioning, Jesus instructs Peter (and, by extension, all Christian leaders) to care for and feed the sheep (21:15-17). The deaths of Peter and the Beloved Disciple are foretold, and the final sentence of the Gospel echoes the final sentence of the Book of Glory: "But there are also many other things that Jesus did; if every one of them were written down, I suppose that the world itself could not contain the books that would be written."

Box 1.1 provides an outline of the Fourth Gospel in greater detail.

Box 1.1: The Gospel of John: An Outline

I. The Prologue (1:1-18)
   A. The Word, the Light, and the Darkness (1:1-4)
   B. The Advent of the Light and Its Reception (1:5-13)
      (Clarification: John Was Not the Light but a Witness to It; vv. 6-8)
   C. The Flesh-Becoming Word Making Manifest the Father (1:14-18)
      (John's Testimony to the Priority of the Word; v. 15)

II. The Book of Signs (1:19—12:50)
   A. The Testimony of the Baptist (1:19-34)
   B. The Calling of the Disciples (1:35-51)
   C. The First Sign in Galilee—the Wedding Feast (2:1-11)
   D. The Inaugural Demonstration in the Temple (2:12-25)
   E. Jesus' Dialogue with Nicodemus (3:1-21)
   F. The Interview with John the Baptist (3:22-36)
   G. Jesus and the Samaritan Woman—an Apostle to the Samaritans (4:1-45)
   H. The Second Sign in Galilee—the Healing from Afar (4:46-54)
   I. Jesus' First Sign in Jerusalem—the Healing of the Invalid; Controversy Ensues (5:1-47)
   J. The Feeding of the Multitude (6:1-15)
   K. The Sea-Crossing Wonder (6:16-21)
   L. The Discussion of the Feeding and Jesus as the Bread of Life (6:22-66)
   M. Peter's Confession (6:67-71)
   N. Jesus' Return to Jerusalem (7:1-13)
   O. Jesus' Address in the Temple and Ensuing Discussion (7:14—8:59)
      (Text insertion: The Woman Caught in Adultery; 7:53—8:11)
   P. Jesus' Second Sign in Judea—the Healing of the Man Born Blind (9:1-41)
   Q. Jesus as the Good Shepherd and the Gate to the Sheepfold—Controversy Continues (10:1-42)
   R. Jesus' Third Judean Sign—the Raising of Lazarus from the Dead (11:1-45)
   S. The Prophecy of Caiaphas the High Priest (11:46-57)
   T. The Anointing of Jesus' Feet by Mary of Bethany (12:1-8)
   U. Jesus' Entry of Jerusalem, Fulfilling Zachariah (12:9-19)
   V. The Visit of the Greeks and the Voice from Heaven (12:20-31)
   W. Jesus' Prediction of his Death and Description of His Missional Agency (12:32-50)

III. The Book of Glory (13:1—20:31)
    A. Jesus Washes His Disciples' Feet (13:1-17)
    B. Jesus' Prediction of His Betrayal and Peter's Denial (13:18-38)
    C. Jesus' First Farewell Discourse and the Promise of the Spirit (14:1-31)
    D. Jesus' Second Farewell Discourse and the Promise of Persecution (15:1-27)
    E. Jesus' Third Farewell Discourse and Promise of Joy and Peace (16:1-33)
    F. Jesus' Prayer for His Followers (17:1-26)
    G. The Arrest and Trials of Jesus (18:1—19:15)
    H. The Crucifixion, Death, and Burial of Jesus (19:16-42)
    I. Visits to the Tomb and Jesus' Appearances to His Followers (20:1-25)
    J. Jesus' Second Appearance to His Followers and the Belief of Thomas (20:26-29)
    K. The First Conclusion of the Gospel (20:30-31)

IV. The Epilogue (21:1-25)
    A. Jesus' Appearance to his Followers in Galilee and the Great Catch of Fish (21:1-14)
    B. Jesus' Dialogue with Peter and the Beloved Disciple (21:15-22)
    C. The Authorship of the Gospel and Its Final Conclusion (21:23-25)

■ Distinctive Features of the Fourth Gospel

In scanning the outline of the Gospel of John, several things become apparent. First, the introduction is presented in the form of a community worship confession: "We beheld his glory!"(1:14). This implies reflection on the impact of Jesus' ministry, and it suggests their attributing cosmic theological significance to the words and works of Jesus. A similar community confession introduces the first Johannine epistle, as one community seeks to draw others into that same experience and confession of faith which had been "seen and heard" from the beginning (1 John 1:1-3). The Prologue to the Gospel seeks to engage hearers and readers experientially in the story that follows.

While less distinctive in its literary form, chapter 21 provides a concluding testimony. It documents the third appearance of Jesus to his disciples after the resurrection, and it emphasizes the authentic witness of the author, attested by a group: "We know his testimony is true!"(21:24). Both the Prologue and the Epilogue reflect a corporate set of claims, introducing and affirming the core of the Gospel narrative.

A second thing to note is that the "Book of Signs" contains a very different presentation of Jesus' ministry over and against the largely unitary view presented in the Synoptics. Only two of Jesus' seven signs in this section (those found in John 6) are found in any of the other Gospels, and the first two signs are numbered. Further, the other three distinctive signs are all performed in Judea—in the South, whereas the miracles of the Synoptic Jesus take place almost entirely in the North. Most characteristic of this material in the Fourth Gospel is its combination of dramatic signs and ensuing developments of their meaning. Interestingly, the great catch of fish in chapter 21 is also found in Luke 5.

Box 1.2: The Signs of Jesus in John

- The first sign in Galilee: The water into wine (2:1-11)
- The second sign in Galilee: The healing of the royal official's son (4:46-54)
- The healing of the invalid by the pool (5:1-15)
- The feeding of the five thousand (6:1-15; also in Matt. 14:14-21; Mark 6:32-44; Luke 9:12-17)
- The sea crossing (6:16-21; also in Matt. 14:22-33 and Mark 6:45-53; not in Luke, although see Luke 8:22-25)
- The healing of the man born blind (9:1-41)
- The raising of Lazarus (11:1-45)
- The great catch of fish (21:1-11; also in Luke 5:1-11)

A third thing to notice is the way the signs in John lead directly into discussions about their significance, which then lead into discourses by Jesus about his identity and mission. The first two are the exceptions—people simply believe on the basis of Jesus' first and second signs. Jesus' two healings in Jerusalem, however, are performed on the Sabbath, resulting in belabored debates over his authority and relation to the Father. It even seems as though the extended debates in chapters 7 and 8 are over the same Sabbath healing narrated in chapter 5 (7:21-23). Most fascinating about these dialogues with Jesus in the Gospel of John is the way that those who hold authority as societal figures, or religious leaders, or imperial officials expose their ignorance as the discussions develop. Time and again, what starts out innocently enough as an inquiry about a simple detail (the significance of signs, drawing water from a well, Sabbath observance, the washing of feet, the authority of a governor) becomes a platform for launching an assault on false understandings of the ways of God, or, simply, of the truth. Irony is heavy in John, and as is often the case in narrative, lack of comprehension on the part of characters is in John always rhetorical. Consider these extended dialogues in John.

Box 1.3: Dialogues with Jesus in John

- Jesus and his first disciples (1:35-51; 4:27, 31-38; 9:1-7; 11:1-16; 14:1-31; 16:17-33)
- Jesus and Nicodemus (a leader among the Jews, 3:1-21)
- Jesus and the Samaritan woman (an apostle to the Samaritans, 4:1-42)
- Jesus and the royal official (4:46-54)
- Jesus and the invalid (5:5-15)
- Jesus and the religious leaders in Jerusalem I (5:16-47; 7:14—8:59)
- Jesus and the crowd, the Jewish leaders, the disciples and Peter (6:25-70)
- Jesus and the seeing blind man (9:35-41)
- Jesus and the sisters of Lazarus (11:17-45)

- Jesus and the Greeks and the Jerusalem crowd (12:20-36)
- Jesus and Peter (13:1-20; 21:15-23)
- Jesus and the high priest and the guard (18:19-24)
- Jesus and Pilate (18:28—19:16)
- Jesus and Mary Magdalene (20:11-18)
- Jesus and Thomas (20:24-29)

A fourth thing to notice is that following directly upon many of these dialogues, the narrator presents Jesus as launching into a discourse about his identity and/or his mission. If, in a dialogue, a character's misunderstanding exposes the "wrong answer" to a given issue, Jesus' discourses set the record straight. From the narrator's perspective, they lay out the "right answer" for an audience to heed. In Jesus' I-am sayings we have the most distinctive features of John's presentation of Jesus. Rather than speaking in short, pithy statements about the kingdom, John's Jesus speaks in long, drawn-out discourses about himself and his mission. Further, the Johannine Jesus sounds a lot like the Johannine narrator, so we must ask whether we really have the words of the historical Jesus here, or do we have more of a paraphrase, or a construction, crafted by the Evangelist? Addressing that question will come later, but note for now the *absolute* presentations of the I-am sayings of Jesus. Some of them seem to present Jesus as the appearance of God before the burning bush (Exod. 3:14), but some of them also function simply as a means of identification: "It is I."

Box 1.4: Absolute I-Am Sayings of Jesus in John

- "I am he!" (the Messiah—Jesus to the Samaritan woman, 4:26)
- "I am—fear not!" (during the sea crossing, 6:20)
- "Where I am you cannot come." (7:34, 36; 8:21)
- "You will die in your sins unless you believe that I am he [that is, he that is from above]." (8:24)
- "When you have lifted up the Son of Man, then you will realize that I am he [that is, the one declaring to the world what I have seen and heard from the Father who sent me]." (8:28)
- "Before Abraham was, I am!" (8:58)
- "I tell you this now, before it occurs, so that when it does occur, you may believe that I am he" (that is, your teacher and lord). (13:19)
- "I desire that they be with me, where I am." (17:24)
- "I am he!" (in response to the guards' statement that they are seeking Jesus of Nazareth; or is this a more absolute use of "I am"? 18:5, 6, 8)

The most weighty question emerging from Jesus' absolute I-am sayings in John is whether all of them, some of them, or none of them present him as the *theophany* (appearance of God) comparable to God's appearance to Moses in the burning bush in Exodus 3:14. The Greek words of the Septuagint translation of the Hebrew text are similar (in John, *egō eimi*; in Exodus, *egō eimi ho ōn*, "I am the one who is"). But these two words together can signify any number of meanings: the evoking of God's self-disclosure to Moses (translated in the King James Version as "I AM THAT I AM"—a theophany); "I am *he*" (the person being spoken of—an identification); "It is *I*" (announcing one's presence—a presentation); or "I *am from* here or there" (describing one's origin or place—location). At stake here is which of these statements might reflect an associating of Jesus with God (6:20 and 8:58 seem most clearly to do this), and whether any of these divine associations might in some way go back to Jesus instead of simply reflecting John's teachings about Jesus.

Interestingly, Mark's Jesus also declares "I am—fear not!" at the sea crossing (Mark 6:50); makes reference to God's "I-am" words to Moses before the burning bush, in disputation with the Sadducees (Mark 12:26); warns of false prophets who claim "I am [the Christ]"(Mark 13:6); and in response to the High Priest's question, "Are you the Messiah, the Son of the Blessed One?" Mark's Jesus declares, "*I am!* And you will see the Son of Man seated at the right hand of the Power, and coming with the clouds of heaven" (Mark 14:62). The point here is that while John's presentation of Jesus' absolute I-am sayings is distinctive, it is not unique. It is also found in similar, though different, forms in Mark.

The other uses of the I-am formula in John relate to the use of the predicate nominative: "I am *this* or *that*," declares the Johannine Jesus. From a theological perspective, Jesus is presented as fulfilling a typology; he is not simply *a* piece of bread, or *a* glimmer of light; he is *the* Bread of Life and *the* Light of the World. In that sense, each of these metaphors also serves a way of speaking about Jesus as the embodiment of the true Israel. John's Jesus is thus radically Jewish, in that he fulfills that of which Moses and the Prophets wrote (5:46). While there is nothing quite like these I-am sayings in the Synoptics, it cannot be claimed that the Jesus of the Synoptics never used such imagery in his speaking. Perhaps they represent a paraphrase of how the purveyors of this particular tradition told their story in their own terms.

Box 1.5: John's I-Am Sayings with the Predicate Nominative

- I am *the bread of life* (6:35, 41, 48, 51).
- I am *the light of the world* (8:12; see also 9:5).
- I am *the gate of the sheepfold* (10:7, 9).
- I am *the good shepherd* (10:11, 14).

- I am *the resurrection* and the *life* (11:25).
- I am *the way, the truth, and the life* (14:6).
- I am *the true vine* (15:1, 5).

A fifth thing to notice involves the presentation of women in John. While women are present in the other Gospels, they are especially featured in the Johannine narrative as being close to Jesus and participating in leadership roles. The mother of Jesus launches his public ministry, but she is also present at the cross. The woman at the well, Mary and Martha (sisters of Lazarus), and Mary Magdalene all play pivotal roles in the narrative. While the male disciples are nowhere to be found at the crucifixion, three women are present (all by the name of "Mary"), and the mother of Jesus becomes entrusted to the Beloved Disciple as a sign of ecclesial authority—a far different image than Jesus' words to Peter in Matthew about the "keys to the kingdom" (Matt 16:19). Martha makes a climactic christological confession in John (11:27), and Mary Magdalene is the first to recognize Jesus after the resurrection and announces to the disciples that she has "seen the Lord" (20:17-18). These are not minor roles; they are major, apostolic ones in so far as the women are "sent forth" with a commission.[2]

Box 1.6: Women in the Fourth Gospel

- The mother of Jesus is present at his first sign (2:1-11) and at the cross (19:25-26).
- The woman at the well becomes the apostle to the Samaritans (4:4-44).
- Mary and Martha feature centrally in the Lazarus narrative and the anointing of Jesus (11:1-45; 12:1-11).
- A woman in labor becomes an image of eschatological travail (16:20-21).
- A woman in the courtyard recognizes Peter (18:15-17).
- Women are present at the cross, and Jesus entrusts his mother to the Beloved Disciple (19:25-26).
- Mary Magdalene encounters first the risen Christ and becomes an apostle to the apostles (20:1-18).

A sixth thing to notice focuses on the Book of Glory (chaps. 13–20) and Jesus' last words with his disciples. Here we have the sense that Jesus' most important teachings to his followers are preserved as a pattern for them to follow in community life and in the world following his departure. Rather than instituting a rite of remembrance, Jesus in John 13 sets an example of servanthood by washing his disciples' feet. The *new commandment* given by Jesus to his followers is that they should love one another as he has loved them (13:34; 15:12). By the time 1 and 2 John were written (the first two Johannine Epistles), the injunction to love one another was regarded as "an old commandment" that they had heard from the beginning (1 John 2:7; 2 John 5-6).

Box 1.7: Love and the Commandments of Jesus

- "My new commandment is that you should love one another as I have loved you (13:34; 15:12).
- "By your love for one another will the world know that you are my disciples" (13:35).
- To love Jesus is to keep his commandments/word (14:15, 21, 23).
- Those who do not love Jesus do not keep his word (14:24).
- Those who love Jesus will be loved by the Father and the Son (14:21, 23).
- Jesus' following the Father's commandments reflects his love for the Father (14:31) and abiding in his love (15:10).
- Believers are invited to abide in Jesus' love (15:9).
- To keep Jesus' commandments is to abide in his love (15:10).
- No greater love is possible than laying down one's life for one's friends (15:13).
- Jesus' commandments are given that his followers might love one another (15:18).
- Jesus has made the name of the Father known to his followers in order that his love might be in them (17:26).
- To love Jesus is to feed his sheep (21:15-17).

A striking feature of Jesus' love command in the Johannine tradition is that it emphasizes loving one another as an expression of one's love for Jesus. First John takes this further and uses the love command as a means of restoring order to community life. How can one claim to love the unseen God if one does not love one's brothers and sisters within community (1 John 4:20)? The commandment of Jesus has now become the community rule: "Beloved, let us love one another."

Continuing with a focus on community life, the promise of the Holy Spirit—a seventh noteworthy feature—is central to this section (chaps. 14–16), and Jesus promises to lead his community through another Advocate or Comforter (both are possible translations of the Greek term *Paraklētos*, which is unique to John's Gospel and first Epistle), the Holy Spirit, the Spirit of Truth, who brings to remembrance his words and leads believers into all truth. This pouring out of the Holy Spirit is promised by Jesus in John 7:39. It will take place at his glorification, which is now impending. Within the narrative, the risen Lord speaks peace to his disciples, breathes on them, and declares, "Receive the Holy Spirit" (20:19-22). Here are the particular references that describe the Holy Spirit's work in John.

Box 1.8: The Promise of the *Paraklētos*—the Holy Spirit—in John

- Jesus promises to ask the Father for another *Paraklētos*, who will be with and in his followers for ever (14:16; cf. 1 John 2:1).
- The *Paraklētos* is the Spirit of Truth, whom the world cannot receive, because it neither sees him nor knows him; but believers know him, because he abides with them and will be in them (14:17).
- The *Paraklētos*, the Holy Spirit, whom the Father will send in Jesus' name, will teach believers everything, and remind them of all that Jesus has said to them (14:26).
- When the *Paraklētos* comes, whom Jesus will send from the Father, the Spirit of Truth who comes from the Father, he will testify on Jesus' behalf (15:26).
- Jesus must depart; otherwise the *Paraklētos* will not come; but if he goes, Jesus will send him to believers (16:7).
- When the Spirit of Truth comes, he will guide believers into all the truth; for he will not speak on his own, but will speak whatever he hears, and he will declare the things that are to come (16:13).

Jesus then closes this section with a programmatic prayer in John 17. Jesus prays that his followers will be protected in the world and that they will be one as a witness to the world. Knowing the Father is the source of life; this is what Jesus has come to effect. Other distinctive features of the Fourth Gospel abound, but these are some of the most significant ones worth considering at the outset.

■ The Central Structure of the Fourth Gospel

In thinking about the central structure of the Fourth Gospel, several passages have been favorites for discerning its core meaning. As well as considering the overall flow of the story, if there is a unit of material that describes the purpose and destination of John's narrative, reading the Gospel through that lens may contribute insights for interpretation. From the back to the front, here are some of the primary passages through which John's central thrust has been interpreted.

John 20:30-31—A Clear Statement of Purpose

As mentioned above, the Fourth Gospel concludes with one of the clearest statements of purpose anywhere in the Bible: these things are written in order that hearers and readers might believe that Jesus is "the Christ, the Son of God," and believing, have life in his name. This is a clearly apologetic function, and that will be reflected in the sort of narrative this is. The Fourth Gospel is not a math equation, nor a poem, nor a political history; it is a religious appeal to its audience, crafting the story in such a way as to evoke a response of faith on their part. It is a narrative designed to engage people in the story, aiming to convince them of its message.

Therefore, to believe in Jesus, according to the Fourth Gospel, involves coming to believe that he is sent from the Father and that he conveys God's message of love to the world authentically. In addition, to believe *in* Jesus is to participate with him relationally—to abide in him and to be indwelt by him through the Holy Spirit. This raises a question, however. Is coming to faith for the first time (one way of understanding what "believe" means in John) the same as abiding in Jesus and remaining in his community? Both of these themes, the apologetic and the pastoral, are present in John, and more will be said on these aspects of the Fourth Gospel's purpose later.

John 17:1-26—The Last Will and Testament of Jesus for the Church

The priestly prayer of Jesus in John 17 is the least original chapter in the entire Gospel of John. Put otherwise, many of its themes are also found in other parts of the Gospel; in that sense, it offers a fitting overview of some of John's leading themes and concerns. While God is the explicit audience of the prayer, hearers and readers in the audience are also drawn into the content by being given a sense of Jesus' central concerns. This is why Ernst Käsemann has called John 17 "the last will and testament" of Jesus for the church.[3]

First, Jesus speaks of the Father's and the Son's mutual *glorification*, praying, "Father, the hour has come; glorify your Son so that the Son may glorify you" (John 17:1). The Father has given the Son authority to give them eternal life, and true life is rooted in relationship—knowing the Father and the one he has sent. Jesus has come that people might *know the Father*, and thereby *have life* through the work that Jesus came to do. Second, Jesus prays for the *protection* of his followers in the world—that they will be in the world, but not of the world. Third, Jesus prays that his followers will be *sanctified—set apart in the truth* and kept in the power of his word. Fourth, Jesus prays that his followers *may be one* in order that the world may believe that he has been sent from the Father. Believers are invited into that same unity which the Son enjoyed with the Father since the beginning of time, and this unity is the love that constitutes the foundation of the earth.

John 3:31-36; 12:44-50—The Central Structure of John's Christology

According to William Loader, two paragraphs conveying the "central structure" of John's Christology[4] especially well are John 3:31-36 and 12:44-50. These passages are very similar in terms of content, but the first appears to follow on the witness of John the Baptist, while the latter features Jesus' closing words as he concludes his public ministry. While the question of whose voice is speaking here is interesting, either way the Fourth Evangelist's convictions come through clearly. These passages together thus pose a compelling outline of the Evangelist's understanding of Jesus' mission, providing also a sense of the thrust of the overall narrative. The following elements are clear in these passages.

Box 1.9: The Central Structure of John's Christology

- The One who comes from above testifies to what he has seen and heard from the Father; he does not speak his own words, only God's, yet the world does not receive his testimony.
- He came as a light into the world so that everyone who believes in him should not remain in darkness.
- Whoever believes in him believes not only in him but in the One who sent him, for he speaks the words of God authentically.
- Whoever accepts his testimony certifies that God is true; that one receives eternal life, but to reject him is to receive judgment on the last day, and that one must endure God's wrath.
- The One whom God has sent gives the Spirit without measure, and the Father loves the Son and has placed all things into his hands; his commandment is eternal life.

Within this central structure of John's Christology, Jesus' mission as the apostolic agent of the Father comes through clearly: the Son is sent from the Father as his representative ambassador. The Son does not do his own bidding, but only what he has seen and heard from the Father. As Peder Borgen has demonstrated,[5] this means that the agent is in all ways like the one who sent him, and to respond to the agent is to respond to the one who sent him. Therefore, while the Son conveys the Father's love, refusal to receive the Light is to incur judgment on oneself. The love of the Father also comes through clearly as the heart of Jesus' commissioned work, and this is the work the Spirit also furthers.

John 1:19-51—An Opening with a Purpose

No reader of John can ignore the ways that the first chapter captivates the reader's attention, conveying the evangelist's purpose and design. However, the opening to the Gospel actually comes to us in two sections: the Prologue (1:1-18), as a communal expression of worship to Christ, and the calling narrative (1:19-51), where disciples receive the invitation to "come and see"—extending that invitation also to the reader. Both sections are highly christological, and this sets the tone for the rest of the narrative to follow.

As in Mark 1:2-3, the Johannine Gospel narrative begins with John the Baptist heralding the ministry of Jesus as the voice of one crying in the wilderness, "Prepare the way of the Lord!" (Isa. 40:3; John 1:23). Very different from the Synoptic presentation, however, John here clearly denies that he is either the Christ, or Elijah, or "the prophet" (that is, Moses, John 1:20-21). Rather, John's witness in the Fourth Gospel is to emphasize that Jesus alone is the Messiah/Christ, and his whole reason for coming is to testify to Jesus' identity and mission. What John professes about Jesus' being "before" him in terms of status (1:30) the Prologue expands into cosmology (1:15→1:1-2; note, here and elsewhere I use an arrow to indicate the direction of influence). John (interestingly, he is not called "the Baptist" in this Gospel) therefore witnesses to Jesus in a striking way, declaring: "Behold, the Lamb of God that takes away the sin of the world!" (1:29, 36).

Another interesting difference between John and the Synoptics is that in John, Jesus is not presented as programmatically calling twelve disciples and naming them all; rather, two disciples who were followers of the Baptist are reported to have left him to become followers of Jesus. One of them, Andrew, went back and brought his brother Peter to Jesus, and the three are invited to "come and see"—an experiential invitation to encounter (1:39) as the basis for discipleship. They see where Jesus is staying and "abide" with him. Philip then finds Nathanael and brings him to Jesus (1:45-51), and with five followers (Nathanael is not listed among the twelve disciples in the Synoptics), now the story of Jesus' ministry gets a firm launching.

Significant here are the messianic references to Jesus in the opening narrative. Jesus is referred to as *Messias* (the Hebrew word for "anointed one"; the Greek word is *Christos*); Jesus is referred to as "the Lord," "the Lamb of God," and "the Son of God"; disciples call him *Rabbi* (meaning "teacher" or "master" in Hebrew); he is called "the one of whom Moses and the prophets wrote," "Jesus son of Joseph from Nazareth," "Son of God," and "King of Israel"; Jesus refers to himself as "the Son of Man." Scholars have called these references *christological titles,* and each of them is packed with rich theological meaning. The reader is thus invited to "come and see," like the first disciples, and also to "abide" with Jesus.

Box 1.10: Titles for Jesus in John 1:19-51

- One whom you do not know (1:26)
- The Lamb of God who takes away the sins of the world (1:29, 36)
- The One who baptizes in the Holy Spirit (1:33)
- The Son of God (1:34, 49)
- *Rabbi,* which means "teacher" (1:38, 49)
- The *Messias,* which means "Christ" (1:41)
- Him of whom Moses and the prophets wrote (1:45)
- Jesus son of Joseph from Nazareth (1:45)
- The King of Israel (1:49)
- The Son of Man (1:51)

While christological references to Jesus are developed elsewhere within the Johannine narrative, nowhere are so many different terms used within such a limited space as the opening chapter of the Fourth Gospel. The Prologue also has its own set of titles, and it likewise draws the reader into the meaning of the text experientially.

John 1:1-18—The Believers' Hymn to the Divine Logos

By far the most common text for assessing the destination and purpose of the Fourth Gospel, however, is the Prologue. If indeed John 1:1-18 reflects an intended introduction to what is to follow in the narrative text, getting a sense of the central thrust of the Prologue will rightly suggest the thrust of the Johannine Gospel.

If this is so, how do we assess the central thrust and meaning of the Prologue? One way is to consider literary and thematic clues. Rudolf Bultmann argued that the pivotal fulcrum of the Prologue is John 1:14a, "And the Word became *flesh*"—a reference to the incarnation. Bultmann's student, Ernst Käsemann, however, argued that the central pivot of the Prologue is 1:14c, "and we beheld his *glory*"—a reference to the supra-human divinity of Jesus.[6] Of course, both cases are arguable, and that is what contributes to the riddle of Jesus' humanity and divinity among John's theological tensions.

Then again, perhaps the thrust of the Prologue is not about Christology at all; perhaps it is about humanity's *response* to Jesus Christ as the Light, being welcomed to becoming children of God—a gift offered to all who believe in his name. This case was argued compellingly by Alan Culpepper, who used a *chiastic* literary analysis of the Prologue's structure as a means of getting at its central meaning.[7] By noting parallels between the beginning and end (A and A$_1$), the second and next-to-last feature (B and B$_1$), and so forth, one finally gets to the center—the pivotal fulcrum of the composition.

Box 1.11 The Chiastic Structure of John's Prologue

A	vv. 1-2		18 The word with God		A'
B	3		17 What came through the Word		B'
C		4-5	16 What was received from the Word		C'
D		6-8	15 John announces the Word		D'
E		9-10	14 The Word enters the world		E'
F		11	13 The Word and his own people		F'
G		12a	12c The Word is accepted		G'
H		12b	The Word's gift to those who accepted him		

In this case, Culpepper argues that the chiastic center of the Prologue is verse 12: "But to all who received him, who believed in his name, he gave power to become children of God." From that standpoint, the whole emphasis of the Prologue is the response of faith to Jesus as the Word and Light, to which all are invited as prospective children of God. This actually makes a good deal of sense, in that it resonates with John 20:31, chapter 17, and also 12:44-50 and 3:31-36. Even the christological imagery and action within the Johannine Prologue serves this missional purpose.

Box 1.12: Christological Titles and References in the Johannine Prologue

- The in-the-beginning Word (1:1, 14)
- God (1:1)
- The Light that overcomes darkness (1:4)
- The true Light that enlightens everyone (1:9)
- The flesh-becoming Word (1:14)
- The Father's only begotten Son (1:14, 18 in later manuscripts)
- The only-begotten God who is at the Father's side (1:14, 18, earlier manuscripts)

In both the Prologue and the rest of John 1, Jesus' agency as the One who is sent from the Father comes through clearly. The central structure of the Fourth Gospel features the divine-human dialogue in which God speaks to humanity through his Word, which is actually a person, Jesus, inviting the world to respond in faith to God's saving/revealing initiative. Those responding in faith are promised the gift of life, welcomed into the fellowship of God's children as members of the divine family. Nonetheless, the Evangelist attempts to explain the unbelieving world's rejecting of the Revealer as a factor of human self-confidence and of being closed off from the workings of God (3:13-21). Within that cosmic story, the audiences of the Fourth Gospel are engaged, and such is the rhetorical interest of John's story of Jesus.

■ Conclusion

In considering the central features of the Fourth Gospel, John's differences with the Synoptic Gospels become apparent. Beginning with a confessional *Logos* hymn, the Johannine Gospel sets a cosmic stage and then quickly brings the focus down to earth on the dusty roads of Palestine. Distinctive within the narrative are John's signs, five of which are unique to John, and also its I-am sayings and dialogues with Jesus. The central thrust of the Fourth Gospel calls its audiences to respond in faith to Jesus as the agency of God's saving/revealing love, promising eternal life for those who believe. Nonetheless, reports of inadequate responses to the Revealer are also noted, and explanations of such disappointments are also offered. Therefore, we find conjoined in this narrative a variety of literary, historical, and theological features, which we shall learn more about as we consider the Johannine riddles.

▣ Questions to Consider

1. How do the distinctive signs in John further its purpose as described in John 20:31?
2. How do the presentations of women and the Holy Spirit in the Fourth Gospel affect an understanding of leadership—in the early church and today?
3. In considering various approaches to the central structure of the Fourth Gospel, is there a single common theme that comes through as the center of John's theological thrust? If so, how would you describe that—in John's terms and in your own terms?

▣ Terms to Understand

- Book of Glory
- Book of Signs
- chiastic structure
- I-am sayings (absolute; with the predicate nominative)
- *Paraklētos*
- theophany

The Theological Riddles
of the Fourth Gospel

I n simply considering the thematic center of the Prologue, the theological riddles of the Fourth Gospel become apparent. Is the central emphasis of John 1:14 the Word becoming *flesh* (featuring the humanity of Jesus), or is it that we have beheld his *glory* (featuring the divinity of Christ)? Is Jesus one with the Father, or subordinate to the Father? After all, he claims, "The Father and I are one," but then he declares, "The Father is greater than I." So, even if one hopes to embrace the plain and direct meaning of the text, how does one decide *what* John's text is saying?

It is no exaggeration to say that the history of Christian theology would have been entirely different had it not been for the Gospel of John. Many a debate in the first four Ecumenical Councils (325, 381, 431, 451 c.e.), convened to find theological unity within a divided Christian empire, featured *both* sides of an argument citing the Fourth Gospel. Most notably, both Arius and Athanasius, leading theologians in the four century c.e., based their opposing convictions largely on material from the Gospel of John. Arius argued for a view of Jesus as the Christ who was not fully divine, privileging the primacy of the Father, based on John; Athanasius (whose position finally won the day) argued that Jesus and the Father were of the same "essence" (*homoousios*), also based on John (though the Greek term *homoousios* does not appear in John). This brings us directly to the theological riddles of the Fourth Gospel.

Of course, John's theological tensions extend beyond its Christology. We also find in John striking differences on virtually every important theme. How about salvation? On one hand, John is the most exclusive of biblical texts, claiming that no one comes to the Father except through Jesus as the Christ; on the other hand, John is the most inclusive and universalistic of biblical texts, claiming Christ as the Light who enlightens all humanity, inviting a response of faith. Can one embrace the saving-revealing work of Christ without knowing the history of Jesus of Nazareth? If so, why tell the story at all? Further, was John anti-Semitic? On one hand, "the Jews" reject Jesus and seek to put him to death with assistance from the Romans; on the other hand, Jesus declares, "salvation is *of the Jews*," and he is presented as the epitome of Jewish ideals. These and other theological riddles deserve consideration as we delve more deeply into the Johannine text.

But where did John's tensions originate, and what is their character? Was the Evangelist senile, repeating himself and reversing himself without noting issues of consistency? Does the text originate from several disparate literary sources or a singular tradition? Was John's narrative written by one person or several? Did a later, final editor modify a few things here and there, or did the same narrator adapt his story as the situation changed? Perhaps we simply have someone who just thought this way—dialectically, looking at things from one angle and then from another. Whatever the case, we must consider first the facts of the text before we can think about what John's theological riddles might imply.

▓ Jesus Christ: Human or Divine?

Was Jesus human or divine? Or, was he both? A common flaw of interpreters is that they tend to take one set of John's polarities without including the other side. The debate between Rudolf Bultmann and Ernst Käsemann on the pivotal fulcrum of the Prologue (and thus the central thrust of the rest of the Gospel) is a prime example (see chap. 1). More on that later; for now, consider these theological tensions regarding John's Christology. In this case and the others, feel free to take the time to look up verses on your own, and note any observations that come to mind.

Box 2.1: The Humanity and Divinity of Jesus

On one hand, Jesus' divinity is pronounced in John:

- ▓ The glory of Jesus is testified to from the beginning of the Gospel (1:14c; 2:11; 11:4; 14:13; 17:1) and his "glorification" is emphasized extensively (1:51; 3:14; 6:62; 8:28; 12:23, 34; 13:1).
- ▓ Jesus is equated with God in John 1:1-2 and 18 (in the earliest manuscripts) and is called "my Lord and my God" by Thomas in John 20:28. Likewise, the "I AM" of Exodus 3:14 is used to point to Jesus in John 8:58—a perceivedly blasphemous claim (see v. 59)—and Jesus' appearance on the lake is presented as a theophany (an appearance of God, 6:20).

■ Further, the divine certainty and sway of Jesus are featured (1:47-51; 2:24-25; 4:17-19; 5:41-42; 6:64; 13:1-3): Jesus knows full well what he will do and what is going to happen to him (6:6; 13:1, 3; 16:19, 30; 18:4; 19:28); his adversaries cannot arrest him unless his time has arrived (7:30; 8:20); and people experience themselves as being "known by the divine" in their encounters with Jesus (1:48; 4:19, 39; 5:6; 9:38; 10:4, 14, 27; 20:16; 21:7).

■ Jesus is presented as God striding over the earth in John.

On the other hand, Jesus' humanity is also unmistakable:

■ The incarnational "flesh" of Jesus is insisted upon in John (1:14a; 6:51, 53-56), and his humanity is acknowledged by others (1:45; 10:33; 18:5-7).

■ His human family references are clear (1:45; 2:1-12; 6:42; 19:19, 25-27), and not even his brothers believed in him (7:5).

■ Out of his side flow physical blood and water (19:34), and Thomas is allowed to touch Jesus' flesh wounds with his finger and hand (20:27). Further, Jesus weeps at Lazarus's tomb (11:35); his heart is deeply troubled (11:33; 12:27; 13:21); he groans (11:33, 38); on the cross he thirsts (19:28); and he loves his own (11:3, 5, 36; 13:1, 23, 34; 14:21; 15:9, 10, 12; 19:26; 20:2; 21:7, 20).

■ The fleshly, pathos-filled Jesus is also a reality in the Johannine text.

These texts reflect a great deal of unity and disunity in John's Christology, and these tensions have influenced the ways interpreters deal with the text. From a narrative standpoint alone, the humanity and divinity of Jesus move the story forward. First, readers are invited to behold his "glory" while also being urged to ingest his "flesh and blood" if they expect to participate with him in life eternal. Jesus' humanity and divinity also play themselves out within the narrative. Jesus not only knows what is in the hearts of people, he knows full well what he is going to do, and he does not allow himself to be captured until his "hour" has arrived. He also weeps at Lazarus's tomb, loves his own, and groans on the cross. These details show the most human side of Jesus in the New Testament as well as the most divine.

■ The Father-Son Relationship: Equal or Subordinate?

Is John's a christocentric theology or a theocentric Christology? New Testament scholar C. K. Barrett put the question sharply in those terms, arguing for the former.[1] The Son's work is important *because* he carries out the Father's work and glorifies the Father. Even the life that the Son has the authority to bestow on others is a factor of having received life from the Father. If John's is a theocentric Christology, however, the Father also glorifies the Son and has entrusted all things into his hands as the agent of God's saving/revealing work. Here the metaphysical presentations of the Father-Son relationship in the first four ecumenical councils run into problems. If believers are to be *one* with the Son as the Son is *one* with the Father, this fits better into an agency-of-commission category than a status-of-being category (17:11, 21). Believers thus share a oneness of agency rather than a metaphysical oneness of being with the Son. Then again, the divinity of Jesus is still asserted within the Father-Son relationship. "The Word was with God, and the Word was God" (1:1) seems pretty clear in terms of being—the church fathers and mothers attested that the Father and the Son are both of the same essence. But if this is so, why is the Father also greater than the Son?

Box 2.2: The Father-Son Relationship

On one hand,

- The Son is equal to the Father (1:18; 5:18; 10:29-30, 33, 38; 12:41; 14:10-11; 16:32; 17:5, 11, 21); "I and the Father are one," declares John's Jesus.
- The Father loves the Son and has placed all things in his hands (3:35; 5:20; 13:3; 16:15); the Son works just as the Father does (on the Sabbath, 5:17); the Father shows the Son all that he is doing and gives him the power to raise the dead (5:19-20, 25-26); all who honor the Son honor the Father (5:23), and the Father glorifies the Son (8:54; 17:1). To know the Father is to know the Son, and to know the Son is to know the Father (8:19; 14:7; 7:1-3); to hate the Son is to hate the Father (15:23-24).
- The Son gives life to whomever he chooses (5:21), and the Father testifies on the Son's behalf (8:16; literally, note the voice from heaven in 12:28).

On the other hand,

- The Son is also subordinate to the Father (5:19, 30; 7:16; 8:16, 28; 12:49; 14:10, 28) and declares, "The Father is greater than I."
- Jesus honors and glorifies the Father (8:49; 17:1) and does whatever the Father commands; he testifies to what he has seen and heard from the Father (3:32; 5:19, 36; 8:26-28, 38, 40; 10:18, 32; 12:49-50; 14:31; 15:15) as one sent from the Father (5:23, 36-37; 6:44, 57; 8:16, 18, 26, 42; 10:36; 12:49; 14:24; 17:21, 25; 20:21).
- The living Father has entrusted life to the Son (5:26), and the Son lives because of the Father (6:57).

So, which is greater—the Father or the Son? A tendency of modern interpreters is to see these as two disparate Christologies in John—one egalitarian, and the other subordinationist. Perhaps the editor has simply patched them together like a literary quiltwork. On the other hand, they still come to us as part of John's overall presentation of Jesus as the Christ, needing to be interpreted as part of a unified text however it came together. What the church theologians of the patristic era addressed in terms of Greek categories of being (the humanity/divinity of Jesus, etc.), modern scholars have sought to address by means of composition theories and historical-critical approaches to John's tradition development. More on that later.

While theories about John's composition will be addressed in Part 2, it is at least worth pondering how Christian theology might have developed if the benefit of modern critical analysis were to have informed their exegesis. We'll save some of those explorations, though, for Part 3. For now, the rhetorical emphasis is important to keep in mind: the reason the Father and Son are presented as being in relationship has to do with the agency of the Son. He is to be equated with the Father precisely because he is sent from the Father; to receive him is to receive the Father, but to reject him is to forfeit the approval of the One who sent him.

▧ Does the Son Judge: Yes or No?

A related but briefer issue is whether the Son judges or not. The answer to this question might not be very significant theologically, but the stark differences of claim are striking. On one hand, the Son judges no one; on the other hand, the Father has entrusted judgment to the Son. So, which is the authentic Johannine opinion? Is the Evangelist self-contradictory here, or might there be another explanation for this apparent theological tension?

Box 2.3: The Judgment of the Son

On one hand,

- ▧ Jesus came not to judge the world (3:17; 12:47), nor does he judge anyone (8:15), although humanity's response to the Revealer brings its own form of judgment (3:18-21; 12:48a).
- ▧ God is the judge (8:50), and the word Jesus has spoken will be experienced as judgment on the last day (12:48b).

On the other hand,

- ▧ The Father has entrusted judgment to the Son (5:22), and it is for judgment that Jesus has come to into the world (9:39); the Father and the Son judge together (8:16).
- ▧ Jesus judges authentically (in contrast to inauthentic judgments, 7:24; 8:15), and thus his judgments are just (5:30; 8:26).

Again, the Fourth Evangelist may be self-contradictory here, or he may simply be operating in a dialectical way—looking at things from one side and then from another. When we look at the particular passages in the light of "judgment" and its functions in John, several things come clear. First, while the Son did not come to be a judge, but to save the world from judgment by means of revealing God's love (3:16-17; 5:22-24), humanity's response to that gift brings its own judgment (3:18-19). Second, as the prophetic agency of the Father, Jesus' speaking the truth precipitates a crisis, as God's truth challenges the scaffolding upon which worldly approaches to life are built (1:9-13; 7:24; 8:16; 9:39). Therefore, truth ultimately threatens the world, and it creates an existential crisis: whether one will acknowledge the frailty of one's platforms (religious, political, social, personal, etc.) or whether one will seek the comfort of darkness lest one's contingent foundations be exposed by the light (3:18-21). Third, the authentic judgment of Jesus condemns the false condemnations of the ruler of this world (either Satan or Caesar, 12:31; 14:30; 16:11), and this work is continued through the convicting/convincing work of the Holy Spirit, who leads people into all truth (16:8-11). Finally, while the truth is indeed liberating (8:31-32), truth itself brings judgment, both now and at the end of the age.

From the perspective of eternity, one's response to the divine Word becomes its own form of judgment—both confirming and disconfirming. In these respects, whether or not the Son judges deserves to be understood as a factor of truth and revelation. Revelation always brings an existential crisis of judgment, which is both liberating and threatening, even when rooted in divine love.

▣ The Holy Spirit: Proceeding from the Father or the Son?

Another topic that has been historically important in the history of Christianity is whether the Spirit proceeds from the Father or the Son. Whereas the Council of Nicea (325 C.E.) made headway on Christology, the Council of Constantinople (381 C.E.) developed a theology of the Spirit and emphasized that the Holy Spirit proceeds from the Father. The Western church, however, centered in Rome, added the word *filioque* ("and from the Son") to the creed in 589 C.E. as a means of affirming that the Holy Spirit is sent by the Son as well as proceeding from the Father.

This view was anathematized (that is, condemned) by the Eastern church at the Council of Constantinople in 879–80 C.E., resulting in the eventual split between Roman Catholicism and Eastern Orthodoxy in 1054 C.E. The point is that both East and West are biblically correct; three passages in John (14:16, 26; 15:26) declare the Holy Spirit is sent or proceeds from the Father, while two passages in John emphasize that it is the Son who sends the Spirit (15:26; 16:7). While "being sent by" and "proceeding from" may have significantly different meanings from a metaphysical perspective, one can also understand why the Western church added the Son's sending of the Spirit to its creed. It is the Spirit of Christ who makes his will known to believers—according to the Fourth Gospel.

Box 2.4: The Procession and Sending of the Spirit

On one hand,

▨ Jesus declares that he will ask the Father to send the Holy Spirit (14:16), and he also declares that the Father will send the Holy Spirit in his name (14:26); as the Son proceeds from the Father, so does the Spirit (15:26).

On the other hand,

▨ Jesus also declares that he will send the Spirit from the Father (15:26), and he promises to send the *Paraklētos* after he departs (16:7); the Holy Spirit is the Spirit of Jesus as the Christ, who reminds believers of Jesus' teachings and who makes his will known (14:26; 16:13-15), testifying on Jesus' behalf (15:26).

As discussions about the Holy Trinity developed further, coming to a grand synthesis at the Council of Chalcedon in 451 c.e., discussions about the Holy Spirit and the Son also continued to develop. While the Fourth Gospel does not contain explicitly a doctrine of the Trinity, the development of Christian theology would be entirely different were it not for the Fourth Gospel. While Christ is considered the first Advocate (*Paraklētos* in Greek) in 1 John 2:1, Jesus promises in John 14:16 that the Father will send "*another* Advocate" to be with his followers forever. As the first Advocate, Jesus serves as a "defender" of those who happen to have sinned, delivering them from judgment; the second Advocate liberates believers as the Spirit of Truth. Perhaps learning more about the Johannine situation will also be instructive on this matter.

▨ The Signs of Jesus: If Embellished, Why Existentialized?

The presentation of Jesus' miracles is very different in John than it is in the Synoptics. Rather than being called "miracles" or "wonders" they are called "signs" (*sēmeia*) in John. So, what do Jesus' works "signify" in this rendering of his ministry? For one thing, they signify that Jesus is sent from the Father. Several passages make that connection—signs confirm that Jesus is sent from God (3:2; 9:16). This, however, leads to a gauntlet being thrown down by those who "test" Jesus—almost as Satan does in the wilderness temptation narratives of Matthew and Luke (Matt. 4:1-11; Luke 4:1-13). When people demand a sign in John, beware! They are exposed as unbelieving and not really open to revelation—that which the signs convey. This is confirmed by the facts that despite seeing signs some refuse to believe, and others, while valuing the signs, fail to see beyond them to that which they signify. This leads to the most distinctive feature of John's presentation of Jesus' signs—their embellishment *and* their diminishment.

Box 2.5: The Tensive Presentation of Jesus' Signs in John

On one hand,

- Jesus' signs lead people to believe in him (2:11, 23; 4:53; 6:2, 14; 11:15, 45, 48; 12:11, 18-19; 20:30-31), and John includes what is arguably the greatest of Jesus' miracles—the raising of Lazarus from the dead (11:1-45).
- Further, the performing of signs seems to confirm that Jesus has been sent from God (3:2; 7:31; 9:16; 10:41-42).

On the other hand,

- Dependence on signs is rebuked (4:48; 6:26), and belief *without* having seen Jesus' signs is considered "blessed" (20:29).
- Those presented as desiring a sign before believing are labeled as non-believing in John (2:18; 6:30), and some refuse to believe despite Jesus' signs (12:37).

Again, John's theological presentation of Jesus and his ministry is distinctive. In contrast to the Synoptic wonder attestations following Jesus' stilling the storm, "Who then is this, that even the wind and the sea obey him?" (Matt. 8:27; Mark 4:41; Luke 8:25), the disciples in John 6:15-21 simply receive him into the boat and arrive directly at the shore. More pointedly, as the valuation of the feeding miracle in all five accounts in the Synoptics is that the crowd "ate and were satisfied" (Matt. 14:20; 15:37; Mark 6:42; 8:8; Luke 9:17), Jesus rebukes the crowd in John 6:26 for seeking him not because they saw the signs, but because they *ate and were satisfied.* Is this departure from the Synoptic wonder attestations intentional in John, or merely a coincidence? Further, John's Jesus rebukes people for seeking a sign (4:48), and he declares, "Blessed are those who have not seen and yet believe" (20:29). Therefore, tensions exist not only within John's narrative but also between John and the Synoptic presentations of Jesus' miracles and their relation to faith.

■ Eschatology in John: Present or Future?

Another set of tensions in John relates to its present and future eschatology (*eschatos* in Greek means "last" or "final"); eschatology has to do with God's saving-revealing action in history *with finality.* The Fourth Gospel displays several sorts of eschatological tension. First, the "hour" is not yet come in some cases (2:4; 7:6, 8, 30; 8:20); then, dramatically, Jesus declares that the "hour" of his glorification has indeed arrived, alluding to his suffering and death (12:23-33) and his last days with his disciples (13:1). Second, while Jesus promises "rivers of living water" flowing from the inner being of the believer (7:37-38), the narrator clarifies that this had not yet happened "because Jesus was not yet glorified" (7:39).

A third time-tension in John involves judgment on the last day and the reward-ing of those who respond to the Son in faith (5:24, 29; 6:39, 40, 44, 54; 11:24; 12:48); and yet, in John 5:25 Jesus declares that "the hour is coming, and *is now here*, when the dead will hear the voice of the Son of God, and those who hear will live." On one hand, abundant life in Jesus begins here and now (5:24; 6:47; 10:10); on the other hand, those who believe will live into eternity (11:25-26).

A final topic for consideration regarding John's eschatological tensions involves the timing of spiritual realities regarding the existential challenges that Jesus' fol-lowers face. On one hand, Jesus tells his disciples that whatever they ask in his name he will do (14:14); on the other hand, the same promise appears to be delayed until "that day," some time in the future (16:23). Jesus promises to speak plainly about himself, not figuratively (16:25); yet he claimed earlier to have been speaking plainly about himself (10:24-25), and he certainly spoke plainly about Lazarus's condition (11:14). "On that day" will Jesus' disciples know that he is in the Father, and he in them and they in him (14:20), but does such a claim imply that their recognition is not fully actualized during the ministry of Jesus itself? The world hates Jesus' fol-lowers (15:19), and yet the hour is coming when Jesus' followers will be put out of the synagogues, and even to death, by those who think they are serving God (16:2). And, while Jesus has fully overcome the world (16:33) and the ruler of this world has been condemned already (16:11), he predicts the coming of "the ruler of this world" (14:30) and declares that he will be driven out (12:31). Like a woman in labor, Jesus' disciples face pain now, but they will be overcome with joy in the future (16:21-22).

Box 2.6: The Tension between Present and Future Eschatology

On one hand,

- In Jesus' ministry salvation, authentic worship, and the work of the Holy Spirit are pre-sented as here-and-now realities (1:33; 3:18a, 34; 4:21-24; 5:24, 28; 6:47, 63; 10:10; 15:3; 16:32; 20:20-22), and the "hour" of Jesus' glorification appears to have been already actualized (12:23, 27; 13:1; 17:1).
- Jesus' hour is coming and is now here (4:23; 5:25), as is the hour of his disciples (16:32). He invites all who are thirsty to come to him and drink, that rivers of living water might flow from the believer's heart (7:37-38).

On the other hand,

- The hour will come in the future when the dead will hear the voice of the Son of God (5:25, 28) and a double resurrection of salvation and condemnation is predicted (5:24, 29; 12:48), as those who believe will on the last day enjoy their final reward (6:39, 40, 44, 54; 11:24).
- Meantime, authentic worship and the outpouring of the Holy Spirit appear to still be in the future (4:21, 23; 7:39; 14:26), and the "hour" of Jesus' glorification is not yet come (2:4; 7:6, 8), thus preventing his arrest (7:30; 8:20).

The complexities of John's time-tensions are extensive, and composition theories attempt their resolution. If John's earlier tradition emphasized the here-and-now saving reality of Jesus' spiritual presence (realized eschatology), we might infer a developing hope in last-day realities as a later set of perspectives (futuristic eschatology). Rudolf Bultmann envisioned the final editor to have introduced futuristic themes to the Evangelist's present emphases, which Robert Kysar calls "the spoiler view." Then again, John's futuristic themes may have been earlier, with later material showing the fulfillment of what had been predicted earlier. Kysar calls this "the preserver view."[2] Either way, movement within John's tradition is one way modern scholars have tried to make sense of these tensions. Then again, were first-century Jewish and Christian thinkers always consistent in their eschatological views? The writings of Paul, the Dead Sea Scrolls, and Jewish apocalyptic literature reveal conflations of the "already" and the "not yet," so John's juxtapositions of these themes might be closer to the norm when compared to contemporary writings rather than an exception.

■ The Saving/Revealing Work of Christ: Universal or Particular?

One of the most pressing questions in the modern and postmodern eras is the question of salvation, or soteriology (*sōtēria* in Greek means "salvation") in the Fourth Gospel—is it particular or universal? Is salvation through Christ alone, or are there other paths that might lead up the mountain to God? If there are other ways to the Father, why did the Son have to come, and why did Jesus have to die? Interestingly, the Fourth Gospel is the greatest source of Christian particularity *and* universalism when it comes to salvation. Jesus is the Way, the Truth, and the Life; no one comes to the Father except by him (14:6). And yet, the Light that enlightens every person was coming into the world (1:9), inviting a salvific response of faith to all—whether they know the outward story of Jesus or not. How can the Light of Christ be accessible to every person, while Jesus is at the same time the only way to the Father? It might be one or the other, but how can it be both?

Box 2.7: Jesus as the Way, the Truth, and the Life, and the Light

On one hand,

- ■ The true Light that enlightens everyone is Jesus (1:9), suggesting *universal access* to God's saving work; and Jesus has many sheep that are "not of this fold" (10:16).

And yet,

- ■ Jesus is the Way, the Truth, and the Life, without whom no one comes to the Father who does so (14:6); and believing in him affords eternal life (3:16; 20:31).

Again, our Evangelist could simply be self-contradictory, or there may be another explanation to this extremely important set of tensions. The way forward in understanding both of these claims is first to ask *why* they are being made. What is being claimed in asserting that all who come to God do so through Jesus, and what is claimed in asserting that all have access to the illuminating work of the eternal Christ? Is the first claim a *prescriptive* statement (all people must . . .), or is it a *descriptive* one (this is how it happens for all . . .)? If the latter is the case, might this affect our understanding of what is being claimed? And, while all might have access to the saving Light of Christ, this is not the same as claiming that all respond equally well to it. Therefore, if the only hope for humanity is God's saving initiative, which Jesus Christ—the Way, the Truth, the Life, *and* the Light—eschatologically was and is, the difference is not that of one religion over another, but one of *revelation over religion*. Might the issue pivot on the insufficiency of human initiative, which religion represents, and the all-sufficiency of the divine initiative, which Jesus embodies?

■ Salvation and the Believer: Determinism or Free Will?

A related subject is John's apparent determinism, which is also accompanied by clear references to free will. Jesus is presented as knowing not only what is in the hearts of humans but also who will receive him and reject him. However, if this is so, why does John emphasize the priority of the human response to the divine initiative, and why does Jesus teach and minister as though it might make a difference? While the Light is accessible to all, not all receive the Light, yet as many as do so receive also the power to become the children of God (1:9-12). One set of texts most commonly yoked into the service of theologies of predestination is John 6:44 and 6:64-65. Here Jesus declares that no one *can* come to him except they be drawn by the Father and except it be given by the Father, commenting on Jesus' knowing from the beginning who would believe and who would betray him.

Box 2.8: Determinism and Free Will in John

On one hand,

■ Jesus knows all people, including who will receive and reject him (2:24-25; 5:42; 6:64, 71; 10:27; 13:11; 16:19), and no one can come to the Father without being drawn by God (6:44, 65).

And yet,

■ As many as believe in Jesus are given the right to become the children of God (1:12), whosoever believes in Jesus receives eternal life (3:14-17), and John is written that all readers and hearers might believe (20:31).

The emphasis upon Jesus' knowledge, however, does not imply that humans have no choice in their response to the gospel. Indeed, any who respond in faith to God's gift of grace through Christ receive eternal life, and Jesus came that the world might believe (3:16-17). Further, the emphasis is upon human incapacity to come to Christ except being drawn by the Father as a gift, which is supposedly available to all. Like the question of salvation, the point is not divine permissibility; it is the insufficiency of the human initiative in apprehending and responding to the Revealer in faith. No one has seen God at any time (1:18; 5:37; 6:46); without God's self-disclosure, human contrivances are of no avail. Therefore, the tension in John is not between determinism and free will; it is between human willingness to respond in faith to the divine initiative, which alone is the way to God, versus the temptation to rely on platforms of human initiative. Revelation, thus, is ever a scandal to religion.

▓ Dualism in John: Prescriptive or Reflective?

Johannine dualism carries its own set of perplexities and puzzlements. Not only does John's dualism pose a striking set of polar opposites—light/darkness, life/death, good/evil, from above/from below, heaven/earth, heavenly/earthly, spirit/flesh, disciples/the world, belief/unbelief, hearing/not hearing, seeing/not seeing, knowing/not knowing, day/night, true/false, right/wrong, saved/lost, Israelites/Jerusalemites, the Judeans (believing)/the Judeans (unbelieving), of divine origin/of creaturely origin, God or the Father/Satan (or the devil or the evil one or the ruler of this world)—but the functions of that dualism also appear to be at odds. On one hand, some dualistic features appear simply to state the way things are and where they are headed. Some people operate in spiritual ways, headed for life; others operate in worldly ways, headed for death. On the other hand, other dualistic features seem to explain the responses of individuals and groups to the Revealer—those who receive Jesus' words and works as being from God show evidence of having been rooted in knowledge of the Father; rejections of the Revealer are explained as factors of not being rooted in the reality from above and not knowing the Father.

Box 2.9: Johannine Dualism—Prescriptive or Reflective?

On one hand,

- ▓ Soteriological realities are highlighted dualistically: God desires life (1:14; 3:15, 16, 36; 4:14, 36; 5:21, 24, 26, 29, 39, 40; 6:27, 33, 35, 40, 47, 48, 51, 54, 63, 68; 8:12; 10:10, 11, 15, 17, 28; 11:25; 12:25, 50; 13:37, 38; 14:6; 15:13; 17:2, 3; 20:31) over death (5:24; 6:49, 50, 53, 58; 8:21, 24, 51, 52; 11:25, 26, 50, 51).

- Jesus desires that none be lost (6:12, 39; 17:12; 18:9), but that all might be saved (3:17; 5:34; 10:9; 12:47).
- God's saving initiative is described in terms of light (1:4, 5, 7, 8, 9; 3:19, 20, 21; 5:35; 8:12; 9:5; 11:9, 12; 12:35, 36, 46), which overcomes darkness (1:5; 3:19; 8:12; 12:35, 46).
- God's loving means of redeeming the world are like living and life-producing water and bread (4:10; 6:27, 51, 57; 7:38) versus death-producing alternatives (6:27, 49, 53, 58; 8:21, 24).
- The way of the Spirit brings life (1:33; 3:6, 34; 4:24; 6:63; 7:39; 14:17, 26; 15:26; 16:13; 20:22), but the flesh profits nothing (1:13; 3:6; 6:63).

On the other hand,

- Dualism serves as an explanation of the world's response to the Revealer: many do not believe (3:12, 18; 4:48; 5:38, 47; 6:36, 64; 8:45, 46; 9:18; 10:25, 26, 38; 12:37, 39; 14:10; 16:9; 20:25).
- Nathanael is a "true Israelite" in whom there is nothing false (1:47), and salvation is "of the Jews" (4:22), and yet the Jewish leaders reject Jesus and seek to kill him (5:18; 7:1; 8:59; 10:31; 11:53—as a fulfillment of Isa. 6:9-10 and 53:1)—therefore, people see but do not perceive (9:39) and listen but do not hear (8:47).
- Responses to Jesus illustrate the incapacity of humanity to know or understand the ways and workings of God (1:10, 26, 31, 33; 2:9; 3:8; 4:22, 32; 5:13; 7:28, 49; 8:14, 55; 9:12, 21, 25, 29, 30; 10:5; 12:35; 13:7; 14:5, 9; 15:15, 21; 16:18; 17:25; 19:10; 20:2, 13, 14; 21:4); people's not knowing God is described as the reason for their not believing in Jesus (1:10; 7:28, 49; 9:29; 12:35; 15:21; 17:25).
- People do not have God's word abiding in them because they do not believe in the One whom God has sent (5:38); Jesus' sheep, however, recognize his voice (10:3-4, 16, 27).
- Some do not believe because they are not among Jesus' sheep (10:26).

Accounting for John's dualism requires understanding its religious background. Before the discovery of the Dead Sea Scrolls in 1947, it was assumed that Judaism was pervasively monistic (meaning that there is one power in the heavens—God). Because Greek cosmology was dualistic, it was assumed that John's dualism must have been Hellenistic rather than Jewish. This led scholars to assume that the Johannine tradition was Greek, but this has changed since the mid-twentieth century. Like the Qumran *Community Rule*, John's ethical dualism is highly motivational. But John's dualism also explains a variety of disappointments.

First, it explains why some responded to the Revealer as they did. Those who received Jesus as the Christ were rooted in God; those who did not were not. This accounts for an uneven history of reception, and it clearly betrays the theological reflection of the Evangelist. Second, it outlines starkly a value-laden set of options—to choose love, life, truth, and glory is to be preferred over lesser (and polar-opposite) alternatives. Third, John's dualism becomes a means of presenting reality in such a way as to provide continuing reinforcement of the community's values—motivating group solidarity and adherence to the truth as it is understood in Johannine perspective. Biblical references are drawn in to support both descriptive and prescriptive functions of John's dualism. In that sense, John's dualism is highly sociological and theological in its function; it establishes the ethos of the religious community and seeks to inculcate its values in the lives of others.

John and Judaism: Anti-Semitic or Pro-Jewish?

Is the Fourth Gospel anti-Semitic or pro-Jewish? John appears at once to be the most pro- and anti-Jewish text in the New Testament, but the question is whether the tensions were over race, religion, power, history, or some other issue. While *hoi Ioudaioi* (translated either as "the Jews" or as "the Judeans") are offended by Jesus' teaching, scandalized by his healings on the Sabbath, threatened by his miracles and their popular effects, protective of their religious investments, and resistant to new ways of seeing God's work in the world, they also believe in Jesus as the Messiah, and he himself fulfills Jewish biblical prophecies and typologies. Moreover, the Fourth Gospel was written by a Jew seeking to convince Jewish audiences that Jesus was indeed the Jewish Messiah. Therefore, the *Ioudaioi* in John are presented in both positive and negative ways.

Box 2.10: The *Ioudaioi* in the Fourth Gospel

On one hand,

- The *Ioudaioi* are presented as adversaries of Jesus (5:16, 18; 7:1, 11, 13; 8:48, 52, 57; 9:18, 22; 10:31, 33; 11:8; 18:31, 36, 38; 19:7, 12, 14, 38; 20:19).
- They are portrayed as types of the disbelieving "world" (3:19; 7:7; 15:18, 19; 16:8; 17:14, 15) who reject Jesus and his ministry.
- The *Ioudaioi* seek to kill Jesus after his miracles in Jerusalem and Bethany (5:18; 7:1, 19-20, 25; 8:37, 40, 59; 10:31-33; 11:8, 53); the chief priests and Pharisees command residents to confess Jesus' whereabouts that they might arrest him (11:57); the crowd and the Jews in Jerusalem accuse Jesus of being demon possessed (7:20; 8:48, 52; 10:20); and Jesus declares the father of the *Ioudaioi* to be the devil, "a murderer from the beginning" and "a liar and the father of lies" (8:44).
- Open followers of Jesus are reported to be excluded from the synagogue both earlier and later (9:22; 12:42; 16:2).

On the other hand,

- The *Ioudaioi* are presented simply as religious leaders (3:1; 18:14—parallel to the Jewish *archoi* [in Greek, "rulers" or "leaders"; 7:26, 48; 12:42]), or simply as inhabitants of southern Palestine—Judea (11:19, 31, 33; 11:54; 12:9, 11; 13:33; 19:20) or Jerusalem (1:19; 2:18, 20; 5:10, 15; 19:31).
- The *Ioudaioi* are also equated with "the world" as the object of God's love and the redemptive mission of Jesus (1:9, 29; 3:16, 17; 4:42; 6:14, 33, 51; 7:4; 8:12, 26; 9:5, 39; 10:36; 11:9, 27; 12:46, 47; 16:28; 17:6, 18, 21, 23; 18:20, 37), and in the I-am sayings and the Son of Man references Jesus fulfills major typologies of biblical Israel.

▓ While some were presented as being divided over Jesus (6:41, 52; 7:35; 8:22; 10:19, 24), many of the *Ioudaioi* are presented as believing in Jesus (7:15, 31; 8:31; 10:42; 11:36, 45; 12:19, 42).

▓ Jesus himself declares that "salvation is of the *Ioudaioi*" (4:22); he is attested as the quintessential Jewish Messiah, fulfilling the typologies of Moses and Elijah.

Because the Fourth Gospel was written by a Jew about a Jewish Messiah, however, charges of anti-Semitism are problematic. It is like saying that because the *War Scroll* of the Qumran community defined its members as the "children of light" versus the Jerusalem priesthood as the "children of darkness" that the Dead Sea Scrolls are anti-Semitic. Further, John's central conviction is that Jesus is the *Jewish* Messiah, citing multiple Jewish Scriptures confirming such a connection. Given that *Ioudaioi* most directly means "Judeans" (not simply "Jews"), the rejection of the Galilean prophet was a factor of long-standing tensions between southern Judeans and northern Israelites—let alone the reluctance of Jerusalem-centered religious leaders to grant authority to small-town messianic pretenders. Therefore, while the Fourth Gospel might have contributed to anti-Semitism within Western history, are such interpretations exegetically solid or are they flawed from day one?

One final note is important here. The asides in John 9:22; 12:42; 16:2, mentioning that open followers of Jesus were excluded from the synagogue even "back then," seem to imply that followers of Jesus were also facing hardship within local Jewish communities at the time the Fourth Gospel was being composed. Within an Asia Minor setting (or elsewhere beyond Palestine), "the Jews" in the Johannine narrative came to represent leaders of the local synagogue whom the Evangelist was trying to reach, albeit with partial success. As the Christologies held by Johannine believers grew higher, full synagogue participation became complicated, plausibly leading to charges of ditheism (having two gods) and their consequences. These later sets of religious tensions provide a backdrop for better understanding the ambivalent presentation of the *Ioudaioi* in the Fourth Gospel. More on this later.

▓ Sacraments in John: Embellished or Deconstructive?

John's sacramentology (understanding of the outward, visible signs of God's grace, such as baptism or communion), is another of those perplexing yet important subjects—is it embellished or deconstructive? On one hand, sacramental associative details are rife within the Fourth Gospel: the role of John the Baptist is even more prominent in John than it is in the other Gospels; being born of "water and the Spirit" is essential for entering the kingdom; believers must eat and drink the flesh and blood of Jesus; Mary (sister of Lazarus) anoints Jesus' feet, and he washes the disciples' feet; water and blood flow from Jesus' side on the cross; and after the resurrection, the risen Lord shares a sacramental meal of bread and fish on the seashore. Nonetheless, if all we had was the Gospel of John, there would be no biblical basis for baptism and communion, or other sacramental forms, in the life of the church. Every time John the Baptist is mentioned alongside Jesus, the emphasis is upon the primacy of Jesus' baptism with the Holy Spirit over and against John's having baptized with water. Further, while it is stated that Jesus and his disciples were baptizing in 3:22 and 4:1, the narrator clarifies in 4:2 that while Jesus' disciples baptized people, Jesus did not. Does this imply a historical correction or a deconstructive slant? Is it an editor's clarification? Most puzzling is the fact that the institution of a meal of remembrance is totally missing from the Last Supper in John. Disciples are invited to eat and drink the flesh and blood of Jesus after the feeding of the five thousand, but if the Evangelist really wanted to insist upon the Eucharist, why not include it at the Last Supper? Rather, if the "bread" Jesus gives is a reference to his flesh being given for the life of the world on the cross (6:51), the invitation is to martyrdom, not a cultic meal.

Box 2.11: John's Sacramentology—Anti- or Pro-Sacramentalist?

On one hand,

- John the Baptist features prominently in John (1:6-8, 15, 19-36; 3:22-30; 10:40-42); Jesus and his disciples are presented as baptizing (3:22); the first sign of Jesus is to produce wine at the wedding (2:1-11); being born of "water and the Spirit" are requisites for entry into the kingdom (3:5); and water and blood flow out of Jesus' side (19:34).
- Eating the flesh and drinking the blood of Jesus are required in order to receive eternal life (6:53-58); Jesus shares table fellowship several times with his disciples (2:1-11; 6:1-15; 13:1-34; 21:9-14); and abiding in him is like the fruit-producing branches connected to the vine (15:1-8).
- In the Fourth Gospel sacramental associations abound.

On the other hand,

- Jesus is greater than John the Baptist (1:6-8, 15, 19-36; 3:22-30); to receive spiritual birth is to be born from above (3:3); and while Jesus' disciples may have baptized, he himself did not (4:2).
- The words of the institution are missing from the Last Supper in John 13, and the "bread" that Jesus gives is his flesh, given for the life of the world on the cross (6:51).
- Perhaps the Fourth Evangelist was an anti-sacramentalist, who sought to dismiss all outward worship forms with the statement "the flesh profits nothing" (6:63).

If John's author was indeed an eyewitness who leaned against Jesus' breast, how could he not include Jesus' main intention at the Last Supper (according to the Synoptics): the setting-up of a meal of remembrance? And, why would an emphasis be made on Jesus' *not* having baptized? Rudolf Bultmann argues that the Evangelist was an anti-sacramentalist, and he interprets John 6:51c-58; 19:34-35; 21:1-25 and other passages (including "water and" in 3:5) as pro-sacramental additions by the redactor. Bultmann's point is a good one, especially if John 6:53 refers to the Eucharist as a requirement for salvation: "*unless* you eat the flesh of the Son of Man and drink his blood, you have no life in you." If John 6:53 implies the necessity of a cultic Eucharist for salvation, this displaces the all-sufficiency of Christ for the salvation of the world (14:6). Especially against a text that claims Jesus is the only way to the Father, the inference of cultic requirements for salvation to be realized is not simply a tension; it is a flat-out contradiction.[3]

▨ The Church in John: Petrified or Dynamic?

A final theological riddle of the Fourth Gospel involves John's ecclesiology (*ekklēsia* means "church")—is it hierarchical or egalitarian? If Peter came to represent hierarchical leadership in the early church (he receives the "keys to the kingdom" from Jesus after his confession in Matthew 16:17-19), how is he portrayed in John? He still comes across as the leader among the apostles, although when paired with the Beloved Disciple, it is the latter who always gets it right. Nonetheless, Peter makes a confession in John 6:68-69, similar to (though quite different from) his leadership role in the Synoptics. And Peter is given the chance to affirm his loyalty to Jesus three times around a charcoal fire (21:15-17), having denied him thrice around a charcoal fire earlier (18:18). So, one could argue that John (like Matthew) affirms Peter's leadership among the Twelve, thus supporting the Petrine apostolic leadership.

On the other hand, in Peter's primary dialogues with Jesus (6:66-71; 13:6-17; 21:15-22) he is presented as misunderstanding Jesus at every turn. Misunderstanding in narrative is always rhetorical (see Box 4.9 and Chapter 6, pp. 150–52). Also, when paired with the Beloved Disciple, the Beloved Disciple *always* gets it right, and his presentation models intimacy with the Lord and faithfulness at the cross. Rather than the "rock" and "keys" as images of the church in Matthew, John's Jesus uses more fluid ones, such as sheep and shepherd (10:1-18) and vine and branches imagery (15:1-17) as more organic metaphors for the church. In addition to Peter's uttering a confession of faith, so does Nathanael (not one of the Twelve, 1:49) and Martha (a woman, 11:27). Jesus *does* entrust something to a disciple, but it is his mother, at the cross (19:26-27)—a relational and familial image of church authority rather than instrumental keys. Further, the risen Lord in John promises to lead believers by means of the Holy Spirit, who will abide in and with his followers. Therefore, the Spirit is accessible to all believers, according to John, seeming to present an egalitarian view of church leadership rather than a structural or hierarchical one. When Peter declares in John 6:68 that Jesus alone has the words of eternal life (not he), it seems like he is presented as "returning the keys of the kingdom to Jesus," where, according to the Fourth Evangelist, they belonged all the while. Does this imply a Johannine-Matthean debate over the character of apostolic leadership at the end of the first century *within* the church?

Box 2.12: John's Ecclesiology

On one hand,

- Peter is called *Kēphas* (1:42), the Aramaic word for "rock," and Jesus affirms Peter's shepherding role (21:15-17).
- The leadership of Peter is central, as he makes a confession as chief of the apostles parallel to his role in the Synoptics (6:68-69), and Jesus accords him three opportunities to amend his threefold denial—also around a charcoal fire (18:15-27; 21:15-17).

On the other hand,

- Images for the church are more dynamic and organic—like a shepherd and his flock (10:1-18) and like a branch abiding in the vine (15:1-17); relational connectedness to Jesus (indeed, as the Beloved Disciple leaned against Jesus' breast in 13:23) is everything!
- Peter is portrayed as affirming Jesus' authority (6:68-69), but also as misunderstanding Jesus on matters of servanthood and leadership (6:70-71; 13:1-34); the Holy Spirit is the second helper—not a human leader (14:25-28; 15:26—16:15).

As John's ecclesiology developed, it must also be considered in its context. Who were the Evangelist's partners in dialogue, and what issues were his audiences facing? Here the memory of Jesus and his approach to leadership within the church relates not only to theology, but also to historical and literary questions. The presentation of Peter and the Beloved Disciple may here point the way forward as a literary construct informing both theological and historical understandings. Therefore, we must move on to considering the other riddles as well.

■ Conclusion

As this overview suggests, John's theological riddles are many and diverse. Some of them might seem incidental, but most of them are highly significant. This makes it important to learn more about the character of these tensions; they cannot be ignored. Already we have seen that one way scholars have dealt with these tensions is to infer different authors or literary sources. Especially Bultmann's attributing of John's material to at least five major sources became one means of assigning particular theological strands to individuated traditions. Another approach is to see the Evangelist himself as being a dialectical thinker, who looked at things from more than one angle. He thought in both-and ways instead of settling for either-or dichotomies. It also is the case that different audiences within the evolving Johannine situation might have called for more than one approach to a subject, and certainly the narrator's employment of rhetorical devices had some impact on the presentation of John's material. Note that approaches to John's composition and tradition development have served the role of accounting for John's theological riddles, and these theories will be addressed directly in Part 2. In simply taking inventory of John's theological riddles, however, you are definitely now swimming with the elephants!

■ Questions to Consider

1. Having looked up at least a selection of the texts listed in this chapter, what impressions do you have regarding the Father, the Son, and the Holy Spirit in John?
2. Look again at the passages related to dualism in John and read some of them in closer detail. How do you think the presentation of polar opposites in the narrative functions reflectively and rhetorically?
3. Regarding John's presentation of sacraments and of Peter and the Beloved Disciple, is there evidence of dialogue with other Christian groups about the character of the church, its organization, structure, and authority? If so, what might that have been like?

■ Terms to Understand

- subordinationism/egalitarianism
- eschatology
- soteriology
- ecclesiology

The Historical Riddles
of the Fourth Gospel

I n addition to theological riddles, John's historical riddles are among the most
perplexing features of any biblical text. Whereas John's theological riddles especially captivated the attention of ancient theologians, John's historical riddles
have evoked some of the most explosive religious and scholarly discussions in modern times. Put bluntly, the "consensus" of modern critical scholarship regarding
John's historicity actually involves two platforms: the *dehistoricization of John* and
the *de-Johannification of Jesus*.[1] First, because John differs so much from the three
Synoptic Gospels, its historicity is often doubted where those differences are the
most pronounced. Second, its pervasively theological thrust eclipses its distinctive
historical features in the judgment of many a critical scholar. Therefore, the three
modern quests for Jesus (the "Original Quest" of the nineteenth century, the "New
Quest" from the 1950s to the present, and the "Third Quest" using more interdisci-
plinary methodologies over the last three decades) have one thing in common: they
leave John on the shelf, and programmatically so.[2] Some reasons for these moves
are understandable, yet they also introduce new sets of critical problems, which
scholars are only recently beginning to address.[3]

In considering John's historical riddles, a good deal of this chapter will involve
comparisons/contrasts between John and the Synoptics. In doing so, the impact
of a classic statement made by Clement of Alexandria around 200 C.E.[4] deserves
consideration: "But, last of all, John, perceiving that the external facts had been
made plain in the Gospel, being urged by his friends, and inspired by the Spirit,

composed a spiritual Gospel." While John indeed is a "spiritual Gospel" written by "the Theologian," from this statement several flawed inferences have followed.

First, the mistranslation of Clement's phrase, *ta somatika* (in Greek, "the bodily things") as "the external facts"[5] gave the English-speaking world the wrong impression about the Synoptics. Matthew, Mark, and Luke are every bit as theological as John, and the "fact-versus-spirit" distinction between the Synoptics and John is wrongheaded from the start. Mark's progression is itself ordered by interests in narrative flow and particular theological investments, and John has more empirically rooted knowledge than scholars have often noted. Second, while John is indeed a spiritual and theological Gospel, this is not to say it is not also interested in outward "facts" and detailed history. Many of John's details serve no symbolic, theological, or narrative-furthering function at all; they appear to represent first-hand knowledge of topography, customs, and empirically derived data.

Third, it is a mistake to assume Clement was claiming factual knowledge about *any* of the Gospels' compositional purposes. In commenting on how and why they appear to be distinctive, that may be *all* he was saying. Clement also speculated that Matthew and Luke were the first Gospels to be written because they are "the Gospels containing the genealogies." No discerning scholar would follow Clement as a trustworthy authority on that account—abandoning Markan priority—so why would entire theories of Gospel composition be based on a faulty translation of Clement's conjectural Synoptic-Johannine distinction? Other issues, of course, are also at stake.

A second set of fallacies arises when comparing and contrasting John against the Synoptics, based upon what I call the *three-to-one fallacy*. If indeed Matthew and Luke built upon Mark, as most scholars rightly believe, the contest is not three against one, with John being the lone Gospel out, but John versus Mark. If Mark got it wrong, so did Matthew and Luke. However, if Mark and John represent two distinctive Gospel traditions, John's rendering may deserve consideration alongside that of the Synoptics, even if it disagrees with all three accounts. This is all the more compelling where John includes material and perspectives that are missing in the Synoptics. Therefore, simply assuming a Synoptic majority "wins" three-to-one against the Johannine witness where John and the other Gospels differ is critically naïve. Their similarities and differences must be sorted out on a case-by-case basis.

■ John's Narrative: Historical or Theological?

This brings us head-on into the first of the Johannine historical riddles—whether John's narrative is theological or historical. Of course, these are not mutually exclusive categories; an explicitly theological detail (such as the name of the pool, "Siloam," meaning "sent," 9:7)[6] may indeed rest on an empirical fact. And, just because a detail is not theologically slanted, this does not confirm its historicity. Nonetheless, the theological character of a detail may suggest an ulterior reason for including it other than historicity, so the inquiry understandably continues. Overall, though, has John's presentation of Jesus' ministry been ordered by theological interests or historical ones? If the Fourth Evangelist was interested in cosmic realities and eternal origins and destinies, how do those interests play themselves out in his construction of a narrative about Jesus of Nazareth? Consider these facts in John's text:

Box 3.1: Theological and Historical Material in John

On one hand, much of John's narrative is theologically weighted:

- Jewish festivals are highlighted (2:13, 23; 4:45; 5:1; 6:4; 7:2, 8, 10, 11, 14, 37; 11:55-56; 12:1, 12, 20; 13:1, 29; 18:28, 39; 19:14); details cast persons in favorable (1:47; 4:39; 9:25; 11:27; 13:23; 20:18) and unfavorable light (3:2; 6:66; 13:2, 30; 18:38; 19:15); Jesus' miracles are referred to as "signs" (seventeen times); and the symbolic meanings of names are highlighted (1:42; 9:7).
- John the Baptist declares Jesus to be "the Lamb of God who takes away the sin of the world" (1:29), and the Passover's nearness is mentioned three times (2:13; 6:4; 11:55).
- Jesus' mission and intentions are noted from beginning to end, both within the narrator's commentary and also in Jesus' own statements of purpose. Given its apologetic purpose (20:31), John's story is highly rhetorical from start to finish.
- Jesus is presented as knowing all things (2:24-25; 5:6; 6:64; 13:1, 11; 16:19) and having full sway over what happens (6:6; 7:30, 44; 8:59; 10:15-18, 39).

On the other hand, much of John is materially grounded and thoroughly mundane:

- John has more archaeologically verified and topographically accurate details (1:28, 43-44; 2:1-11, 12, 13-22; 3:23-24, 26; 4:3-9, 43-54; 5:1-3; 6:1, 23, 59; 7:1, 9, 14; 8:20; 9:7; 10:22-23, 40; 11:1, 18, 54; 12:1-8; 18:1, 15-20, 28-29; 19:13, 17, 20, 41; 20:1, 8; 21:1) and more information derived from apparent empirical-sensory means than all the other Gospels put together.
- All five senses are reported as having been used in John (seeing ninety-eight times, hearing thirty times, smelling twice, tasting once, and touching four times); temperature is mentioned (18:18).
- Illustrative details are rife in John (1:32-34, 48; 2:6, 15; 4:4-6; 6:9-13; 8:59; 9:6-15; 11:39, 44; 12:3, 5, 12:13; 13:4-5, 30; 18:3, 10, 18, 27; 19:2, 5, 20, 23-24, 29-30; 19:34, 39; 20:1, 5-7, 19, 25-27; 21:6-7, 9, 11).
- Personal knowledge is implied (1:40, 44; 6:8; 11:5; 12:22; 18:10, 13, 15-16, 26; 19:25, 38; 21:2).
- Places of people's origin are mentioned (1:44, 48; 6:71; 7:41-52; 11:1, 18; 12:14, 20-21; 13:2, 26; 14:22; 18:7; 19:25-26, 38; 20:1, 18; 21:2), as are particular distances (6:19; 11:18; 21:8), weights (19:39), languages (5:2; 19:13, 17, 20), measurements (2:6; 12:3), costs (6:7; 12:5), topographical references (2:12-13; 3:23; 4:5, 19-24, 47, 49; 5:1-3, 7; 6:1, 15-16, 22-25, 59; 7:8-14; 11:38, 54-55; 12:1-8, 12, 20; 21:1), and alternative names of places (5:2; 6:1; 19:13).
- Time intervals are highlighted in the narrative in terms of hours (1:39; 4:6, 52-53; 19:14), times of day (6:16; 18:28; 20:1, 19; 21:4), days (2:1, 12, 19-20; 4:40, 43; 5:9; 11:6, 17; 12:1; 20:19, 26), years (2:20; 5:5; 11:49, 51; 18:13), and the season (10:22).
- Jesus is presented as being forced to do certain things because of outward circumstances (4:1-4; 9:4; 10:16).

Indeed, John's presentation is highly theological, but to say it is "only" or "primarily" theological misses the mark on at least twenty categories of apparent historical knowledge listed above. For this reason, a both-and approach to John's history and theology is more critically sound than an either-or approach. The fact of a theological association does not preclude the possibility of a historical origin. Thus, explaining all or most of John's distinctive material as a factor of "the theological interest of the Evangelist" is a flimsy procedure critically.[7] A detail may have been such, but claiming that it was *not* historical must be argued with the same rigor as required of claims that something *was* historical. Simply questioning an inference does not demonstrate the opposite. History and theology in John must be considered critically to discern both their character and their relation to each other.

▓ The Source of John's Tradition: An Eyewitness or Not?

This, of course, leads to a more pointed question: Was the source of John's tradition an eyewitness or not? If the Beloved Disciple was indeed an eyewitness source of John's material, however, why is he left unnamed? The critical opinion on this matter is negative, and yet the evidence is somewhat mixed. Gospel texts, of course, were not produced with their present names attached to them; these were added later. So, given that the Fourth Gospel bears the later-added title "according to John," how might one assess the Gospel's own claims to be rooted in firsthand memory of Jesus' ministry? Strong arguments abound for and against such a possibility.

Box 3.2: Eyewitness Claims and Their Problems

On one hand:

- John contains more direct claims to eyewitness origins and apostolic authorship than any of the other Gospel traditions—canonical or otherwise. The Beloved Disciple is named as the author or source of the Fourth Gospel (21:24); this person is identified as the one who leaned against Jesus' breast at the Last Supper (13:23), was entrusted with custody of Jesus' mother (19:26-27), was present at the empty tomb (20:2-10), and pointed out the resurrected Lord to Peter (21:7); Peter questioned Jesus regarding his destiny (21:20-23).
- The "eyewitness" is also attested to having seen the water and blood flowing forth from Jesus' side (19:34-35) just after Jesus' mother had been entrusted to the Beloved Disciple. If the Beloved Disciple is indeed present in John 21, it bears note that the named disciples in that chapter other than Peter include Thomas, Nathanael, the sons of Zebedee, and two unnamed disciples (21:2)—thus providing a possible link between the Beloved Disciple and one of the Zebedee brothers.
- The Beloved Disciple (or the "other" disciple) and Peter are paired together in the Fourth Gospel (1:35-42; 13:23-38; 18:15-16; 20:2-4; 21:1-7, 15-23), and Peter and John are paired together in the Synoptics and Acts (Matt. 10:2; 17:1; Mark 5:37; 9:2; 13:3; 14:33; Luke 8:51; 9:28; 22:8; Acts 3:1-11; 4:1-20; 8:14-25).

- Therefore, one can understand how John the son of Zebedee came to be connected with the source of the Fourth Gospel's tradition as an eyewitness and with the Beloved Disciple, who leaned against Jesus' breast at the Last Supper, and who was present at Jesus' crucifixion and postresurrection appearances.

On the other hand:

- All of the above references are in the third person; the clarification that Jesus never said the Beloved Disciple would not die (21:23) implies that he had died by the time John was finalized, and the attestation that "we know his testimony is true" (21:24) implies a plurality of witnesses rather than a singular one (see also 1 John 1:1-3). Likewise, "We beheld his glory" implies a community's contribution also behind the Johannine Prologue at least (1:14).
- And, while the veracity of the eyewitnesses testimony is asserted at the cross (19:35), the identities of that witness and the Beloved Disciple are finally left anonymous, and the connection between the two is not explicitly made. Further, does one eyewitness claim at the crucifixion imply that the rest of the Fourth Gospel entirely consists of eyewitness testimony? Not necessarily.
- On the particular person(s) involved, neither the disciple John nor his brother James is mentioned by name in this Gospel (although "those of Zebedee" are mentioned in 21:2), and the unnamed disciple is not necessarily the Beloved Disciple. Further, virtually every scene in which the sons of Zebedee are mentioned in the Synoptics is missing from John. This includes James and John being called away from their fishing nets and boat to follow Jesus (Mark 1:19); the healing of Simon's mother-in-law (Mark 1:29-31); the calling of the Twelve (Mark 3:16-19); the request for privilege by the sons of Zebedee (Mark 10:35-45); the raising of Jairus's daughter (Mark 5:22-43); the transfiguration (Mark 9:2-10); John's personal discomfort with other exorcists (Mark 9:38-41); James's and John's inquiry regarding calling down fire from heaven (Luke 9:54); Peter's and John's being commissioned to arrange the upper room for the Last Supper (Luke 22:8); the apocalyptic discourse on the Mount of Olives (Mark 13:3-37); and the disciples' slumber in Gethsemane (Mark 14:32-34).
- Given that much of John's distinctive material is Judean, many scholars claim that its author cannot have been the Galilean John, son of Zebedee.

While it is impossible to know whether all of John's tradition comes from an autonomous eyewitness source (or sources), two things are clear. The narrator testifies that an eyewitness had indeed seen the water and blood come forth from Jesus' side, and if the Beloved Disciple was on the scene, as suggested eight verses earlier, this is an understandable connection. Second, the final editor attests that the Beloved Disciple is the credited author of the Johannine Gospel, although it seems that he had died by the time the Gospel was finalized. Of course, firsthand information could have originated from more than one person or source, and the Fourth Gospel may contain other traditional material as well; the main question is whether John's distinctive material has its own claim to historical memory, or whether it originated otherwise.

▓ John and the Synoptics: Why Such Different Introductions and Conclusions?

When considering the beginnings of John and the Synoptics, their dissimilarities are significant, but so are their similarities. Unlike Matthew and Luke, John has no birth narrative. John's Prologue, though, also sketches the divine origin of the man Jesus, but in a different way. Like the Johannine Prologue, Luke's three hymns—by Mary (1:46-55), Zechariah (1:68-79), and Simeon (2:29-32)—were probably used in the worship life of the early church before being drawn into the written Jesus narrative. And, while the genealogies of Matthew and Luke connect Jesus' earthly lineage with his role as a Davidic Messiah, the Johannine Prologue presents the "genesis" of Jesus, showing his cosmic origin *from the beginning*. Following the Johannine Prologue, the story begins in John as it does in Mark—John the Baptist comes ministering, and he points people to Jesus. In these ways, John's narrative is similar, yet dissimilar, to the beginnings of the Synoptic stories of Jesus, so it is not surprising that John's developing story is also distinctive.

Box 3.3: Distinctive Beginnings and Endings

On one hand:

- ▓ Differences abound when considering the beginnings of the Synoptics and John. John has no birth narratives, but Matthew begins with the virgin birth of Jesus, the visit of the Magi, and the flight to Egypt (Matt. 1:18—2:23). Luke begins with the wondrous births of John the Baptist and Jesus, the hymns of Mary, Zechariah, and Simeon, and Jesus' teaching in the Temple as a twelve-year-old (Luke 1:1—2:52). John, on the other hand, begins with a Prologue to Christ the eternal *Logos* (John 1:1-18). Matthew and Luke also include genealogies of Jesus, and Mark begins with the ministry of John the Baptist (Matt. 1:1-17; Luke 3:23-38; Mark 1:1-15).
- ▓ The first conclusion of Mark (16:1-8) shows Jesus promising to go ahead of his disciples into Galilee, and his followers are smitten with fear. Mark's added ending (vv. 9-20) contributes a far more robust presentation of the postresurrection disciples and their evangelistic ministries, and while Matthew 28:16-20 describes the eleven meeting Jesus in Galilee, only John 21:1-25 provides an extended narration of the Galilean rendezvous. Only Luke and John present Jesus as eating bread and fish with his disciples after the resurrection, and only in Luke and John does Jesus show his disciples his hands and his flesh wounds.

On the other hand:

- ▓ One notes general similarities between the beginnings of John and the Synoptics: the birth narratives and the Johannine Prologue do present in different manners the story of the divine and human Jesus; the genealogies emphasize his human lineage and heritage, but the Johannine Prologue emphasizes his "genesis" from a cosmic perspective (*egeneto*, meaning "came into being," is used six times in the Prologue: 1:3 [2x], 6, 10, 14, 17); and John also begins with the ministry of John the Baptist—emphasizing that he was neither the Light, the Prophet, Elijah, nor the Christ, but that he pointed to Jesus as the Christ (1:6-8, 15, 19-36).

▧ All four Gospels portray Jesus' appearing to women (especially Mary Magdalene) and other disciples (especially Peter) after the resurrection, and he gives something of a commission to his followers as a continuation of the movement (Matt. 28:18-20; Mark 16:15-18; Luke 24:46-49; John 20:21-23). The disciples' fear is overcome by the presence of the risen Lord, and their boldness is presented as a continuing reality into the apostolic era.

While the details are largely different, the beginnings and endings of John and the Synoptics still play similar roles. They begin by pointing to Jesus' divine commission and origin, and they conclude by featuring his appearances to his followers after the resurrection. These features are especially theological, and their supernatural character locates them in categories of faith rather than naturalistic history for most scholars. In addition, more mundane issues also call for consideration.

▧ John and the Synoptics: Why Such Differences and Similarities in Order and Chronology?

Impressive differences in order and chronology also exist between John and the Synoptics, as well as some similarities. While some of these can be harmonized, others cannot. The dating of the Last Supper, for instance, is sometimes addressed by inquiring as to whether different calendars were used, although scholars also disagree on that point. It also is a fact that while the Last Supper is presented as a Passover remembrance in the Synoptics, Jesus is *not* crucified on the Passover in the Synoptics, so even Mark differs from Mark, not just John, on the specifics of the date (see below). In general, scholars side with John on the dating of the Last Supper. On the Temple cleansing, however, which John places early in Jesus' ministry (John 2:13-25), most scholars side with the Synoptics, which locate the event during Jesus' last days (following Mark 11:15-18), arguing that such a Temple disturbance would not have gone unpunished for two or three years; discipline would have been swift and decisive. The point is a good one, although the Jerusalem authorities are presented as wanting to kill Jesus already in John 5 on his second visit. Further, even in the Synoptics, several days follow the Temple incident before Jesus is arrested, so the Synoptics share the same problem of the delayed response by the authorities, though less egregiously. While other differences abound, general similarities also confirm the general coherence of the two traditions.

Box 3.4: Differences and Similarities in Order and Chronology

On one hand, note these differences in order and chronology:

- Jesus cleanses the Temple at the end of his ministry in the Synoptics (Mark 11:15-18); in John he does so at the beginning (John 2:13-25).
- Three Passovers are mentioned only in John (2:13; 6:4; 11:55), suggesting a two- or three-year ministry of Jesus; only one Passover is mentioned in the Synoptics (Mark 14:1), implying that Jesus ministered less than a year.
- In Mark, Jesus begins his ministry after John the Baptist had been arrested (Mark 1:14); in the Fourth Gospel, their ministries overlap (John 1:19-42; 3:22-30).
- Jesus' first two miracles in Mark involve an exorcism and the healing of Simon Peter's mother-in-law (Mark 1:23-31); the first two miracles of Jesus in John involve the turning of water into wine at the Cana wedding (John 2:1-11) and the healing of the royal official's son from afar (4:46-54).
- Jesus visits Jerusalem only once during his ministry in the Synoptics (Mark 10:32), where-upon he is killed; in John, Jesus goes to and from Jerusalem four times (John 2:23; 5:1; 7:14; 12:12), as any observant and active Jewish leader would have done.
- In the Synoptics, the Last Supper appears to have been held as the Passover meal (Mark 14:16); in John it is held on the *day before* the Passover (John 13:1), on the day of Preparation.
- Jesus agonizes about "this cup" in the garden of Gethsemane after the Last Supper in the Synoptics (Mark 14:36); in John, he agonizes about "this hour" before the Last Supper (John 12:27)—both alluding to his impending death.

On the other hand, note these similarities:

- First, a general similarity in the overall chronology of the ministry of Jesus is clear: Jesus begins his ministry in Galilee, having been introduced by John the Baptist; Jesus performs healings and other miracles and teaches about the ways God works; animosity with reli-gious authorities grows; Jesus marches to Jerusalem, where he is betrayed, tried, killed, and buried; Jesus appears to disciples on the first day of the week.
- Second, a number of similarities surround the events narrated in John 6 and Synoptic paral-lels: Jesus feeds the five thousand, performs a sea-deliverance miracle, and discusses the feeding and Peter utters a christological confession leading to a response by Jesus.
- Third, the similarities during the final week of Jesus are impressive: Jesus is welcomed in Jerusalem by crowds shouting "Hosanna" as he enters the city riding on a donkey; Jesus and his disciples share a last supper together; Jesus predicts his betrayal and Peter's denial; Jesus is arrested and tried (a Jewish trial and a Roman trial); Judas betrays Jesus, and Peter denies him; Jesus is abused, sentenced, and crucified; Jesus dies and is buried; Jesus appears to disciples on the first day of the week.

On the face of it, John's larger itinerary seems more realistic. Any observant and active Jewish leader would have attended festivals in Jerusalem several times a year, and it is odd that scribes and Pharisees would come from Jerusalem to see Jesus (Mark 3:22; 7:1) if he had never visited the city. Further, as Paula Fredriksen has questioned, why did the Romans *not* arrest Jesus after his triumphal entry into Jerusalem with crowds shouting "Hosanna"? Her explanation is a good one: Jesus must have been there before, and they perceived him to be no threat. It also seems that Jesus' ministry would have taken more than one year to have the impact that it did, so on matters of chronology and order, John's rendering seems more plausible.[8]

Despite differences, John's general similarities with the Synoptics are also impressive. The general beginning, middle, and end of Jesus' ministry come through in all four Gospels, and the same is also true for the events around the feeding and the Passion events. From the similarities in the Passion narratives some scholars infer the use of a similar source. However, this is not the only explanation possible; they also could represent knowledge of generally similar historical events. Either way, it is hard to imagine any of the sequence being different. The trials of Jesus cannot have come before the arrest; the appearance narratives must follow the crucifixion; the supper must precede the arrest and denials of Peter; and so on. On matters of chronology and sequence, John's presentation of Jesus' ministry raises a good number of questions, but it cannot be ruled out as an alternative rendering with knowing intentionality.

▨ John and the Synoptics: Why Such Differences of Inclusion?

John also differs from the Synoptics on matters of inclusion. That is, a good deal of material in the Synoptics is missing in John, and a good deal of John's material is missing in the Synoptics. The question is, *why*? While space will not allow a full listing of both categories, and some of these will be listed later in fuller detail, some of the more notable omissions are as follows:

Box 3.5: Materials Missing from John and from the Synoptics

On one hand, a good deal of material in the Synoptics is completely missing from John:

- ▨ Exorcisms and encounters with demoniacs
- ▨ The healing of the deaf, the dumb, or the leprous
- ▨ The formal calling of the Twelve
- ▨ The healing of Simon Peter's mother-in-law
- ▨ John the Baptist's immersing Jesus in the Jordan
- ▨ The temptation in the wilderness
- ▨ The transfiguration on Mount Tabor
- ▨ Kingdom teachings in parables
- ▨ The Sermon on the Mount, including the Beatitudes and the Lord's Prayer
- ▨ Jesus' dining with "sinners" and tax gatherers (and Pharisees)
- ▨ The institution of the Eucharist at the Last Supper
- ▨ Jesus' apocalyptic discourse and agony in Gethsemane

■ The cry of dereliction on the cross

On the other hand, a good deal of John's material is completely missing from the Synoptics:

■ John the Baptist's witness: "Behold, the Lamb of God!"
■ The informal calling of the four
■ The wedding at Cana—the first sign
■ Jesus' ministry among the Samaritans
■ Multiple visits to Jerusalem, including debates with the Jewish leaders there
■ The crowd's challenging Jesus to provide more bread
■ Jesus' I-am sayings
■ Two healings in Jerusalem (the lame man and the man born blind)
■ The raising of Lazarus in Bethany
■ Jesus' washing of his disciples' feet at the Last Supper
■ Jesus' final discourses and his High Priestly Prayer
■ The piercing of Jesus' side
■ The mentioning of nails and Jesus' flesh wounds
■ Peter's being asked three times if he loved Jesus

Differences in inclusion between John and the Synoptics are difficult to explain if John represents a tradition rooted in history. If the items listed in the first group indeed happened, how could the Johannine Evangelist leave them out if he really was an eyewitness? And, if the second list of items actually took place in history, how could the Synoptic writers *not* know of them? If they knew of them, how could they leave them out? Of course, Gospel traditions developed in different geographical contexts, and no one person or tradition knew all the circulating stories about or teachings of Jesus, but these differences in inclusion continue to perplex historians on all sides of the issues.

■ John and the Synoptics: Why Such Differences in Detail and Theological Emphasis?

Beyond matters of inclusion, an impressive set of differences present themselves when considering both the details and the theological emphases of John and the Synoptics. While differences in theological emphasis are clearly rooted in the views of the Evangelists and/or their traditions, significant differences in detail raise historical questions. Like questions of chronology, differences in detail may press for siding with either John or the Synoptics, and sometimes there is agreement with John by one or more of the other Gospels against another tradition or two. These data may even illumine relations between Synoptic traditions as well.

Box 3.6: John and the Synoptics—Differences in Detail and Emphasis

Interestingly, differences in detail between John and one or two of the Synoptic Gospels are striking:

- Was there one feeding miracle (John 6:1-15 and Luke 9:10-17) or two (Mark 6:32-44; 8:1-9 and Matt. 14:14-21; 15:29-39)?
- Was there one miraculous sea crossing (John 6:16-21 and Luke 8:22-25) or two (Mark 4:35-41; 6:45-52 and Matt. 8:23-27; 14:22-34)?
- Was Peter's confession after the feeding of the five thousand (John and Luke) or after the feeding of the four thousand (Mark and Matthew)?
- Was it an anointing of Jesus' feet (John and Luke) or of his head (Mark and Matthew)?
- Why are details in Mark and John, such as two hundred and three hundred denarii (Mark 6:37; 14:5; John 6:7; 12:5) and green grass/much grass at the feeding (Mark 6:39; John 6:10) omitted in Matthew and Luke (although Matt. 14:19 has "grass" without the modifier)?
- Why are the great catch of fish (with the sons of Zebedee present), presentations of Mary and Martha, references to a dead man named Lazarus, the embracing of Samaritans, the amputation of the right ear of the servant, Satan's "entering" Judas, Pilate's declaring "I find no crime" in Jesus, an unused tomb, Peter's witnessing the linen cloths, Jesus' showing his followers his wounds, and the postresurrection eating of fish and bread with Jesus missing from Mark and Matthew while being present only in John and Luke?
- Did John come baptizing in order to point Jesus out (John), or did he come preaching a baptism of repentance and the forgiveness of sins (Mark and Luke)?
- Did Jesus declare that he would raise up "this temple" (the one made with human hands) three days after it was destroyed (John 2:19), or is that the allegation raised by co-opted witnesses in the attempt to put Jesus to death (Matt. 28:61; Mark 14:58)?

Likewise conspicuously, the theological emphases of the Synoptics and John are distinctive—perhaps even in dialogue:

- How is the kingdom of God furthered: by binding the "strong man" and plundering his household (Matt. 12:29; Mark 3:27), or by advancing the truth? (John 18:36-37)
- Is the value of the miracles their physical effect (Mark 6:42; 8:8) or their revelational significance (John 6:26)?
- Did Jesus come to supplant Jewish cult and rites and inaugurate new ones that would become Christian rites (water baptism and eucharistic communion: Matt. 28:19; Luke 22:19-20), or to transcend such creaturely endeavors in the name of the religion-transcending Father (4:21-24)?
- Did Jesus promise to return before the last of the eyewitnesses had died (Mark 9:1; 13:30), or does such a belief reflect a misunderstanding of Jesus' words conveyed by Peter and others (John 21:20-24)?
- Did Jesus intend to establish a hierarchical structure (Matt. 16:17-19), or did he intend divine leadership to be effected by the Holy Spirit (John 14–16)?
- Are apostolic ministry and discernment limited to a few, or are they extended to every believer (Matt. 18:18-20; John 20:21-23)?

While differences in detail may suggest differences in particular historical knowledge, theological differences reflect distinctive perspectives and understandings. Of course, details influence theology, and theology has a bearing on the presentation of details. Likewise, theological dialogue may have existed within Gospel traditions as well as between them. This being the case, the Johannine tradition appears to have been engaged dialectically with other traditions as to not only what Jesus said and did, but also what these things meant. Therefore, the compiler's assertion that the Beloved Disciple's testimony is true would have had theological overtones as well as historical ones (21:24). Such dialogues may be reflected also in similarities and differences in the presentation of Jesus' ministry.

▤ John and the Synoptics: Why Such Distinctive Presentations of Jesus' Ministry?

Differences and similarities between Gospel traditions, and indeed between all historical presentations, are factors of any of three sources: memory and tradition, the author's theology and perspective, and the author's rhetorical interests in addressing an audience. While significant similarities abound between John and the Synoptics, impressive differences also present themselves when these texts are read closely. Again, differences in theological presentation could be rooted in historical memory, but they might be influenced by other factors as well, such as the needs of the audience.

Box 3.7: Similarities and Differences in the Presentation of Jesus' Ministry

On one hand, similarities between John and the Synoptics in their presentation of Jesus' ministry are many:

- In both John and the Synoptics, Jesus hails from Galilee (Nazareth) and is rejected in Jerusalem.
- Jesus' closest disciples are described as "the Twelve" in all four Gospels.
- John the Baptist is the forerunner of Jesus in the Synoptics and in John.
- Jesus is declared to be the Son of God in both the Synoptics and in John, as well as the Messiah/Christ, and in all four Gospels he refers to himself as the Son of Man.
- Peter makes a christological confession in all four Gospels and plays the role of the leader among the apostles.
- Jesus declares the cost of following him in all four Gospels.
- Jesus ministers in Capernaum early in his ministry in the Synoptics and John, and he also teaches in its synagogue.
- In the Synoptics and John, Isaiah 40:3 ("the voice of one crying in the wilderness, 'Prepare the way of the Lord!'") is associated with the mission of John the Baptist.

On the other hand, differences between John and the Synoptics in their presentation of Jesus' ministry also abound:

- Jesus is born in Bethlehem in Matthew and Luke (Matt. 2:1; Luke 2:4-7); John's Jerusalem authorities reject Jesus because he has not come from Bethlehem (John 7:42).
- John the Baptist denies that he is either Elijah or the Prophet in John (1:19-24); he is clearly associated with both of them in the Synoptics (Matt. 11:12-14; 17:10-13; Mark 6:14-15; 8:28; 9:11-13).
- To whom does Jesus command, "Rise, take up your mat and walk!"—the paralytic in Capernaum (Mark 2:9) or the lame man in Jerusalem (John 5:8)?
- Who is it that declares Jesus to be the Son of God: was it John the Baptist (John 1:34), Nathanael (1:49), Jesus (3:18; 5:25; 11:4), and Martha (11:27); or was it the angel (Luke 1:35), Peter (Matt. 16:16), the Gadarene demoniacs (Matt. 8:29), other unclean spirits or demoniacs (Mark 3:11), other disciples (Matt. 14:33), and the centurion at the crucifixion (Matt. 27:54; Mark 15:39)?
- Who hails Jesus as the Holy One of God: the demoniac (Mark 1:24; Luke 4:34), Peter (John 6:69), or both?
- In Mark 1:16, it appears that the home of Andrew and Simon Peter is in Capernaum (near the synagogue), but in John 1:44, Peter and Andrew hail from Bethsaida, nearby.
- In the Synoptics, Jesus contrasts John the Baptist's disciples and the Pharisees to the wedding guests who do not fast as long as the bridegroom is present (Mark 2:19-20); John the Baptist is presented in the Fourth Gospel as the friend of the bridegroom who rejoices at the bridegroom's voice (John 3:29).
- Are Jesus' followers "the light of the world" (Matt. 5:14), or is this designation reserved for Jesus (John 8:12; 9:5)?
- A voice from heaven is sounded at Jesus' baptism and at the transfiguration in the Synoptics (Matt. 3:17; 17:5; Mark 1:11; 9:7; Luke 3:22; 9:35); in John it is sounded after the triumphal entry (John 12:28).
- In the Synoptics, Jesus is accused as casting out demons by Beelzebul, the prince of demons (Matt. 12:24; Mark 3:22; Luke 11:15); in John, Jesus is accused of having a demon because he claims the authority of the Father (John 8:48, 52; 10:20).
- In Mark and Matthew, followers of Jesus will be delivered up to councils and beaten in synagogues (Matt. 10:17; 23:34; Mark 13:9); in John they will be cast out of the synagogues (John 16:2).
- Jesus says, "Rise, let us leave," at the Last Supper in John (John 14:31); in Mark and Matthew he says, "Rise, let us leave," in the garden of Gethsemane, just before the betrayer arrives (Matt. 26:46; Mark 14:42).

Again, similarities of detail and presentation often cohere when comparing and contrasting John with the Synoptics, but at other times the presentations of Jesus' ministry are very different. Some of this could be a factor of Jesus' having done or said something more than once, in different contexts, but it also could reflect ways that traditions have developed in distinctive ways. As stories were told and written, and retold and rewritten, associations developed around particular stories, and connections with audiences likely affected the crafting of the material. Sometimes a narrator's theology influenced the crafting, and this can be seen especially when an Evangelist's presentation of Jesus' ministry resembles his own points and emphases.

■ **John and the Synoptics: Why Such Distinctive Presentations of Jesus'
Teachings and Intentions?**

Especially with reference to the teachings of Jesus, we have considerable differences
between the Synoptic Jesus and the Johannine Jesus. The Synoptic Jesus teaches
in parables about the kingdom of God and speaks in short, aphoristic sayings.
John's Jesus, however, speaks in long, drawn-out discourses about the Son's being
sent from the Father and the world's responses to the Revealer. Can this really be
the same Jesus, or is one of these presentations less historical than the other? Then
again, remarkable similarities also abound.

Box 3.8: Similarities and Differences in the Presentation
of Jesus' Teachings and Intentions

On one hand, differences in the presentations of Jesus' teachings and intentions are striking:

- Did the historical Jesus really speak in parables? If so, why are they totally missing from
  John, at least in their Synoptic form?
- If the primary focus of Jesus' teachings was the kingdom of God, why is this theme largely
  missing in the speech of the Johannine Jesus?
- If Jesus really spoke in the grand "I-am" speeches as depicted in John, how is it possible that
  all three Synoptic Gospels would have largely missed these declarations?
- If Jesus spoke in short, pithy, agrarian aphorisms, as presented in the Synoptics, why does
  the Johannine Jesus speak in such long, extended discourses?
- If Jesus taught about righteousness and the fulfilling of the Law, as portrayed in the Synoptics, why does the Johannine Jesus emphasize revelation and enlightenment as means
  of redemption?
- If Jesus' followers are called to love enemies and neighbors, why has this injunction gone
  missing in John?
- If the Markan Jesus emphasizes messianic secrecy, why does the Johannine Jesus emphasize messianic disclosure?

On the other hand, aspects in the presentation of Jesus' teachings in John that are generally
similar to that in the Synoptics also abound:

- The Johannine Jesus still employs metaphors and speaks in figures of speech (10:6; 16:25),
  causing consternation among the disciples (16:29).
- The Johannine Jesus does indeed address the kingdom in two pivotal passages (3:3-8; 18:36-
  37), and the focus in the narrative is on Jesus the King (1:49; 6:15; 12:13-15; 18:33—19:22).
- Each of the nine Johannine I-am metaphors are also present in the Synoptics, and "I-am"
  language is clearly used by the Markan Jesus (Mark 6:50; 8:27-29; 13:6; 14:62)—including references to the I-am language of Exodus 3:14 (12:26).
- Has the presence of short, pithy, agrarian aphorisms in John (3:3-8; 4:32-38; 12:24-36; 16:19-22),
  been overlooked by Jesus scholars and is it likely that the historical Jesus gave no extended
  discourses but spoke only in staccato one-liners?

- Like the Synoptic Jesus, John's Jesus is also presented as fulfilling the Law of Moses (1:17), and the claim is made that Moses wrote of Jesus (1:45; 5:46).
- How can we claim to love God and neighbor (Mark 12:30-31) if we are unwilling to love one another (13:34-35; 15:12-17)?
- The Johannine Jesus also withdraws into solitude (6:15; 10:40-43; 11:54), as does the Synoptic Jesus, and he likewise prefers secrecy over sensationalism (6:15; 7:4-10).

While Jesus' kingdom teachings cohere more in the Synoptics, the Johannine Jesus speaks conspicuously in the Evangelist's language and thought-forms. Then again, all of the Johannine I-am metaphors are present in the teachings of the Synoptic Jesus, so one cannot rule out the possibility of Johannine paraphrasing of actual words of Jesus. Further, some differences are exaggerated, such as the distance between loving one's neighbor and loving one another, and a common fallacy is to limit all of Jesus' teaching to traits of his "characteristic" speech. Likewise, some agrarian aphorisms and kingdom sayings are present in John, and the Synoptics also feature the owner of a vineyard sending his *son*, only to be killed by the unreceptive tenants (Mark 12:1-12; Matt. 21:33-46; Luke 20:9-19). Therefore, the agency of the Son, sent by the Father, is not a uniquely Johannine construction.

John and the Synoptics: Why Such Distinctive Presentations of Jesus' Miracles?

Differences in Jesus' teachings between John and the Synoptics also extend to presentations of his miracles. While only three of John's eight miracles are found in the Synoptics, similarities still abound when viewing John's distinctive signs side-by-side with their Synoptic counterparts. Significant also are the differences regarding the meaning of the miracles and their importance for later audiences. In the Synoptics, faith generally leads to seeing the wondrous (without faith miracles do not happen), while in John the signs of Jesus function to lead people to faith (they are performed "that you might believe"). Again, similarities and differences between the Synoptic and Johannine renderings of Jesus' miracles abound.

Box 3.9: Similarities and Differences in the Presentations of Jesus' Miracles

On one hand, similarities regarding the miracles of Jesus are many:

- Jesus heals the sick in both John and the Synoptics, including healing the blind and the lame, and he also raises the dead.
- Many of Jesus' miracles are performed on the Sabbath, challenging Sabbath regulations.

- Jesus performs nature miracles in John and the Synoptics—in particular, the feeding of multitudes and rescuing his disciples from the wind and the waves.
- Jesus performs a healing from afar in Capernaum in Matthew and Luke (Matt. 8:5-13; Luke 7:1-10), and also in John (John 4:46-54).
- A great catch of fish is found in John and Luke (Luke 5:1-11; John 21:1-14).
- Human faith is central to Jesus' miracles in both facilitative and reflective ways.

On the other hand, differences regarding the presentations of Jesus' miracles are also many:

- All of Jesus' miracles in the Synoptics are performed in the North, in Galilee and its environs (except for the healings of the blind in Jericho: Matt. 20:29-34; Mark 10:46-52; Luke 18:35-43); whereas three of Jesus' eight signs in John were performed in the South, in Jerusalem or Bethany (John 5:1-8; 9:1-41; 11:1-45).
- If John purports eyewitness connectedness to Jesus, why have all the exorcisms (the most common form of miracle in the Synoptics) gone missing?
- Likewise, John includes no healings of lepers, nor does the treatment of lepers and outcasts figure at all in the Johannine presentation of Jesus' ministry.
- Five of John's eight miracles are not found in the Synoptics. Why not—especially when some of them, such as turning the water into wine (2:1-11) and the raising of Lazarus (11:1-44), are among the most memorable?
- Have the attestations about Jesus' miracles being wondrous been omitted from John's tradition, or have they been added to Mark's? Rather than miracles hinging on people's faith as in the Synoptics, signs are performed in John to lead people to faith, suggesting two distinctive theological trajectories in the Johannine and Synoptic traditions.

While three of John's eight signs are also narrated in the Synoptics, John's presentation of Jesus' miracles is considerably different. In the Synoptics, miracles are the result of faith; in John, signs generally lead to faith. One can even detect a Johannine challenge to Synoptic valuations of the feeding as a wonder of satisfaction, when in Johannine perspective it is a vehicle of revelation (6:26). John both omits standard Synoptic miracles while also including others not found in the Synoptics. Indeed, some of the Johannine signs are also similar enough to those performed by the Synoptic Jesus to provide something of a corroboration of his wondrous ministry, although the fact of their having no external validation makes it hard to confirm their historicity with certainty.

■ The Origin of the Johannine Signs: A Religion of History or the History of Religions?

In the modern era, miracles in the Bible have presented a problem for critical scholars. Unless there is a natural explanation for "the wondrous," scholars have tried to find alternative ways of accounting for their presence in the text—other than history. Given that John's miracles are among the most wondrous in the Gospels, they are among the most questioned subjects in biblical studies in terms of historicity. How, for instance, could water really be turned into wine, or how could a man who was dead for four days be raised from the dead, as two of John's distinctive miracles claim? As an answer to the naturalism-versus-supernaturalism problem in the Fourth Gospel, since the nineteenth century scholars have proposed that the origin of John's distinctive signs was not the historical ministry of Jesus, but mythic folklore from contemporary religions in the Mediterranean world. From a strict rationalist perspective, scholars have argued for a History-of-Religions explanation for the origin of Gospel miracles. In John's case, some of these might have come from an adaptation of Synoptic miracles of Jesus or from Hellenistic religious folklore. Consider these parallels.

Box 3.10: Johannine Wonders and Contemporary Parallels—the Synoptics or Hellenistic Religions?

On one hand, Jesus' signs in John are similar to his miracles in the Synoptics, if not identical:

- Healing a sick person from afar (Matt. 8:5-13; Luke 7:1-10; John 4:46-54)
- Healing the lame or the paralyzed (Matt. 9:1-8; Mark 2:1-12; Luke 5:17-26; John 5:1-9)
- Feeding the multitude with loaves and fishes (Matt. 14:14-21; 15:29-39; Mark 6:33-44; 8:1-9; Luke 9:10-17; John 6:1-15)
- Calming the wind and the waves (Matt. 8:23-27; 14:22-33; Mark 4:35-41; 6:45-56; Luke 8:22-26; John 6:16-24)
- Healing the blind (Matt. 9:27-31; 12:22-23; 20:29-34; 21:14; Mark 8:22-26; 10:46-52; Luke 18:35-43; John 9:1-7)
- Raising the dead (Matt. 9:18-26; Mark 5:21-43; Luke 7:11-17; 8:40-56; John 11:1-45)
- A voice is sounded from heaven (Matt. 3:17; Mark 1:11; Luke 3:22; John 12:28)
- Helping his disciples net a great catch of fish (Luke 5:1-11; John 21:1-14)
- Healing on the Sabbath (Matt. 12:1-23; Mark 1:21-34; 3:1-8; 6:2-5; Luke 6:6-11; 13:10-17; 14:1-6; John 5:1-18; 9:1-17)

On the other hand, Jesus' distinctive signs in John bear echoes of Jewish and Hellenistic wonder stories:

- Turning water into wine was performed by Apollonius of Tyana, a second-century c.e. miracle worker in Asia Minor; Jesus turned the water into wine as his first miracle in Cana of Galilee in John (Philostratus, *Life of Apollonius of Tyana* 6.10; John 2:1-11).
- When the son of Rabban Gamaliel was ill, Hanina ben Dosa prayed for him from afar, and he was made well that very hour (*Berakoth* 34B; John 4:46-54).
- The well in Asclepius's temple had healing powers when its waters were stirred (Aelius Aristides, *Speech* 39.14-15; John 5:1-9).
- At the consummation of time, the treasuries of heaven were expected to open, and manna would descend from heaven (2 *Baruch* 28.2; John 6:1-32).
- Suetonius and Tacitus report the Emperor Vespasian's applying spittle to a blind man's eyes and the resultant recovery (Suetonius, *Lives of Caesar* 7; Tacitus, *Histories* 4.89; John 9:1-7).
- Homer describes a thundering response from heaven as the prayer of Odysseus was apparently well received by Zeus (Homer, *The Odyssey* 20.97-104; John 12:29).

As historical-critical scholars have challenged everything that appears wondrous as either a fabrication or an adaptation of religious folklore or myth from Jewish or Hellenistic sources, connections in the second list have been levied to argue that the origin of John's miracles lay not in the history of Jesus' ministry but in the history of ancient religions and their myths. However, the features of John's wondrous material nearly always show greater coherence with the miracles of Jesus as rendered in the Synoptics than interreligious parallels. Therefore, the thesis that the Johannine Evangelist simply borrowed his Jesus stories from pagan mythology is fraught with new critical problems, as none of the parallels are identical, and most are more distant from the Johannine renderings than those of the Synoptics. Naturalistic historians will struggle with miracles, but mythic-dependence theories face their own sets of new problems from a literary-critical standpoint.

■ Cross-Cultural Elements in John: A Diachronicity of Situation?

Whether or not John's material comes from a single source or multiple ones, it does reflect a diachronicity of situation. That is, it features translating Palestinian Jewish customs and Aramaic words for a Greek audience to understand. Therefore, the tradition seems to have had both Palestinian and Hellenistic histories of development, as its Jewish customs and content are crafted for a Gentile audience. Consider two aspects of cross-cultural deliveries within the Johannine narrative.

Box 3.11: Jewish Terms and Customs "Translated" for Gentile Audiences

For one thing, firsthand knowledge of Palestinian customs is reflected in the text:

■ Explanations of Jewish customs and traits are provided for those not familiar with Jewish ways: the size of stone jars used for Jewish purification (holding about two or three *metrētēs*—twenty or thirty gallons, 2:6); Jews do not share things with Samaritans (4:9); the day on which something took place was the Sabbath (5:9; 9:14); the Jewish leaders did not enter the Roman palace to avoid ceremonial uncleanness, as they wanted to be able to eat the Passover (18:28); since it was the day of Preparation, the Jewish leaders did not want the bodies left on the cross during the Sabbath (19:31); they prepared Jesus' body according to the burial customs of the Jews (19:40).

In addition, the delivery of John's material involves cross-cultural translation, reflecting delivery in a Hellenistic setting:

■ Aramaic terms are translated into Greek for non-Jewish audiences: *Rabbi*, which means "teacher" (1:38); *Messias*, which is translated "Christ" (the word for "anointed one" 1:41; 4:25); *Kēphas*, which is translated "Peter" (the word for "rock" 1:42); Thomas, also known as *Didymus* (the word for "twin," 11:16; 20:24; 21:2); the place of the Skull is called in Aramaic *Golgotha* (meaning "place of the skull," 19:17); Mary said to him in Aramaic, *Rabbouni*, which is translated for the audience as "teacher" (20:16).

The question is what these cross-cultural elements suggest. These features are most common in John and Mark but are largely missing from Luke and Matthew, probably for opposite reasons. As Matthew was delivered to a primarily Jewish audience, Jewish customs and words did not need to be explained to the audience. On the other hand, Luke was written to a Hellenistic audience, and in his borrowing from Mark, Luke apparently chose to omit the distinctively Jewish details, despite the fact that his audience may have had some Hellenistic Jews within it. The bulk of Luke's tradition, however, did not originate in Palestinian settings in quite the same way that John's and Mark's did, and this feature likely suggests Johannine and Markan proximity to Palestinian oral traditions, where Aramaic sayings of Jesus are still discernible within the telling of the stories. In that sense, the Johannine and Markan traditions appear to have originated within Palestinian settings and to have been finalized in Hellenistic settings.

▓ Johannine Narrative: Rooted in History or the Historical Johannine Situation?

One of the major questions in Johannine studies over the last four decades is the issue of whether John's presentation of the Jesus story says more about the Jesus of history or the history of the narrator and his audience. J. Louis Martyn argues compellingly in his *History and Theology in the Fourth Gospel* that the Fourth Gospel must be read against the situation history of Johannine Christianity.[9] Several statements explaining the way things were, so to speak, "even back then," suggest ongoing realities for the Evangelist and his audience. Therefore, inferences of the Johannine situation history have somewhat displaced scholars' interest in its originative history, calling into further question any Johannine historical memory of Jesus of Nazareth. At least six or seven crises in the Johannine situation can be inferred behind the Johannine text, and four of these later ones are referenced explicitly in the Johannine epistles and the letters of Ignatius of Antioch.

Box 3.12: Originative History versus Situation History in the Fourth Gospel

On one hand, John's narrative may provide information about the Jesus of history, as its originative history is considered:

- ▓ While the Samaritans and Galileans received Jesus as the messianic prophet and king (4:39-45; 6:14-15), the Judean leaders did not (5:10-47; 7:11—8:59).
- ▓ John the Baptist heralds the ministry of Jesus and even declares that the reason he came baptizing was to reveal Jesus to Israel (1:31).
- ▓ Not only in Jerusalem, but also in local synagogues, open followers of Jesus were beginning to be ostracized by the Jewish leaders (9:22; 12:42; 16:2).

- Fear of Roman retaliation is palpable among the Jewish residents of Palestine, especially with reference to the Passover, the Temple, and Jerusalem (2:13; 6:4; 11:48, 55).
- Many of Jesus' followers withdrew and followed him no longer when it became apparent that he was not leading them to political or economic triumph, but the way of the cross (6:66; 19:25).
- Jesus' teachings on the kingdom in John emphasize being born "from above" and moving with the "wind" of the Spirit, because his reign is one of truth, not coercion or power (3:3-8; 18:36-37).

On the other hand, much in John seems to represent several crises in the history of the evolving Johannine situation:

- While some Judean leaders and members of the populace believed in Jesus, others did not, suggesting that the southern rejection of the northern prophet and his movement probably continued for several decades (7:41-52; 8:31-32; 11:45; 12:35-43).
- The witness of John the Baptist points away from himself and directly to Jesus, channeling later Baptist adherents to Jesus as the authentic Messiah (1:6-8, 15, 19-37; 3:22-30).
- Not only in Palestine, but elsewhere among the mission churches, those who confessed Jesus openly were in danger of being marginalized from the synagogue (John 9:22; 12:42; 16:2); those who refused to believe in Jesus as the Jewish Messiah apparently left the community of the "Elder" (see 1 John 2:18-25) and were labeled "antichrists."
- In defiance of Roman imperialism, Pilate is presented as neither knowing the truth nor having the power or courage to release Jesus (18:36—19:16), and in anti-imperial defiance Thomas declares of Jesus, "My Lord and my God!" (20:28); the Johannine Elder puts it bluntly: "Little children, stay away from idols" (1 John 5:21).
- Apparently combating Christian Docetism (the belief that Jesus' physical body and crucifixion were illusions), the fleshly, suffering of Jesus is emphasized (John 1:14; 6:51-58; 19:34); this countered false teachers arguing that Jesus did not come in the flesh (1 John 4:1-3; 2 John 1:7).
- As a counter to rising institutionalism in the late-first-century church, Jesus is presented as leading his followers by means of the Holy Spirit, who is accessible to all (chaps. 14–16), Peter is thus presented as "returning the keys of the kingdom" to Jesus (6:68-69), and Jesus commissions a plurality of Spirit-filled, apostolic, and priestly ministers (20:21-23). By contrast, the church leader Diotrephes loves primacy, excludes Johannine ministers, and excommunicates members of his own church who take them in (3 John 1:9-10).

Whether John's story of Jesus says more about the later history of the Johannine situation or represents an independent memory of the Jesus of history is a weighty question. While some scholars in recent years have been willing to sacrifice John's originative history to see what can be learned about John's situation history, are both quests mutually exclusive? Indeed, John's narrative is highly theological, but does that mean it is not historical? And while it does cast light on the later history of Johannine Christianity, especially with parallels from the Johannine epistles, to what degree does it illumine anything about Jesus? Does one aspect of historicity eclipse all others, or might both of these windows be translucent? At stake here is not only the ways we envision John's riddles but also the ways we envision the character of history itself.

Conclusion

While the historical riddles of the Fourth Gospel can largely be explained on the basis that the Evangelist either makes use of an independent tradition or has an individuated perspective on the meaning of Jesus' ministry, one of these points being true does not eliminate the other. Much of John corroborates the presentation of Jesus in the Synoptic Gospels, but much of it also challenges such presentations. Are these differences featured knowingly or unwittingly? Either way, do some differences force a choice between the Synoptic presentation of Jesus and the Johannine version, or can some be harmonized as factors of distinctive perspective or knowledge? Here is where the literary riddles assert themselves into the discussion. Views of John's composition and dependence on, or independence from, other sources must now be addressed, as one set of riddles impinges upon the others.

Questions to Consider

1. Consider the tension between history and theology within the Johannine narrative; does something being historical mean it cannot be theological, and does something being theological mean it cannot be historical?
2. Consider the extensive similarities and differences between John and the Synoptics; how should one account for these sets of facts?
3. If the Johannine narrative was delivered within a developing set of situations over several decades, how would that affect the formation of the content?

Terms to Understand

- the dehistoricization of John
- the de-Johannification of Jesus
- aphorism
- Docetism

4

The Literary Riddles
of the Fourth Gospel

n addition to theological tensions and historical riddles, a host of literary perplexities confront the reader of the Fourth Gospel. Scholars call these *aporias* (meaning "impasses" or "puzzlements"), and in seeking to address them, they also look for ways to make sense of the other riddles we have already addressed. From odd transitions to apparent additions to the text, John's literary perplexities must also be considered before posing an adequate theory of composition and tradition history. While leading theories of Johannine composition will be engaged in following chapters, the bases for those theories will be explored in this chapter outlining the literary riddles of the Fourth Gospel. Like John's theological and historical riddles, its literary aporias move us from wading pools to deeper waters.

■ The Johannine Prologue: An Original Introduction or a Later Add-On?

At the outset we are faced with the question of the relation of the Prologue to the rest of the Gospel. John 1:1-18 introduces the narrative in a personally engaging way; the hearer/reader is welcomed into the family of God by means of responding in faith to the saving/revealing Light, Life, and Word of God made flesh (1:9-14). Uses of the first-person plural, "we," invite the audience into transformative community, and membership in this grace-filled fellowship transcends the bounds of space and time. Indeed, the Prologue serves as an engaging entrée to the reception of the narrative, but was it composed at the outset as an initial introduction, or was it added later as a corporate response to the message? After all, the form and content of the Prologue are closer to the beginning of the first Johannine epistle than to the rest of the Gospel. Some of its vocabulary and features are also not found in the rest of the Gospel.

Box 4.1: Form and Vocabulary Differences between John's Prologue and Narrative

On one hand, form and vocabulary differences exist between the Prologue (1:1-18) and the rest of John's narrative:

- The Prologue is poetic and strophic in its form (suggesting a worship setting as its origin), whereas the rest of the narrative is more prosaic. Note also the "we" references in verses 14 and 16, reflecting the experience of a community (these same references appear twenty-two times in the ten verses of 1 John 1).
- Distinctive terms, such as "Word" (*Logos*), "fullness" (*plēroma*), "grace" (*charis*), and "came into being" (*egeneto*), are present in the Prologue, but these are found with greater prevalence in 1 John (especially 1 John 1:1-4) than in the rest of the Johannine Gospel.
- Form-critically, the poetic form of the Gospel's Prologue finds few parallels elsewhere in the narrative.

On the other hand, the Johannine Prologue is germane to the rest of the narrative:

- Within the Prologue, narrative asides mention the ministry of John the Baptist (1:6-8, 15), which is developed more fully in chapters 1 and 3.
- Such terms as "light" (*phōs*), "darkness" (*skotia*), "glory" (*doxa*), and "truth" (*alētheia*), however, *are* rife within the rest of John's narrative, so these themes both echo and announce the central thrust of the Johannine Gospel.
- In welcoming into the *family* of God as *children* any who *believe* in Jesus as *the Christ*, this pivotal thrust of the Prologue matches the announced purpose of the Gospel—that hearers and readers might *believe* (20:31).
- The first-person plural language of the Prologue ("we," 1:14, 16) is also replicated in the final words of the editor in the epilogue (21:24) and found ninety times in the seven chapters of the Johannine Epistles.

While the Fourth Gospel must be read and treated as a completed document, understanding something of the history of its development assists the reader in understanding its meaning. If the Prologue marks the first strokes of the narrator's pen, we have in this narrative a cosmic and eternal story playing itself out on the dusty roads and towns of ancient Palestine. If, however, we have in John 1:1-18 a community's late-first-century worship response to that story, which has been added as a later introduction, the narrative need not be stripped of its mundane perspectives and historical voice. Especially if there is some connection with the Johannine epistles, we may also infer something of the Johannine situation-history within the later material. Certainly its content would have reached out to Greco-Roman audiences as well as Jewish ones, and we see in the Johannine Prologue something of a translation of the Jewish prophet's mission into that of the cosmic *Logos* of God.

▨ The Johannine Epilogue: A Fresh Start or a Second Ending?

Because John 20:31 appears to be an original ending of the narrative, scholars have wondered whether chapter 21 was added to an earlier edition of the Gospel. Indeed, the last verse of the last chapter appears to echo the last verse of the previous chapter, so it even seems that the final compiler has imitated the style of the first ending. This suggests a conservative interest, rather than an innovative one. It also is interesting that the author of the final chapter refers to the Beloved Disciple in the third person as the author of the narrative, and that he explains that Jesus never said that the Beloved Disciple would not die (21:20-24). Does this imply that John's final chapter was added by another hand after the death of the Evangelist? Telling also is the fact that the final editor uses the first-person plural, "we," as a corporate attestation of the Beloved Disciple's truthful witness. Again, this style of writing is very close to 1 John 1, so it appears that the author of the epistles may be the final compiler of the Johannine Gospel. This being the case, does the return of the disciples and Jesus to Galilee in John 21 reflect a fresh start for the Jesus movement, or does it serve as a later ending to an earlier edition?

Box 4.2: The Place of John 21 as a First or Second Ending

On one hand, the thrust of John 21 seems to reflect a second ending to the Gospel:

- ▨ The clear statement of John's apologetic purpose in 20:30-31 appears to have served as an original conclusion to the narrative; 21:1-25 appears more pastoral in its thrust.
- ▨ The narrator in John 21 acknowledges the death of the Gospel's author (21:23-24), and John 21:25 echoes the first ending in John 20:31.
- ▨ The final compiler represents the corporate testimony of Johannine Christians, that his "testimony is true" (19:35; 21:24), echoing the claims of the narrator (5:32; 8:14) and the epistles (3 John 1:12).

On the other hand, John 21 poses a fitting conclusion to the rest of the narrative:

- ▨ Major themes of the Fourth Gospel are replicated in chapter 21 (the arrows here point to an echo of an earlier theme): a lake scene on Tiberias (21:1→6:1); familiar disciples (Peter, Thomas, Nathanael, unnamed disciples, 21:2); the Beloved Disciple (21:7, 20→13:23; 19:26; 20:2); a charcoal fire (21:9→18:18); the eating of bread and prepared fish (21:9→6:9); Jesus' emphasizing love for others (the lambs/sheep, 21:15-17→10:11-12; 13:34-35; 15:12, 17); Jesus' declaring "Follow me!" (21:18, 22→1:43; 10:27; 12:26); God's glorification in the death of the faithful (Peter, 21:19→Jesus, 12:28; 13:32; 16:14; 17:1-5); Peter's asking the Beloved Disciple about a reference (21:20→13:23-25); and the verifying claim that "his testimony is true" (21:24→Jesus, 5:32; the eyewitness, 19:35).

- Like John 20:30-31, John 21:25 defends Johannine selectivity if contrasted to other reports of Jesus' ministry.
- Whoever wrote and/or added it, John 21 makes a fitting conclusion to the Fourth Gospel.

If John 21 represents an epilogue added to an earlier edition of the Johannine Gospel, this would account for several of these features. Further, it appears that a hand *other* than the Evangelist's added it after his death. Given the similarities with the Johannine epistles, whose author calls himself "the Elder" (2 John 1:1; 3 John 1:1), it appears that we at least have a Johannine Evangelist and a compiler involved in the finalization of the Gospel. If the epilogue was added at a later time, however, might other material also have been added, and might such a feature account for some of John's distinctive characteristics? Assuming John 20:31 represents a first ending, the thrust of the earlier edition appears to have been more evangelistic and apologetic—leading people to come to faith in Jesus as the Christ. The later material, however, seems more pastoral—calling for adherence and faithfulness to Jesus and his followers during times of adversity. The implications of such a distinction will be explored later.

■ John 7:53—8:11: A Text Caught in Adultery (and Other Textual Indiscretions)?

Interestingly, the Fourth Gospel includes several passages not found in the earliest Greek editions of the text. Most notably, the woman-caught-in-adultery passage (7:53—8:11, which might actually be called "the *text* caught in adultery"), was added to the Johannine Gospel sometime in the middle of the second century; earliest Greek manuscripts do not include it. Further, its vocabulary and sentence structure differ from the rest of the Johannine narrative, so it clearly reflects a traditional unit that was added to the Johannine text at a later time. Some early manuscripts feature this passage within the Gospel of Luke. In addition, several other shorter passages were added to John's text, usually as clarifications or expansions of a theme. Apart from these clearly later additions to the text, other explanatory asides are apparent, and the question is whether they were added by the narrator or by a later editor.

Box 4.3: Textual Additions and Narrative Asides in John

On one hand, the Gospel of John features additions to the text not included in the earliest manuscripts:

- The "Woman Caught in Adultery" passage (7:53—8:11) is missing in the earliest manuscripts.

- The statement that the Spirit troubled the waters at the Pool of Bethzatha as a factor in healing (5:4, though not in earliest manuscripts) explains the sick man's dilemma.
- The clarification that it was the "only-begotten *Son*" who was at the Father's side alleviates the theological problem of the earlier rendering: "the only-begotten *God*, who is at the Father's side" (1:18): some scholars see this change moving in the opposite direction, supporting trinitarian developments.
- Several minute additions or changes found in some early manuscripts reflect developments in the later tradition: the adding of *eucharistēsantos* (where the Lord "gave thanks," 6:23) connects the feeding with later eucharistic practices; the apparent changing of *pisteusēte* to *pisteuēte* (that you may "believe"→"continue believing," 20:31) suggests a change from apologetic to pastoral interests.

On the other hand, the Gospel of John possesses a variety of explanatory asides that clarify what Jesus was really doing or saying—asides that are *not* textual variants:

- Jesus was speaking of the "temple" of his body, a reference to his death and resurrection, though people failed to understand it at the time (2:21).
- A clarification is made that Jesus himself did not baptize (contra 3:26; 4:1); only his disciples did (4:2).
- Jesus was speaking *not* of Peter, but of Judas—the one who would eventually betray Jesus (6:71).
- Jesus was referring to the Holy Spirit, which had not yet been poured out (7:39).
- Jesus was speaking to them of the Father, but they did not understand it (8:27).
- Jesus was speaking of Lazarus's death, although the disciples did not understand (11:13).
- Jesus spoke of these things in order to explain by what means he would die (12:33).
- Clarification: it was not Judas the traitor, but *another* Judas (14:22) that was asking the question.
- Jesus spoke of Peter's death to show by what means he would die (21:19).
- A clarification is made that Jesus never promised that the Beloved Disciple would not die before his return (21:23); he said something else to Peter elsewhere.

Despite the presence of later textual interpolations, however, this does not prove that a later editor added disparate material to the Johannine text instead of the Evangelist. If the editor wanted to add material, he could have done a much better job at smoothing over rough transitions and filling gaping holes with Synoptic-type material, which has not been done overall. Clarifications of Jesus' words could have been added by the original Evangelist. Then again, the compiler appears to clarify in John 6:71 that Jesus did not mean Peter: he meant Judas, the one who would betray him. Indeed, the Johannine narrator adds a good number of clarifying asides, shedding light on Jewish customs and language and making explicit otherwise overlooked references in the text. While the Evangelist and the compiler did a good deal of such clarifying, inferring additions of disparate material should be limited to cases involving compelling manuscript evidence—a fact that is missing in the second list.

◼ Odd Progressions and Contextual Perplexities in John: Reflecting on the Future?

Several odd progressions and textual anomalies in the Johannine narrative require attention, especially because the narrator also often refers to earlier events. Put directly, do the out-of-sequence references in John suggest a disrupted text or editorial seams? If Jesus' ministry in Galilee in John 4 and 6 go together (living water complements living bread), and if Jerusalem leaders in John 7 are still debating the Sabbath healing in John 5, might the original chapter order have been 4, 6, 5, 7, before major displacements of the text? Also, why does Jesus say "let us depart" at the end of John 14 while failing to arrive at the garden until John 18? Mary is introduced in John 11 as the one who had anointed Jesus' feet, but that scene does not come until John 12. Jesus asks in John 16 why none of his disciples had asked where he was going, but Thomas had just asked that question (or one like it) in John 14. As other odd progressions are also present, how should these literary perplexities be approached?

Box 4.4: Textual Anomalies and Reflective References

On one hand, odd progressions and textual anomalies abound in John:

- John the Baptist is presented as having testified that Jesus was before him (1:15), and yet the narrative does not state this until fifteen verses later (1:30).
- People at the first Passover in Jerusalem believed in Jesus on account of the "signs" he was doing (2:23, plural), but the second sign (in Galilee) is not mentioned until John 4:46-54.
- People come to Jesus on the other side of Galilee having seen the signs he had performed on the sick (6:2), but the second healing was in Jerusalem (5:1-9), a hundred miles away.
- Jesus and his disciples enter "the land of Judea" (3:22) after apparently having been there all along (2:12-25).
- The world cannot hate Jesus' brothers (7:7), but it does hate Jesus' followers (15:18-19).
- Chapters 5 and 7 are in Jerusalem, while chapters 4 and 6 are in Galilee, with little transitional commentary; further, the debate in John 5:16-47 appears to continue in 7:14-52.
- Following the feeding, the Tiberias crowd asks *when* Jesus had arrived on the opposite shore, but his response addresses a different issue: *why* they seek him (6:25-26).
- After Jesus says, "Let us leave," in 14:31, it takes three chapters for them to arrive at the garden (18:1). Were Jesus' discourses and prayer in John 15–17 originally connected with that setting or with another?
- Mary is mentioned in 11:2 as the one who anointed the feet of Jesus, but the narrative does not describe her doing so until 12:3.
- Jesus says, "None of you asks where I am going," in 16:5, and yet Thomas had just asked him where he was going and how to know the way (14:5).
- At the Jewish trials, Jesus is sent first to Annas, the father-in-law of Caiaphas the high priest (18:13), but he is then questioned by the high priest (18:19) before he is sent to Caiaphas in verse 24.

On the other hand, the narrative's self-reflective and anticipatory comments upon past and future events, within proper narrative sequence, are characteristically Johannine:

- John the Baptist's later statements about Jesus refer to his earlier ones (arrows here reflect references to earlier events: 1:30, 40→1:26-27, 29-34).
- Discussants in the narrative comment on what Jesus had said or done (3:2→2:1-22; 5:10→5:9; 9:16→9:14).
- Jesus' knowing words about the Samaritan woman are recalled later (4:29, 39→4:18-19).
- The Galilean crowd had seen the signs Jesus had performed in Jerusalem (4:45→2:13-23).
- Once more Jesus visits Cana of Galilee, where he had turned the water into wine (4:46→2:1-11).
- The healing of the royal official's son from afar is reported as the second sign performed after coming into Galilee from Judea (4:54→2:11).
- Jesus' healing on the Sabbath is referenced later (5:16, 18→5:9).
- The signs performed on the sick motivate the crowds to follow after Jesus (6:2→4:46-54; 5:1-9).
- Boatloads of people from Tiberias come to the place near where they had eaten the loaves after the Lord had given thanks (6:23→6:1-15).
- Judas's betrayal is anticipated (6:71; 12:4; 13:2→13:21-30) and reflected upon later (18:2, 5).
- Jesus is reluctant to return to Jerusalem because the Judeans were trying to kill him (7:1→5:18), and references to this concern continue (7:19-25; 8:37-40).
- Jesus comments on what he had said or done (7:22-23→5:1-15; 15:20→13:16).
- Nicodemus, who had first come to Jesus before/by night, is referenced later in the narrative (7:50; 19:39→3:1-2).
- Jesus speaks to the Judeans who had earlier believed (8:31→2:23; 7:31; 8:30).
- Jesus speaks of his departure again (8:21→7:33; 8:14).
- The Judean leaders are again divided over Jesus' words (10:19→9:16).
- The Jewish leaders try again to arrest Jesus (10:39→7:30, 44) but are unsuccessful.
- Jesus returns to the trans-Jordan place where John had been baptizing earlier (10:40→1:28).
- Jesus discusses returning to Judea, where religious leaders had attempted to stone him earlier (11:8→10:31-33).
- Lazarus, whom Jesus had raised from the dead, is referenced in the next chapter (12:1, 9→11:43-44).
- The hope that none of those given to Jesus should be lost is fulfilled in the narrative (18:9→6:39).
- Caiaphas is described as having uttered a prophecy earlier regarding Jesus' sacrificial death (18:14→11:49-53).
- A relative of the man whose ear Peter had severed is mentioned (18:26→18:10).
- The place where Jesus was crucified is mentioned as also the site of the garden tomb (19:41→19:17-20).
- The other disciple is referenced as the one who had reached the tomb first, before Peter (20:8→20:4).
- The reader is reminded of momentous events on the first day of the week (20:19→20:1).
- A week later Jesus comes again to the house where he had appeared to the disciples in Jerusalem (20:26→20:19-25).
- The postresurrection lakeside appearance is referred to as the third appearance after Jesus' being raised from the dead (21:14→20:19, 26).
- A later reference is made to Peter's earlier asking the Beloved Disciple to ask Jesus to expand on who would betray him (21:20→13:21-27).

While not all of John's odd progressions pose serious problems ("the land" in 3:22 may refer to wilderness rather than region; 6:26 reflects an ironic statement; Annas could have been called "the high priest" due to his enduring tenure, even after Caiaphas had assumed the position), they nonetheless pose a challenge for any theory of John's composition. Did earlier texts get displaced and reordered wrongly? Did the Evangelist use different sources? Did the final editor alter an earlier text or "restore" a disordered one? Might later material have been added, either by the Evangelist or the editor? Do some contextual problems reflect oral deliveries of material gathered later into written form? These are the sorts of questions that present themselves when we seek to make sense of John's literary puzzles. Of course, composition theories need to solve more problems than they create, so a modest approach to composition history is always preferable over more elaborate ones.

■ "Play It Again, Sam" (But in a Different Key): Whence the Repetitions and Variations in John's Narrative?

What should we make of repetitions and variations in the Johannine narrative and where do they come from? Time and again, the narrator repeats himself, or introduces a familiar theme again, leaving the reader to feel that ground has been covered before. Nonetheless, familiar themes are never simply repeated in exactly the same way; new themes and associations are added, also moving the story forward. Therefore, cyclical repetition and linear progression suggest the development and expansion of particular themes. Again, this raises questions about the composition and editing of John's material. Why the repetition of familiar themes? Did the work not undergo a proper editing? Or were developments of material in the oral stages of tradition perhaps gathered together by a later hand? Does the inclusion of somewhat similar renderings suggest conservative or intrusive operations by either the author or the editor? Consider these examples.

Box 4.5: Repetition and Contextual Perplexities

On one hand, repetitions and variations abound:

- John 3:31-36 sounds like Jesus or the Evangelist, but a break is not made following the words of John the Baptist in 3:27-30 (might the original connection have been with 3:1-21?); further, this summation of Jesus' agency from the Father is very similar to Jesus' concluding words at the end of his ministry in 12:44-50. So, *who* is speaking in 3:31-36—the Baptist, the Evangelist, or Jesus?
- The narrator gives a summary statement twice at the end of Jesus' ministry, first declaring that after performing his signs many people believed (10:40-42); later it is claimed that

despite witnessing his signs many did not believe (12:37-43). Why the uneven reception and differing reports? Do we have earlier and later endings of different sections here?

▨ The Bread of Life discourse in John 6 progresses in repetitive-cyclical ways, raising questions about the meaning of bread and eating the flesh and drinking the blood of Jesus (6:51-58) as themes from 6:26-50 are recapped climactically. Does Jesus as the "Bread of Life" find new relevance in later phases of the tradition's history?

▨ The mixing of metaphors between 10:1-10 and 10:11-19 raises questions about the unity of this passage; is Jesus the gate, or the shepherd, or both?

▨ A fair amount of repetition exists in the controversies between Jesus and the Jewish leaders in John (5:16-47; 7:14-52; 8:12-59; 10:19-39); does John 6–10 reflect one long controversy with Jerusalem authorities that is interrupted by John 6, 7:53—8:11 and John 9, or a gathered series of debates in which similar themes are covered?

▨ Several of the *Paraklētos* passages of John 14–16 appear to develop similar themes in somewhat redundant ways; do we have one long address by Jesus here, or a compilation of several renderings of his last words to the faithful?

On the other hand, recurring themes reinforce each other and are developed progressively:

▨ The agency of Jesus as "having been sent by the Father" is developed extensively throughout the Fourth Gospel as he is described as the One of whom Moses and the prophets wrote, the commissioned Son of Man, and the One who incarnates God's love in the world.

▨ People respond unevenly to Jesus and his mission—some believing and others not—moving the narrative plot forward toward its culminative events.

▨ Metaphors describing Jesus' saving-revealing work draw on typologies of ancient Israel, showing him to be the Jewish Messiah, ironically rejected even by his own.

▨ The text is rife with commentary on earlier (inadequate) and later (fuller) understandings, suggesting development of perspective within the Johannine tradition.

▨ Between the Johannine Gospel and epistles, common themes include emphases on eyewitness continuity with Jesus' ministry, loving one another, abiding in Jesus and his fellowship, and remaining apart from the world.

Repetition and variation may reflect renewed emphases of familiar points, or they may suggest a gathering of similar material that had been developed in more than one setting. Whatever the case, the final editorial process of John's narrative allows repetitions to stand without eliminating redundancies. The repetition of important themes impresses them upon the consciousness of the hearer/reader, and the adding of new associations develops themes dialogically. Themes such as life, light, glory, truth, believing, abiding, loving, and the world connect with each other in impressively reinforcing ways. Might there have been some intentionality in the narrator's cyclical-repetitive and progressive-developing approach? Indeed, these themes bolster each other in repetitive-progressive ways; just when the hearer/reader masters comprehension of a theme, it is turned and reintroduced as a mysterious stranger, yet at the same time a welcome friend.

■ The Johannine Gospel, Epistles, and Apocalypse: Close Relations or Distant Cousins?

In considering relations between the Johannine Gospel, epistles, and Revelation (Apocalypse), how close were they? While thematic and linguistic similarities between the Gospel and the epistles abound, Revelation is the most distinctive among the Johannine writings—largely as a result of its apocalyptic genre. Nonetheless, it still has enough echoes of Johannine themes that it deserves inclusion among the Johannine corpus—echoes that may reflect its origins in the setting of Johannine Christianity. In all of these writings, several larger themes abound: the Word of God comes to humanity inviting a response of faith, hardship is experienced from the world, and walking in the light is central. Much closer to the Johannine Gospel than Revelation, however, are the Johannine epistles. They emphasize such themes as loving one another and knowing the truth, and the issues they represent suggest a good deal about the situation and audience of the Gospel.

Box 4.6: Johannine Gospel, Epistles, and Revelation: Similarities and Differences

On one hand:

■ Similarities between the Johannine Gospel, epistles, and Revelation abound: the Word of God comes to humanity in redemptive ways (John 1:1; 10:35; 1 John 2:14; Rev. 1:2, 9; 6:9; 19:13; 20:4); emphasis is made on things being in or from the beginning (John 1:1-2; 8:44; 15:27; 16:4; 1 John 1:1; 2:7, 13-14, 24; 3:8, 11; 2 John 1:5-6; Rev. 21:6; 22:13); walking in the light is commended (John 11:9-10; 12:35; 1 John 1:7; Rev. 21:24); the witness/testimony motif is strong (John 1:7, 15, 19, 32-34; 3:11, 26-33; 4:39; 5:31-36; 8:13-18; 19:35; 21:24; 1 John 5:9-11; 3 John 1:3, 6, 12; Rev. 1:2, 5, 9; 2:13; 3:14; 6:9; 11:3, 7; 12:11, 17; 17:6; 19:10; 20:4; 22:16, 20); "darkness" is a pejorative reference (John 1:5; 3:19; 8:12; 12:35, 46; 1 John 1:5-6; 2:8-11; Rev. 16:10), while "abiding" is extolled (John 1:38-39; 5:38; 6:56; 9:41; 14:17; 15:4-10; 21:22-23; 1 John 2:6, 14, 24-28; 3:6, 9, 14-17, 24; 4:14-16; 2 John 1:2, 9; Rev. 3:2).

■ Similarities between the Gospel and the epistles are clear: what is seen and heard carries authority (John 3:32; 1 John 1:1, 3); the injunction to love one another is abundant (John 13:34-35; 15:12, 17; 1 John 3:11, 14, 16, 23; 4:11-12; 2 John 1:5); adversaries are referred to as "liars" (John 8:44, 55; 1 John 1:10; 2:4, 22; 5:10); eternal life is promised (John 3:15-16, 36; 4:14, 36; 5:24, 39; 6:27, 40, 47, 54, 68; 10:38; 12:25, 50; 17:2-3; 1 John 1:2; 2:25; 3:15; 5:11, 13, 20); the relation of the Father and the Son is emphasized (John 3:35; 5:19-26; 6:40; 14:13; 17:1; 1 John 1:3; 2:22-24; 4:14; 2 John 1:3, 9); water and blood carry testimonial weight (John 13:34; 1 John 5:6-8); one's testimony being "true" carries distinctive rhetorical weight (John 5:32; 19:35; 21:24; 3 John 1:12); loving the world is disparaged (John 12:25; 15:19; 1 John 2:15), but Jesus' followers are in the world (John 13:1; 16:33; 17:11-13; 1 John 4:17); knowing the truth is valued (John 8:32; 1 John 2:21; 2 John 1:1); the Holy Spirit is referred to as "the Spirit of Truth" (John 14:17; 15:26; 16:13; 1 John 4:6), and believers have an advocate before the Father (the Spirit—John 14:16, 26; 15:26; 16:7; Jesus—1 John 2:1).

▪ In addition, distinctive similarities between the Gospel and Revelation are also impressive: Jesus is referred to as "the Lamb of God" (John 1:29, 36; Rev. 19:9; 21:22-23); a voice from heaven is heard (John 12:28; Rev. 4:1; 10:4, 8; 11:12; 12:10; 14:2, 7, 13; 18:4; of a multitude in heaven—19:1); the voice of the bridegroom is featured (John 3:29; Rev. 18:23); references to "this book" are distinctively made (John 20:30; Rev. 22:18-19).

On the other hand:

▪ The thought forms of the Fourth Evangelist are characterized by dialectical thought forms, whereas the author of the epistles thinks in largely monological ways. For the Fourth Evangelist, Jesus is both human and divine, equal and subordinate to the Father, and judging while not judging; for the Elder, if one does not believe Jesus is the Christ, that person is the antichrist (1 John 2:18-25); likewise, if one does not believe Jesus came in the flesh (1 John 4:1-3). It could be that a conjunctive (both-and) approach is more conducive to narrative, while a disjunctive (either-or) stance serves the purpose of an epistle. However, it seems that the Fourth Evangelist is an inductive, first-order thinker, while the Elder is an authority-citing, second-order leader. For the Evangelist, abiding in Jesus is key (John 15:1-8); the Elder advocates abiding in the teaching *about* Jesus. Those are very different realities.

▪ While some similarities of setting, theme, and exhortative thrust exist between the Johannine Gospel and Revelation, the striking differences in form account for most of the stylistic and contextual differences. Revelation uses rougher Greek, and while Johannine in general, it seems best to see it as being rendered in a different hand. If either of these pieces were finalized by another person, however, this could account for some dissimilarities of style. Interestingly, Revelation is the only Johannine writing to contain the name "John" within its text as an authorial reference (Rev. 1:1, 4, 9; 22:8).

▪ Some parts of the epistles seem to be written after the Gospel; some before. The "new commandment" of Jesus (John 13:34) is no longer "new" but an "old commandment" heard from the beginning (1 John 2:7; 2 John 1:5). This makes it appear that the epistles are later. However, Jesus' being the Advocate (*Paraklētos*; 1 John 2:1) is followed by "another Advocate" (John 14:16, 26; 15:26; 16:7) as a later reference. John 1:1-18 also seems to be a fuller expansion of 1 John 1:1-3.

For these reasons, the basic connections between the five Johannine writings seem strong, although Revelation is clearly the most distinctive. As more than one author seems to have contributed to the Gospel's composition, a plurality of authors likely contributed to these writings overall. It could even be that the author of the epistles played a role in the finalizing of the Gospel, and the work of another hand would explain the third-person references to the Beloved Disciple in John 21. Might it even be that the epistles were written between different stages of the Gospel's composition? That would be a plausible inference, especially if the Beloved Disciple continued to preach and teach (and perhaps write) after an earlier edition was written. Regarding Revelation, though, the establishment of particular literary relations with the other Johannine writings is speculative at best.

◼ Intratraditional and Intertraditional Dialogues in John: Reflective or Corrective?

The Johannine tradition is marked by several dialogical features. *Intratraditionally*, the narrator describes earlier understandings of disciples that changed as a factor of later insights and experiences. The narrator also presents more than one perspective on both themes and events, suggesting a dialectical mode of remembering and reflecting on the past. We also see some apparent commentary between the final editor and the Evangelist, as clarifying asides and explanations are added to the narrative. These features suggest an intratraditional set of dialogues within the Johannine tradition. In addition, however, *intertraditional* dialogues are also apparent, suggesting an extended set of dialogues between the developing Johannine tradition and those of the Synoptics. Did the Fourth Evangelist know the Synoptics, or did the Synoptic Evangelists (or their sources) know the Johannine tradition? If so, what sort of relationships might these have been? While we have the three Synoptic Gospels together in a finalized collection, they probably were not known together by anyone in the early church before the mid-second century C.E., and intertraditional contact may have taken place between earlier or different forms of any of the finalized works we have now. And, while we have a finalized Gospel of John to peruse, if this material did not come together until the end of the first century C.E., any Synoptic familiarity with the Johannine tradition was likely partial and varied. Therefore, the particular character of the apparent contacts between the Johannine and each of the Synoptic traditions must be considered individually. While some similarities might suggest intertraditional familiarity, differences of inclusion and presentation might suggest the same as well.

Box 4.7: Intratraditional and Intertraditional Dialogues in John

On one hand, connectedness between impressions within the Johannine tradition abounds:

◼ Parallel to the Markan traditions, where the memory of Jesus' followers is mentioned (Mark 11:21; 14:72; Luke 24:8), John also records instances of the disciples' memory (they remembered the Scripture that fulfilled Jesus' demonstration in the Temple, John 2:17; they remembered after the resurrection his prophecy about building up the "temple" in three days, 2:22; they perceived the triumphal entry differently after Jesus had been glorified, 12:16).

◼ Jesus' disciples and others reportedly "did not understand" what he was saying at the time, but later they did, regarding the Father who sent him (8:27); the sheep knowing the voice of the true shepherd (10:6); Jesus' riding into Jerusalem on a donkey (12:16); the washing of Peter's feet by Jesus (13:7); and the Scripture that Jesus would rise from the dead (20:9).

◼ Explanations of actions and developments in the narrative are added to elucidate internal outcomes and turns of events whereby the narrator sheds light on why things happened the way they did, regarding Jesus and the woman being alone because disciples had gone to buy food (4:8); Jesus' not wanting to go to Judea because leaders there were seeking to kill him (7:1); the blind man's parents' giving an indirect answer because those confessing Jesus had already been put out of the synagogue (9:23); the significance of Caiaphas's statement as the high priest that year making it a prophetic utterance (11:51-52); Judas's not really caring for the poor (he dipped into the common purse, 12:6); Jesus' disciples misunderstanding his betrayal prediction because they thought he was referring to Judas's paying for the meal (13:29); Barabbas's being a thief (18:40); gambling for Jesus' robe because it was a seamless garment (19:23).

▨ Later understandings refer to outcomes actualized well beyond the events reported in the narrative itself, extending into the life of the early church (7:39; 9:22; 12:42-43), and Jesus predicts hardships that his followers would face in the world (16:2, 33), including the deaths of Peter and the Beloved Disciple (21:19, 23).

On the other hand, apparent contacts *between* the Johannine and Synoptic traditions are intriguing:

▨ Mark and John possess a good deal of distinctive material in common, including Jewish words and customs and nonsymbolic illustrative details; the influence may thus have gone either or both ways (two hundred and three hundred denarii, Mark 6:37; 14:5⟵⟶John 6:7; 12:5; the amount of grass at the feeding, Mark 6:39⟵⟶John 6:10). Elsewhere, the Johannine narrator appears to set the record straight regarding the sequence of the Baptist's and Jesus' ministries as presented in Mark (John 3:24→Mark 1:14, arrow indicating possible correction); the prophet's receiving no honor in his hometown (John 4:44→Mark 6:4); Jesus' receiving the wine (John 19:30→Mark 15:36), and what he did and did not say regarding the death of the apostles and the second coming (John 21:22-23→Mark 9:1).

▨ In addition to the adding of Johannine details and traditional units, Luke departs from Mark and sides with John dozens of times—reflecting John's influence: including only one sea crossing and one feeding instead of two (John 6:1-15→Luke 9:10-17, arrow indicating possible influence); moving the confession of Peter to follow the *other* feeding (the five thousand—as it is in John) and conflating "the Christ" with "the Holy One of God" to become "the Christ of God" (Mark 8:29 and John 6:69→Luke 9:20); changing the anointing of Jesus' head to Jesus' feet (John 12:1-8→Luke 7:36-50); and moving the discussion of servanthood to the Last Supper (John 13:1-17→Luke 22:24-30).

▨ The Q tradition (a hypothetical source that scholars infer accounts for material common to Matthew and Luke, but not found in Mark) includes a remarkably Johannine saying (reflecting Johannine influence?): "All things have been handed over to me by my Father; and no one knows the Son except the Father, and no one knows the Father except the Son and anyone to whom the Son chooses to reveal him" (John 3:35; 7:28-29; 10:14-15; 13:3-4; 17:1-3, 22-25→Matt. 11:27 and Luke 10:22) and several other Johannine motifs.

▨ The Johannine presentation of inclusive and inspired ministry, as effected by the Holy Spirit's empowerment and direction, appears in dialogue with Matthew's presentation of the church and its leadership (John 6:68-69; 20:21-23⟵⟶Matt. 16:17-19; 18:18-20).

Within the Johannine tradition developments are apparent. Earlier impressions are confirmed or modified by later ones, and memory thus develops reflectively. More primitive perspectives are challenged by later experiences, and truth is held in tension within the cognitive operation of a dialectical theologian/historian—the Fourth Evangelist. In addition, the Johannine Evangelist seems engaged in corrective and reinforcing dialogues with other traditions as represented in the Synoptics. While none of John's similarities with Synoptic traditions are identical, some contact is still likely. Yet, how is it known which direction influence may have flowed? Might the Johannine tradition have influenced Synoptic ones, and might influence have extended in multiple directions? With different sorts of contacts emerging with different forms and phases of traditional developments being likely, particular contacts between the Johannine and other traditions must be considered individually. The mistake is to limit possibilities to one type of intertraditional relationship, as though one plausible inference excludes all others. Therefore, intratraditional *and* intertraditional dialogical relationships are likely and must be considered critically.

■ The Johannine Collection of Materials: Leftover Fragments or a Seamless Robe?

If the Synoptic traditions pose a basis for understanding the development of the Johannine tradition, might John's material have developed in similar diachronic ways? Put otherwise, do we have signs of disparate units or clusters of material that had their own tradition-histories before finding a place in John's narrative? This interest is especially relevant to studies of the Synoptics, as Mark contains a good number of short paragraphs that the Evangelist appears to have gathered together as a collector and organizer of Gospel material. Luke and Matthew added their own bits here and there, perhaps also drawing from a second source, Q. Does this imply that the Johannine Evangelist may have operated in this way as well? Did he draw from Synoptic-type reservoirs of tradition, including such units within his own tradition, or did he draw from earlier Johannine clusters of tradition, perhaps having their own literary history earlier on? Whatever the case, note also the distinctive Johannine material listed below in categories of literary form.

Box 4.8: Distinctive Sets of Material in John and their Relations

On one hand, distinctive Synoptic-like forms of material abound in John:

■ The I-am sayings of Jesus: (1) *with a predicate nominative*—"the life-producing bread" (6:35, 48, 51); "the light of the world" (8:12; 9:5); "the gate to the sheepfold" (10:7, 9); "the good shepherd" (10:11, 14); "the resurrection and the life" (11:25); "the way, the truth, and the life" (14:6); "the authentic vine" (15:1, 5); (2) *without a nominative*—identification (4:26; 8:24, 28; 13:13, 19; 18:5, 6, 8, 37); (3) *without a nominative*—theophanic (6:20; 8:58); (4) *descriptive of place*—originative/destinative/relative (7:28, 29, 34, 36; 8:16, 23; 10:36; 12:26; 13:33; 14:3; 16:32; 17:11, 14, 16, 24). Note other uses as well: (5) *the associative*—the blind man (9:9); and (6) *the negative*—John the Baptist's denying that he is the Messiah (1:20, 21, 27; 3:28). Note also that I-am sayings are not entirely missing from Mark (Mark 1:7; 6:50; 13:6; 14:62).

■ As a distinctive mark of emphasis, the double *amēn* highlights the importance of many sayings in John, sometimes introducing longer sayings or making an individuated claim (3:3, 5; 5:19; 6:26, 32, 53; 8:34, 58; 10:1, 7; 13:21, 38); sometimes making points of emphasis within a larger unit (3:11; 5:24, 25; 6:47; 12:24; 13:16; 14:12; 16:20, 23); and sometimes concluding sayings (1:51; 8:51; 13:20; 21:18). Mark has fourteen single-*amēn* sayings, and Matthew features over thirty, but John alone in the New Testament attributes double-*amēn* sayings to Jesus, numbering twenty-five.

■ Quite distinctive are the Johannine presentations of dialogues of Jesus: with John's disciples (1:35-43); Nathanael (1:47-51); the mother of Jesus and the servants (2:1-11); Jewish leaders in Jerusalem (2:13-23; 5:16-47; 7:15-52; 8:12-59; 10:22-39); Nicodemus (3:1-21); the Samaritan woman (4:4-26, 28-30, 39-42); Jesus' disciples (431-38; 6:5-13, 60-66; 9:1-7; 11:1-16; 14:1-31; 16:17-33; 21:1-14); the royal official (4:46-54); the invalid (5:5-15); the Galilean crowd (6:25-40); the *Ioudaioi* (6:41-59); Peter (6:67-70; 13:1-20, 31-38; 21:15-23); the brothers of Jesus (7:1-10); the man born blind and the Judean Pharisees (9:35—10:21); Mary and Martha (11:17-45); Judas (12:4-7); the Hellenists and the Jerusalem crowd (12:20-36); the Beloved Disciple and Judas (13:21-30); the soldiers (18:1-9); the High Priest and the guard (18:19-24); Pilate (18:28—19:16); Mary Magdalene (20:11-18); and Thomas (20:24-29).

■ Jesus' signs are also featured with distinctive prominence in John, often becoming a platform for an extended dialogue or discourse: the turning of water into wine in Cana (2:1-11); the healing of the Capernaum official's son from afar (4:46-54); the healing of the invalid in Jerusalem (5:1-15); the multiplication of the loaves (6:1-15); the Galilean sea-crossing (6:16-21); the healing of the Judean blind man (9:1-41); the raising of Lazarus of Bethany from the dead (11:1-44); and the great catch of fish on the sea of Tiberias (21:1-14).

On the other hand, the Johannine narrative shows an impressive interwovenness between the different types of material:

■ The signs of Jesus flow readily into discourses and dialogues, appearing to have an integrated history: after the first healing on the Sabbath, debates follow over Jesus' authorization leading to discourses on his relation to the Father (5:1-9→5:10-47); the feeding leads into discussions of the loaves and Jesus' discourses on being the Bread of Life (6:1-15→6:25-71); following the healing of the blind man, discussions emerge leading to an assertion of the blindness of those who claim to see (9:1-7→9:41); preceding Jesus' raising of Lazarus, discussions arise leading to Jesus' claiming to be the resurrection and the life (11:1—12:11←→11:25).

■ The double-*amēn* sayings occur not as separate sayings but as emphases within the narrative, most often emerging either within dialogues or discourses: with Nicodemus (3:3, 5, 11); with the Jerusalem authorities (5:19, 24, 25; 8:34, 51, 58; 10:1, 7); with the Galilean crowd (6:26, 32, 47, 53); and with his disciples (1:51; 13:16, 20, 21, 38; 14:12; 16:20, 23; 21:21).

■ Likewise, dialogues and discourses tend to flow into each other with remarkable ease, with misunderstanding being set straight by the I-am sayings of the Johannine Jesus: Jesus' being the Bread of Life (6:35, 41, 48, 51) fits in with his discussions with the crowd and the Jews; his being the Light of the World (8:12; see also 9:5), the Gate of the Sheepfold (10:7, 9), and the Good Shepherd (10:11, 14) inform his discussions with the Jerusalem authorities; his being the Resurrection and the Life (11:25) culminates his discussions with Mary and Martha; his being the Way, the Truth, and the Life (14:6) and the true Vine (15:1, 5) punctuate his discussions with his disciples.

While the Fourth Gospel contains different literary forms of material, there is no indication its distinctive forms enjoyed separate histories of development, for example, clusters of sayings or dialogues enjoying histories separate from those of the signs or other material. Rather, the Johannine sayings, dialogues, and signs seem to have been interwoven from the early stages of the Johannine tradition rather than cobbled together by a later editor. Therefore, instead of reflecting a gathered-up collection of leftover fragments, the Johannine narrative displays something closer to a seamless robe woven from top to bottom. There is no evidence of a later merging of disparate literary forms or sources, and in that respect, the unity of the Johannine tradition is very different from the conjoined traditions of the Synoptic Gospels.

■ Comprehension and Miscomprehension in John: They Just Don't Get It . . . Do You?

The knowledge of Jesus is presented as a factor in the development of the narrated events, contrasted with the misunderstandings of his audiences. The protagonist of the story shares the omniscience of the narrator, and from the perspective of the known outcome, the progression of the plot is interpreted accordingly. Not only does the narrator declare that Jesus understands hidden motives and stances of his subjects; Jesus also declares his knowledge in his teachings. The lack of comprehension among others is also highlighted, and in narrative, misunderstanding always functions rhetorically. Sometimes human responses to Jesus determine what happens next in the narrative; because of their belief or unbelief, Jesus' actions take a particular turn. On the other hand, sometimes Jesus makes a move based entirely upon his knowing what was in human thoughts or inclinations; therefore, he did not entrust himself to unbelieving crowds, or he challenged oppositional religious leaders. In that sense, Jesus never makes an unknowing blunder, and the hearer/reader is thereby drawn into the fellowship of the insiders by the narrator.

Box 4.9: The Knowledge of Jesus and the Misunderstanding of Characters

On one hand, the "knowledge of Jesus" is presented as a factor in how things developed in the narrative:

- Jesus knows full well what he will do (4:1; 5:6; 6:6; 13:1-3; 18:4; 19:28); he also declares his knowledge in his teachings (5:32, 42; 8:55; 10:14-15, 27; 11:42; 12:50; 17:25).
- Jesus' "knowledge" of the situation of others is presented as a factor in their becoming convinced (2:24-25; 6:64; 11:42; 13:11; 16:19), as people feel themselves intimately "known" in their encounters with Jesus, they come to believe in his being the Messiah (1:45-51; 4:17-19, 25-30, 53; 20:15-16).

- Knowing and not knowing are presented straightforwardly in the narrative (1:26-34; 3:10; 5:13; 8:37; 9:12, 20-21; 11:57; 13:35; 18:2; 20:2, 13).
- Knowledge and understanding are presented as positive examples for others to follow (4:10, 25, 42; 6:69; 7:17; 8:32; 9:25; 10:4-5, 38; 11:22-24; 13:12, 17; 14:31; 16:30; 17:3, 7-8, 23; 19:35; 21:24).

On the other hand, the world's lack of knowledge or faith also plays a role in the development of the Johannine plot:

- Jesus' "knowledge" of inadequate faith or understanding is also presented as a factor in his own reactions to others or the outcomes of events (2:24-25; 6:15, 64; 7:28-29; 8:14, 19, 55; 13:7, 11, 18; 14:7, 9, 17; 15:21; 16:3, 19).
- Conversely, people's lack of understanding or knowledge at the time is presented as a factor in the development of events or Jesus' actions (1:10; 2:22; 3:10; 8:55; 10:6; 11:13; 12:16; 13:28; 16:18; 17:25; 20:9; 20:14; 21:4).
- Knowing and not knowing are presented ironically within the narrative (2:9; 3:2, 8; 6:42; 7:26-27, 49; 8:52; 9:24, 29-31; 11:49-50; 13:28; 18:21; 19:10; 21:9, 12, 15-17).
- Not knowing or understanding is presented rhetorically: it portrays negative examples for others not to follow (4:22, 32; 8:27, 43; 12:35; 15:15).

In addition to the narrative function of the transcendent knowledge of Jesus, people's responses to him also play distinctive roles. Whenever Jesus' audiences get it right and receive him knowingly, this provides a positive example for others to follow. However, whenever others get it wrong or fail to comprehend entirely what Jesus is doing or saying, such presentations serve rhetorical and corrective functions. Even partial understanding plays a corrective role, and the hearer/reader is thereby motivated to get it right by contrast. Especially powerful is Johannine irony, which in both local and extended presentations moves the story forward with compelling rhetorical thrust. Whenever political or religious figures of higher status are presented as claiming knowledge, while at the same time being exposed as ignorant, such reversals are particularly striking. Likewise, when the sick, the unsophisticated, or the underprivileged get it right, such reversals are also compelling. Thus, noting the function of varying responses to Jesus serves one's comprehension of the Johannine narrative well. When characters get it right, the example is a positive one to follow; when they get wrong, reader beware! That is an option to avoid.

Scripture Fulfillment in John: Implicit or Explicit?

Scripture and its fulfillment are connected in various ways in the Fourth Gospel—some implicitly and others more explicitly. As literary features, echoes of biblical themes connect Jesus to Israel's heroes of old, yoking their authority to his mission. Some are subtle, such as the mention of barley loaves (the same food with which

Elijah fed the multitude, 2 Kgs. 4:42→John 6:9, 13), while others are more explicit, such as Moses' lifting up the serpent on a pole (those who looked to it were healed/saved, Num. 21:9→John 3:14-15). By contrast, biblical texts are also fulfilled explicitly, either by citing a reference or by using biblical language. Sometimes Scripture is cited by Jesus, sometimes by characters in the story, and sometimes by the narrator. In every instance the use of Scripture furthers the rhetorical interests of the Evangelist.

Box 4.10: Typological and Textual Fulfillments of Scripture

On one hand, Jewish Scripture finds its fulfillment in John implicitly and typologically:

- The Word and Wisdom of God are the source of creation and redemption in Hebrew Scripture (arrows here showing influence, Gen. 1:1—2:4; Prov. 8:22-30→John 1:1-18).
- Being children of Abraham is asserted by Jews in Jerusalem, who claim they were slaves to no one; Yahweh's promise to bless the world is fulfilled in the Greeks' coming to Jesus (Genesis 12–22→John 8:12-59; 12:20-21).
- Parallels to the ascending and descending angels of Jacob's ladder are referenced by Jesus, and in contrast to the water from Jacob's well, the water Jesus avails is living and life-producing (Gen. 28:12→John 1:51; 4:5-12).
- Just as Moses brought the law and anticipated Jesus, Jesus brought grace and truth. Just as Moses raised a serpent on a pole, provided manna in the wilderness, and produced a wondrous sea crossing, Jesus was raised on a cross, fed the multitude, and delivered his disciples safely to the shore of the lake. The fulfilled word of the authentic prophet confirms that a messenger has been sent by God and that he should be responded to as to God.
- While Jesus' coming from the city of David is debated, he indeed rides into Jerusalem on a donkey, fulfilling the Davidic prophecies of Zechariah. (Zech. 9:9→John 12:14)
- Just as Elijah raised the son of the widow of Zarephath and parted the water with his mantle, and just as Elisha raised the son of the Shunammite woman from the dead and fed the crowd of one hundred with barley loaves, so Jesus raised Lazarus from the dead, fed the five thousand with barley loaves and fish, and delivered his disciples across the sea (1 Kgs. 17:17-24; 2 Kgs. 2:8; 4:8-44→John 11:1-44; 6:1-21).
- Just as Ezekiel referred to his lowly obedience to God with "Son of Man" language, and just as Daniel used the same term with reference to the heavenly agent of God coming to judge the earth, Jesus as the Son of Man in John obeys whatever the Father commands and is paradoxically lifted up on the cross as a result of his divine commission.

On the other hand, explicit references to Scripture being fulfilled are many:

- The reader is told that disciples later found anticipated in Scripture a particular meaning for what Jesus had done or said (arrows here showing reference: the Temple incident, John 2:17→Ps. 69:9; the resurrection, John 2:22→20:9 and Hebrew Scripture in general; the triumphal entry, John 12:13-16→Zech. 9:9); generally, the disciples and Jesus both point to Scripture as that which testifies to his mission and authenticity (John 1:45; 5:39→Deut. 18:15-22).
- Hebrew Scripture is cited by a person or group (John the Baptist declaring his mission, John 1:23→Isa. 40:3; the crowd at the entry to Jerusalem, John 12:13→Ps. 118:25-26), at times in

flawed ways (the Jewish leaders after the feeding, John 6:31→Exod. 16:4; Neh. 9:15; Ps. 78:24-25; the Jerusalem authorities in seeking a Davidic Messiah, John 7:41-42→Mic. 5:2).

▣ Jesus cites Scripture directly at times (John 6:45→Isa. 54:13; John 7:38→possibly Zech. 14:8; Isa. 44:3; John 8:17→Deut. 17:6; 19:15; John 10:34-35→Ps. 82:6; John 13:18→Ps. 41:9; John 15:24-25→Pss. 35:19 and 69:4; John 17:12→possibly Pss. 41:9 and 42:10) in the course of explaining his actions and teachings.

▣ The narrator cites the fulfillment of a particular Scripture passage (John 12:14-15→Zech. 9:9; John 12:38→Isa. 53:1; John 12:39-41→Isa. 6:10; John 19:24→Ps. 22:18; John 19:28-29→Ps. 69:21; John 19:31-36→Exod. 12:10, 46; Num. 9:12; and Ps. 34:20; John 19:34-37→Zech. 12:10) as the culmination of Jesus' ministry, reflecting a special set of connections between events and scriptural associations.

While some Scripture allusions are presented as emerging out of Jesus' ministry and its reception, several of them are presented as a factor of connections made in postresurrection consciousness—probably emerging from worship settings that connected the narration of stories about Jesus and the reading of texts from Hebrew Scripture. At first disciples did not understand, but later, upon reading Hebrew Scripture, connections were made between Jesus' actions and words and biblical references (2:22). These unfolding discoveries within the Johannine tradition eventually became part of the Johannine apologetic thrust, wherein Jesus is presented as fulfilling Scripture both implicitly and explicitly. The interest, of course, is to show that Jesus indeed was the Jewish Messiah as prophesied in Scripture.

▣ The Purpose of the Fourth Gospel: Apologetic or Pastoral?

John's statement of purpose in 20:31 ("these things are written that you might *believe*") is the clearest statement of literary intentionality anywhere in the Bible, but what does "believing" really mean? While the end result is clear, that believers have life in Jesus' name, controversy has revolved around what is meant by the verb *believe*. On the face of it, believing seems to involve accepting that Jesus is sent from the Father as the Messiah/Christ, whom believers receive as the Son of God and the way to the Father. Therefore, believing involves coming to faith for the first time—receiving the *evangel*, the good news—a response to an apologetic thrust. On the other hand, believing is at times associated with abiding and remaining in Jesus as a matter of faithfulness—not abandoning the community as the schismatics of the epistles appear to have done. That would involve a pastoral thrust. Intrigue is compounded by the fact that some Greek texts (see Box 4.3, above) suggest first-time belief, while others suggest continuing belief. These themes are also evident in the text.

Box 4.11: John 20:31—Coming to Faith, or Continuing in Faithfulness?

On one hand, the material in John is crafted so that the hearer/reader might believe that Jesus is the Christ, the Son of God:

- *Witnesses* testify that Jesus has been authentically sent from God: John the Baptist came to testify to Jesus (1:6-8, 15, 26-36; 3:27-30); others include the Samaritan woman (4:2-42), the man born blind (9:9-38), and Lazarus (11:45—12:9); in addition, the Father (5:37; 8:18), the *Paraklētos* (14:26; 15:26), Jesus' works (5:36; 10:26), the Scriptures and Moses (5:39, 46), and Jesus' followers witness to Jesus' being sent from God (15:27). Finally, the eyewitness (19:35) and the Beloved Disciple (21:24) testify truly about Jesus' divine commission.
- The *signs* of Jesus testify to his having been sent from God: Jesus provides merriment that purification jars otherwise never could (2:1-11); heals the official's son from afar (4:46-54); commands power to heal on the Sabbath (5:1-15); feeds the multitude and calms the storm (6:1-21); restores the sight of the blind (9:1-7); raises the dead (11:1-45); and directs a great catch of fish (21:1-11). No one could do such signs unless he were sent from God (3:2; 9:33; 10:41-42)—the signs of Jesus invite belief in his divine agency.
- The *fulfilled word* confirms the authenticity of Jesus' mission: First, the fulfilled word of Scripture shows that he is the Christ (see Box 4.10, above); note especially Jerusalem events—the Temple incident (arrows imply reference: 2:17→Ps. 69:9) and entry into Jerusalem (12:13-15→Ps. 118:25-26; Zech. 9:9); the unbelief of the crowds (12:38-41→Isa. 53:1; 6:10) and rejection in Jerusalem (15:24-25→Ps. 109:3); his betrayal by Judas (13:18→Ps. 41:9); the casting of lots for his robe (19:24→Ps. 22:18) and the piercing of Jesus' side (19:37→Zech. 12:10) rather than the breaking of his legs (19:36→Exod. 12:10, 46; Num. 9:12; Ps. 34:20). Second, the fulfilled words of Jesus show that he truly is the prophet like Moses (whose word always comes true, Deut. 18:15-22)—regarding the raised-up "temple" of his body (arrows imply prediction: 2:19, 22→20:1-28); the official's son, who will live (4:50→4:53); Jesus' death on the cross (6:51→19:16-30); the prediction of his abandonment (6:64→66), betrayal (6:64, 71→18:2-5) and denial (13:38→18:17-27); Lazarus's sickness, which will not end in death (11:4, 23→11:43-44); the arresting of Jesus only and not his disciples (6:39; 17:12→18:8-9). Jesus declares explicitly that he predicts things ahead of time so that when they are fulfilled people will believe (13:19→18:2-5), including his means of death (3:14; 8:28; 12:32-33→18:31-32; 19:16). Third, Caiaphas's fulfilled word as the high priest that year comes across as an unwitting prophecy regarding Jesus' death on behalf of the world (11:47-53→12:20-36).

On the other hand, the Johannine Gospel calls for believers to stay with Jesus in solidarity with him and his community:

- Jesus admonishes his followers to abide (remain) in him and he in them: by eating and drinking Jesus' flesh and blood (6:56); as the branch is connected to the vine (15:4-10); being mutually indwelt by the Spirit of Truth (14:17).
- The fleshly suffering of Jesus foreshadows the way of the cross for future believers: in the flesh-becoming-Word is the glory of God experienced (1:14); by ingesting the martyrological bread that Jesus gives and is (6:48-58); finding life by willingness to die—as a buried kernel of wheat (12:24-25); loving one another as Jesus has loved them and has laid down his life for them (13:34; 15:13); enduring the hatred of the world (15:18-25; 17:14); the eyewitness testifies that water and blood poured forth from the side of the suffering Lord (19:34-35).

▓ The guidance and empowerment of the Holy Spirit is promised as a resource bolstering believers' faith and faithfulness: the Spirit will be poured out in fullness after Jesus' glorification (7:39); another Advocate will be sent—the Spirit of Truth, to be with believers forever and in them (14:16-17); the Advocate—the Holy Spirit—will teach and remind them all that Jesus has taught them (14:26); the Advocate will testify on Jesus' behalf (15:26); Jesus must depart in order for the Advocate to come—convicting the world of sin and righteousness and judgment (16:7-11); the Spirit of Truth will guide believers into all truth as he glorifies Jesus by declaring his word faithfully (16:13-14).

Ample evidence supports the view that the Gospel of John calls the audience to come to faith in Jesus as the Messiah/Christ, sent from the Father in love to the world. Then again, to believe in Jesus is also to remain with him and his followers, in solidarity with the Christian community in the face of later hardship and hostility from the world. The fulfilled word of Jesus not only applies to events that were verified during his earthly ministry, but it also extends to postresurrection experience. Jesus predicts that the world and his disciples will no longer see him, but then that they will later see him (14:19; 16:10→20:19), and his promise to send the Holy Spirit after he has departed indeed comes true (14:16-17; 15:26; 16:7→20:22), which confirms his being the authentic prophet like Moses (Deut. 18:15-22). Even the deaths of Peter and the Beloved Disciple are understood to have been prophesied earlier by Jesus, confirming his authority in the light of later realities (21:18-24). Might we have *two* main purposes of the Johannine Gospel instead of only one? Especially if some parts of John were added to an earlier edition (such as 1:1-18, chaps. 6, 15–17, and 21, and 19:34-35, etc.), the purposes of earlier and later editions of John may indeed have been different. The first edition seems to be apologetic—leading people to believe in Jesus as the Jewish Messiah/Christ; the later material seems to call for solidarity with Jesus and his community in the face of later hardship. So, in response to whether John's rhetorical thrust is apologetic or pastoral, the answer may well be "Yes."

▓ The Beloved Disciple: A Dead Author or a Literary Device?

Scholars in recent years have been interested not only in who the Beloved Disciple might have been, but also in the figure's literary function within the narrative. As the purported author, the Beloved Disciple is referred to as the source of the Gospel's writing (21:24); some of its material comes from him (19:34-35); but the figure plays other roles, too. As a character in the story, this figure always gets it right, thus exemplifying ideal discipleship. He enjoys an intimate relationship with Jesus (13:23); is the only one of the Twelve present at the cross; becomes the custodian of the Lord's mother (19:26-27); beats Peter to the tomb but graciously allows him to enter first

(20:2-8); and he even becomes a bridge between Peter and the resurrected Lord (21:7). Thus playing an exemplary role within the narrative—whoever he might have been—his implied death is even "explained" by the final editor (21:20-24). That being the case, however, his unnamed identity is puzzling. If his identity were indeed known, why is it not stated clearly? Perhaps this disciple's anonymity allows the reader to "fill in the blank," inserting his or her own name in his place. Then again, references to the person seem explicit—including a reference to his having died.

Box 4.12: The Beloved Disciple and Anonymity in the Fourth Gospel

On one hand, references to the Beloved Disciple as a specific person seem intentional in John:

- He leaned against Jesus' breast, showing intimacy with the Lord (13:23).
- If he is "the other disciple" associated with the Beloved Disciple elsewhere (20:2-8), his being known to the High Priest facilitates entrance into the courtyard (18:16).
- He is present at the crucifixion, whereupon Jesus entrusts his mother to his care (19:26-27).
- He arrives at the tomb before Peter but allows Peter to enter first; there he believes (20:2-8).
- He is the first to recognize the risen Lord in Galilee and serves as a bridge between Peter and Jesus (21:7).
- Jesus explains the timing of the Beloved Disciple's death in relation to his return (21:20-23).
- The Beloved Disciple is referenced as the author of the Johannine narrative, and his witness is attested corporately as true (21:24).

On the other hand, anonymity plays a subtle role within the narrative:

- One of the two disciples who first left John the Baptist and followed Jesus at the beginning is left unnamed (1:35, 37).
- Individuals in the story are left unnamed—the steward of the feast, the Samaritan woman, the invalid by the pool, the man born blind, etc.
- Groups of people are left unnamed—the disciples, Jesus' brothers, the Judeans, the crowd, the Pharisees, the Temple police, etc.
- The mother of Jesus is left unnamed (2:1-12; 6:42; 19:25-27).
- The eyewitness who testifies to the blood and water pouring forth from Jesus' side at the crucifixion is left unnamed (19:34-35).
- The "other disciple" is left unnamed although associated with the Beloved Disciple (18:16; 20:2-8).
- The Beloved Disciple is left unnamed (13:23; 19:26; 20:2; 21:7, 20).

These instances suggest two things: first, the Beloved Disciple is clearly credited with being the source of the Johannine tradition, and his prominence is telling. He is linked with Peter in several important scenes, and his actions prove exemplary for later generations. It also appears that he has died by the time the narrative is final-ized, so a second hand seems at work in finalizing the text he began. Therefore, not only do the final editor and his community attest to the truth of his witness, but he seems to be an esteemed fountain and source of John's distinctive memory of Jesus.

Second, anonymity is also a common feature in the Fourth Gospel, but assum-ing it to diminish the identity of the author is problematic. Indeed, all characters in the story invite readers into their places and thereby into transformative, imaginary dialogues with Jesus. The Beloved Disciple is no different, except that he always gets it right. It would be wrong, though, to infer anonymity to reflect a diminishment of the Beloved Disciple's identity. If the mother of Jesus can be taken as a parallel, the fact of her remaining anonymous does not prove that she was not "Mary" who is known to the Judeans (6:42); nor does the anonymity of Jesus' brothers prove they were not James or Jude; nor does the general reference to "those of Zebedee" (21:2) prove that they were neither James nor John. As in Mary's case, three features stand out: (a) there were other women named "Mary" in the narrative, so the descriptor "his mother" is clearer; (b) she was familiar to the audience—at least in earlier renderings; (c) she was highly respected within the narrative and its audience: here anonymity implies esteem. If we extend these three features of Mary's anonymity to the case of the Beloved Disciple—being distinguished from others bearing the same name ("disciple"), presumed familiarity to the audience, and evident respect—far from disconfirming his particular identity, they may confirm not only the tradition but its personal source.

■ Conclusion

So, is John a seamless robe, woven from top to bottom as a unitive construction—to be gambled over but not to be torn (19:24)? Or is John a collection of literary fragments—gathered into distinctive literary baskets, to be broken, bound, and blessed as disparate parts of a seeming whole (6:13)? Overall we have a synchronic-ity of tradition with a diachronicity of development, as John deserves consideration as an autonomous composition. John's theological tensions, combined with its liter-ary perplexities, make an explosive mix! Indeed, the varied features of John's liter-ary riddles challenge easy answers to its composition and development, which is why good scholars have disagreed with each other over the years on such matters.

■ Questions to Consider

1. Why does the author of the last few verses of John refer to *another* person as the author and Beloved Disciple (someone not himself), commenting also on Jesus' never having said that this disciple "would not die" (21:23)?

2. What do you think of the evidence for dialogues *within* the Johannine tradition (intratraditionally) and *between* the Johannine and other traditions (intertraditionally)?

3. If there was an earlier and a later edition of the Johannine narrative, might there also have been a difference in purpose between these editions—and if so, how so?

▇ Terms to Understand

- aporia
- intratraditional dialogue
- intertraditional dialogue
- typological

Summation of Part 1

W hen considering even the basic features of the Fourth Gospel, its riddles quickly become apparent. Theologically, nearly every major theme
appears to have more than one side to it, and these poles must be held
together in tension lest the material be overlooked or misunderstood. It is therefore
understandable that some of the leading theological controversies in Christian history have revolved around seeking to understand issues of which the Fourth Gospel
represents both sides.

In the modern era, this same Gospel has contributed to some of the most
intense historical debates in the Western world, as proponents of all three historical quests for Jesus have programmatically excluded the one Gospel that claims
firsthand contact with Jesus and his ministry. Then again, the Johannine Gospel is
highly theological as well as historical, which is a major reason why its differences
with the Synoptics have rendered it the historical loser when push comes to shove.

Literarily, the Fourth Gospel also has its own set of challenges, however, as
rough transitions in the text raise questions of its composition history, and similarities and differences with the Synoptics evoke questions as to potential relations with
other traditions. Given the fact of John's theological, historical, and literary riddles,
one can understand how even the best of biblical scholars have come to different
perspectives on the origin and development of its tradition. We turn to a consideration of these perspectives in Part 2.

PART 2

Addressing the Johannine Riddles

H aving outlined the riddles of the Fourth Gospel, the question now is how to address them and how to interpret the Gospel of John in light of the issues they raise. Of course, the ultimate goal of reading any classic text, especially this favorite Gospel text, is to open oneself to its message and to allow its story to engage us personally. Otherwise, can we really claim that we are taking a text seriously? So, I ask you to read over the Gospel of John again, having noted its riddles and tensions, but this time asking yourself how the message speaks to you. Are there particular characters in the story with whom you resonate? Are there notions and opinions that Jesus affirms or challenges that you feel may affirm or challenge readers today in similar ways? Does the work inspire or offend you? Either way, why?

As we address the Johannine riddles in the second part of this book, the place to begin is to survey some of the leading ways the Gospel of John has been approached by religious leaders and by scholars over the centuries (chapter 5), followed by what I think is the best way do so, which I describe as the *dialogical autonomy of the Fourth Gospel* (chapter 6). Of course, we could have started with these two chapters and outlined the riddles later, but a fuller understanding of the issues addressed by each of these approaches builds a good deal of empathy for it, even if a particular view is not finally embraced. These discussions will lead us to consider the origin and character of the riddles of the Fourth Gospel (chapter 7), leading to guidelines for interpretation.

Scholarly Approaches to John

pproaches to the Fourth Gospel are often divided into two larger categories: traditional and critical approaches to John. But this simplistic division fails to do justice to astute scholarship on more than one front. While it is largely true that scholarly approaches to John before the nineteenth century were fairly uniform in their appraisals, it cannot be said that they were uncritical. And, while a great number of scholarly approaches to John have developed over the last two centuries, it cannot be said that there is a general consensus about one particular way to approach the Fourth Gospel. This analysis will attempt an overview of the leading theories regarding John's origin and development, including appraisals of each view. It will become readily apparent how each approach has attempted to address particular aspects of the Johannine riddles, albeit with varying degrees of engagement and success. As all approaches have their own sets of strengths and weaknesses, appreciating both sets of features will help us address the Johannine riddles in service to meaningful interpretation of the biblical text.

While many more theories of John's composition could be included, this chapter will limit itself to a dozen leading views regarding John's origin, character, and development, noting leading scholars who have furthered each of these views. While some approaches will be relevant regardless of who wrote the Gospel of John, some of them rely specifically on what a scholar does with the question of authorship. Put otherwise, if one believes that the Gospel of John represents an independent memory of, and reflection upon, Jesus' ministry, that will determine the approach one takes. Conversely, if a scholar believes the Fourth Gospel cannot represent an independent tradition with its own perspective on Jesus and his ministry, that posture will require alternative explanations as to how the Johannine tradition came together. A third set of approaches reflects theories developed on the basis of textual features themselves, regardless of who might have written the narrative. Considering the strengths and weaknesses of these theories within each of these categories will then provide a basis for a new synthesis for which I will argue in the following chapter.

■ The Author as the Source of the Johannine Tradition

The "traditional view" that John the son of Zebedee was the source of the Johannine tradition fits within the larger rubric of an individuated memory about the ministry of Jesus, which is parallel to the Markan traditions but not dependent on them. This certainly was the second-century view. John the son of Zebedee is not the only person connected with the personal source of John's material as a firsthand witness, however. Other members of the Twelve have also been proposed for the figure of the Beloved Disciple, as well as other first-generation Christians who might not have been among the Twelve. That being the case, the following four theories represent leading approaches to the origin and development of the Johannine tradition that assume the Beloved Disciple enjoyed a firsthand relationship with Jesus, and that his memory is represented in the Johannine witness. It might be said that whoever the Evangelist might have been, he himself *was* the tradition!

The "Traditional" View—John the Son of Zebedee as the Beloved Disciple

The traditional view of the Fourth Gospel, held consistently from the second century through the eighteenth century, is built on the view that the Fourth Gospel was written by John the son of Zebedee, who, after the Synoptics were written, produced his own presentation of Jesus' ministry with its own emphases and content. He also is credited with having written the three Johannine epistles and Revelation, which alone bears the name John within the text. The Muratorian Canon (ca. 170 C.E.), an ancient list of New Testament canonical books, affirms John the son of Zebedee as the author of the Johannine Gospel and epistles as follows:[1]

> When his [that is, John's] fellow-disciples and bishops urged him, he said: "Fast with me from today for three days, and what will be revealed to each one let us relate to one another." In the same night it was revealed to Andrew, one of the apostles, that, whilst all were to go over (it), John in his own name should write everything down. . . . What wonder then if John, being thus always true to himself, adduces particular points in his epistles also, where he says of himself: "What we have seen with our eyes and have heard with our ears and our hands have handled, that have we written to you." For so he

confesses (himself) not merely an eye and ear witness, but also a writer of all the marvels of the Lord in order.

Even Ptolemy, the student of the Gnostic leader Valentinius, in his commentary on the Prologue to the Gospel of John attributes it clearly to "John, the disciple of the Lord," although his exegesis is questioned rather pointedly by the church father Irenaeus. Interestingly, Irenaeus does not challenge Gnostic threats by disparaging the authorship of the Fourth Gospel; he argues for a fourfold Gospel on the basis that John, the disciple of the Lord, was indeed the author of the Fourth Gospel, and he also argues that he was the author of the Johannine epistles and Revelation. When some second-century Christians grew uncomfortable with what some interpreters were doing with Revelation (that is, arguing a millenarian form of apocalyptic speculation) and others with the Gospel of John (for example, the controversial Montanus claimed the authority of the Johannine *Paraklētos* for his "New Prophecy"), Epiphanius, a stalwart defender of orthodoxy, labeled these interpreters as *alogoi* (that is, against the *Logos*, or even "irrational"). In this process, the authority of Revelation was bolstered by its being connected to the Johannine Gospel. This connection later helped to secure Revelation's place among the canonical writings of the New Testament; likewise the second and third Johannine epistles.

In his *Ecclesiastical History* (ca. 325 C.E.), Eusebius cites earlier traditions claiming that after the destruction of Jerusalem by the Romans (70 C.E.), the apostles drew lots, and John's lot fell to go to Asia Minor, where he later died under the reign of Trajan (post-98 C.E.). John's ministry was reportedly interrupted when the Roman emperor Domitian exiled him to Patmos in 84 C.E., although John is said to have returned to Ephesus after Domitian's death (d. 96 C.E.). The traditional view therefore is that John the disciple wrote the Gospel and epistles of John from Ephesus, and then wrote the bulk of Revelation while on Patmos.

While critical biblical scholarship arguably has challenged the traditional view of John's authorship more than any other, that view also has a variety of staunch defenders. B. F. Westcott argued concentrically (from generality to specificity) that internal and external evidence demonstrated that the Johannine Evangelist was: (a) a Jew, (b) from Palestine, (c) an eyewitness, (d) an apostle, and finally (e) John the son of Zebedee.[2] Meantime, Leon Morris, Donald Carson, Ramsey Michaels, and Andreas Köstenberger, among others, have also maintained John the apostle as the source and author of the Johannine Gospel, although some diversity remains on whether he may have been the conceptual source of the material with another doing the final writing, or whether he was the authorial source of all five Johannine writings: the Gospel, the epistles, and the Apocalypse. More scholars take the former stance than the latter one.

Box 5.1: Westcott's Concentric Defense of the Traditional View

Moving from larger circles, or sets, to smaller ones, the Fourth Evangelist was:

- *a Jew*—his explanations of Jewish customs and religious realities, use of Aramaic language, and knowledge of Hebrew Scripture make this clear.
- *from Palestine*—the Gospel's archaeological and topographical details show firsthand familiarity with Palestine, particularly Jerusalem, and bear the stamp of authenticity.
- *an eyewitness*—references to persons, time, number, place, and measure seem to be rooted in firsthand memory of Jesus' ministry.
- *an apostle*—the Johannine insights about the feelings, imperfections, and erroneous-yet-corrected impressions of the disciples, as well as insights into Jesus' intentions, suggest proximity to the Lord.
- *John the son of Zebedee*—the Beloved Disciple's relation to Peter, connections with the sons of Zebedee in John 21, and the unanimous second-century testimony to John's being the author of the Fourth Gospel confirm this view.

The *strengths* of the traditional view include the following:

- The second-century testimonies to the apostle John's connection to the Johannine writings are largely unanimous, and there is no other person in early church memory directly connected with the authorship of the Fourth Gospel than John the son of Zebedee.
- The Gospel of John appears to be presenting its own perspective on the ministry of Jesus, perhaps even in dialogue with the Markan Gospels, which argues strongly for someone like John being the authorial source of this distinctive witness.
- Personal knowledge of people, their places of origin, relationships, and the regions of Galilee and Judea argue strongly that the Johannine narrative reflects a firsthand witness.
- If John the apostle was uncomfortable with exorcism work being done by others (Mark 9:38; Luke 9:49), his discomfort might account for the absence of exorcisms in the Fourth Gospel; his being paired with Peter in the Synoptics matches the Beloved Disciple's association with Peter in the Fourth Gospel.
- Given that Mary the mother of Jesus is connected with John in later traditions; that second-century Orthodox and Gnostic leaders hold the same opinion on John's authorship; that Polycarp claims to have been tutored by John the apostle in Smyrna; and that much of John's presentation seems preferable historically to the Synoptic renderings, the enduring strength of this view is understandable.

Weaknesses, however, are also many:

- The final editor refers to the Beloved Disciple in third-person ways—an unlikely approach to self-reference.
- It appears that the Beloved Disciple had died by the time the Fourth Gospel was finalized (John 21:20-24), and that it was circulated by a community claiming "his testimony" was true.
- Papias and others argued in the second century that there were two Christian leaders buried at Ephesus named "John"—John the disciple and John the Elder; Irenaeus and others may have conflated these two into one person, unaware that there may have been a plurality of Christian leadership in Ephesus during the late first century.
- The stylistic differences between Revelation and the other writings are highly problematic, making it highly unlikely that the same person authored all five writings.
- The dialectical tensions so prevalent in the Johannine Gospel are largely missing from the Johannine epistles. While linguistic and thematic similarities exist, it seems like we have a first-order creative thinker as the source of the Gospel and a second-order domesticating organizer as the source of the epistles.

So, if John the apostle was involved with Johannine authorship, he likely was not the author of all five Johannine writings, and it appears that an editor finished the Gospel after his death.

The "Elder" John as Compiler and Finalizer of the Gospel and Epistles

While the preaching, teaching, and writing of John the apostle may have underlain much of the Gospel, this is not to say that he was its final editor or even its primary narrator. A leading modification of the traditional view is that John the son of Zebedee's preaching and/or writing may have been gathered by another and was finalized after his death by another John, John the Elder. Alternatively, a co-leader in the Johannine situation may have rendered his own story of Jesus, not as one of the Twelve but as a leader within John's community. If the identification of "two Johns at Ephesus" by Papias and other second-century writers suggests that there was more than one leader within that situation, and if they shared the same name (*Iōannēs* was a common Greek name), it is not at all unlikely that they would have been distinguished by the appellations *disciple* and *elder*. The question is which authorial roles each played.

Scholars adopting this view are fairly numerous, and speculations regarding the contribution of the Elder (in Greek, *ho presbyteros*) go back to the fourth century and earlier. Eusebius, for instance, "solves" the problem of the differences between Revelation and the Gospel by relegating the authorship of Revelation to John the Elder (as distinct from the disciple who wrote the Gospel), and Jerome later expands the Elder's authorial role to include the second and third Johannine epistles. After all, their author introduces himself as "the Elder" (2 John 1:1; 2 John 1:1). In recent years, attributing the Gospel's authorship to the Elder has also been a way of getting around the historical problems in the Fourth Gospel—especially its differences with the Synoptics. Martin Hengel, for instance, questions whether a Galilean fisherman could have used such good Greek and have been so familiar with the environs and religious leadership of Jerusalem. Answer: the Johannine Evangelist was a member of a priestly family in Jerusalem and a younger partner in leadership, who continued the ministry of John the apostle with his own accounts of Jesus' ministry.[3] This would explain why this narrative is so different from the Synoptics, how someone could have produced it so late, why it contains abundant Jerusalem material, and why later confusions of the "two Johns at Ephesus" emerged.

The *strengths* of his view are several.

- It seeks to account for the distinctive material in the Fourth Gospel in a plausible way, and it makes sense of "the Johannine questions" efficiently— especially differences with the Synoptics and a late finalization date. Some second-century traditions recall "John" as wearing priestly garments, and a Jerusalem connection with a priestly family would account not only for John's Jerusalem familiarity, but also for the so-called "other disciple's" being known to the high priest (John 18:15).
- In holding open the possibility that the claims to firsthand connections to Jesus' ministry in 1 John 1:1-3 are tenable, this proposal reinforces the point that more than one eyewitness memory of Jesus may have conveyed Gospel traditions, including the Johannine.[4]
- It would account for the fact that there is a strong link between the testimony of Irenaeus, the memory of Polycarp, and material in the Fourth Gospel— in particular, the ordered naming of the disciples. It also accounts for the apparent confusion of "Johns" at Ephesus, while still promoting an alternative explanation for the autonomous historicity of the Johannine tradition: that is, eyewitness tradition was preserved by an apostle's companion.

Weaknesses, however, are also noted.

- The Fourth Gospel's Jerusalem material and connections are not so specific as to be unattainable on the part of a Galilean leader, who might well have been familiar with the religious and economic center of the nation. After all, visits to Jerusalem were common, and if a twenty-year-old visited Jerusalem two or three times a year, that would make fifty visits before Jesus' last Passover! If, on the strength of Luke 1, the Baptist's father was a priest (and thus known to John's followers who took after Jesus, according to John 1:35-37), and if Jesus' family was related to both the Baptist's family and to the Zebedee family (a possible inference from Jesus' words in John 19:26-27 and Matthew's locating the wife of Zebedee at the crucifixion scene in Matthew 27:56), this could also explain the connection.

- Too much is often made about what a "Galilean fisherman" could or could not have mastered. If Peter and others worked for Zebedee, his was a business owner's household; as well as being prejudicial, assuming that James and John were illiterate because of their occupation may also be wrong. Further, the exclamation that Peter and John were "unschooled and ordinary" in Acts 4:13 refers not to their inadequacy but to their theological proficiency (despite not having been schooled in a rabbinic school); it is *not* a claim that they could not read or write. In that scene, the Jewish leaders then noted *why* Peter and John were so advanced theologically—they had studied under Rabbi Jesus. A similar charge is levied about Jesus in John 7:15, but few would argue that Jesus thus could not read or write.

- Even if John the Elder was an active leader in the Johannine situation, he may have been more of a compiler than the source of the material. On this matter, the particulars remain open for consideration.

While John the Elder may indeed have played a role in the transmission and recording of the Johannine writings, ascertaining the particulars is a challenge. The author of the second and third epistles calls himself "the Elder," and the compiler of the Gospel at least shows impressive similarities with that hand. The identities of the Beloved Disciple and "John" of Revelation, however, have yet to be established.

The Johannine Evangelist as an Alternative Member of the Twelve

Even if John the Elder were the final editor of the Gospel and author of the Johannine epistles, a different eyewitness and member of the Twelve may have been the authorial source of the Johannine tradition. This would accommodate the facts that the Zebedee brothers are mentioned only once in the Gospel of John and that all the references to the sons of Zebedee found in the Synoptics are missing in John. In the most extensive treatment of the Beloved Disciple in recent years, James Charlesworth asks the probing question: Whose testimony stands behind the Johannine witness? Upon rejecting other possibilities, Charlesworth argues that Thomas fits the bill better than any other figure. For one thing, Thomas is present in John 21, where one of the disciples mentioned in that scene is identified as the Beloved Disciple. It cannot be Peter, as he is engaged in a dialogue with the Beloved Disciple, and Charlesworth finds John the son of Zebedee too problematic to be considered a possibility. Given that Thomas makes the concluding confession, "My Lord and my God!" (20:28), and that he plays a climactic role in the narrative, Charlesworth argues that he deserves to be identified as the Beloved Disciple.[5] Other connections might be made between the Beloved Disciple and Andrew, or Philip, as well.

The strengths of this proposal orbit around the fact that an independent eye-witness tradition is forwarded without the liabilities associated with John the son of Zebedee or the problematic departures from the Synoptic accounts. Especially strong is Charlesworth's inference that the Johannine tradition has its roots in the memory and preaching of a *person*, as Gospel traditions were humans, not clusters of ideas circulating in disembodied ways. Therefore, his question as to *whose* testimony represents the Johannine account matches the unitive and distinctive character of the Johannine witness, whoever that person or persons might have been. More pointedly, if Thomas were the Beloved Disciple, we have in the narrative a dramatic transformation of the *doubter* (20:24-27) to the *believer* (20:28). Given that Thomas has the "last word" in the first edition of the material, Charlesworth's case is a strong one.

The general *weakness* with this overall view, however, is that many of the vulnerabilities of the traditional view are also shared by this view, as even an alternative apostolic presentation of Jesus' ministry is so different from the Synoptic presentations. The particular weakness with this specific proposal is that the Johannine narrator declares in John 20:8 that he had believed, while Thomas declares in 20:25 his refusal to believe unless he sees and touches the flesh-wounds of Jesus. Charlesworth accounts for this discrepancy by explaining that the grammar of the text diminishes the apparent contradiction; it remains to be seen whether or not other scholars follow his lead. Other possibilities along these lines include Philip and Andrew, but these cases are not argued as strongly; James the son of Zebedee was killed by Herod Agrippa in 44 c.e. (Acts 12:2), so he is not an option for consideration.

A First-Generation Source, But Not a Member of the Twelve

If the Beloved Disciple was not a member of the Twelve, this would account not only for the Johannine differences with the Synoptics, but also the Evangelist's apparent diminishment of the Twelve, the presentation of Peter as miscomprehending the nature of leadership in John 13 and 21, and the more informal and Spirit-based approach to church leadership. Raymond Brown moved toward this view between his commentaries on the Johannine Gospel and epistles (1966–70, 1984), and Rudolf Schnackenburg made a somewhat similar move between his first volume on John and his later work.[6] However, asserting that the son of Zebedee was "not necessarily" the Johannine Evangelist is a far cry from establishing that he was "necessarily not."

A leading particular candidate that was a first-generation source, but not a member of the Twelve, is Lazarus. After all, Jesus is said to have "loved" Lazarus

(John 11:5, 36), and if the Last Supper was held near Jerusalem—perhaps in Lazarus's home, as the setting of the foot anointing had been—it follows that the host of the home should have been seated next to the honored guest (13:23). The Lazarus theory would also explain:

- The plentitude of Jerusalem and Judean material, given that Bethany was near Jerusalem;
- The "outsider" perspective regarding Peter and the Twelve;
- The "other" disciple's having been known to the high priest in Jerusalem (18:16, assuming this was the Beloved Disciple);
- The climactic featuring of the Lazarus family in John 11–12;
- And even the Johannine narrative's transcendent perspective if the Evangelist had experienced being brought forth from the tomb.

While such scholars as Floyd Filson, Vernard Eller, and Mark Stibbe have argued the Lazarus hypothesis with gusto, Ben Witherington III has led the advance of the Lazarus hypothesis in recent years.[7]

Several other particular theories identify the following candidates for the source of the Johannine tradition:

- Simon the leper; since Mark locates the anointing of Jesus in his home (Mark 14:3), the host would have had a place of honor next to Jesus. It could even be that he was related to Lazarus and his sisters, possibly explaining their single status as adults and Lazarus's illness.
- A Jerusalem priest or Sadducee, following on some second-century traditions describing John the Evangelist as wearing the clothes of a Jewish priest.
- Pierson Parker and Herman Waetjen propose that the "John" of the Johannine tradition was actually "John Mark" of Alexandria, the companion of Paul, making connections with the *Logos* doctrine of Philo of Alexandria.
- Robert Fortna, Thomas Butler, and Sandra Schneiders argue that the Beloved Disciple may have been a *woman*.
- Michael Goulder argues that the Beloved Disciple was none other than the apostle Paul incognito, featuring the gospel of grace upon grace, received by faith, argued in a narrative form.

Each of these theories[8] has its particular *strengths*:

- They account for departures from the Synoptics, omitting Synoptic scenes featuring the sons of Zebedee, and posing something of a critical view of Peter and the Twelve.
- Some of them account for the Judean material distinctive to the Gospel of John by assuming the author was a Judean (Lazarus, his sister Mary, or Simon the leper).

- Others account for distinctive theological features, making connections with similar bodies of literature (*Logos* and Philo; faith and Paul).

Weaknesses of these views include the facts that:

- None of these theories were argued by the early church, or even before the modern era.
- The Beloved Disciple is presented as a companion of Peter in John (13:23-24; 18:15-16; 20:2-4; 21:7, 18-24), but none of these figures is presented distinctively alongside Peter in other canonical or extracanonical sources; however, James and John are grouped together with Peter in the Synoptics, and Peter and John are presented as traveling together in both Jerusalem and Samaria in Acts (3:1, 3, 4, 11; 4:1, 13, 19; 8:14, 17, 25).
- While some of them account for John's less plausible differences from the Synoptics, they fail to account for the ways in which John seems historically more plausible than the Synoptics.

While some problems are solved by identifying the Beloved Disciple as a leader who was not one of the Twelve, new problems arise, such as the fact that he is presented in close relationship with Peter. No ancient traditions make such a move, so charges of revisionism are not without merit. We are still faced with the fact that John and the Synoptics are very different.

■ Composition Theories Distinguishing the Author from an Eyewitness and from John Son of Zebedee

While some theories of the Gospel's origin are based upon inferences of who the Beloved Disciple or the source of the Gospel's material might have been, a second set of theories hinges upon the assumption that whoever the Fourth Evangelist was, he *cannot* have been an eyewitness, and certainly was not John the son of Zebedee. Theories along these lines are exclusively modern in their emergence, and they are largely rooted in attempts to make sense of the Johannine riddles laid out in the first part of this book. Especially significant in this respect are the Fourth Gospel's historical and literary riddles, although its theological tensions also play a role in the construction of several theories. Another factor in excluding John the son of Zebedee in particular is the view that he died early, at the same time as his brother James (44 C.E.). This is first alluded to by Philip of Sides in the fifth century (*History,* codex Baroccianus 142) and echoed by George Hamartolos ("the Sinner") in the ninth century (*Chronicon,* codex Coislinianus 305), but this view faces huge critical problems. First, neither Philip nor George state that James and John died at the same time; they only make reference to Jesus' words in Mark 10:38-39 being fulfilled, that the Zebedee brothers would indeed suffer martyrdom. Second, both claim that Papias (d. 150 C.E.) was an "earwitness" to John the theologian and apostle, who was followed by John the Elder (conversely, Eusebius claims that Papias did not know the apostles but was a companion of their followers—that is, John the Elder). Third, George goes on to report that John the apostle died as a martyr in Ephesus (*not* in Jerusalem, with James) after the death of Domitian (96 C.E.—over fifty years *after* the death of James), as Papias also reported. Therefore, John the apostle may have died early, but no one believed or claimed that until the modern era—a terribly wrong reading of ancient sources on all accounts! Even the supposed fifth and ninth century sources of such a view *did not believe it*. Nonetheless, beliefs that neither John the apostle nor an eyewitness can have been the Fourth Evangelist have required other composition theories to be devised. Although these proposals are often distinguished from alternative views as being "critical" rather than "traditional," such designations fail to do justice to either set of approaches.

The "Concocted" Gospel

Karl Gottlieb Bretschneider was not the first scholar to argue that, whoever John's author was, he likely concocted his work, but he launched the debate in Germany in 1820. Nevertheless, Bretschneider's book, *Probabilia de evangelii et epistolarum Joannis Apostoli indole et origine eruditorum iudiciis modeste subiecit* ("Probable conclusions about the type and origin of the Gospel and Epistles of the Apostle John, modestly submitted to the judgment of the scholarly world" [Leipzig: J. A. Barth, 1820]),[9] published in Latin for the intelligentsia in Germany, created a stir that has not yet subsided in biblical studies. Noting the many differences between John and the Synoptics, as well as John's literary perplexities, Bretschneider concluded that the reasonable scholar must choose between the Synoptics and John, and that, given three versus one, the Synoptics win. Matthew, Mark, and Luke could not have all concocted their unitary perspective on Jesus, but given John's theological bent, the Johannine Evangelist undoubtedly concocted his Gospel. While Friedrich Schleiermacher and Johann Neander opposed the questioning of John's historicity, F. C. Baur and David Strauss carried this skeptical view further. Strauss argued that John's distinctive stories were rooted in the Jewish and Hellenistic mythologies of the day, and he sought to overturn Schleiermacher's approach to the historical Jesus based on the Gospel of John, calling Bretschneider the "strong man of science."[10] Given parallels with Justin Martyr's writings, many nineteenth-century German scholars assumed that the Fourth Gospel was finalized in the second half of the second century C.E.

The *strengths* of this approach include the following features:

- Distinguishing the Christ of faith from the Jesus of history has made an enduring contribution to historical and theological studies alike, calling for a focusing on one of these issues without being unduly influenced by the other.

- It accounts for the development of the Johannine tradition without needing to reconcile it with the Synoptic presentations.
- It furthers a largely naturalistic approach that argues for a History-of-Religions origin of the Johannine material, as reported miracles need not have happened in history but purportedly reflect the assimilation of folkloric religious typologies.
- It explains the Hellenistic character of the Johannine material, having a reach beyond Palestinian Judaism.
- Strauss appropriates the mantle of scientific authority against Schleiermacher's view, proclaiming Bretschneider to be the true "man of science," contributing to a decisively critical approach to biblical studies.

Weaknesses of this approach include the following:

- Simply assuming John to be "concocted" does not account adequately for the ways that the Fourth Gospel is historically as plausible as, or even superior to, the Synoptics, nor does it contribute a larger theory of Johannine composition that is critically plausible.
- It overlooks the facts that none of the comparative-religion parallels with John are identical or even all that close to the material in John, and that most later Gnostic parallels reflect the assimilation of Johannine material rather than a Gnostic prefiguring of it.
- It assumes wrongly that Palestinian Judaism was not dualistic and this fails to recognize the many ways in which the Fourth Gospel belongs in a Jewish milieu.
- It fails to account for Schleiermacher's scientific literary analysis, which accurately noted the conceptual and literary unity of the Johannine witness in contrast to the disjointed and fragmentary character of the Synoptic witness.
- Discoveries of the Rylands Papyrus fragment (dated around 125 c.e. or slightly later) move the finalization of the Fourth Gospel closer to the turn of the first century rather than later in the second century.

It is fair to say that in both Johannine and Jesus studies, the view that John is a concocted Gospel—divorced from the Jesus of history—has won the day within the leading set of critical platforms for interpreting the Gospels in the modern era. The question is how solid these new platforms are.

John, the Diachronic Gospel

More than a century of critical Johannine scholarship was drawn together by Rudolf Bultmann in a landmark synthesis whereby perplexing literary, historical, and theological features of the Johannine text were accounted for as factors of a highly diachronic process. In Bultmann's view, the composition of John involved the use of at least three disparate sources, the work of the Evangelist, a disordering and reordering of the text, and the redactor's adding of alternative material in his finalization of the Fourth Gospel. While appraisals of Bultmann's 1941 commentary on the Gospel of John (English translation, 1971) have been varied, this monograph was arguably the most significant contribution to biblical studies in the twentieth century (save, perhaps, Albert Schweitzer's 1906 *Quest of the Historical Jesus*). Ernst Haenchen called it a giant oak tree under which nothing could grow for a generation of scholarly work, at least.[11] Most impressive is the extent to which Bultmann addressed many of the Johannine riddles, posing an intricate yet arguable theory of the origin and composition of the Fourth Gospel.

As a historical skeptic, Bultmann saw all claims to miracles and high Christology as rooted not in the Jesus of history, but originating in the religious environment of the Evangelist. As a committed biblical theologian, he believed that Christians are saved by faith, not by history, elevating the theology of the Bible over its premodern historical claims. While the Evangelist could not have been an apostle, in Bultmann's judgment, this is not to say that the material he used did not have historical connections with Jesus. Assuming that the Evangelist had been a follower of John the Baptist who came to believe that Jesus was the Messiah, Bultmann surmised that the Johannine Evangelist co-opted a Gnostic revelation-sayings source (containing the poetic material underlying the Johannine Prologue as well as the I-am sayings of Jesus) and recrafted it into the teachings of Jesus. Therefore, the distinctive teachings of Jesus in the Fourth Gospel, as well as their high Christology and revelatory thrust—given the Evangelist's low Christology—reflect not the Jesus of history but the Gnostic redeemer myth, which the Evangelist featured but also counterbalanced theologically. Bultmann identified other poetic features in the Johannine sayings material, even if he had to apply also an extensive disordering/reordering program to "expose" the strophic form of a hypothetical source.

A second source argued by Bultmann is a *sēmeia* (signs) source, which explains the origin of John's distinctive miracles, as well as the fact that they fail to include the wonder attestations of the Markan Gospels. According to Bultmann, the numeration of the first two signs (2:11; 4:54) reflects the numbering of signs within this source, and its conclusion is found in John 20:30-31: "Jesus did many other signs . . . not written in this book, but these are written that you might believe that Jesus is the Christ . . ." Thus, the function of this hypothetical source, showcasing Jesus doing miracles in ways reminiscent of the Hebrew prophets, was targeted at Jewish audiences in hopes of convincing them that Jesus was the Jewish Messiah. This also accounts for the theological tension between the elevated presentations of miracles in John and the existential inclination of the Evangelist, who wrote, "Blessed are those who have not seen, and yet believe" (20:29).

While Bultmann argued stylistic and linguistic bases for demarcating these first two sources, Robert Fortna carried this hypothesis further, applying further linguistic criteria for distinguishing this hypothetical source. Fortna, however, expanded it into a "Signs Gospel," adding the Passion narrative. Under Fortna's analysis, the Johannine Signs Gospel was similar to Mark in its wonder attestations, but these have been removed by the Johannine Evangelist, who supplanted them instead with his critical stance toward signs-faith. In Bultmann's and Fortna's approaches to the inferred source of John's distinctive miracle tradition, the Fourth Gospel's literary, historical, and theological riddles are addressed extensively.[12]

A third major source inferred by Bultmann is a Passion source, although it is indistinguishable from the Evangelist's work on the basis of either linguistic or theological criteria. Bultmann must infer the existence of such a source, however, given his rejection of the Evangelist's being a firsthand witness to the ministry of Jesus—even its final events. Bultmann is aware of how different the Johannine Passion narrative is from those presented in the Synoptics, so he does not infer a co-opting of any of the Synoptic traditions. Therefore, a source for John's Passion narrative must be inferred because of its seemingly historical, yet distinctive, presentation of the culminating events in Jesus' ministry. Especially compelling is the presentation of topographical and political realities in Jerusalem, as rendered distinctively with a sense of historical realism in the Johannine presentation.

As a means of addressing contextual and transitional difficulties in the Johannine text, Bultmann infers an extensive history of text disordering (for "unmotivated" reasons—in other words, it happened by accident rather than the text's being disrupted on purpose), only to be reordered (incorrectly) by the redactor. In Bultmann's view, the ordering of chapters 4–7 was originally 4, 6, 5, 7, and dozens of other textual anomalies are accounted for by inferring an extensive displacement/reordering scheme. Given Bultmann's restoring of the "original" order of the text, two primary results are that the "literary seams" in the underlying texts are exposed and that the poetic structure of the Revelation-sayings source material is restored. Bultmann also attributes apparent editorial additions to the final text of the Fourth Gospel to the redactor, who also added his own material emphasizing futuristic eschatology, conventional sacramentology, Synoptic-like material, and Peter' restoration after his denial of Jesus. These elements posed a corrective to the Evangelist's present eschatology, anti-sacramentalism, dearth of Synoptic material, and disparaging of Peter and the Twelve. In so doing, Bultmann infers that the redactor must have been motivated by ecclesial concerns. He argues that the redactor made his additions to the Johannine text in order to make the Fourth Gospel more palatable for Christian audiences no later than the second century, given the Gospel's relative absence of attention to the institutional and sacramental interests of the later church. He also infers that the linguistic similarities between the Johannine epistles and the apparent work of the redactor imply the same hand at work.

Box 5.2: Bultmann's Diachronic Theory of the Origin and Composition of John

- Three major sources underlie the Johannine Gospel:
  - *A Revelation-sayings source*—Form: poetic worship material from the Baptist's community; Content: the Prologue and I-am Sayings; *Tendenz* (or tendency): the Gnostic revealer myth and high Christology
  - *A Sēmeia [signs] source*—Form: an apologetic wonder tract presenting Jesus as the Jewish Messiah; Content: the Johannine signs; *Tendenz*: a God-Man (*theos anēr* in Greek) typology shows Jesus to be a wonder worker
  - *A Passion source*—Form: Gospel narrative parallel to the Synoptics; Content: the Johannine Passion narrative; *Tendenz*: similar to the rest of the Johannine narrative

- The Evangelist's contribution in forming a Gospel as a first edition:
  - Arranging the disparate sources into an overall narrative progression
  - Connecting revelation sayings with thematically related signs material
  - Counterbalancing the sayings material with incarnational and low Christology emphases
  - Counterbalancing the signs material with existentializing emphases
  - Presenting his own theology, including anti-sacramental and realized eschatology themes

- A disordering of the text—occurring for "unmotivated" reasons:
  - Chapters 4–7 and 14–17 were disordered
  - Other out-of-sequence presentations are thus explained
  - Especially the sayings material was disrupted

- A reordering of the text and the redactor's adding of material:
  - An incorrect reordering of chapters 4–7 and many other passages in ways that occlude the original poetic structure of the sayings material
  - The addition of sections that restore sacramental and future-eschatology themes (6:51c-58; 21:1-25, etc.)
  - The addition of sections and details that harmonize the Johannine Gospel with the Synoptics

---

The *strengths* of Bultmann's paradigm are extensive! More incisively and thoroughly than any scholar before him, Bultmann's way of addressing many of the Johannine riddles commanded notice and established unprecedented critical authority in so doing.

- John's theological tensions are largely explained on the basis that we have a set of literary dialogues external to the Evangelist's thinking, whereby he used but corrected the theological tendencies of the Revelation-sayings source and the signs source, and the redactor counterbalanced the Evangelist's theological tendencies.
- John's historical riddles are accounted for on the basis that the Evangelist employed independent traditional sources, allowing some historical background for the Johannine material without requiring one to accept the eyewitness claims of the text, which were added to bolster the appeal of the material rhetorically.
- John's literary aporias are accounted for on the basis that the stylistic differences in the text reflect disparate sources, contextual difficulties reflect editorial seams and the disordering and reordering of the material, as well as the finalization of the text by another hand.
- Inferring the author of the epistles to be the final editor of the Gospel is confirmed by several types of evidence.
- The Johannine rendering of Jesus' ministry indeed reflects independent traditional memory rather than Synoptic derivation.

While the inferred theology of the Evangelist may "preach well" in some circles—allowing the modern interpreter to embrace the Evangelist's existential and incarnation theology without being encumbered by the scandal of miracles and supernaturalism—Bultmann's paradigm also has its own share of critical *weaknesses*:

- When all of Bultmann's stylistic evidence for disparate sources is applied to John 6 (the place where four of his five major sources are supposedly present), the distribution is random and inconclusive.[13] *All* of John is what Bultmann calls "Semitizing Greek."
- While a theory of disordering and reordering is theoretically possible, the claim that John's material became disordered and reordered as extensively as Bultmann claims (including "unmotivated" breaks falling exactly between sentences and sentences of uneven length) makes this part of his theory critically implausible.
- The form-critical and source-critical approaches to the Synoptics fare less well when applied to the Johannine tradition, as it seems that the signs and the discourse material were integrated earlier in the tradition history than Bultmann allows.
- Bultmann fails to consider the possibility that the theological tension may have been internal to the thinking of the Johannine Evangelist and his tradition, as first-century theologians (Jesus, Paul, the Fourth Evangelist) were probably every bit as much dialectical thinkers as modern theologians have been.[14]

- Bultmann fails to account for the synchronistic and unitary features of the Johannine narrative, as many terms and themes are found in all parts of the Johannine Gospel, not just a few.

The most enduring feature of Bultmann's paradigm has been the inference of a signs source, furthered most vigorously by Robert Fortna and his Signs-Gospel theory.[15] Is an inferred alien source, however, for which there is no hard evidence preferable to the hypothesis of a more likely first *Johannine* edition that was later augmented by supplementary material? Most of the major aporias Bultmann detects can be addressed with such an approach.

John as a Spiritualization of Mark and the Synoptics

If the Fourth Evangelist was not an independent witness to Jesus' ministry, and if a scholar finds little evidence for alien sources underlying John, the leading remaining option for explaining the origin of John's material is to see it as a theological reflection upon Mark and other Synoptic traditions. The leading single theorist along these lines is C. K. Barrett, whose 1978 commentary on John (second edition) is one of the finest commentaries available in English.[16] Given dozens of textual similarities between the Greek texts of Mark and John, Barrett argues that there must be some traditional dependence at work here, although John cannot be said to have borrowed from Mark as closely, or in the same way, as Matthew and Luke did. Given the theological and dialectical character of the Evangelist's work,[17] Barrett takes the connections with Mark as indicators of a derivative relationship; contacts with Luke are less telling. Frans Neirynck and the Leuven School have carried this program further, arguing that because John was finalized last, all contacts between John and the Synoptics show some form of literary dependence. Tom Brodie has also argued this view extensively.[18]

The *strengths* of John as a spiritualization of Mark and other traditions are several:

- While we have no real evidence of the hypothetical sources underlying the Johannine narrative, we do have the Synoptic Gospels that can be compared directly.
- If Mark was finalized and circulated as the first of the Gospels, it is more likely that the Fourth Evangelist would have been familiar with Mark than with either of the other two Synoptic Gospels, and this might have influenced his project.
- The Greek-language similarities between Mark and John are conspicuous, in that a good number of details and theological insights are shared between them.[19]

- Several echoes of features of Mark suggest that the Fourth Evangelist at least was familiar with Mark's material,[20] and perhaps also Luke and Matthew.
- Since the Johannine Evangelist was clearly theological in his interests, expanding on details imagining his using but modifying other material to suit his purposes becomes attractive.

Weaknesses of this view, however, are also considerable:

- Despite numerous similarities between John and Mark, *none* of these involve identical material, making a conscious-employment-of-Mark theory implausible.[21]
- While some contact may have existed between the Markan and Johannine traditions, dependence in one direction is not the only possibility—contact between the oral stages of traditions could have involved influence in either direction.[22]
- Gospel-dependence theories fail to account for the multiplicity of ways that intertraditional contact could have emerged between the Johannine and other traditions as they developed within a variety of forms.[23]
- Solely intertraditional theories fail to account for intratraditional dialogue within the Johannine tradition. In other words, some of John's theological tensions may be rooted in the Evangelist's dialogues with his own tradition rather than simply between the Johannine and other traditions.[24]
- Most devastatingly, Synoptic-dependence theories make no account of over 80 percent of John, which has no direct Synoptic parallels, and they fail to account for the fact that the most memorable of Synoptic passages are missing from John.

Scholars who remain unconvinced that the Fourth Gospel represents an independent tradition or that the Evangelist made use of alien sources find themselves turning to the Synoptics (especially Mark) as the likely source of John's traditional material. But can all of John's distinctive material therefore be attributed to "the theological interests of the Evangelist"—even the mundane and topographical detail? That is a critically inadequate stance.[25]

John as a Historicized Drama

While not an isolated element in his own larger theory, Bultmann accounted for the apparent historical detail in the Fourth Gospel by describing it as a "historicized drama." This view has been expanded into an overall approach in two particular ways. First, virtually all differences between John and the Synoptics are attributed to "the theological interests of the Evangelist." Within this approach, the three Passovers in John, the early Temple cleansing, the locating of the Last

Supper on the day of Preparation (when the paschal lambs were killed), and other distinctive features reflect theological interests, not historical knowledge, or even opinion. Therefore, the Fourth Gospel presents no historical challenge to the other three, and the bulk of John's historical riddles are thereby expunged from historical-critical consideration. Second, given that it is highly theological, John's distinctive features are explained as factors of theological interests, which scholars take ample license to elucidate. Within the overall schema of interpretation, then, the larger features of John's narrative are allegorized, and mundane references are assigned to "mimetic imitations of reality"—as any fictive narrator would also have sought to make his story graphic and compelling for later audiences.[26] Thus, the dramatic features of the story are elevated over historical ones, and literary-theological inferences here displace history altogether.

This approach is often combined with others. Its *strengths* are several:

- From a naturalistic standpoint, the presence of miracles in the Johannine text may be explained as the co-opting of folkloric wonder stories and the divinization of a heroic figure (such as Dionysius legends or stories of Apollonius of Tyana, recorded by Philostratus).[27]
- The presence of empirical references is explained on the basis of a literary feature not requiring a historical connection—either to narrated events or their subject.
- Claims to historicity and eyewitness testimony are seen as rhetorical only, in the tradition of pseudepigraphic literature; that is, spurious claims to have been written by authoritative figures.
- Explaining symbolic features of the Johannine details allows extensive theologizing interpretations of those details—numbers, places, times, names, and ironic developments in the narrative.
- As the narrator's literary purpose is stated in 20:31, connections between the narrative's contents and its rhetorical function provide extensive possibilities for interpretation.

The *weaknesses* of this approach, however, are notable:

- Despite some similarities with the story of Apollonius and other mythic literature of the time, none of the parallels are all that close, as John seems closer to the Synoptics, while also different from them.[28]
- When the three closest parallels to John are compared (the Synoptic Gospels), they demonstrate the *opposite* operation regarding a supposed "mimetic imitation of reality"—that is, Matthew and Luke omit much of Mark's graphic detail when using a narrative source, so arguing that the Fourth Evangelist added detail goes against the two closest literary parallels.[29]

- While some adding of details and embellishment of stories is plausible, to claim that *all* of the lofty stories and *all* the mundane, gritty detail in John had *no* root in historical knowledge and were simply made up stretches this argument too far.[30]
- The "theologizing interests of the Evangelist" becomes a basis for rife symbolizing speculation upon Johannine scenarios and details, often with no critical controls expected or employed.[31]
- The many appeals to historical memory and firsthand acquaintance with the events in the narrative must be denied or ignored, when eyewitness claims are a literary fact in John.

While the Johannine narrative is clearly theological and different, are *all* of its details to be regarded as aspects of the author's effort to "historicize" the narrative, that is, fictively to add elements of verisimilitude? If we imagine an author operating in ways similar to the authors of Matthew and Luke, we observe that while Matthew and Luke add units to Mark, they tend to omit nonsymbolic, illustrative details. Unless John's operation was diametrically opposed to its closest contemporary parallels, we should conclude that it reflects a dramatized history rather than a historicized drama.

▨ Composition Theories Regardless of Authorship

A genuine advance in Johannine scholarship over the last half-century or so is evident in a number of approaches that have sought to produce a thoughtful analysis of the Fourth Gospel regardless of who might or might not have written it. This is an important advance on the previous two centuries of scholarship, as the question of authorship invariably became an impasse in scholars' approaches. While most scholars whose contributions are described in this category do indeed have opinions on Johannine authorship, their interpretive platforms do not require adherence to that particular view, nor are they designed to establish it. This is a tremendous strength in an approach, as it allows for the literary, theological, and historical evidence to speak for itself without limiting any of those features to preformed commitments as to who the Evangelist must or cannot have been.

An Independent Tradition Developing in Two or More Editions

If the Fourth Gospel was not dependent on alien sources or Synoptic traditions, and if it does appear to be rooted in historical tradition, an analysis of how that tradition developed must follow. In 1938, Percival Gardner-Smith wrote a book on John and the Synoptics, wherein he notes dozens of similarities between John and the Synoptics but also notes that all of these parallels are highly different. From this he concludes that the Johannine Evangelist could not have employed the Synoptics as direct sources; if he did know the Synoptics, he must have gone against them at nearly every turn. Therefore, for Gardner-Smith, a more plausible conjecture is that John's story of Jesus was largely independent of the Synoptics. D. Moody Smith, arguably the leading authority on the Johannine-Synoptic question, has registered his agreement that the Johannine tradition appears on all accounts to be an independent one.[32]

Constructing a robust two-volume approach to John's origin and development, C. H. Dodd, in his *Historical Tradition in the Fourth Gospel* (1963), outlines the Hellenistic and Jewish milieu in which the Fourth Gospel was produced; he also sketches the development of its underlying historical tradition. Beginning with the most certain evidence and moving to the least, Dodd analyzes John's presentations of the Passion narrative, the works of Jesus, and the words of Jesus, concluding that we have an independent tradition developing with its own claims to historicity. The multivolume commentaries of Raymond Brown and Rudolf Schnackenburg develop more detailed analyses of how the Johannine tradition emerged from an independent oral tradition into written forms, and then into a finalized Gospel. While both of them start with the belief that the human source of that tradition was John the apostle, their theories evolve into a place where his role is not needed for their paradigms to stand. Among multiple-edition theorists, Barnabas Lindars argues most compellingly for a first Johannine edition to which supplementary material was added. Most influential within American settings over the last four decades, however, has been Brown's contribution, and his revised introduction to the Fourth Gospel (prepared after his death by Frank Moloney in 2003) reduces his original five stages in the Johannine tradition's development into three.[33]

Box 5.3: Raymond Brown's Theory of John's Composition

Stage One: Origin in the public ministry or activity of Jesus of Nazareth

- Selective memories of Jesus' ministry developed within the experience of the Beloved Disciple, who left John the Baptist to become a follower of Jesus and traveled to Galilee.
- Independent from the Synoptics from day one, the dualistic background of Qumran set the stage for what this unnamed disciple saw in Jesus as a teacher of personified Wisdom.

Stage Two: Proclaiming Jesus in the postresurrection context of community history

- The Johannine community's situation-history engagements with followers of the Baptist, incorporated Samaritans who held anti-Judean biases (which caused Johannine Christians no longer to think of themselves as "Jews"), leaders among Asia Minor synagogues, Docetizing believers, and members of "the larger church" influenced testimonial character of the narrative.

Stage Three: The writing of the Gospel

▨ The "Evangelist" composed the body of the existing Johannine Gospel narrative after the death of the Beloved Disciple, calling for abiding in Jesus and his community, crafting compelling discourses and dialogues, integrating sayings with the signs, employing irony and other literary devices, and perhaps even retouching his own work here and there.

▨ As a follower of the Beloved Disciple and the Evangelist, the "redactor" finalized the Fourth Gospel, adding unused material from stages one and two, marked not by lateness (some of it may indeed be primitive) but by the intrusive features of apparent repetitions and duplications, seeking to conserve material going back to the Beloved Disciple's teachings about Jesus.

Strengths of this approach are considerable:

- Given that none of the similarities between John and the Synoptics are identical, and given that evidence for alien sources underlying John is minimal, it stands to reason that we have an independent tradition underlying the Fourth Gospel.
- It is also likely that this tradition developed first in oral forms before it was crafted into a foundational document, representing the Fourth Evangelist's teaching and preaching about Jesus for later generations.
- It is likely that at least one more edition followed, although there may have been others, and it is plausible that this material was added by another hand.
- We likely have an autonomous Palestinian tradition that was finalized within a Hellenistic setting.
- Such a history of the Johannine tradition is likely regardless of who the Evangelist and final editor might have been.

Weaknesses include the following:

- Even if the Johannine tradition is considered an independent one, particular relations to the Synoptic traditions remain to be explained, as total isolation seems unlikely.
- If oral tradition was crafted into written tradition, clarifying how those movements developed and whether there were more than one earlier edition remains to be explored.
- While a final edition may be inferred, it is difficult to know if there were other editions or literary phases before that and whether the Evangelist or the editor added them.[34]
- The relation of the Johannine Gospel to the epistles still requires consideration, especially in relation to the addition of later material.
- The question of the relation of the final editor to the Evangelist still demands analysis; this involves especially references by a third person as to who the

eyewitness and Evangelist might have been. If the text was finalized by the author, why did he not say, "I was the eyewitness or the author" instead of asserting, "*his* testimony is true" (19:35; 21:24)?

The theory that the Fourth Gospel represents an independent tradition, gathered over at least two editions, deals with the most pressing literary problems in the Johannine text. Among such theories, the approach by Barnabas Lindars is the simplest and most compelling (John Ashton and I came to this same conclusion independently), wherein supplementary material was added to an earlier edition of the Johannine Gospel.[35]

The Two-Level Gospel

Nearly three decades ago, John Ashton referred to the work of J. Louis Martyn as the most significant work on John since Rudolf Bultmann wrote his commentary.[36] Central to Martyn's contribution is the thesis that the Gospel of John should be read on two levels: the level of what happened (history) and the level of its meaning (theology) for the Evangelist and his audience. While Martyn largely adopted Bultmann's paradigm of the Fourth Gospel being constructed upon earlier sources, his central thesis is that the dialogue between the local synagogue and Johannine Christians was the primary issue being addressed by John's story of Jesus, presenting him vigorously as the Jewish Messiah (20:31).

Under Martyn's paradigm, as Johannine Christians' belief in Jesus evolved into a higher set of christological beliefs, this became a threat to Jewish monotheism. Jesus adherents were thus likely labeled "ditheists" and were conceivably expelled from local synagogues, the plausibility of which is corroborated by the twelfth of eighteen Benedictions drafted at the Jamnia councils between 80 and 90 c.e. In that liturgical recitation, the *Birkat ha-Minim* (the blessing against the heretics) condemned followers of "the Nazarene"—likely targeting Jesus adherents. If this was recited corporately in weekly meetings for worship, followers of Jesus would have felt confronted. Therefore, three seemingly anachronistic statements in John 9:22, 12:42 and 16:2 should be understood as implying: "*even back then* (as now), those who claimed adherence to Jesus openly as the Messiah/Christ were cast out of the synagogue." Martyn sees the term for being "cast out of the synagogue" (*aposynagōgos* in Greek) as a technical term for Jewish excommunication, or at least marginalization from fellowship by the local Jewish community of faith. Therefore, John's presentation of "history" is primarily apologetic in character—crafted to convince later audiences that Jesus was indeed the Messiah/Christ. That accounts for many of John's distinctive elements and particular emphases.

Martyn's contributions, accompanied by Raymond Brown's sketching a history of the Johannine situation in which tensions with the Synagogue were also acute, shifted the primary historical interest in Johannine studies from the history of the tradition and its subject (Jesus) to the history of the Johannine situation (its community). In the meantime, appreciation for John's thorough Jewishness (aided by the discovery of the Dead Sea Scrolls in 1947)[37] bolstered the conviction of most Johannine scholars over the last four decades that Jewish-Christian dialogues were central to John's presentation of Jesus. In the meantime, however, several Jewish scholars have challenged the Martyn hypothesis with the fact that Jewish and Christians were really quite close during this time period, making it unlikely that a total separation of the two movements would have happened. At the same time, the consideration of other crises in the Johannine situation (Roman hegemony— Richard Cassidy [1991] and Warren Carter [2008]; Docetist teachers—Peder Borgen [1965] and Udo Schnelle [1992]; Christians working to institutionalize the churches—Ernst Käsemann [1968] and Arthur Maynard [1984]) have expanded the dialogical partners in the Johannine situation to include other groups in addition to Jewish audiences. These critiques and additional analyses have softened the Martyn hypothesis in the views of many scholars, but most still embrace at least some level of dialectical engagement with Jewish audiences.[38]

A notable challenge to the entire enterprise of seeing John and other Gospels as written for particular communities was levied by Richard Bauckham and others, arguing that the Gospels were written for all Christians. Within his treatment of John, Bauckham argues that the Johannine Gospel was written for readers of Mark, and that it was meant to be engaged in the broader Christian movement rather than in an isolated community. Bauckham also challenges the tendency to displace the originative history of a Gospel narrative with the situation-history of its author and audience, seeing the Gospel of John as being more historical than recent scholars have thought. While he sees the anonymity of the Beloved Disciple as a literary device drawing all readers into a place of intimacy with Jesus, he argues for firsthand knowledge of Jesus' ministry as being foundational for the Johannine witness that John the Elder finalized at Ephesus.

Strengths of a two-level approach include:

- The Martyn-Brown hypothesis accounts for an impressive connection between three texts that are difficult to explain otherwise (9:22; 12:42; 16:2) and the Twelfth Benediction against followers of "the Nazarene"; fraternal proximity to Judaism does not demolish this theory, it qualifies it.
- It explains why Jesus is presented as the Jewish Messiah/Christ with such apologetic fervor and design in the Fourth Gospel.
- It heightens awareness of the role of the Johannine audience in the Evangelist's crafting his distinctive story of Jesus—some of John's distinctive presentation of Jesus is indeed a factor of its audiences and their needs.
- Unlike the case with other Gospels, this reconstruction benefits from corroboration by the Johannine epistles, Revelation, and even the writings of Ignatius as these appear to confirm a larger, dialectical Johannine situation.

- This approach accounts for the Fourth Gospel's Jewishness, despite its being finalized within a Gentile setting.

Weaknesses of a two-level approach include:

- The tendency of the second level of history to eclipse the first; while the Johannine text was finalized in a Hellenistic setting, it also shows signs of Palestinian phases of development.
- While extensive excommunication of Jesus adherents from synagogues is unlikely, some marginalization of "ditheists" cannot be ruled out (for example, would Jewish communities at the time *really* accept their members reciting something like the Johannine Prologue within meetings for worship?).
- The tendency of some scholars to argue for only one set of dialectical tensions (that is, with Jewish members of the audience only) fails to acknowledge other groups in dialectical relationship within the Johannine situation.
- Martyn distances the Johannine epistles from the Gospel (perhaps feeling the Docetizing "antichrists" of 1 John 4:1-3 might diminish his case), although the "antichrists" of 1 John 2:18-25, who denied Jesus was the Jewish Messiah, actually corroborate his theory.[39]
- While the Fourth Gospel does appear written *from* a community, its thrust is not confined to being *for* a particular community or situation; its features and influence imply a larger readership within early Christianity.[40]

While the history of the Johannine situation must be taken into account when reading the Johannine literature, its second level of history should not displace the first. Among plausible settings for Johannine Christianity, Brown's contention that Ephesus has no compelling rivals (even Alexandria) is a worthy judgment, and multiple partners in dialogue over a seven-decade period are likely.

The Literary Anatomy of the Fourth Gospel

In my view, the most important Johannine work in the last quarter-century is R. Alan Culpepper's *Anatomy of the Fourth Gospel* (1983).[41] A quick scan of the number of doctoral dissertations posing new literary approaches to John in recent years will confirm this judgment. Culpepper's approach applies the literary-critical approaches of Frank Kermode and others to the narrative characteristics of the Fourth Gospel, including the narrator and his point of view, narrative time, the plot, characterization, implicit commentary, and the implied reader. The great attraction of Culpepper's approach is that he outlines how a biblical narrative can be considered "true" apart from history. By analyzing its rhetorical ploys and literary devices, Culpepper also makes significant advances for contemporary interpretation. By noting misunderstanding and partial comprehension among the characters of the text, not only are they set straight and guided toward the path of truth, but so are later readers, whose flawed platforms and scaffoldings of life are challenged by John's timeless message. Here the narrator's implicit commentary reaches the implied reader by connecting with his or her experience as an invitation to faith. By setting the history-theology debates aside and focusing simply on the literary features of the text, Culpepper provides a way for the text to be read and engaged today as it was intended to for its original audiences. Such is the promise of the new literary approaches to the Fourth Gospel.

In addition to Culpepper's work, other new literary approaches to John have provided an extremely helpful set of ways forward in addressing the Johannine riddles, especially its literary ones.[42] Within this movement other hermeneutical approaches, such as ideological, feminist, autobiographical, postcolonial, and new-historicist readings of John, open new vistas on how to take the literary text of the Fourth Gospel seriously and personally. On the question of genre, however, Richard Burridge has recently argued that the genre of the Gospel was not fictive; it should be read as Greco-Roman biography, implying historical interests on the part of the Fourth Evangelist.[43] Then again, even historical narrative benefits from suitable narrative analysis; history is constructed rhetorically as well as fiction.

Strengths of the new literary approaches to John are many:

- The impasses of history and theology, origin and composition, relation to the Synoptics, and source and redaction questions are dealt with by means of focusing on the literary features of the completed text as it stands, *whoever* the author(s) might have been.
- The treatment of Gospel narrative *as* narrative (rather than as a theological treatise, for instance) allows the text to be read and experienced as it was designed to be.
- This first-century text can be liberated from modernist questions regarding naturalistic and empirical approaches to truth, enhancing symbolic and spiritual meanings where applicable.
- By exploring new literary approaches to John, we learn to appreciate *what* the Gospel says by better understanding *how* it says what it says.
- Rather than focusing on getting "behind the text," the text is read as it is, as a whole, allowing one to focus on the place of the audiences "in front of the text."

Weaknesses to this approach include the following:

- While addressing primarily the literary riddles and features of the Fourth Gospel, its historical and theological features are too easily sidestepped, requiring their fuller consideration.

- Comparisons and contrasts with the Synoptics and parallel literature may indeed inform one's appreciation of the literary thrust of the Fourth Gospel, so they should not be ignored.
- While the text is rightly interpreted as a final unity, markers of the traditions' development and composition may also enhance appreciations of its meaning and should not be overlooked.
- While some hermeneutical approaches to a Gospel text serve its meaning, highly ideological readings of John threaten to usurp the meaning of a text in distortive ways.
- If the genre of a Gospel narrative is biographical and it makes claims to first-hand historicity, not just theology, the literary interpreter must find ways of addressing those realities eventually.

New literary approaches to Gospel studies are here to stay, and analyses of the Fourth Gospel are certainly strengthened by their fitting application. In providing ways to interpret the Johannine narrative, whoever its author and whatever its historical origin and development may have been, Culpepper and others provide ways forward for our appreciation of the narrative character of the Gospels. Historical and theological issues still must be sorted out, but these literary advances are serviceable indeed.

The Priority of John

In 1985, John A. T. Robinson's book, *The Priority of John,* was published posthumously,[44] challenging the posteriority of John as the "Fourth" Gospel in modern scholarship. In Robinson's view, not only is John's tradition both primitive and historically reliable, but it deserves to be considered the first among the Gospels instead of the last. He also challenges modern attempts at dating the New Testament writings in general, calling for a much earlier dating of all the Gospels, not just John. Robinson believes the modern challenges to John's apostolic authorship have been unimpressive, and while he argues that John the son of Zebedee is indeed the authorial source of the Gospel bearing his name, his overall approach does not depend on a particular person being the author. Because of the great deal of primitive tradition, archaeological detail, and firsthand familiarity with Palestine and Jerusalem, Robinson argues that John's differences from the Synoptics were the result of John's being the *first* Gospel to be written, not the last. If Mark was written without knowledge of an earlier Johannine text, it is easier to imagine that one Gospel (John) was overlooked by Mark than that all three Synoptic Gospels were overlooked by a later writer, the Fourth Evangelist.

While most scholars have not followed Robinson's lead in arguing that the Johannine Gospel was finalized early (admittedly it may contain early material, but it is difficult to demonstrate that it contains no later material), several scholars in Europe have built upon his work. Peter Hofrichter of Salzburg, for instance, has argued that the Gospel of John was an early pattern for Mark and shows in his work how contacts between John and Mark suggest Markan dependence on the Johannine narrative, not the other way around. Especially if the christological hymns of Paul's writings antedated his writing of Philippians and Colossians, John's Prologue, with its high Christology, far from being the latest of compositions might plausibly have been the earliest! Hofrichter's title, "In the Beginning was the Johannine Prologue," argues that very point. Klaus Berger has argued that the Fourth Gospel was the first of the Gospels to be written, and James Charlesworth of Princeton poses that the first edition of John's Gospel may have been produced in 68 c.e., before the destruction of Jerusalem and before the writing of Mark.[45] These cases for John's "priority" can be argued without reference to who the author might or might not have been.

Strengths of this approach are as follows:

- It takes seriously the primitive material in the Johannine text and works creatively with the givens to propose new approaches to familiar issues.
- The idea that John may have influenced Mark and other Synoptic traditions is an issue at least worth considering and testing, and Hofrichter argues that case extensively.
- If John was written before the Synoptics in a Hellenistic context, its extensive differences are less problematic, given that the other Evangelists may simply have overlooked it.
- The high christological themes in John may indeed have been early instead of late and only late.
- "Letting John be John," as James Dunn calls for, is easier if John's witness is considered on its own without being regarded a stepsibling to the Synoptics.[46]

Weaknesses of this approach are as follows:

- Just because there is early material in the Johannine Gospel, this does not prove that it was finalized early.
- Apparent contacts with Mark might or might not imply literary dependence in one direction or another, as contact may have extended to the oral and pre-literary stages of the Markan and Johannine traditions.
- References to the predicted destruction of the Temple seem to imply that readers would have recognized that the prophecy of Jesus had apparently come true, making a pre-70 c.e. dating of the finalized Gospel unlikely.

- Particular ways that John's story appears to engage Mark as a written text seem to imply Johannine familiarity with Mark and even a dialogical relationship with later Matthean themes (see Box 4.7).
- The Johannine epistles cast valuable light also on the Johannine Gospel and its situation-history, and while they seem to be written after at least some of the Gospel's material, it also appears that the Gospel was addressing some of the issues reflected in the epistles.

The value of considering Johannine priority is that one is liberated from Synoptic straitjackets of interpretation, allowing the Johannine rendering of Jesus and his mission to speak with its own voice. While the Fourth Gospel does indeed seem to have been finalized later, noting its primitive tradition and autonomous voice is essential for adequate interpretation. Regardless who the author was, the memory of earlier Palestinian events rendered in a subsequent Hellenistic setting fits the literary and historical character of this distinctive work.

■ Conclusion

As shown in each of these major approaches to the Fourth Gospel's origin and development, attempts to address the Johannine riddles are central to each approach. Also apparent is the fact that each approach accounts for some aspects of the Johannine riddles, but few attempt to engage them all. This may be why good scholars disagree with each other as to the character and history of the Johannine tradition. It is fair to say that Rudolf Bultmann has probably done the most thorough job of addressing Johannine riddles, and yet he does so by minimizing John's historical claims and apparently historical material. Just as limiting as theories arguing who the Fourth Evangelist "must have been" are views assuming who he "cannot have been." This is what forces such a fine scholar as C. K. Barrett to infer Markan dependence, and yet such a view leaves most of John's material unaccounted for. Whatever one's approach, the perspective of Alan Culpepper and Raymond Brown poses the best way forward: the Gospel of John is best interpreted as a literary narrative with its own claims to memory and interpretation of Jesus' ministry, *whoever* its author might have been. Such is my conviction as I pose a new set of paradigms for addressing the Johannine riddles in the next chapter.

■ Questions to Consider

1. How does assuming who the Johannine author was—or cannot have been—affect the theory of Johannine composition and development that one adopts or develops?

2. Choosing at least three theories of John's composition, describe how each of them addresses or does not address particular Johannine riddles (theological, historical, literary).

3. What are the strongest features of these approaches to Johannine composition, and can any of them be combined together to form a new synthesis or paradigm?

▨ Terms to Understand

- diachronic/synchronic
- interfluence
- *Birkat ha-Minim*
- historicized drama/dramatized history

The Dialogical Autonomy
of the Fourth Gospel

A Plausible Theory

Reflecting on a dozen leading approaches to the origin and composition of the Fourth Gospel, we see that each of them has its own set of strengths—and likewise weaknesses. Impressive also is the way each of these approaches to John seeks to make sense of the Johannine riddles, with varying degrees of success. In this chapter, I shall lay out what I believe to be the best way to handle the classic Johannine questions, always seeking to move from the strongest evidence available to other inferences. In my view, first- and second-century opinions should be given priority of consideration until challenged by compelling evidence or formidable problems, although modern scientific analysis should also be followed when it is genuinely compelling. As both traditional and critical views can be either firm or flawed, however, they must all be tested against evidence in and around the text, and an overall synthesis should be attempted in addressing the Johannine riddles. That is what my theory of *the dialogical autonomy of the Fourth Gospel* aims to achieve.

At the outset, the third general approach listed in the previous chapter seems the strongest way to proceed—developing a worthy approach to reading the Fourth Gospel and addressing its riddles *whoever* the author(s) may or may not have been. The text deserves to be interpreted as it stands, whoever wrote it, whenever and wherever it was written. Put otherwise, just as traditional approaches have suffered on the basis of clinging to a particular view of who the author *must have been*, so modern approaches have suffered on the basis of claiming who the author *must not have been*. We might even have a combination of firsthand memory and alternative traditional material in the Fourth Gospel; but again, we should let the evidence of the text speak for itself.

▧ An Autonomous Tradition Developing Alongside Mark—The Other Bi-Optic Gospel

The Johannine tradition shows every sign of having developed independently, emerging alongside Mark, but not dependent upon it. Put otherwise, unlike Matthew and Luke, which depend extensively upon Mark, the Gospel of John shows a radical independence from Mark. The main reason scholars do not believe Matthew represents an independent memory of Jesus—its word-for-word similarities with Mark in over six hundred verses—is precisely why the same cannot be claimed for John. Of its many similarities with Mark, *none* of them are identical, although signs of at least some familiarity are also present. This is why Mark and John deserve to be called the *Bi-Optic Gospels*—they represent similar, but autonomous, impressions of Jesus from day one, developing in distinctive and individuated ways.

In that respect, the perspectives underlying Mark and John represent two separate sets of impressions about Jesus and his ministry, formed also by their oral delivery within the early Jesus movement. In so doing, the pre-Markan and early Johannine traditions both addressed the needs of the churches with the message of Jesus in ways that also conformed to the gifts and ministry inclinations of the early preachers themselves. As with any historical project, the main interests of these early preachers were not simply in "what happened," as though all events were equally significant or memorable. Rather, selection of materials and slant in presentation were primarily influenced by the purpose of connecting "what happened" during Jesus' ministry with "what was happening" among their audiences—as mediated through the preachers themselves. While it is impossible to know exactly who these preachers might have been, something like the presentation of Peter and John traveling through Samaria in Acts 8, preaching about Jesus as the Messiah/Christ, is reinforced by textual evidence and traditional memory. Of course, this is not to claim that the particular preachers were Peter and John—these traditions may represent a dozen different preachers. The point is, rather, that this narrative suggests how some contacts during oral stages of respective traditions may have developed. Purveyors of Gospel traditions were *persons*, and different cognitive operations and styles of communication likely played a role in how their material developed and was delivered.[1]

When the similarities and differences between Mark and John are considered in detail, several features become apparent. First, a variety of buzzwords and illustrative details are preserved in these two Gospels distinctively that are omitted by Matthew and Luke in their incorporations of Mark. These instances argue against the view that Evangelists added details to bolster "mimetic imitations of reality" as a means of making stories more graphic and accessible. Apparently, Matthew and Luke did not operate that way; they often omitted names of places and people, as well as illustrative, nonsymbolic details, although they did tend to add units of material.[2] Therefore, explaining the prevalence of such material in Mark and John as reflecting graphic embellishment on the part of those Evangelists falls flat critically. Rather, for example, references to two hundred and three hundred denarii as the costs of feeding the multitude and of the woman's perfume (John 6:7; 12:5; Mark 6:37; 14:5) are only found in John and Mark, as are the descriptions of the grass where people sat down to receive the feeding (John 6:10; Mark 6:39). These features suggest intertraditional contact between the oral stages of the Markan and the Johannine traditions—details remembered by preachers and reinforced by hearing others mention them. Because it is impossible to know which direction the influence may have traveled, the early contacts are regarded more accurately as reflections of "interfluence."[3]

Second, in addition to non-identical similarities of detail in John and Mark, some non-identical similarities in speech also can be found, although often Matthew and sometimes Luke also follow Mark along these lines. In both Gospels, Jesus says something like:

- "Stand up, take your mat and walk" (Mark 2:9-11; John 5:8-12—to a sick person)
- "A prophet is not without honor, except in his home town." (Mark 6:4; John 4:44—to his disciples)
- "Follow me." (Mark 1:16-17; 2:14; 8:32-34; John 1:43; 21:19-22—to Peter and other disciples)
- "I am [it is I]; fear not!" (Mark 6:50; John 6:20—to the disciples in the storm-tossed boat)
- The Temple will be destroyed and rebuilt in three days (Mark 14:58; 15:29; John 2:19—in Jerusalem)
- One of his disciples will betray him (Mark 14:18; John 13:21—Judas) and Peter will deny him thrice before the cock crows (twice in Mark 14:30; once in John 13:38)
- Those who wish to preserve their lives will lose them (Mark 8:35; John 12:25)
- "You always have the poor with you." (Mark 14:7; John 12:8)
- "Rise, let us be going." (Mark 14:42; John 14:31)

Similar, yet different, sayings by others include:

- Jesus' being confessed as "the Holy One of God" (by the demoniac in Mark 1:24; by Peter in John 6:69)
- "Hosanna, blessed is he who comes in the name of the Lord!" is declared by the crowd upon Jesus' entry into Jerusalem (Mark 11:9; John 12:13)
- Pilate asks Jesus if he is "the king of the Jews" (Mark 15:2; John 18:33) and Roman soldiers mockingly declare, "Hail, King of the Jews!" (Mark 15:18-20; John 19:2-3)
- The crowd yells, "Crucify him!" (Mark 15:13-14; John 19:15—at the trial before Pilate)

Because these details are also presented distinctively in Mark and John (although sometimes Matthew and/or Luke will follow Mark), they likely reflect parallel associative memories of Jesus' ministry developing in individuated ways.

Third, some details in John suggest both familiarity with written Mark and at the same time a corrective and alternative rendering to Mark. Beginning with the ministry of John the Baptist, leading to healings and teachings in Galilee, followed by a final trip to Jerusalem, the Johannine narrative follows at least some of Mark's general order of things. On the other hand, real differences are also asserted. The clarification that John "had not yet been thrown into prison" in John 3:24 assumes that the Gospel's hearers and readers know something like Mark 1:14, which declares that Jesus began his ministry *after* John had been thrown into prison.

Another marker of John's knowing contrast to Mark's rendering is Jesus' saying that a prophet is not without honor except in his hometown (Mark 6:4; John 4:44). Unlike the unbelieving Nazarenes in Mark, John's presentation of believing Samaritans and the royal official's household poses a strikingly different account of how Jesus' ministry was received in Galilee. Finally, the first ending of the Johannine Gospel reflects apparent criticism for omitting some material (like Mark's), and the intentionality of its approach is asserted: "Now Jesus did many other signs in the presence of his disciples, which are not written in *this* book; but these are written that you may believe" (John 20:30-31). Could this be read, "I know Mark is out there; don't fault me for leaving things out; I've done so on purpose"? Read this way, the first edition of John appears to be clarifying, correcting, and complementing Mark.

In these ways John's tradition appears to rectify a variety of things for readers and hearers of Mark.[4] Some contact during the oral stages of their respective traditions is apparent, but the Johannine narrator appears also to be setting the record straight here and there with relation to Mark's presentation of Jesus and his ministry. This is not surprising; Matthew and Luke added material to Mark's narrative, while depending on it centrally. Even Mark's second ending (Mark 16:9-20) attempts to "fix" its less-than-inspiring first ending, but the Johannine Evangelist has his own way of presenting an alternative story of Jesus, and his project is distinctive because he has his own tradition to convey and story to tell. While Matthew and Luke built *upon* Mark, John builds *around* Mark; John's alternative rendering of Jesus' ministry appears knowing and intentional.

■ The Dialectical Thinking of the Evangelist

The theological tensions in the Fourth Gospel do not represent a multiplicity of sources and authors; they reflect a pervasively dialectical approach to most issues as embraced by the Fourth Evangelist. Dialectical thinking represents an advanced form of reflection in which issues are considered from more than one perspective. While there is truth in one aspect of an issue, other sides of that issue also ring true, and a dialectical approach holds truths together in tension. Plato described "thinking" as the conversation that the soul has with itself, considering something from one side, and then another, until it has finally achieved its "glory" (or "opinion," *doxa*, *Theaetetus* 189).[5] How well the Johannine Evangelist knew Plato is uncertain, but he certainly exemplifies the mode of dialectical thinking Socrates advocated, and the constructed dialogues with Jesus in John mirror Plato's instructive dialogues. From this perspective, several other features become clear.

First, regarding the human and divine presentations of Jesus, the Evangelist seeks to hold these polarities together in tension. This is not a matter of disparate literary sources, whereby a later editor existentializes a high-Christology sayings source; rather, the narrator presents Jesus as the Revealer, who scandalizes Jewish religious leaders with mystery and likewise challenges advocates of high Christology with an incarnate and suffering Lord. It is also unlikely that we simply have a movement from a low regard for a Galilean prophet to Gentile adoration of Jesus as a Hellenistic god over a span of several decades. High appraisals of Jesus also seem to be early, and incarnational emphases upon his suffering and humanity appear also to be late. Therefore, high and low views of Jesus appear to have been both early and late, although different emphases can also be inferred. For instance, theophanic (the burning bush or I-Am) associations with Jesus of Galilee may even have roots in encounters with something of the numinous in the presence of the man, Jesus; these impressions were later formalized in the worship material of the Johannine community, as they came to embrace Jesus as the Word and Son of God.[6] Conversely, memories of Jesus' material presence with his followers, including displays of emotion and pathos, appear to have been followed decades later by emphases that he really did suffer and die. The Evangelist appears to have held these poles together in tension over a sustained period of time. Christological features also are emphasized correctively later, as members of the Johannine audience might have come to privilege one polarity over the other.[7]

A second feature of the Evangelist's dialectical thought is his elevated, yet existentialized, presentation of Jesus' signs. Rather than reflecting a corrective to an imagined Mark-like miracle source, of which there is neither evidence nor any compelling indicator, it appears a good deal of this tension was internal to the Johannine tradition itself. On one hand, Jesus performs a wedding miracle, performs Sabbath healings of the lame man and the blind man in Jerusalem, and brings Lazarus forth from the tomb after four days' death, glorifying God in the process. On the other hand, the Johannine Jesus rebukes people for seeking signs, and he declares climactically in John 20:29: "Have you believed because you have seen me? Blessed are those who have not seen and yet have come to believe." One can even infer a corrective to the prevalent valuation of the feeding miracle in all five Synoptic feeding accounts when Jesus declares in John 6:26: "Very truly, I tell you, you are looking for me, not because you saw signs, but because you ate your fill of the loaves." Rather than amending a backwater signs source, the Johannine Jesus appears to be taking on the prevalent Christian valuation of Jesus' miracles: it is what they *signify as signs* that is significant, not their materiality alone.[8]

In addition to these primary theological tensions in John, we also note the Evangelist's addressing just about every other theological issue dialectically as well. While the Son did not come to judge the world, truth itself brings a judgment; therefore, the advent of the Son creates a crisis for the world: whether humans will receive or reject the Revealer. While the Father sends the Holy Spirit, just as he has sent the Son, the Son also sends the Spirit, who brings Jesus' words to later believers as needed. Jesus is the epoch-changing means by which the world is drawn to the Father, and his enlightening work is accessible to all humanity if people will but respond receptively to the divine initiative. The coming of the kingdom is both now and on the last day—the *already* and the *not yet*. Salvation is "of the Jews," and yet many of the Judeans reject Jesus as the Messiah. While Jesus opened the eyes of the blind man, could he not keep another from dying? Jesus warns the once-lame man to live right, lest something worse befall him, yet he also declares that the blind man's illness is not due to any person's sin, but for the glory of God to be revealed (5:14; 9:3). The Son is equal to the Father, and yet he can do nothing except what the Father commands. And, while no one can come except being drawn by the Father, as many as believe in him receive the power to become the children of God—as many as believe in his name.[9]

In these and other ways, the Johannine Evangelist shows himself to work in both-and ways instead of either-or ways. Therefore, his presentation of theological themes must be interpreted dialectically, lest the content be misapprehended. From a cognitive-critical standpoint, his dialectical thinking reflects proximity to a subject rather than distance. With relation to Jesus, this could imply firsthand encounter with the actual ministry of Jesus, although such is impossible to demonstrate. At the very least, however, it represents experiential engagement with the spiritual reality of the postresurrection Christ, whereby older understandings find new meanings as mediated by the *Paraklētos*.

One way to understand this proposal regarding dialectical thinking in John is to consider it within James Fowler's six stages of faith development. The dialectical approach to theology described here reflects Fowler's Stage 5 faith (Conjunctive Faith) rather than Stage 3 (Synthetic-Conventional Faith) or Stage 4 faith (Individuative-Reflective Faith).[10] While modern dialectical theologians have readily seen the best of theological reflection taking place dialectically, believing that few propositions can contain the entirety of truth on a given matter, it is a critical failure to be unwilling to envision a first-century Evangelist as demonstrating the same capacity. John's theological tensions reflect dialogues internal to the Evangelist's thought, not external dialogues alone. In that sense, the author of the Johannine Gospel operates far more conjunctively (in both-and ways instead of either-or, disjunctive ways) than the author of the epistles, thus providing a dialogical complement to some features of Mark and perhaps Matthew slightly later.

▨ The History-of-Religions Origins of John's Human-Divine Dialectic

One thing that Rudolf Bultmann got right in his depiction of the Fourth Gospel's dominant theme is his inference of the agency of the Revealer—one who comes from and returns to the Father, calling for a response to the divine initiative as the epitome of redemptive faith. His judgment is wrong, however, that this theme originated as a Gnostic Redeemer myth conveyed by followers of John the Baptist, who Bultmann believed was a leader in an early Gnostic community. Following the discovery of the Dead Sea Scrolls in 1947, the dualistic character of first-century Judaism has decimated the modern judgment that Judaism was monistic and that any dualism in John must have represented Hellenism rather than Judaism. Given that the Qumran community was highly dualistic (seeing themselves as "children of light" versus Jerusalem leaders as "children of darkness"), John's dualism need not be ascribed to Hellenistic or Gnostic sources in its origin, although it would certainly find a home within such audiences eventually. By far, the closest parallels to the Johannine sending motif are found in the prophet-like-Moses agency schema as represented in Deuteronomy 18:15-22. The Greek rendering of this passage reveals at least twenty-four parallels in the Fourth Gospel,[11] but the basic outline is as follows:

Box 6.1: The Prophet Like Moses in Deuteronomy 18:15-22 and the Divine Agency of Jesus in John

■ God will raise up a prophet like Moses from amidst the brethren—Israel must listen to him (Deut. 18:15).

Moses wrote of Jesus (John 1:45; 5:46); people experience him as a prophet or the Mosaic Prophet/Messiah (the Samaritan woman, 4:19; the crowd, 6:14; the Jews, 7:40; and the blind man, 9:17); to receive the agent is to receive the one who sent him (13:20).

■ God will put God's own words into this prophet's mouth, and he will speak only the words that God has commanded him to speak (Deut. 18:18).

The Son speaks not his own words but says and does only what the Father has commanded him to say and do (John 3:11; 5:19, 30; 6:38; 7:28; 8:28; 12:49-50; 14:10, 31).

■ Humans are accountable to respond to God's agent and will be judged by God accordingly (Deut. 18:19).

Those who do not believe are already condemned (John 3:18) and will be held accountable ultimately for their response to the Son (5:37-38; 12:47-48).

■ Anyone who speaks on behalf of other gods or speaks presumptuously a word God has not commanded is a false prophet who should be put to death (Deut. 18:20).

The Jewish leaders accuse Jesus of speaking presumptuously (John 10:33), and they seek to put Jesus to death (5:18; 7:1, 25; 8:37, 40, 59).

■ The authentic prophet is identified by his word always coming true; if his word does not come true, that prophet has spoken presumptuously and may be disregarded (Deut. 18:22).

Jesus' predictive word comes true, showing that he is the authentic prophet whom Moses predicted (John 2:22; 4:41; 13:19, 38; 14:29; 18:9).

The Johannine Mosaic agency schema appears to have had at least three stages in its development. First, it is likely that Jesus of Nazareth saw his own mission more in terms of a prophet like Moses than a king like David. While Luke doubles the six Davidic references in Mark, and Matthew triples them, the Mosaic prophet references do not appear to have been a part of the earliest Christian theological development. In Acts they appear in the proclamation of Peter (Acts 3:22) and the witness of Stephen (Acts 7:37), but references to Moses do not appear in Christian hymnic or christological material. Therefore, Mosaic associations with Jesus were likely earlier rather than later, making it plausible that their origin was closer to the Jesus of history than later Christian embellishments. The crowd at the feeding seeks to rush him off for a coronation as a prophet-king like Moses, but Jesus is presented as fleeing their designs on his political future (John 6:14-15). Ironically, however, when Jesus claims to speak on behalf of the Father, this gets him into trouble time after time with the Jerusalem authorities. That Jesus understood his mission in terms of the prophet like Moses as predicted in Deuteronomy 18 is a strong likelihood; it also suggests one reason why the religious authorities of Jerusalem may have mistaken his agency claims for blasphemy, when they were something closer to the Galilean's prophetic assertions to be speaking as God's representative.

Second, Torah-oriented Judaism, keen to emphasize the oneness of God and the priority of Scripture adherence, resisted emerging Christian claims that Jesus was the Messiah/Christ after the fall of Jerusalem in 70 C.E. Here Jesus is accused of being the presumptuous prophet of Deuteronomy 18:20, evoking an apologetic emphasis on his authenticity confirmed by his proleptic words coming true: for instance, "I tell you this now, before it occurs, so that when it does occur, you may believe that I am he" (John 13:19). In the Johannine and Matthean traditions alike, an apologetic emphasis on Jesus' authentic agency representing the Father authoritatively can be inferred in hopes of reaching Jewish audiences in Asia Minor and elsewhere. Emphases that Moses wrote of Jesus and that he fulfills the typologies of Moses and Elijah would have been asserted during these phases of the traditions' development history.

A third development can be seen in the later Johannine tradition, whereupon Jesus' agency from the Father became recast in the form of a *Logos* theology within the worship life of Johannine Christianity. Here the creative agency of God in Genesis 1:1—2:4 and the *Logos* teachings of Heraclitus of Ephesus and Philo of Alexandria are adopted as a Hellenism-friendly means of conveying Jesus' divine agency from the Father. While levels of particular knowledge of Heraclitus and Philo are debatable, John's employment of *Logos* motifs similar to their constructs is uncontroversial.[12] Already within the beginning of the first Johannine epistle, the word of life is embraced as the subject of revelation (1 John 1:1-3), and the worship hymn underlying the Johannine Prologue reflects the community's response to the message that has been heard from the beginning. Combined with the personification of divine Wisdom motifs, one can understand how John's Christology evolved later into Gnostic Revealer schemas. Therefore, the Gnostic Redeemer myth, characteristic of second- and third-century Gnosticism, drew from the Jewish agency schema in its conception of Jesus as the Christ rather than being its originative source.

Whatever its origin, Jesus is one with the Father in the Fourth Gospel precisely because he subordinates his will to his divine commissioning as the authentic agent from God. Therefore, the Son's equal and subordinate relation to the Father does not betray two disparate Christologies; rather these two representations of the Son reflect flip-sides of the same coin—a Jewish agency schema rooted in Deuteronomy 18:15-22.

◼ Dialogical Engagements within the Johannine Situation: Seven Crises over Seven Decades

Building on what Wayne Meeks describes as the dialectical Johannine situation,[13] a longitudinal approach is the most compelling. The following views are flawed: that the Johannine situation cannot be known; that there is no relationship between the situation of the Johannine epistles and that of the Gospel; that there was only one crisis to be dealt with over a seventy-year (or even a thirty-year) period; and that if one partner in dialogue is inferred, it necessarily displaces all others. More adequate is a broader perspective that infers no fewer than seven crises over seven decades, including three phases with at least two major crises in each. A seventh crisis spanned all three phases—engaging Synoptic and other Christian traditions regarding interpretations of Jesus' ministry—but the other six crises were largely sequential, though also somewhat overlapping. Put otherwise, crises in real life rarely entirely disappear; they simply are crowded out by other, more pressingly acute ones. Further, an impending problem rarely waits until present ones have eased before presenting itself. Real life is messier than that! Rather, a series of intramural and extramural crises within the evolving Johannine situation can be inferred from a variety of angles, as follows.

Period I: The Palestinian Period (30–70 C.E.)

While the Johannine Gospel was finalized in a Hellenistic setting, it shows clear evidence of Palestinian developments reflecting at least two crises within the first phase of the Johannine situation. Within this phase, community issues are less evident, but references to Jesus and his ministry are clearly asserted.

1. The first crisis involved a running set of dialogues between Judean religious leaders and the Galilean prophet and his followers. Not only do the religious leaders in Jerusalem, who are reportedly seeking to kill Jesus (5:18; 7:1, 19-25; 8:37-40, 59; 10:31-33; 11:8), reject him, but they do so because he comes from Galilee, in the North, rather than from Bethlehem, the city of David, in the South (7:41-52). This crisis was especially acute during Jesus' actual ministry, but it likely continued after that for several decades, as Jesus and his followers were also accused disparagingly of being Galileans, and even Samaritans (7:52; 8:48).

2. The second crisis involved followers of John the Baptist, seeking to convince them that Jesus, rather than John, was the Messiah. This is why John is presented as pointing centrally to Jesus as the Messiah rather than himself (1:6-8, 15, 19-37; 3:27-30; 10:41). Especially if the Johannine Evangelist and some of the other disciples left John and followed Jesus (1:37-42), the importance given to this transfer of loyalty is understandable. The Baptist thus is presented as the central witness to Jesus in the Johannine Gospel, and his elevating Jesus rather than himself functions to point any Baptist adherents in Palestine (and later in

Asia Minor; see Acts 18:24—19:7) to Jesus as the true Messiah. Following the destruction of Jerusalem by the Romans in 70 C.E., the Johannine Evangelist and other followers of Jesus likely relocated to one of the churches in the Pauline mission, and there is no site as compelling as that of Ephesus in Asia Minor—now modern-day Turkey.

Period II: The First Asia Minor Period—A Johannine Community (70–85 C.E.)

With the move to Asia Minor, the Johannine leadership joined an existing community of Jesus adherents, which enjoyed fellowship with the local synagogue, while also including Gentile believers. This being the case, the community into which the Evangelist settled probably straddled Jewish and Gentile groups, perhaps meeting within the synagogue on the Sabbath and meeting with Gentile believers on the first day of the week. As Johannine believers in Jesus sought to convince Jewish family and friends that he was the Messiah, this led to a third crisis within the Johannine situation.

3. Dialogues with the local synagogue probably did not result in the total expulsion from the synagogue that some have connected with the *Birkat ha-Minim*, but unconvinced Jewish leaders must have felt consternation over belief in Jesus as the Christ, which developed into a *Logos* Christology claiming him to be the Son of God. While recent scholars have challenged J. Louis Martyn's hypothesis that the twelfth of the eighteen benedictions, ostensibly crafted at the Jamnia council between 70–90 C.E., cursed the "Nazarenes" as heretics and marginalized Jesus adherents, such challenges do not mean there were no tensions at all. Rather, the very Jewish-Christian proximity argued by Martyn's critics, far from demonstrating a dearth of friction between the synagogue and Johannine believers, arguably created the opposite. Territoriality exists *only* among members of the same species. What likely happened was an ongoing set of dialogues, whereby Johannine believers sought to convince Jewish community members that Jesus was the Messiah based on his prophetic signs and fulfilled words. While some likely believed, the public confession of Jesus as the Messiah/Christ was probably subjected to discipline within the synagogue, causing believers either to withdraw from fellowship or to go underground (John 9:22; 12:42; 16:2). Jewish family and friends, however, probably felt their departure was a loss (and possibly a surprise), and they apparently appealed for departed Jesus adherents to return to the synagogue in the name of loyalty to one God, the Father. This is reflected in 1 John 2:18-25, as Johannine community members appear to have departed and rejoined the synagogue. The Johannine Elder labeled them as "antichrists," and their refusal to accept Jesus as the Messiah/Christ was countered by arguing that if they rejected the Son they would lose the Father (their very interest in returning to the synagogue—recovering Jewish monotheism), but if they received the Son they would retain the Father

who sent him. Therefore, *because* relations remained intact, there was likely a good deal of interchange—and tension—between Johannine believers and the local synagogue.

4. Pressures on the community related to the Roman imperial presence appear to have increased a decade or two after the Johannine leadership relocated in Asia Minor. These can be correlated with developments under Domitian (81–96 c.e.). At the entrance of Domitian's temple in Ephesus stands a monument to the goddess Nike (meaning "victory"), celebrating the emperor's victory over subjugated peoples. Where emperor worship had not previously been a widespread practice since the days of Caesar Augustus (19 b.c.e.–14 c.e.), Domitian reinstated it as a means of bolstering imperial power and loyalty. He even required his own lieutenants to regard him as "lord and god,"[14] which suggests that the confession of Thomas, "My lord and my God!" (John 20:28), conveys a decisively anti-imperial thrust. Indeed, the last verse of 1 John (5:21) admonishes believers to "stay away from idols" as a more pointed injunction to "love not the world."[15] It would have been a direct statement against offering sacrifices to Caesar (either incense or a more substantive animal or grain offering), but it would also have challenged participation in civic festivals, which sometimes went on for days at a time. While demonstrating loyalty to the empire on the emperor's birthday would have been a standard expectation under Domitian's reign, pressure to support civic life would have come from fellow citizens, not just Roman occupiers. Further, as Ephesus vied with Pergamum for Roman favors, seeking to attain *neokoros* (temple guardian) status, anything less than an enthusiastic demonstration of support for the Roman presence might have jeopardized Rome's favor—including the bestowing of such favors as roads, water systems, bath houses, and marketplaces. While Jewish members of the synagogue were exempted from emperor-worship requirements, if one was put "out of the synagogue," as a Jesus adherent or otherwise, one would have been expected again to participate in emperor worship—sometimes even on pain of death.[16] Therefore, growing pressure from Roman imperial policy created a fourth crisis in the Johannine situation as its leaders relocated to the heart of the imperial presence in Asia Minor.

Period III: The Second Asia Minor Period—Johannine (and other) Communities (85–100 c.e.)

The third phase of the Johannine situation involves the Johannine "community" diversifying and developing into a cluster of communities, still in Asia Minor. Some of these Christian communities had already been in existence, but as the Christian movement grew, new communities were also formed. While proximity to the local synagogue would have characterized most of these believers in the 50s, 60s, and 70s of the first century c.e., the adding of Gentile converts to the Jesus movement, as well as growing distance from the synagogue in the 70s and 80s, prompted a transition within the leadership from what Martyn calls being "Christian Jews" to becoming "Jewish Christians." A parting of the ways between Judaism and Christianity is suggested by the reference to the writings of those who persecute Jesus followers, for instance, as "your law" (Jesus, 8:17; 10:34) and "their law" (the narrator, 15:25). This led to two further crises within the Johannine situation involving the emergence of Gentile Christian leadership and its consequences.

5. With the emergence of traveling ministry among the churches of Asia Minor and beyond, in addition to more orthodox Jewish Christian preachers, Gentile Christian leaders also circulated in ministry, but they were more given to assimilation with the local culture and its practices. Given a backdrop of increasing pressures to participate in the imperial cult, including associated festive activities, they likely were accused of loving the world by the Johannine leadership (1 John 2:15-17; see also John 16:33; 17:11-17).[17] The additional problem of Roman disciplining of Christians who did not offer worship to Caesar or confess "Caesar is lord" when required to do so produced divisions among Christians. In Governor Pliny's correspondence with the Emperor Trajan (*Letters* 10.96-97) around 110 C.E., he complained against an apparent standing policy requiring him to put to death Christians that neither reverenced Caesar's idol, nor denied Christ, nor confessed Caesar as lord. He had just killed two young women, who had been directly warned of a capital penalty, but they refused to deny Christ and confess Caesar; he had them killed but felt troubled having done so. However, he then described others who were willing to submit to imperial demands and declared that he understood such people *could not* be Christians. Such demands would have made a Docetic Christology (that is, one that claimed that Jesus had not suffered death) attractive among Gentile believers. If Jesus did not suffer, neither would his followers need to do so, especially when confronted with Roman imperial demands and the consequences of conscientious resistance. Therefore, the antichristic language of the Johannine epistles should actually be seen as referring to two different threats, not one.

In contrast to the prevalent view of scholars that simply lump all three antichristic passages into the same crisis, the pejorative term "antichrists" is used at this stage of a different group—those who refused to believe Jesus *came in the flesh* (1 John 4:1-3; 2 John 1:7). Note three major differences with the first "antichristic" threat mentioned in 1 John 2:18-25.[18] First, in contrast to the previous "antichrists," this group reflects not a schism but an invasion. The danger is not that they might depart and leave one's community; the danger is that they might come to one's community with a false set of teachings—therefore, they must not be let in. Second, it is not a crisis in the past but in the impending present—look out, here it comes! Third, the content of their error is not the refusal to believe Jesus was the Messiah/Christ, but their refusal to believe he came in the flesh—they thus teach a costless discipleship. These features make it clear that this is *not* the same group described earlier, despite the similar use of the ultimate pejorative label within this Christ-centered community. When the antichristic passages of 1 John are lumped together, as most scholars tend to do, they wrongly equate all adversaries with schismatics (which the second group is not) and they infer that all "antichrists" were Docetists (which the first group was not). Another flawed conjecture among scholars is that these teachers must have been Gnostics. While all Gnostics were Docetists, not all Docetists were Gnostics. That is, the false teachers of 1 John 4:1-3 and 2 John 1:7—when put to the test—might simply have denied that Jesus came in the flesh, a false teaching that later evolved into second-century Gnosticism, but which was not yet a full-blown heresy at this period in the Johannine community's experience. In contrast to the first antichristic schism, where former community members denied Jesus was the Messiah/Christ, the second antichristic threat more likely involved Gentile Christian leaders who were not convinced that the gospel demanded a total renunciation of the world and its customs. These probably attended civic festivals, perhaps showed tribute to the emperor cult, and likely participated in other aspects of Greco-Roman society that Jewish Christians would have opposed.

Actually, a Docetic Christology might not even have been their lead doctrine, but a means by which their assimilative teachings were singled out for scrutiny in terms of their implications. If withdrawing from civic life and imperial festivals would have involved suffering (physically or socially), the Elder's rhetoric probably referenced Jesus' suffering as a costly example to follow. If challenged on such a standard, the Gentile Christian leaders might have diminished his suffering as the divine Son of God, seizing upon the implications—if Jesus did not suffer, neither need his followers do the same. That is where the Elder warns communities to beware of assimilative teaching that might sound innocent but is not: "Just ask the preacher if Jesus *really* came in the flesh." If the teacher hesitates or denies the human suffering of Jesus, his threat is to be spurned with the same intensity that the schismatic actions of those who deny Jesus as the Christ were rejected. Beware, the antichristic threat is back—not as a return to religious certainty, but with the promise of easy discipleship. Such is a false gospel to be recognized and rejected.[19]

6. As other Christian communities sought to discipline the faith and practice of false teachers and their assimilative message, the emergence of hierarchical structures of leadership created new sets of crises within the Johannine situation. As seen in the epistles of Ignatius of Antioch (who died at the hands of the Romans ca. 115 C.E. as a persecuted Christian leader), Judaizing and Docetist threats were dealt with by the assertion of community solidarity and the admonition to appoint one bishop in every church—an episcopal leader who would wield the keys to the kingdom, continuing the legacy of Peter (Matt. 16:17-19) and holding both schismatics and false teachers at bay. Apparently, Diotrephes, who "loves to be first"

(3 John 1:9-10), was one of these emerging leaders, although the Johannine Elder experienced the ways in which he wielded his authority as problematic. Diotrephes reportedly spread malicious rumors about Johannine Christians, forbidding his own church members from extending them hospitality, and he even excommunicated any who took them in. If he claimed Petrine authority as a means of staving off other threats, one can see how the Fourth Evangelist would seek to correct such abuses by showing Peter as affirming Jesus' singular authority (John 6:68-69) and being challenged to lovingly shepherd the sheep (21:15-17). More positively, the Johannine Jesus promised to lead the (entire) church by means of availing the Holy Spirit to all (John 14–17), and Jesus commissioned his disciples (plural) as his apostolic ministers rather than just a select few (20:21-23). The priesthood of every believer in the Fourth Gospel thus functioned to counter the narrowing of apostolic authority to a hierarchical few within the growing Christian movement in the late-first-century situation.[20]

7. A seventh crisis spanned all the other six, namely: the felt need to correct dialectically some of the presentations of Jesus and his ministry among other emerging traditions. While the Johannine Evangelist's familiarity with Mark apparently led to his effort, at least in his first edition, to set the record straight regarding sequence and inclusion of material, more weighty concerns extended to theology, Christology, ecclesiology, sacramentology, and eschatology. While "crisis" might be too strong a description of these intertraditional dialogues, the perceived need to clarify the meaning and emphasis of Jesus' ministry did have some urgency to it despite involving a friendly dialogue within the larger Christian community.

Briefly, for example, in addition to a *theological* clarification as to the true value of the feeding as a revelatory sign rather than a wonder satisfying human hunger (John 6:26 versus Matt. 14:20; 15:37; Mark 6:42; 8:8; Luke 9:17), the emphasis in John is on the king rather than the kingdom (John 1:49). Thus Johannine messianic disclosure counterbalances Markan messianic secrecy. *Christologically*, the Fourth Evangelist presents Moses and Elijah coming neither in the ministry of John the Baptist nor on Mount Tabor, but in the ministry of Jesus—fulfilling both typologies by his words and deeds. *Ecclesiologically*, the Johannine Jesus sends his Spirit to guide and empower a multiplicity of believers rather than an apostolic few, and Peter is presented as affirming Jesus' sole authority. *Sacramentally*, the assertion is that "it was not Jesus himself but his disciples who baptized" (John 4:2), and the institution of a meal of remembrance is totally missing from the Last Supper in John 13. Such presentations appear to counter the development of sacraments in the late first-century Church in the interest of a more primitive view of the Jesus movement. Another possibility is that the Evangelist might simply have been "sacramentally innocent," as it cannot be assumed that movement toward institutionalization in the early church happened at the same time or the same way within all sectors of the movement. *Eschatologically*, the Fourth Evangelist appears to correct the claim that "there are some standing here who will not taste death until they see that the kingdom of God has come with power" (Mark 9:1). He refers to that expectation as a misunderstanding, purveyed wrongly, when Jesus actually said something else to Peter and those around him: "'If it is my will that he remain until I come, what is that to you? Follow me!' So the rumor spread in the community that this disciple would not die. Yet Jesus did not say to him that he would not die, but, 'If it is my will that he remain until I come, what is that to you?'" (John 21:22-23).

In these and other ways, the Fourth Evangelist seems to be clarifying the meaning and significance of Jesus' ministry over and against, as well as in support of, prevalent parallel presentations in the Synoptics. Unlike the other crises, however, this running dialogue with Synoptic valuations and interpretations of Jesus' ministry extended from the earliest stages of Gospel-tradition formation to the latest. It is located as the final dialogical crisis, however, because the finalization of John features much of the intertraditional dialogue—especially as familiarity with all three Synoptic Gospels would have been most likely in the final stages of its composition. And, in our analyses of Johannine-Synoptic comparison-contrasts, those dialogues continue to this day!

Box 6.2: Three Periods in the History of the Johannine Situation

Period I: The Palestinian Period, the Developing of an Autonomous Johannine Jesus Tradition (ca. 30–70 C.E.)
    Crisis A: Dealing with North/South Tensions (Galileans/Judeans)
    Crisis B: Reaching Followers of John the Baptist
    (*The oral Johannine tradition develops*)

Period II: The First Asia Minor Phase, the Forging of a Johannine Community (ca. 70–85 C.E.)
    Crisis A: Engaging Local Jewish Family and Friends
    Crisis B: Dealing with the Local Roman Presence
    (*The first edition of the Johannine Gospel is prepared*)

Period III: The Second Asia Minor Phase, Dialogues between Christian Communities (ca. 85–100 C.E.)
    Crisis A: Engaging Docetizing Gentile Christians and Their Teachings
    Crisis B: Engaging Christian Institutionalizing Tendencies (Diotrephes and his kin)
    Crisis C: Engaging Dialectically Christians' Presentations of Jesus and His Ministry (actually reflecting a running dialogue over *all three* periods)
        (*The Evangelist continues to teach and perhaps write; the epistles are written by the Johannine Elder, who then finalizes and circulates the testimony of the Beloved Disciple after his death*)

As the Johannine tradition developed over seven decades, at least these seven dialogical crises in the evolving Johannine situation seem likely. There may have been more, in addition to these (such as dialogues with Samaritans), but these are the most likely. Some of them were more intramural, while others were more extramural. For instance, North-South tensions between northern Galileans and southern Judeans were more likely extramural, as were the later tensions with the Roman presence in Asia Minor. The rest of the crises were largely intramural, although some of them also involved partners in dialogue outside the immediate Johannine situation.

▤ A Two-Edition Theory of Composition

Among the various theories of Johannine composition, the least complex means of accounting for the major literary perplexities involves a basic two-edition theory of composition. Of course, there could have been several editions, but ascertaining the particulars beyond a likely early edition and what may have been added to it is elusive at best. Therefore, a basic first edition, followed by the adding of supplementary material culminating in a final edition, seems the most plausible way to approach the issue. Also likely is the inference of the Evangelist's continued preaching and teaching, and the writing of the Johannine epistles by the Elder, between the first and final editions of the Johannine Gospel. Therefore, in response to the question, "Were the epistles written before or after the Gospel?" the answer is *Yes!* They were written after the first edition, but before the final edition. Further, the final editor of the Gospel appears to have been the author of the epistles, and on this matter Bultmann's literary judgments are indeed sound.

A First Edition of the Johannine Gospel (80–85 c.e.)

Assuming that material added to the final edition of the Gospel of John included the Prologue (1:1-18), the Epilogue (21:1-25), and chapters 6 and 15–17 (as well as Beloved Disciple and eyewitness references), the original Johannine Gospel narrative began with the ministry of John the Baptist—parallel to that of the Gospel of Mark. If John 5 was originally followed by John 7, however, and if John 21 was added to the first ending in 20:31, this would have involved five signs instead of eight. Given that the first edition of John closes with inviting the hearer/reader to believe in Jesus as the Jewish Messiah/Christ, the five signs of Jesus likely functioned as a parallel to the five books of Moses. Further, these are precisely the five signs that are neither in Mark nor any of the other Gospels. Thus, the first edition of John played a role similar to Bultmann's inferred *sēmeia* source, or Robert Fortna's Signs Gospel; it simply reflects the earlier Johannine edition rather than co-opted alien material. Rather than inferring that this edition involved the dialectical correction of an imaginary source comparable to Mark, however, it makes more sense to see this edition as engaging Mark, and perhaps other parts of gospel traditions, dialectically. As such, it likely represents a distinctive rendering of Jesus' ministry, as attested by the Muratorian fragment around 170 C.E., where local leaders encouraged John the apostle to produce his own account of Jesus' ministry as an alternative to circulating Gospels. Whether or not the particulars of authorship were accurate, this is precisely what the first Johannine edition seems to have been. Whoever the author may have been, the Johannine narrative provides a meaningful rendering of Jesus' ministry as a knowing alternative to Mark and eventually other Gospels dependent on Mark.

The Continued Preaching of the Evangelist and the Writing of the Epistles by the Elder (85–95 C.E.)

While the Johannine Evangelist is credited with "writing" the Gospel, he may have dictated the material or employed a scribe in its production; that editor may even have been its final editor as well. Nonetheless, the Evangelist probably continued to preach and teach about Jesus even after completing the first edition, and some of this material was probably preserved in written form either by himself or by members of his community. When noting the character of the material likely to have been added to the first edition of the Gospel, it includes the community's worship material (the Prologue), narrations of Jesus' miracles also found in the other Gospel traditions (the feeding, the sea crossing, the confession of Peter), especially Jesus' teachings about the ongoing work of the Holy Spirit leading believers into truth and in unity, and emphasis on the servant character of apostolic leadership in caring for the flock of Christ. Similar issues were being addressed by the Johannine Elder, the author of the epistles, as he calls for loving one another in unity, staving off false teachings and their assimilative inclinations, challenging the love of the world instead of the community, and confronting abrupt leaders in the name of more gracious and inclusive approaches to leadership. 1 John was probably written as a circular to be read within various churches in Asia Minor (ca. 85 C.E.); 2 John was written to a community—"the chosen lady and her children"—calling for the opposing of false teachers and their Docetizing inclinations (ca. 90 C.E.); 3 John was written to Gaius, an individual leader, encouraging him to continue extending hospitality to others despite its having been denied members of Johannine Christianity by Diotrephes who "loves to be first" (ca. 95 C.E.). The "new command" of Jesus, to love one another (John 13:34), has become the "old commandment that you have had from the beginning" by the time of 1 John 2:7-8 and 2 John 1:5-6.

The Death of the Beloved Disciple and the Finalization of the Fourth Gospel by the Johannine Elder (100 C.E.)

Several features make it difficult to assume that the Johannine Gospel was finalized by the original Evangelist. First, "the Beloved Disciple" is referenced in the third person (John 13:23; 19:26; 20:2; 21:7, 20) as an actor in the narrative alongside Peter; it is unlikely that one would refer to oneself in such a way. Likewise, the third-person reference to "the eyewitness" at the cross appears to imply someone other than the narrator, although no direct claim is made that this person is the Evangelist (19:35). Second, the death of the Beloved Disciple is "explained" as though he had died by the time the text is finalized (21:23). This implies at least a final editor's hand. Third, the Beloved Disciple is explicitly credited as the source of the narrative by another, implying that the editor also wrote those words. Fourth, some of the material apparently added to the final edition of the Johannine Gospel, such as the Prologue, is both unlike the rest of the Gospel material in terms of poetic form and vocabulary and similar to 1 John 1:1-3. Fifth, some of the issues that are palpable in the material added to the first edition (1:1-18; chaps. 6, 15–17, 21) are also pressing issues in the epistles: church order, abiding in unity, emphases upon the flesh and blood of Jesus, and the need to love one another. For these reasons, it is highly likely that after the death of the Beloved Disciple, who was either the traditional or authorial source of the Johannine narrative, the Johannine Elder finalized the Gospel and sent it off as the witness of the Beloved Disciple, "whose testimony is true" (21:24). Apparently, the first edition's differences from the Synoptics have evoked a number of critiques, and two reactions are apparent. First, the addition of John 6 squares the account with the best known of Jesus' miracles; second, its selectivity is defended in the last verse: "there are also many other things that Jesus did" (21:25)—which might be paraphrased: "Yes, I know the Synoptics are available, but this complementary selection of material is intentional."

Box 6.3: A Two-Edition Theory of Johannine Composition

The First Edition of the Johannine Gospel (80–85 c.e.)
  Following several decades of Johannine preaching (and perhaps some writing), a first edition of John is completed between 80 and 85 c.e. as an augmentation of and a response to Mark. This "second" Gospel (chronologically) is not distributed widely, but it begins with the ministry of John the Baptist (1:6-8, 15, 19-42) and concludes with 20:31, declaring the apologetic purpose of the Johannine Gospel.

The Writing of the Johannine Epistles (85–95 c.e.)
  The teaching/preaching ministry of the Beloved Disciple (and possibly other Johannine leaders) continues over the next decade or two, and during this time (85–100 c.e.), the three Johannine epistles are written by the Elder (85, 90, 95 c.e.).

The Finalization of the Johannine Gospel (100 c.e.)
  After the death of the Beloved Disciple (around 100 c.e.), the Elder compiles the Gospel, adding to it the worship material of the Prologue (1:1-18), inserting the feeding and sea-

crossing narrative (chap. 6) between chapters 5 and 7, and inserting additional discourse material (chaps. 15–17) between Jesus saying "Let us depart" (14:31), and his arrival with his disciples at the garden (18:1). The Elder also apparently attached additional appearance narratives (chap. 21) and eyewitness/Beloved Disciple passages (13:23; 19:26, 34-35; 20:2; 21:7, 24), and crafted a second ending (21:25) in the pattern of the first. Then, he circulated the finalized witness of the Beloved Disciple, "whose testimony is true," as an encouragement and challenge to the larger Christian movement.

This theory of Johannine composition assumes that the early traditional material had its own history of development, but rather than inferring disparate sources from which a later editor assembled unrelated sayings and signs, their connection seems to have been more integral to their development. As the signs of Jesus were narrated, their meaning was developed theologically in the discussions and discourses that followed. Therefore, the Johannine tradition developed in its own autonomous way, showing itself to be an independent rendering of Jesus' ministry and finding connections with the needs of audiences along the way. Following the completion of the Fourth Gospel, it becomes a favorite within the Christian movement in the early to middle second century, finding also a home among some second-century Gnostics and Montanists, as well as in orthodox centers of Christianity.[21]

■ Aspects of Interfluentiality between John and Other Traditions

The questions whether or not the Fourth Evangelist knew the Synoptic Gospels, and whether their authors knew his work, are difficult to answer. Too often the Synoptics are discussed as a single group, when they were probably not gathered together until the mid-second century C.E. at the earliest. Likewise, earlier and later stages of the Johannine tradition may have had different sorts of contact with other traditions at different times. Therefore, the Fourth Gospel must be compared and contrasted with each of the other Gospels individually, and the basic elements of the Synoptic hypothesis are assumed: (a) Mark was the first Gospel to be finalized (ca. 70 C.E.), and some Hellenistic setting (such as Rome or elsewhere) is a strong inference. (b) Matthew and Luke both drew from Mark as a source (ca. 90 and 85 C.E.), while also adding traditional material to which they had access. (c) Material common to Matthew and Luke, but not found in Mark, may suggest a second source, "Q" (called "Q" for the German word for "fountain" or "source"—*Quelle*), consisting primarily of sayings material. More refined approaches to these issues can be argued, but a basic theory such as this makes the most sense to most scholars. Therefore, comparing John to each of these traditions, and making inferences accordingly, seems the best way to proceed.

John and Mark: Interfluential, Augmentive, and Corrective

As the Bi-Optic Gospels, John and Mark represent two distinctive and individuated impressions of Jesus and his ministry, developing in ways parallel to each other
without either tradition being derivative from the other. As listed above, the Johannine and Markan traditions show an impressive set of similarities, suggesting several
sorts of contact during the oral stages of their traditions. First, there appears to have
been *interfluence* (mutual influence, back and forth) between the oral stages of their
traditions. This would account for similarities of detail—the sorts of details Matthew and Luke omitted in their incorporations of Mark. Second, a good deal of traditional associations abound, as many phrases and short sayings attributed to Jesus
are shared, although used in different ways. Third, parallel renderings of Aramaic
sayings translated for later Gentile audiences show the cross-cultural reach of these
two traditions. Fourth, connections between Jesus' works and words develop in parallel though different ways in these traditions, reflecting their development in the
oral preaching of the material. Fifth, parallels between John's and Mark's Passion
narratives are many, suggesting similar memories or a common bank of preaching
material about the last days of Jesus. While influence in one direction only is impossible to establish, a theory of mutual influence is far more plausible, and it may be
extended to theories of secondary orality (influence from how a story was told, even
if second- or third-hand) as well as primary access to the preaching itself.

Second, the first edition of John appears to betray familiarity with written
Mark at least, and this evoked *augmentive and corrective responses*. The first edition
of John augments Mark by introducing the earlier ministry of Jesus and adding
three southern signs as a complement to Mark's northern presentation of Jesus'
ministry. Multiple visits to Jerusalem also show how Jesus challenged and was
rejected by the religious leaders in Jerusalem, and John also appears to correct Mark
chronologically and topographically. The Temple cleansing is intentionally placed
early (instead of at the end of Jesus' ministry); the ministry of John the Baptist is
presented alongside that of Jesus (instead of his being imprisoned before Jesus' ministry began); the Samaritans and the household of the royal official received Jesus
(in contrast to his rejection in Nazareth); Jesus is presented as going to and from
Jerusalem (instead of only one visit, leading to his death); only one feeding and sea
crossing are mentioned (instead of two), followed by a confession of Peter; and like
the later second ending of Mark, in John 21 Jesus appears to his followers after the
resurrection, emboldening them (instead of leaving them in fear).

While this set of observations is constructed primarily upon close analyses
of the biblical texts, it coheres remarkably with the earliest commentary on the
Markan and Johannine traditions. In his *Ecclesiastical History* (ca. 325 C.E.), Eusebius describes several things about John and Mark that cohere with the facts of

the Gospels ascribed to them. Eusebius cites Papias, the Bishop of Hierapolis (ca. 60–135 C.E.), who attributed to "the Elder" (*ho presbyteros*) the tradition that

> Mark, having become the interpreter of Peter, wrote down accurately, though not indeed in order, whatsoever he remembered of the things done or said by Christ. For he neither heard the Lord nor followed him, but afterward, as I said, he followed Peter, who adapted his teaching to the needs of his hearers, but with no intention of giving a connected account of the Lord's discourses, so that Mark committed no error while he thus wrote some things as he remembered them. For he was careful of one thing, not to omit any of the things which he had heard, and not to state any of them falsely. (*Eccles. Hist.* 3.39)

Note several things here. First, claiming that Mark (likely John Mark, the follower of Paul) was not an eyewitness but a recorder of other persons' material is not likely to have been invented. Papias may have been wrong, but such a point is corroborated by the way the main elements of Mark match the outline of 1 Cor. 15:3-8 quite well. Second, stating that Mark recorded Peter's (and other) preaching "accurately, though not . . . in order" is also not likely to have been concocted for rhetorical reasons. It plausibly refers to a traditional opinion. Third, Papias cites John the Elder (whom he distinguishes elsewhere from John the apostle) as the source of this opinion, which implies that it was at home among the Johannine leadership. A second-century memory of a Johannine critique of Mark's chronological order is interesting indeed! Fourth, Papias notes the applied interest in the material's being crafted as it was—addressing the needs of his hearers—and he notes also that Mark followed Peter's example in crafting his written narrative according to the needs of his emerging audiences. The Johannine tradition shows signs of doing the same. Fifth, Papias acknowledges duplicate material (the feeding of the five thousand and of the four thousand?) plus other apparent redundancies in Mark, but defends Mark, claiming that he was operating conservatively, seeking to not leave anything out. Again, a single feeding and sea crossing in John would have set the record straight.

In that light, the evidence in the Johannine text conforms well to Papias's report that the Johannine Elder held the view (as the Evangelist plausibly did as well) that Mark did a commendable job, but neither did he get it down in the right order, nor did he include everything he could have, nor did he successfully provide a report free of redundancies or editorial bias. These views correlate well with the appearance of John's alternative rendering of Jesus' ministry. This earliest external opinion of Mark's composition and Johannine perspective coheres entirely with seeing Mark and John as the Bi-Optic Gospels—each putting forward an individuated presentation of Jesus, while also being somewhat in dialogue with each other. Therefore, John's relation to the Markan tradition was interfluential, augmentive, and corrective.

John's Contribution to Luke: Formative, Orderly, and Theological

The relation of John and Luke is most fittingly analyzed from the perspective that Luke employed Mark as his primary source. This is uncontroversial among scholars, as over 350 verses in Mark are reproduced, often word for word, in Luke. Therefore, distinctive similarities between Luke and John (Luke's agreeing with John alone) should be seen as Luke's *departure* from Mark and *siding* with John. This happens at least six dozen times, and therefore the Johannine tradition (probably in its oral stages) should be seen as a formative source for Luke. In terms of detail, Luke includes such Johannine features as the slave's "right" ear being the one that was severed; the change of the anointing from Jesus' head to Jesus' feet (an unlikely change without a traditional basis); the point that the tomb of Jesus had never been used; the identification of Mary and Martha as sisters connected with Jesus' ministry; the feature of a dead man named Lazarus; the report that Satan "entered" Judas; and at Jesus' transfiguration, that the disciples "beheld his glory." While predominant Lukan motifs and units are missing from John (making it highly unlikely that the Fourth Evangelist had access to the Lukan tradition), these Johannine details have been added to Mark's material in ways that imply Luke's access to the Johannine rendering of Jesus' ministry.

Luke also changes his account to fit the Johannine order in some cases, although not in others. He includes a great catch of fish, for instance, although he places it at the original calling of the disciples (Luke 5) rather than at the end of the narrative (John 21). Likewise, he moves the servanthood motif to the Last Supper, and includes only one feeding (the five thousand) and sea rescue rather than the two presented in Mark. He also moves the confession of Peter to follow the *other* feeding (as it is in John), and he harmonizes the Markan and Johannine renderings of Peter's confession: "the Christ" (in Mark) + "the Holy One of God" (in John) = "the Christ of God" (in Luke). Luke also embellishes theological detail found in John: his heightened treatments of the Holy Spirit (the Spirit as "wind" is found in John 3:8 and Acts 2:2) as the gift of God through Christ; a high view of women in close relationship with Jesus; and Samaritans playing exemplary roles in the ministry of Jesus all reflect indebtedness to the ethos of the Johannine tradition. Again, the fact that Luke does not place the Temple incident at the beginning of Jesus' ministry, in addition to his not including the majority of the Johannine witness, suggests that his access to the Johannine rendering is only partial—likely within the oral stages of the tradition. Luke may even have mistakenly "heard" the wrong "Mary" associated with the anointing of Jesus, which may account for his mentioning Mary Magdalene (not the sister of Martha) directly after the anointing of Jesus' feet.

Given the likelihood that Luke had access to the Johannine tradition, his introduction seems even to acknowledge such indebtedness. That is, Luke's prologue might be read as expressing his familiarity with such written projects as Mark and perhaps Q ("many have undertaken to set down an orderly account of the events that have been fulfilled among us," Luke 1:1), but it also seems to acknowledge Johannine input in particular ("just as they were handed on to us by those who from the beginning were eyewitnesses and servants of the *logos*," 1:2), reflecting even a bit of Johannine ethos in the process (investigating everything "from the very beginning," 1:3), writing an "orderly account" for the benefit of his audience ("so that you may know the truth," 1:4). Luke's dependence on the Johannine tradition during its oral stages of delivery was thus plausibly formative, orderly, and theological.

Johannine Influence on the Q Tradition?

Most scholars have explained the distinctive agreements between Matthew and Luke (passages and details not in Mark) as the result of access to a hypothetical first-century source to which we no longer have access, calling it the "Q" source. This seems a plausible inference if not a likely one. Of course, there could have been a dozen different sources to which Matthew and Luke had common access instead of one, or there may have been a fuller presentation of Mark that is no longer available, or Luke may have had access to Matthew's tradition, which would explain (better in some ways) the minor agreements between Matthew and Luke (one- or two-word identical additions to Mark). However, the Q hypothesis has strong merits to it, and most scholars accept it in some form. What is interesting is that one of the passages attributed to Q is entirely reminiscent of the Johannine presentation of the Father-Son relationship (see John 3:35; 5:19-27). For this reason, this passage is even referred to by Q scholars as "the bolt out of the Johannine blue."

> All things have been handed over to me by my Father; and no one knows the Son except the Father, and no one/or who knows the Father except the Son and anyone to whom the Son chooses to reveal him. (Matt. 11:27; Luke 10:22)

Again, the predominant features of the Q tradition are missing from John, but this distinctively Johannine feature appears conspicuously in Q. Several other similarities between the Johannine and Q traditions (the healing from afar of the royal official's son/the Centurion's servant in Capernaum, saving and losing one's life sayings, etc.) may suggest other sorts of contact between the Johannine and the Q traditions (hence, some degree of mutual influence), but the least implausible inference is that the Q tradition, if there was a Q tradition, has incorporated a typical Johannine motif. This could have gone back to Jesus, of course, or an alternative earlier tradition, but since we do not have direct access to either, the strongest inference is that Q drew from the Johannine tradition—also probably in its oral stages of development. Given the uncertainty of Q and the evidence itself, this possibility should be tagged with a question mark; still, it is an arguable view and the strongest way to account for the textual facts. Alternative explanations are less worthy. Therefore, Q appears dependent on the early Johannine oral tradition regarding at least the Father-Son relationship.

The Johannine and Matthean Traditions: Dialogical, Reinforcing, and Corrective

When comparing and contrasting the distinctive Matthean and Johannine material, several things become apparent. First, both traditions address issues relevant to the second- and third-generation church: the formation of Christian lives as disciples of Jesus; apologetic interests in showing that Jesus was the Jewish Messiah; concerns for church leadership and how it is implemented; and taking the gospel further, to the world beyond Judaism. In these ways, the Matthean and Johannine traditions appear to be reinforcing each other, although contacts do not suggest much direct literary contact or influence. On the other hand, secondary orality between these traditions is likely, and it is even more telling that the later material added to the final edition of the Johannine Gospel seems to contain most of the implicit connections with Matthean Christianity. Therefore, a series of dialogical relations between these traditions is likely.

Some level of mutual influence may be inferred in Matthew's locating the Capernaum healing from afar just before the healing of Simon Peter's mother-in-law, hence seeing the "first" and "second" signs of Jesus as presenting material earlier than events reported in Mark 1. Matthew may even have assimilated the Johannine doctrine of the spiritual presence of Christ through the Holy Spirit (John 14–17) in his emphasis that where two or three are gathered in the name of Jesus, he is present in their midst (Matt. 18:18-20). And, the second ending of John restores Peter in a threefold way, parallel to his threefold denial, apparently affirming his leadership in ways the Matthean tradition would also support. On leadership, however, the Johannine tradition appears to be correcting rising institutionalism in the late-first-century situation, challenging the entrusting to Peter (and those who follow in his wake, cf. Matt. 16:17-19) of apostolic power and authority. While direct engagement of the Matthean text is less than evident, the Fourth Evangelist does seem to be challenging at least the inhospitable employment of this tradition—likely by someone like Diotrephes (who "loves to be first") in 3 John 1:9-10. In somewhat overstated terms, when Peter declares that Jesus alone has "the words of eternal life" in John 6:68, this appears to present him as "returning the keys of the kingdom" to Jesus.[22] Put constructively, this is because the post-resurrection Lord leads through the Holy Spirit, who is accessible to all. It is thus a plurality of leadership that is given an apostolic commission in John (John 20:21-23), and the priesthood of all believers functioned to expand the leadership of the apostles against early Ignatian tendencies to constrict it. Therefore, John's relation to the Matthean tradition was dialogical, reinforcing, and corrective.

When the Johannine tradition is compared and contrasted to each of the four Synoptic traditions, including Q as one of them, the particular bases for the above theory become apparent. Given the likelihood that this theory is too complex, or not complex enough, I believe the latter is more the case. Interchange between Gospel traditions probably involved dozens more types and occasions of contact and, in that sense, the above paradigm is primarily suggestive of some of the most likely basic elements within a larger history of intertraditional dialogue. The assumption that contacts and influences happened all in one way, or at one time, or in only one direction, is wrong. Therefore, there may be many exceptions to such a paradigm, even if the basic outline does seem plausible. The *Gospel of Thomas* could also be drawn into such an analysis, but as a clearly second-century document, most of its parallels with the canonical Gospels are arguably derivative from them. The same is true with other noncanonical Gospels, although traces of independent traditions could also be analyzed in a similar way. For now, however, this theory of mutual influence will stay with the four canonical Gospels, which are also arguably the earliest. Below is a diagram, which lays out these relationships in graphic form.

■ Revelation and Rhetoric: Two Dialogical Modes in the Johannine Narrative

While the primary mode of John's narrative progression is revelatory, a secondary mode is rhetorical. Within the revelatory mode, God's saving agency comes to the world, inviting a response of faith to the divine initiative. Moses and the prophets wrote of God's revelatory work, John the Baptist comes as a witness to Jesus, Jesus' revelatory signs and fulfilled words reveal the Father's love for the world, a voice sounds from heaven, and the Father and the Spirit witness to the authenticity of Jesus' mission. Therefore, revelation creates an existential crisis for humanity—forcing a judgment as to whether or not one will respond receptively to the saving/revealing initiative of God. In essence, that is also the message of the gospel: the good news that God has acted toward humanity in saving/revealing love. One need not know the particulars, although the news of God's irrupting into human history confirms that God has indeed acted on humanity's behalf. Therefore, the narrator simply announces that God has acted in saving/revealing ways, and the reception of that message is the beginning of the redemptive/empowering response of faith to the gospel. This divine-human dialogue is the heart of the Johannine gospel, and describing the details of God's saving/revealing work is the main content of the Johannine Jesus' words and works.

A second dialogical mode, however, involves a rhetorical means of engaging the hearer/reader in an imaginary dialogue with Jesus, whereby one's conventional understandings are corrected and one's misconceptions are exposed. Here misunderstanding in the narrative is key. Whenever an individual or group is portrayed as

Johannine-Synoptic Interfluential Relationships

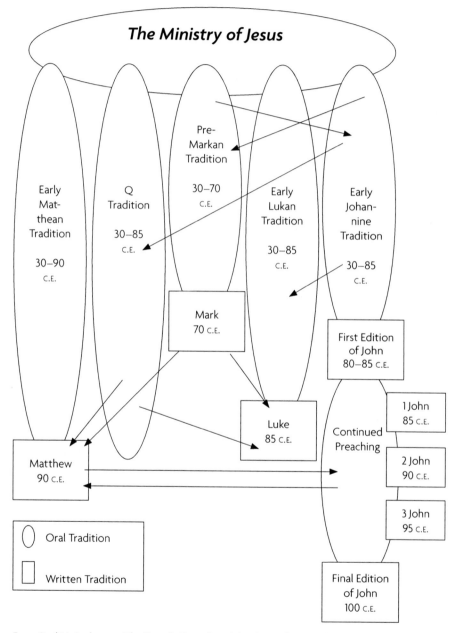

From Paul N. Anderson, *The Fourth Gospel and the Quest for Jesus* (London: T&T Clark, 2006), 126.

miscomprehending the protagonist or some important theme, such a presentation is always corrective. As literary critic Mikhail Bakhtin puts it, stupidity in the novel (and I would add "in historical narrative") is always rhetorical.[23] By presenting such lofty and authoritative figures as Pilate, Nicodemus, the crowd, the Judean leaders, and even Peter as non-comprehending, the narrator corrects members of John's audience who might share similar misapprehensions of the truth. Irony functions powerfully within narrative, and there is nothing quite as ironic as the presentation of those who should know better but do not. As the Fourth Gospel is filled with dialogues, and as most of them function to correct some aspect of miscomprehension, appreciating their rhetorical function is essential for reading John rightly.

Between these two dialogical modes, an interesting interplay is involved related to who takes the initiative in the narrative. Invariably, when God or God's agent takes the initiative, or is described by Jesus or the narrator, the dialogical mode is *revelational*—inviting a response to the divine initiative in faith. When the initiative shifts, though, to the discussant or an actor in the narrative—someone who declares a wise-sounding statement or asks Jesus a question—reader beware! The mode becomes *rhetorical*, and that actor in the narrative is about to be exposed as miscomprehending and coming up short in his or her estimation of the truth. Further, because particular individuals and groups in the audience are intentionally targeted by the text, the hearer/reader is about to be engaged correctively, wittingly or not.

While such a narrative device was designed to reach members of the original audience in the Johannine situation, it also draws readers in other contexts and settings into an imaginary dialogue with Jesus, whereby conventions are challenged and misconceptions are exposed. Nicodemus and Pilate are long gone, but the Johannine narrative engages religious and political leaders of every generation if they will but respond to the convicting power of truth. In that sense, there is neither a first word nor a last word, as revelational and rhetorical modes extend their reach. When the rhetorical mode functions effectively, a response to the revelational mode, and better yet, the Revelation itself, is effected. Such is the character of life-producing faith according to the Fourth Gospel, as truth is always liberating.

Conclusion

As an overall paradigm for interpreting the Fourth Gospel, appreciating its dialogical autonomy offers a suitable way forward. As an independent tradition, the Johannine witness works way alongside other traditions, but it tells the story of Jesus with its own voice and distinctive emphases. It represents a dialectical reflection of a theologian who also appears to have encountered Jesus of Nazareth and who develops his understanding of the significance of his mission over several decades of Christian history and experience. As such, his story dialectically engages members of the Johannine community and issues within their situation, including at least seven crises over seven decades. It also engages other traditions dialectically; while autonomous in its origin, it was not isolated in its development. Therefore, particular types of contacts between the Johannine and the Synoptic traditions can be discerned when assessed individually. Finally, the subject of the narrative involves the time-changing divine-human dialogue, wherein God speaks to humanity in love, inviting a response of faith. That dialogue, reported in the text, continues through the text, but it also extends beyond it. Ultimately, this dialogue has the capacity to produce a spiritual encounter in the experience of the hearer/reader, which itself is a transformative encounter of the first order. Therefore, from one dialogue to another, the reach of the Johannine narrative extends, which is why this classic narrative continues to scandalize and redeem.

Post-Script: Acts 4:19-20—An Overlooked First-Century Clue to Johannine Authorship?

The larger theory of John's composition, situation, relation to the Synoptics, and rhetorical artistry just presented hangs together on its own, whoever the author might or might not have been. This theory thus fits into the third category discussed in chapter 5—"Composition Theories Regardless of Authorship." It seeks to build on the strongest critical approaches to the Fourth Gospel, while also learning from their limitations. As a distinctive perspective, the Fourth Gospel thus has its own story to tell, and while it is highly theological, many of its claims appear to be made in the service of historical memory.

But can we say more about authorship? Assuming that John the Elder was both the author of the epistles and the final compiler of the Gospel, there is no substantive evidence, critical or otherwise, that disproves his attributing the (oral or written) authorial source of the narrative to a figure such as the Beloved Disciple. Further, each new proposal for identifying the Beloved Disciple as someone other than John the son of Zebedee bears within itself a new set of problems; that fact invites a renewed consideration of the univocal second-century identification of the Beloved Disciple as John the son of Zebedee.

A primary reason for denying the possibility of the Beloved Disciple being John the apostle is the claim that the earliest clear identification of the son of Zebedee *with Johannine authorship* was Irenaeus, who confronted Marcion's favoring of Luke among the Gospels with a four-fold Gospel around 180 C.E. Critics argue that if John the apostle really were the author of the Gospel bearing his name, earlier and surer references would doubtless have been made.

This judgment is problematic for several reasons. First, just because Irenaeus's argument involved both religious motivation and questionable logic (four winds, four corners of the earth, four creatures in Revelation, four covenants requires four

Gospels—including one by John the apostle, *Against Heresies* 3.11.8), this does not mean his historical claim was itself wrong. Second, Irenaeus was not the first to connect John the apostle with the Gospel bearing his name.[24] According to Alan Culpepper, attributions are also made between 150–180 C.E. by the *Epistula Apostolorum*, the Quartodecimans, Melito of Sardis, Tatian, and Theophilus.[25] These pre-Irenaeus writings clearly associate John the apostle with the Johannine writings, and Papias's references to two tombs in Ephesus, those of John the disciple and John the Elder (*Eccles. Hist.* 3.39), makes it understandable that their close association might have led to confusion—even while they were both involved in ministry. This might explain why the terms "the disciple" and "the Elder" were used to distinguish them—with "beloved" (*agapētos* in Greek) being added following the death of the former in much the same way we speak of "the dearly departed."

A third problem with claiming that Irenaeus was the first to make the connection between John the disciple and the Johannine writings is that Luke may be seen to make this connection *a full century earlier* in a first-century clue to Johannine authorship that has been totally missed by all sides of the debate. In Acts 4:19-20 Peter and John speak. This is the only time John the apostle is cited as speaking in Acts. The fact that he is quoted along with Peter, though, may explain why this connection has been missed. Far from presenting a unison chorus, however, when these two statements are studied more closely, they reveal two individuated statements reflecting two recognizably different associations. The first statement, "Whether it is right in God's sight to listen to you rather than to God, you must judge" (Acts 4:19), is Petrine in association—echoed in the God-versus-human authority rhetoric attributed to Peter elsewhere in Acts (5:29; 11:17). Luke may have been wrong, but the Petrine association in verse 19 is clear.

The second statement, however, is more typically Johannine: "For we cannot keep from speaking about *what we have seen and heard*" (Gk *ha eidamen kai ēkousamen*: Acts 4:20). Consider: while Luke employs "seeing" verbs over 250 times in Luke-Acts and "hearing" references over 150 times (and sometimes together), the first-person plural reference to *seeing and hearing* (in that order) what has transpired in the past occurs nowhere else in Luke's writings. Therefore, it is not a typical Lukan phrase. The closest New Testament parallel, though, is 1 John 1:3, "We declare to you *what we have seen and heard* (Gk *ho heōrakamen kai akēkoamen*) so that you also may have fellowship with us; and truly our fellowship is with the Father and with his Son Jesus Christ." Furthermore, John 3:32 says that the Son declares what he has "seen and heard" from the Father (*ho heōraken kai ēkousen*). These verbs are characteristically Johannine in other ways as well. While the Greek words in Acts 4:20 and 1 John 1:3 are not identical (*eidamen* vs. *heōrakamen*), the association is clear: Luke portrays John the apostle as uttering an unmistakably Johannine saying *a full century before* Irenaeus makes his explicit claims regarding

Johannine authorship. Therefore, we can no longer maintain that there was no clear linking of John the apostle and the Johannine tradition before Irenaeus.

Of course, this does not prove that John the apostle was indeed the Beloved Disciple, whose witness the compiler and his community attest is "true" (John 21:24). What this overlooked first-century clue to Johannine authorship does contribute, however, is a contemporary external basis for affirming the Johannine tradition as an alternative memory of Jesus and his ministry, possessing its own authority and voice. It corroborates the basis for the Johannine Evangelist's and compiler's boldness in presenting an individuated account as an alternative rendering of Jesus' ministry.

Therefore, while a theory of John's dialogical autonomy coheres on the basis of the strongest literary evidence available, whoever the author(s) might have been, given the fact that the Johannine narrative possesses its own claims to historical knowledge and first-hand encounter with the ministry of Jesus, this overlooked first-century clue to Johannine authorship bolsters that likelihood in terms of external verification. While it might not prove the specifics of Johannine authorship, it does overturn the view that there was no explicit connecting of John the apostle with the tradition bearing his name until the late second century. Luke's connecting of John the apostle with a characteristically Johannine phrase, a full century before Irenaeus, approximates a fact[26] deserving of open-minded critical consideration.

■ Questions to Consider

1. Name three dialectical or dialogical features of the Johannine tradition and describe how each of them accounts for the origin, development, or presentation of the Johannine witness.

2. Describe the apparent autonomy of the Johannine tradition, but try to account also for particular types of contact or relationship with other Gospel traditions.

3. Describe how the developing history of the Johannine situation may have affected the Fourth Gospel's presentation of Jesus' ministry and its reception by others in the narrative.

■ Terms to Understand

- the dialogical autonomy of the Fourth Gospel
- a Bi-Optic Hypothesis
- dialectical/dialogical
- cognitive-critical biblical scholarship

The Origin and Character
of the Johannine Riddles

A Guide to Interpretation

We return now to the Johannine riddles and how to address them. The two previous chapters showed how composition theories and analyses of the Johannine tradition and its situation have sought to provide ways forward. In the light of John's dialogical autonomy, we have here an independent tradition that developed alongside Mark and the other Gospels but is not dependent on them. Further, some of the contacts, in oral stages of the traditions and otherwise, may have been dialogical—and even corrective—instead of simply repeating the same thing. In history as well as theology and literature, points reflecting contact are often made by means of contrast rather than imitation. Furthermore, some of John's distinctive presentations of Jesus imply a historical opinion, not simply a theological insight. While we now have a closed canon, with a fitting selection of four authorized Gospel narratives, we must remember that first-century engagements with these traditions were variable and in flux. Differing forms of material may also have been circulating, so even our best work in the twenty-first century must remain modest in its claims.

Nonetheless, this chapter briefly outlines three sets of factors contributing to the tensions underlying the Johannine riddles. This discussion may not solve every issue, but an outline at least is offered as a means of making sense of John's enduring perplexities in terms of its theological, historical, and literary riddles. Here I encourage the reader to take a look again at chapters 2–4 of this book, considering how each set of John's riddles might be approached from the perspective of one or more of these interpretive keys. Of course, secondary factors could also be mentioned,[1] but this discussion will limit itself to primary factors underlying each of the Johannine riddles. The connections between these factors and the riddles of the Fourth Gospel will be developed further in Part 3, as they inform one's interpretation of John's presentations of both the Jesus of history and the Christ of faith. This chapter will involve some repetition, as earlier discussions of riddles and approaches will here be integrated and explored in relation to each other.

■ The Origin and Character of John's Theological Tensions

As I argue in *The Christology of the Fourth Gospel*, there are four primary sources of John's theological tensions,[2] and these factors are best approached in terms of how they influenced those tensions. While the church fathers sought to interpret John's theological tensions in terms of essence and categories of being, modern scholars have sought to understand those tensions as expressions of more mundane realities. What would the history of Christian theology look like if we sought to understand John's theological content in terms of its epistemological origins and character? That is, rather than seeing John's theological tensions as the results of ontological thinking alone, what if we saw them as having their roots in such mundane origins as the Evangelist's patterns of thinking and the changing situation in which his material was delivered? On one hand, the basics of Christian theology might remain the same; but then again, we might come to a fuller grasp of what the biblical texts are saying and, perhaps more importantly, what they are not.

Box 7.1: Origins of John's Theological Riddles

■ *The dialectical thinking of the Evangelist.* The texture of the Gospel indicates that the Evangelist was a first-order thinker, characterized by a cognitive dialogue between earlier experiences and perceptions and later ones. His is a both-and approach to theology rather than an either-or stance; he thinks dialogically rather than monologically. As a first-century dialectical theologian, his thought is characterized by a highly theologized memory of Jesus and his ministry.

■ *The Prophet-like-Moses agency schema.* Rooted in Deuteronomy 18:15-22, the Evangelist presents Jesus as fulfilling the promise that God would raise up a prophet like Moses from amidst the brethren of Israel. Jesus would not speak of his own agenda but only what God told him to say; therefore, the Sender and his Agent are one and the same. To reject or receive the Agent is to reject or receive the Sender, for the former is in all ways like the latter. The prophetic agent is proven authentic in his commission because his word invariably comes true.

▪ *The dialectical Johannine situation.* Because (as we saw above) the Johannine tradition faced at least seven dialogical crises over seven decades, the Evangelist and the compiler of the Gospel can be seen to be addressing issues that were of acute relevance to an evolving audience. Apologetic attempts to show that Jesus was indeed the Messiah/Christ pushed Christology higher; pastoral attempts to call for solidarity with Jesus and his community during times of suffering made the human suffering of Jesus keenly relevant for a slightly later audience. With the epistles as a backdrop, the situation of the Johannine Gospel is much clearer than any or all of the other Gospel traditions.

▪ *The rhetorical designs of the Evangelist.* By means of several literary devices, the Evangelist draws the reader into an imaginary dialogue with Jesus wherein one's flawed conceptions and errant ways are challenged, and one's valid and authentic views and actions are affirmed. The motif of misunderstanding in a dialogue is the primary means of engaging the audience dialogically with the protagonist, although irony, symbolism, repetition, and hyperbole in the plot and discourses also play important rhetorical roles within the narrative. Whereas the rhetorical thrust of the first-edition material is evangelistic—seeking to convince hearers and readers that Jesus is the Christ—the later material is more pastoral, seeking to convince audience members to abide with Jesus and his community in the face of hardship in the world.

The Dialectical Thinking of the Evangelist

If the Fourth Evangelist was clearly a dialectical thinker, as argued in the previous chapter, apparent contradictions in John's theology should first be considered as factors of a dialectical approach to memory and truth. Here the presentation of Jesus as the Christ as both divine and human (Box 2.1) should be seen as a factor of encounter and reflection—both in the presence of the Galilean prophet on the dusty roads of Palestine and in the post-resurrection experience of the developing Christian movement. As a first-order thinker, the Evangelist reflected upon transformative spiritual encounters both in earlier and later stages of the Johannine tradition. He also rhetorically asserted both christological poles several decades later, pushing christological claims higher in seeking to reach later audiences with his message, and then emphasizing Jesus' fleshly humanity as Gentile believers found a suffering Lord problematic.

Regarding the question of whether the Son judges or not (Box 2.3), the Evangelist holds these two issues together in tension. On one hand, the Son reveals the love of the Father and judges no one; on the other hand, revelation always creates an existential crisis—whether one will respond for or against the Revealer. Truth itself evokes judgment, in that humanity's inclination toward the truth is tested by one's response to the light.[3] Humanity's response to the saving/revealing initiative of God is further measured by one's response to Jesus' signs (Box 2.5). On one hand, the signs demonstrate that Jesus indeed has been sent from God, and features of his redemptive mission are disclosed in his deeds. On the other hand, dependence on signs and wonders shows not that one has embraced the revelation, but that one has missed it entirely. Given the relative dearth of the wondrous in the "real life" of later generations, especially a firsthand witness can affirm to later generations of believers: "Blessed are those who have not seen, and yet believe!"[4]

Present and future eschatology are also held in tension dialectically by the Evangelist (Box 2.7), as the present is viewed in the perspective of eternity, and as one's eternal destiny is set by one's existential decisions.[5] The presence of the future is already accessible within the Spirit-imbued community of faith, as abundant life is experienced as a dynamic encounter with the *Shekinah* presence of the divine (*Shekinah* is the Hebrew word for the glory of the Lord, Exodus 24:16-17). Eternal fellowship within that loving community which knows no beginning or end has yet to be actualized, however, and the anticipation of such remains a hope for believers in a hostile world. Here the dialectical operation of the Evangelist's thought addresses acute issues unfolding within the later Johannine situation, bringing the relevance of Jesus' words to bear upon the needs of his emerging audiences.

The Prophet-like-Moses Agency Schema

Rather than seeing the Son's relationship with the Father as representing two disparate Christologies (Box 2.2) or in terms of essence, we see that he is one with the Father precisely because he submits entirely to the Father's will. The Mosaic agency schema provides the central missional thrust of the Fourth Gospel, and the origin of this presentation may include both Jesus' historic understanding of his work—at odds with Judean religious leaders—as well as later debates with Jewish leaders in Asia Minor over whether the Nazarene really was worthy of being regarded as the Messiah/Christ. In addition, the universality-particularity question regarding God's saving/revealing work (Box 2.7) should also be considered through this lens. The issue is not one of divine exclusivity, but of human capacity.[6] There is no hope for humanity except the redemptive initiative of God, and where humans respond fully in faithful authenticity they receive God's grace fully in spirit and in truth.

Related here is the question of whether the Fourth Gospel puts forward a view of determinism or free will (Box 2.8). Again, the issue is one of human capacity to apprehend the divine, as no one has seen the Father except the Son. The question is whether humans will open themselves to the divine initiative, responding to God's saving/revealing Word communicated at many times and in many ways. Those inclined to do so will be given the grace to recognize divine openings in the future; but closed receptivity to the workings of God reveals one's spiritual inclination and investments. Therefore, the issue of Johannine sacramentalism (Box 2.11) must also be viewed from the perspective of God's saving/revealing work. When the Father sought to communicate divine love, light, and life to the world, he chose not an inanimate form or text; God sent a person—an incarnate communication—and such is the ultimate sacramental *topos* (place) in every generation. To focus on formal means of conveying God's presence and grace, like an undue focus on the signs or cult, misses the point entirely. The Fourth Gospel challenges emerging Christian forms of worship not as an affront to sacramentality, but by arguing for an incarnational and directly mediated sacramental reality—the divine presence conveyed and encountered in the community and lives of believers.[7]

The Dialectical Johannine Situation

While the dialectical Johannine situation played at least a secondary role in many of John's theological tensions, it played a primary role in at least two of them: the question of the Holy Spirit's proceeding from the Father and the Son (Box 2.4), and whether John's presentation of the Jews was pro-Semitic or anti-Semitic (Box 2.10). On the first question, it is interesting that the two passages in which it is asserted that the Father will send the Spirit occur in John 14, part of the first edition of the Gospel. The emphasis there may have been more primitive, asserting continuity between the Father's sending the Son and also the Holy Spirit as a means of reaching out in loving guidance to the world. In the later Johannine situation, however, the emphasis apparently shifts to the ongoing relevance of Jesus' teachings for the community of faith as believers face challenges and unforeseen hardships. Here the first Advocate (Christ, 1 John 2:1) promises to send the second Advocate (the Holy Spirit, John 15:26; 16:7), who will provide believers with the guidance and empowerment they need to face the challenges of the world. Continuity with Jesus' ministry is asserted in the later material, as special relevance is associated with Jesus' earlier teachings, called to the present in a later situation.

The Johannine presentation of "the Jews" must be approached from the perspective of the evolving history of the Johannine situation. While the Evangelist and his subject (Jesus) are clearly Jewish in the narrative, a distancing from Judaism can be observed between affirming an Israelite in whom there is nothing false (1:47) and salvation being "of the Jews" (4:22), and referring to Jewish approaches to Scripture as "your law" (Jesus to the Jerusalem leaders, 8:17; 10:34—the same way Pilate refers to the Jews in 18:31) and seeing Jesus' words as a fulfillment of "their law" (15:25). Two main sets of dialogues with Jewish leaders are here implied: the first involving North-South dialectical tensions with religious leaders of Jerusalem (taking *Ioudaioi* to mean "Judeans"), and the second involving Jewish-Christian debates within a Diaspora setting over whether Jesus could be regarded as the Messiah/Christ. Reflected also in the crafting of the Johannine narrative, it is interesting that the most intense debates with the Judean leaders are presented in the first-edition material of the Johannine narrative. By the time the later material is added (John 6, etc.), those tensions appear to have cooled.

The Rhetorical Design of the Evangelist

While the dialectical history of the Johannine situation is also reflected in the presentation of John's dualism (Box 2.9) and ecclesiology (Box 2.12), the primary source of these riddles is their rhetorical design within the Evangelist's presentation.[8] While the Fourth Evangelist employs dualistic inferences to explain uneven responses to the Revealer, even by "his own" (1:10-13), the primary thrust of John's dualistic categories is rhetorical. Audiences are admonished to choose the life-producing path versus its death-producing alternatives (6:27). And, while Johannine diminishments of Petrine leadership in deference to more egalitarian and spirit-based alternatives reflect a challenge to rising institutionalism in the late first-century Christian situation, the artistic design of the Evangelist's presentation of such ecclesial images as the Shepherd and the flock and the Vine and the branches reflects his rhetorical interests. The dynamic presentation of Christ's desire to lead the church by means of the Holy Spirit reflects the theological convictions and didactic preaching of the Evangelist, but it is also crafted in such a way as to provide sustenance and direction for later generations. Indeed, it has functioned that way, and such is a testimony to the Fourth Gospel's rhetorical design.

■ The Origin and Character of John's Historical Conundrums

Given the fact that most of John's historical problems are factors of its divergence from the Synoptic traditions, most of these riddles are explicable as factors of an alternative Jesus tradition developing alongside the Synoptic Gospels in parallel, yet autonomous, ways.[9] Of course, intratraditional factors were involved, as well as intertraditional ones, as correctives and adjustments to known perspectives are always a part of historical narration. As theological history, the tradition unfolds to disclose new meanings within familiar stories and events; as historical theology, the tradition responds to new challenges and crises by emphasizing older or newer themes in its narration of the past. Nonrelevant history is rarely worth repeating. Therefore, appreciating the inextricability of history and theology within all Gospel narrative is essential for understanding the meaning and character of these texts—especially the Gospel of John.

Box 7.2: Origins of John's Historical Riddles

■ *An alternative Jesus tradition with its own perceptions and reflections.* If the Fourth Gospel does indeed reflect an independent Jesus tradition, developed theologically, its similarities and differences compared to the Synoptic renderings of Jesus' ministry must be considered as historical contributions to understanding Jesus' ministry. It is highly unlikely that all followers of Jesus understood his actions and teachings identically, and the ministries of the preachers of Gospel material, as well as the needs of the audiences they addressed, played considerable roles in the selection and development of Jesus-tradition material.

▪ *Intratraditional dialogue.* Within the Johannine tradition, dialogues can be seen between earlier and later understandings unfolding within its development. As earlier perceptions were challenged by later experiences, connections were made between sayings and actions of Jesus and later events. In the light of post-resurrection consciousness, new insights emerged regarding Jesus' teachings about his death and resurrection; in the light of later hardship suffered at the hands of religious and political adversaries, new insights emerged regarding Jesus' teachings on the way of the cross; in the light of the Temple's destruction and yet another Jewish Diaspora, the memory of Jesus' prophetic challenge in the Temple affirmed his being the authentic prophet like Moses. Fulfillments of Scripture continued to emerge within worship, as texts were read and reflected upon in the light of memories of Jesus' words and deeds; Spirit-inspired "remembering" also played a role in calling to present the ministry of Jesus with special relevance to a later situation.

▪ *Intertraditional dialogue.* If at least Mark was familiar to the Johannine Evangelist, the first edition of John appears to be crafted as an augmentation and a modest correction of Mark. The five distinctive signs of Jesus in John contribute both earlier and southern signs not included in Mark as a chronological and geographical augmentation; the early Temple incident, multiple trips to Jerusalem, and the dating of the Last Supper may reflect modest corrections in the presentation of Jesus' itinerary. Mutual influence between the Johannine tradition and the oral pre-Markan and later Matthean stages of tradition is likely, and the best explanation for the Lukan and Q contacts is that these traditions had access to (and were influenced by) the Johannine tradition in its oral or developing forms.

▪ *Theology as history; history as theology.* Even though the Johannine presentation of Jesus and his ministry is highly theological, this does not mean it is not historical. On one hand, the Evangelist's theological understandings, language, and convictions come through palpably within the narrative, but claiming that something is historical is invariably linked to its perceived significance; therefore, we can say that John's history is presented theologically. On the other hand, the Evangelist's theological investments are furthered through his narration, so his theology is presented within the history of the ministry of Jesus and its reception. Of course, even the word *historical* is itself a rhetorical term, and *any* historical account is always rhetorical. The Synoptics are also theological with particular rhetorical agendas, as are the works of Philo, Josephus, and Roman historians, so the Johannine narrative is not unique in its conjoining of history and theology.

An Alternative Jesus Tradition

As at least something of an independent memory of Jesus' ministry, an alternative Jesus tradition would account for at least some of John's material being different from that included in the Synoptic Gospels (Box 3.2). While the final editor attributes the testimony at the cross to an eyewitness and the Gospel narrative to the Beloved Disciple, this of course does not imply that all of the Fourth Gospel originated in direct, independent, eyewitness memory. Much of it reflects later theological development, and some of its reports may have stemmed from other sources despite the dearth of evidence to that effect. The point, however, is that because

John's tradition represents an alternative Jesus tradition, ways should be explored to account for its corroborative, distinctive, and alternative renderings of Jesus' ministry.[10] The dialectical character of the Evangelist's thought suggests firsthand contact with his subject, and while Johannine claims to firsthand memory of Jesus and his ministry are problematic, they have not exactly been critically overturned. Put otherwise, the Johannine Gospel may be the only complete story of Jesus to involve narration by an eyewitness. This does not mean it is always accurate or free of bias; it does call for a fresh historiographic consideration of Jesus of Nazareth in Johannine perspective.[11]

In particular, the archaeological and topographical details of John's narrative suggest firsthand familiarity with at least the places Jesus ministered, although many of the theological emphases must be attributed to the constructive work of the Evangelist (Box 3.6). Rather than inferring a historicized drama, however, we have in the Johannine narrative more of a dramatized history. Therefore, incidental details otherwise easily left behind by later editors seem to be the stuff of original insights and developing meanings.[12] Within this tradition, distinctive understandings of Jesus' words and works lent themselves to creative associations, which were developed further in the Evangelist's preaching and teaching about Jesus (Box 3.8). While the Jesus of history probably never uttered the I-am discourses as presented in the Fourth Gospel, it cannot be said that any of these themes are missing from the Synoptics. And, while the Jesus of history probably never claimed to be the pre-existent deity, the burning-bush motif is developed by the Markan Jesus, who also declares several times "I am." The Johannine paraphrase developed these motifs further, representing the convictions and experiences of the Evangelist, but not entirely truncated from Jesus' ministry. Therefore, as an alternative Jesus tradition, John's is also a developed tradition, presenting Jesus' work and words in the Evangelist's theological framework, addressing the needs of his emerging situation accordingly.

John's Intratraditional Dialogue

Within the Johannine tradition, intratraditional dialogues can be seen, especially in John's distinctive Prologue and Epilogue (Box 3.3). While John 1:1-18 reflects the community's faithful response to the Johannine narrative, it also comes to serve as a new introduction preparing hearers/readers for its reception.[13] Likewise, chapter 21 brings several other issues to closure, including the death of the Beloved Disciple and the pastoral character of authentic Christian leadership.

While the History of Religions shows some parallels with the distinctive signs of Jesus in the Fourth Gospel (Box 3.10), these are largely closer to Jesus' miracles performed in the Synoptics, though proof of their historical origin is impossible to establish. Distinctive within the Johannine presentation, though, is the narration of Jesus' signs in ways that address the concerns of the unfolding Johannine situation

(Box 3.12). Presenting Jesus in the typologies of Moses and Elijah enhances his appeal before later Jewish audiences; presenting him as a performer of wonders enhances his appeal also before Hellenistic audiences. Against these features, however, the existentializing thrust of the Evangelist's interpretation poses a corrective not only to other traditions, but to the embellishment of wonders within the Johannine tradition itself.

Johannine-Synoptic Intertraditional Dialogue

While it cannot be assumed that Johannine familiarity with some Synoptic material implies exhaustive familiarity with all of it, a good deal of intertraditional dialogue is likely. Plausibly, if the Fourth Evangelist had a general familiarity with at least Mark, his following a general chronological pattern, while taking issue with several features of Mark's order and chronology (Box 3.4), suggests knowing intentionality. Such a view goes against the prevalent scholarly opinion of the day, but it is reinforced by Papias's citing of the Johannine Elder's opinion. A to-and-from-Jerusalem itinerary is certainly more historically plausible than the single visit of the Synoptic Jesus. If we do have here an independent historical tradition, the Evangelist appears to have deferred to Mark in not duplicating material already presented effectively, while at the same time including distinctive material as an augmentation of Mark (Box 3.5).

Distinctive presentations of Jesus' ministry, however, can also be seen in the Johannine presentation of such themes as ministry, worship, the advance of the kingdom, and the work of the Holy Spirit (Box 3.7). Here the Johannine Jesus speaks with his own voice thereby suggesting the Evangelist's convictions as to the significance of his ministry. In the Johannine selection of Jesus' signs, exorcisms are left out—either because of the Evangelist's discomfort (note who objects to other exorcists in Mark 9:38: none other than John the apostle!) or due to their lack of suitability within a Hellenistic setting. Alternatively, a more celebrative Jesus is presented (Box 3.9). Again, such moves do reflect the Fourth Evangelist's preferences within his narration of Jesus' ministry, but a good deal of his nonduplicative rendering is an apparent attempt to augment Mark with underutilized material.

Theology as History; History as Theology

The history-theology relationship has been a longstanding question in biblical studies, and nowhere is it more acute than in Johannine studies (Box 3.1). In answer to the question as to whether John's narrative is historical *or* theological, the answer must be *yes*. It is both historical and theological, as are the other Gospel narratives. Therefore, applying critical theory regarding historicity is important for biblical scholarship; such resources have too long been ignored. In particular, we have in the Johannine narrative a set of cross-cultural elements, whereby Palestinian details and Jewish words and customs are "explained" within a non-Jewish setting (Box

3.11). This may have been done by either the Evangelist or the final compiler, but it does reflect Palestinian origins of the material's earlier delivery, either as the preaching of firsthand recollections of Jesus' ministry or teachings about Jesus by Jewish followers in Palestine, crafted for a Hellenistic audience later. Just as Mark shows evidence of the same, the cross-cultural translation of the Palestinian Jesus into the language and thought-forms of more distanced audiences suggests the type of history and theology that is here at work.

▉ The Origin and Character of John's Literary Perplexities

Appreciating *how* a text says what it says helps one appreciate *what* it says and what it means; this is especially the case when seeking to comprehend the origin and character of John's literary perplexities. While it cannot be said that the Fourth Gospel is a seamless robe, woven from top to bottom, neither do we have here a collection of leftover fragments to be gathered into disparate literary baskets or imagined alien sources. Here we have a largely synchronic tradition in terms of its Johannine origin, developing diachronically within an evolving situation. Most of John's literary aporias can be accounted for within a basic two-edition theory of composition, and while the text was finalized by a second hand, the compiler appears to have been conservative in his attempts to preserve the authentic witness of the Beloved Disciple. The oral and written presentation of the Johannine witness can be inferred in its development, and the history of the Johannine situation provides a backdrop for appreciating its original relevance and delivery.

Box 7.3: Origins of John's Literary Riddles

- *Orality and literacy in the formation of the Johannine tradition.* The Johannine rendering of Jesus and his ministry began, as with all Gospel traditions, in the preaching and teaching about Jesus. It was not until first-generation apostolic leaders began to die that interest coalesced around preserving their testimonies in written form, although units of oral and written tradition were likely in circulation, used within meetings for worship and teaching settings. Johannine repetitions and variations reflect the gathering of orally delivered material into written forms, and the Beloved Disciple likely developed Jesus' I-am sayings christologically, as they represented his understanding of Jesus as the embodiment of true Israel and Jesus' being the Jewish Messiah/Christ. Connections were made with Jesus' signs and ensuing dialogues, crafted into larger units for teaching and preaching within early Christian settings.
- *The "Second Gospel" as an apologetic Jesus narrative.* Given a general familiarity with Mark (perhaps heard delivered in one or more meetings for worship), the Beloved Disciple was encouraged to gather his own rendering of Jesus' ministry into a written whole, probably enjoying only a limited circulation. Gathered around 80 to 85 C.E., it was the "Second Gospel" and an alternative rendering as a complement to Mark. Designed to be

an apologetic outreach to Jewish family and friends in Asia Minor, the five signs of Jesus would have played on the five books of Moses, and his fulfilled word would have explicitly shown that he was indeed the prophet predicted by Moses in Deuteronomy 18. The ending of the first edition accounts for Markan omissions, acknowledging Jesus' other signs not written in *this* book (that is, signs known to appear in Mark), and the apologetic thrust of the narrative is declared directly (John 20:30-31).

▩ *Continuing preaching within the Johannine situation.* After gathering a Gospel narrative, the Beloved Disciple (the Evangelist) continued to preach and to teach, and the later Johannine material reflects the addressing of concerns elucidated by the Johannine epistles. By then, adversity from the *Ioudaioi* had softened (1 John 2:18-25), but acute pressures from "the world" within an imperial-worship context (1 John 2:15-17; 5:4-5, 21), dealing with the false teachings of assimilative (and Docetic) Gentile Christians (1 John 4:1-3; 2 John 1:7), and struggling with emerging hierarchical leaders such as Diotrephes and his kin (3 John 1:9-10) became important issues to address. The later Johannine material emphasizes a call to abide with Jesus and his community, in the face of such issues.

▩ *A final edition as the Fourth Gospel.* After the death of the Beloved Disciple, the Johannine Elder (author of the epistles, and perhaps even a scribe recording some of the first edition or earlier material) adds a selection of later material (John 1:1-18; chaps. 6, 15–17, 21; and "Beloved Disciple" and "eyewitness" references) to the earlier edition. His work is "conservative" in that he sought to preserve material, letting it stand, despite duplications and rough transitions. Most of John's major literary aporias can be addressed in this way, and the Fourth Gospel was then circulated among the churches for believers and others to receive. As such, the compiler added a worship hymn as an engaging introduction to the narrative, the feeding and sea-crossing narrative as a means of filling out the story, Jesus' final discourses and prayer as his "last will and testament" for the church, and an eyewitness/Beloved Disciple attestation as a means of asserting the text's authority. Imitating the first ending, the compiler again defended Johannine selectivity in the light of differences with other Gospels in addition to Mark (John 21:25).

Orality and Literacy in the Formation of the Johannine Tradition

While the Fourth Gospel includes a few texts that were added later by copyists in the second century or later (Box 4.3), this does not mean that other sections of the Johannine text were added by an alien hand. Indeed, editorial asides and clarifying comments appear to have been inserted by either the Evangelist or the editor, and some of these features may reflect clarifications made during oral deliveries of the material as well. Within the oral stages of the Johannine material's development, repetitions and variations are also conceivable (Box 4.5), as earlier renderings of similar themes are repeated and included in the eventual written form. This need not be a reflection of later additions to the text, as though an earlier edition had no repetitive duplications; any preservation of orally delivered material in written form will likely include some redundancies. It also is the case that references to a familiar theme or event in the narrative may involve clarifying who is being referred to even if that event has not yet been reported within the narrative. Therefore, the movement from orality to literary forms of the material accounts for a good deal of the Johannine repetitions and variations.

The "Second Gospel" as an Apologetic Jesus Narrative

As the second Gospel to be crafted, following Mark's general pattern but not depending on its content, the Johannine first edition betrays both intratraditional and intertraditional sets of dialogues (Box 4.7). Reflecting on the ministry of Jesus and its significance for later generations, the Johannine witness presents its own rendering as an autonomous narrative, while setting the record straight here and there with reference to Mark. In addition to filling in Markan gaps, the Johannine Evangelist is keen to present Jesus as fulfilling Hebrew Scripture both typologically and explicitly (Box 4.10). This being the case, the typologies of Elijah and Moses are wrested from their Markan presentations and presented as being fulfilled by Jesus. As an apologetic narrative, the first Johannine edition is designed to convince its audiences that Jesus is indeed the Jewish Messiah/Christ, thus serving a function similar to that of Bultmann's and Fortna's inferred Signs source.

Continuing Preaching within the Johannine Situation

As the Beloved Disciple continues to minister within the Johannine situation, the Johannine *Logos* hymn reflects the community's response to his message (Box 4.1). While the Johannine epistles represent a variety of issues faced in the Johannine situation between the first and final editions of the Gospel (Box 4.6), such issues as Jewish-Christian conflicts, the imperial Roman presence, assimilative Gentile-Christian teachings, and even rising institutionalism seem apparent in all the Johannine writings (Box 4.9, likewise in the letters of Ignatius). Therefore, they reflect at least the same sector of early Christianity, and commonalities between their larger situation-history may be generally inferred.

This being the case, as defectors had broken off from the Johannine community (1 John 2:18-25) and as hardship within an empire-dominated setting can be inferred, one can see how the thrust of the Evangelist's message shifted from apologetic outreach to pastoral community concerns (Box 4.11). Interestingly, nearly all the anti-Docetic (incarnational) material, emphases upon the Advocate's empowering and sustaining help during hardship, and calls for abiding solidarity with Jesus and his community can be found in the later material. Such is not a criterion for its selection, but it confirms the identification of apparently later material otherwise identified almost exclusively upon literary bases.

A Final Edition as the Fourth Gospel

Imitating the style of the Evangelist's first ending, the compiler adds a second ending to the narrative, bringing closure to its authorization, authorship, and witness

(Box 4.2). The deaths of Peter and the Beloved Disciple are accounted for, and the ongoing ministry of the church is bolstered. The compiler's addition of the Evangelist's later material, either in oral or written forms, is preserved in such a way as to fill out the larger picture and to harmonize the narrative with the Synoptics by the adding of John 6. In addition, the Prologue provides an engaging new introduction, and the adding of Jesus' instructions for the church in John 15–17 accounts for several literary aporias in the text (Box 4.4).

Within this modest approach to John's composition most of the major perplexities are addressed (Box 4.8), including the third-person references to the Beloved Disciple as the original author (Box 4.12). While traditional approaches seek to explain this feature as an indirect means of self-reference, the mention of his death suggests that another hand prepared a final edition after his death. Given the similarities between the supplementary material and the content of the Johannine epistles, Bultmann's judgment that the final redactor was the author of the epistles is a worthy one. His interest, however, was not that of an ecclesiastical traditionalist; he seems willing to challenge Petrine hierarchy along with the Evangelist. Of course, Brown saw such tendencies as evidence that the Beloved Disciple was not a member of the Twelve; I believe it could be taken as evidence that he *was*. If institutionalizing tendencies arose in the late first-century church as a means of confronting Docetism and other threats by claiming the mantle of apostolic authority, who would be more motivated to set the record straight than an apostle who still remembered the informal and egalitarian leadership style of the Master of Galilee?[14]

But that gets us into interpretation, which will now be developed in Part 3.

■ Conclusion

While not all aspects of the Johannine riddles are accounted for in the above discussions, a sustained effort to understand the character and origins of these phenomena has been pursued employing the most compelling evidence of which we are aware. In the light of John's dialogical autonomy, we have reviewed its theological tensions, historical conundrums, and literary perplexities and proposed a new set of platforms to advance more adequate interpretation. While not all features of the riddles are addressed, many of the most pressing ones are, with a few new problems created along the way. As interpretation is carried out in the remaining chapters, this set of paradigms will provide a solid platform upon which to carry forward our investigations.

■ Questions to Consider

1. What difference does it make in the development and presentation of the Johannine tradition if we think of the Evangelist as a dialectical thinker?

2. If Jesus is presented as fulfilling the prophet typology of Deuteronomy 18:15-22, how does this affect the Father-Son relationship and the presentation of Jesus as the Messiah/Christ?

3. If the Johannine tradition developed as a complement to and augmentation of Mark, how might this account for its alternative rendering of Jesus' ministry?

▇ Terms to Understand

- agency schema
- *Ioudaioi*
- apologetic
- rhetorical

Summation of Part 2

While attempts to address the riddles of the Fourth Gospel have been rigorous and sustained, not all paradigms have fared equally well. Most have addressed some riddles but neglected others. Likewise, addressing one set of problems critically often leads to a new set of critical problems, which scholars have sometimes then ignored. Interestingly, traditional and critical approaches to John's origin and development have often been driven by a conviction as to who the author must, or must not, have been. Such a delimiting of options then forces other issues and choices, which sometimes occasion other, unforeseen sets of problems. Therefore, I have argued that the best way forward is to examine the literary character of the material, independent of questions of the author's identity, and to proceed from there toward plausible approaches to addressing the Johannine riddles.

On that basis, I believe a view of John's dialogical autonomy poses the best way forward. A two-edition theory of composition makes sense of most of John's literary perplexities; a three-phase theory of the history of the Johannine situation in longitudinal perspective accounts for six or seven dialogical engagements over seven decades; and a Bi-Optic Hypothesis builds a larger theory of Johannine-Synoptic relations based on particular contacts (including similarities and differences) between these traditions. In this way, a more detailed and exacting set of inferences assist the interpreter in understanding the Johannine rendering of Jesus' ministry as an alternative perspective within the emerging history of the early church.

In the light of John's dialogical autonomy, we can better understand the origin and character of the Gospel's riddles, and this assists further interpretation. Regarding the Fourth Evangelist as a dialectical thinker helps us to understand why his approaches to most theological issues involve tensions. He thought in both-and, conjunctive ways instead of either-or, disjunctive ways. In addition, the Mosaic agency schema allows us to understand many of John's theological emphases as factors of God's initiative and human responses to it. As these themes were played out within the evolving Johannine situation, the literary artistry of the Evangelist also becomes an interesting feature to consider, as we see points being made with rhetorical thrust and nuance. But this point moves us toward the interpretation of the riddles, the subject of Part 3.

Interpreting the Johannine Riddles

A s we turn now to the interpretation of the Fourth Gospel, as well as its riddles and related themes, a theory of John's dialogical autonomy provides a solid basis on which to build. Beginning with leading themes in John's theology, a question to ponder is whether the theological conclusions of the church fathers and mothers would have been any different if explored in terms of John's dialogical autonomy. The next chapter deals not only with John's historicity, but also its implications for the historical quest for Jesus. What would happen if the Fourth Gospel were included in Jesus research instead of being programmatically excluded from the venture? Might this approach require a "fourth quest" for Jesus? The final chapter addresses corporate implications of John's message for the life of the church. As authenticity, love, and mutuality are central to John's relational approach to worship and ministry, one wonders what would happen if members of today's churches really took John's ecclesiology seriously. Might it change the ways they do business within community, and might it also affect the ways its members live their lives in the world?

In all these interests, I invite the reader to go back to the outline of John's riddles in Part 1 and to read again the biblical texts that we are seeking to interpret in Part 3. Some repetition of familiar issues and texts will be required here, but taking things further in the light of the analyses in Part 2, I hope that truth-seeking inquiry will be advanced.

The Christ of Faith
and Johannine Theology

John's presentation of Jesus as the Christ is central to the Evangelist's theology, and one is mindful of Oscar Cullmann's view that for the early Christians, Christology *was* theology.[1] This is especially true for the Fourth Gospel. In addition to the nature of Christ and the Son's relation to the Father, however, John's perspective on Jesus' signs, the means of salvation, the presentation of "the Jews," and dualism deserve to be addressed. In considering the origin and character of John's theological tensions, primary factors have in each case been put forward (see chap. 7, above), although secondary factors may also have been involved. Therefore, primary and secondary factors will be discussed in this chapter and the tensions outlined in chapters 2–4 will be engaged more thoroughly, as the origin and character of John's theological riddles do make a difference for our ongoing efforts to interpret them.

■ Johannine Christology: Is Jesus Human, Divine, or Both?

Nowhere in the New Testament is Jesus presented as both more thoroughly human and more thoroughly divine than in John; thoughtful interpreters cannot ignore such tensions. While modern attempts to see these tensions as a factor of multiple sources fall short in terms of evidence, the primary source of these tensions is *the Evangelist's dialectical thinking*. Appreciation of Jesus' elevated status did not simply begin several generations into the Johannine tradition; rather, some elements appear to have had their origin early in the tradition's history—perhaps even as a factor of transformative encounters with Jesus of Nazareth. While "recognition scenes" (*anagnorisis*—a discovery scene in Greek drama or literature)[2] certainly played rhetorical functions for later audiences in showing Jesus to be the Messiah, how would actual followers of Jesus have experienced his ministry? Might they have sensed something special about him from day one? If so, memory of such firsthand encounters may be embedded within the Johannine tradition.

Might *any* of these stories be rooted in actual events: what caused the disciples of the Baptist to leave him and follow Jesus? Why did Nathanael describe himself as being known by Jesus from afar? How did the Samaritan woman feel as Jesus told her about her past and present situation? How did the disciples reflect upon the multitude being fed and Jesus' appearing to them on the water? In both John and Mark, God's words to Moses before the burning bush are cited in identical Greek (*Egō eimi* Exod. 3:14 LXX; Mark 6:50; John 6:20). Yet in Mark the statement comes across as an *identification* (it is *not* a ghost; it is I—do not be afraid), while in John it comes across as a *theophany* (I am—fear not!). These represent two radically different perceptions and experiences (perhaps between different people in the boat?) from day one. If Peter's strong language elsewhere (Matt. 26:74) might have characterized the pre-Markan rendering, whoever its human source(s) might have been, the perception of a striking encounter in that case might have been expressed in an utterance like, "My God; it's a ghost!" Conversely, the human source of the Johannine memory might have responded to the appearance of Jesus by exclaiming, "My Lord and my God!" Therefore, at least one of the disciples experiencing a theophanic encounter in the presence of the man Jesus may account for an early memory of high christological associations inferring who Jesus was and what he came to do.

Box 8.1: Similar *Egō Eimi* Sayings of Jesus in Mark and John[3]

- *Egō eimi! Mē phobeisthe!* An epiphany (Mark 6:50—"It is not a ghost; It is I!")

  Egō eimi! Mē phobeisthe! A theophany (John 6:20—"I am!") on the lake.

- Jesus makes an I-am reference to the burning bush theophany and Abraham (Exod. 3:14-15) before Jerusalem leaders: "I am the God of Abraham, the God of Isaac, and the God of Jacob." (Mark 12:26)

  Jesus makes an I-Am reference to the burning bush theophany and Abraham (Exod. 3:14-15) before Jerusalem leaders: "Before Abraham was, I Am!" (John 8:58)

- I-am claims are mentioned regarding alternative Messiah figures: false Messiahs will say "I am the Christ" or "I am [he]" (Mark 13:6)

  I-am claims are mentioned regarding alternative Messiah figures: John the Baptist confessed "I am not the Christ" (John 1:20); Jesus calls for belief that he is the one he claims to be (John 8:24, 28).

▦ Jesus makes an I-am response to the high priest's or Pilate's question: "Are you the Messiah, the Son of the Blessed One?" Jesus replies, "I am. . . !" (Mark 14:62)

Jesus makes an I-am response to the high priest's or Pilate's question: "Are you a king, then?" Jesus replies, "You say that I am . . ." (John 18:37)

Given such an early association with the theophany of Moses before the burning bush, one can also imagine this disciple's gathering Jesus' words and works into this interpretive set. Even in Mark Jesus is presented as quoting God's words to Moses before the burning bush (Mark 12:26), so it cannot be claimed that Jesus never associated himself with the I-am motif of Exodus outside of the Johannine witness. In addition, all nine of the I-am metaphors in John (bread, light, shepherd, gate, resurrection, life, way, truth, vine) are also found in Matthew or Mark, so it also cannot be said that these themes are totally absent from Jesus' teaching ministry in the Synoptics.

Box 8.2: Johannine I-Am Metaphors in the Synoptic Jesus' Teachings

▦ *Artos*—Jesus is tempted to turn stones into *bread* (Matt. 4:1-4; Luke 4:1-4), and he feeds the multitudes with *bread* (Matt. 14:13-21; 15:32-39; Mark 6:32-44; 8:1-10; Luke 9:10-17).

▦ *Phōs*—Jesus' disciples are the *light of the world* (Matt. 5:14-16).

▦ *Thyra*—Negotiating the (narrow or locked) *gate/door* is emphasized (Matt. 25:10; Luke 11:7; *thyra* is similar to *pylē* in Matt. 7:13-14 and Luke 13:23-27 as the way to life).

▦ *Poimēn*—The parable of the *shepherd* and the sheep (Matt. 18:10-14; Luke 15:3-7) emphasizes the care of Jesus for his fold, individually and collectively.

▦ *Anastasis*—Debates over the *resurrection* arise between Jesus and Jewish leaders (Matt. 22:23-33; Mark 12:18-27; Luke 20:27-40), and the raising of Jarius's daughter (Matt. 9:18-26; Mark 5:21-43; Luke 8:40-56) and the Nain widow's son (Luke 7:11-17) brings life out of death.

▦ *Hodos*—The "*way* of righteousness" (Matt. 21:28-32) is advocated over "the *way* that leads to destruction" (Matt. 7:13-14).

▦ *Alētheia*—The way of God in *truth* is what Jesus teaches (Matt. 22:16; Mark 12:14, 32); the account of which helps others know the truth (Luke 1:4).

▦ *Zōē*—The narrow way leads to *life* (Matt. 7:14), and Jesus discusses what it means to inherit eternal life (Matt. 19:16, 23-30; 10:17; Mark 10:23-31; Luke 18:18, 24-30).

▦ *Ampelos*—The owner of the *vineyard* sends his son to the tenants (Matt. 21:33-41; Luke 20:9-16); Jesus drinks of the fruit of the *vine* one last time (Matt. 26:29; Mark 14:25; Luke 22:18).

Nonetheless, the Johannine presentation of these motifs in clear christological forms is distinctive, and it most likely represents the constructive work of the Evangelist in crafting his own understanding of Jesus' spoken ministry. That being the case, one can understand how he might have crafted an apparent theophanic claim in John 8:58 for rhetorical effect ("Before Abraham was, I am!") as well as crafting the arrest in the garden with theophanic associations, as the soldiers fall to the ground at Jesus' declaration, "I am!" (18:5-6). Whereas the Markan tradition betrays memory of epiphanic encounters in Jesus' presence, John's tradition shows traces of theophanic encounters during his ministry, and these early high christological associations come across vividly, though they were finalized in written form several decades later.

Also palpable in the Johannine witness are human and fleshly presentations of Jesus. Jesus eats real food with his disciples even after the resurrection; his mother and father are known; his brothers did not yet believe in him; he needs a familial custodian for his mother; water and blood flow from his side; Thomas is allowed to touch the flesh wounds of the risen Lord. Further, Jesus is presented in human anguish—a striking contrast to the one who knows full well what he is going to do. He weeps at Lazarus's tomb; his heart is deeply troubled; he groans; on the cross he thirsts; he loves his own until the end. These depictions of the human Jesus likewise appear to have had their origin in firsthand contact with his mundane existence, and the dusty roads of Palestine can even be sensed in the master's washing of his disciples' feet. Jesus' followers refer to him as "rabbi" in John twice as many times as in Mark—a mundane reference to Jesus as a Jewish teacher leading his band (1:38, 49; 3:2, 26; 4:31; 6:25; 9:2; 11:8). Therefore, we have here a pathos-filled Jesus, and his fleshly humanity is even more pronounced than it is in any of the other Gospel traditions—seeming to reflect the recollections of ones who walked and talked with Jesus of Nazareth.

Therefore, both the flesh and glory of Jesus seem to have emerged from this firsthand memory of his ministry, and those polarities are engaged dialectically in the experience and reflection of the Fourth Evangelist. They also were experienced later, however, in the life of his community. As members of the Johannine situation heard the stories of Jesus conveyed in the first edition of the Gospel, they too came to encounter experientially the subject of the narrative. In hearing stories about Jesus' earthly ministry and dwelling "among us," they came to confess, ". . . and *we* beheld his glory" (1:14). Later encounters with the Holy Spirit, bringing to mind the wisdom and teachings of Jesus as needed for the occasion, also became a source of firsthand encounter for members of the community. Therefore, later spiritual encounters reinforced earlier historical ones, as the Johannine Evangelist sought to connect the original story of Jesus with the emerging history of his community living under the Word.

A second source of the human-divine polarity in John relates to *the dialectical Johannine situation*, as the Evangelist seeks to tell his story of Jesus in ways that will address the needs of his evolving audiences. In seeking to convince later Jewish and Gentile audiences that Jesus really was the Messiah/Christ and Son of God, embellishing his ministry raised christological motifs higher. Not only was the Word in the beginning with God; the Word *was* God (1:1). The cross is rendered as the paradoxical glorification of the Son, and the christological confessions of Nathanael, Martha, and Thomas signal Jesus' divine agency in whom humanity should put its faith. Especially the first ending of the Gospel makes it clear that its purpose is to evoke belief in Jesus as "the Christ, the Son of God" in order that believers might experience life in his name. Therefore, an elevated Christology furthers the evangelistic and apologetic work of the Gospel both in its preliminary and final forms.

An interesting fact emerges, however, when noting the incarnational and fleshly character of John's later material. Virtually all the direct emphases upon the fleshly humanity of Jesus occur in what is likely to be considered supplementary material added to the first edition of the Gospel. The Word-become-flesh is a central element of the Prologue (1:14); the emphasis upon eating and drinking the flesh and blood of Jesus is emphasized in John 6:51-58; the world's hatred of Jesus and his followers—leading to inevitable suffering—is found in the last discourse and prayer (15:18; 17:14); an eyewitness testifies to water and blood flowing out of Jesus' side (19:34-35); Jesus eats real fish and bread with his disciples after the resurrection (21:9-12). If the second and third antichristic passages of the Johannine epistles (1 John 4:1-3; 2 John 1:7) reflect the threat of Docetizing teachers—those who refuse to believe that Jesus came in the flesh—this may explain the incarnational thrust of the later material in John. It emphasizes that Jesus really did suffer and die, and the practical implication is that his followers must be willing to do the same if they expect to share with him the eternal life he offers. The Son of Man title in John, however, is not a reference to Jesus' humanity; rather, it refers to his divine agency and his paradoxical glorification on the cross.

Therefore, the human/divine presentation of Jesus as the Christ reflects a set of tensions first originating in experiential encounter, followed by dialectical reflection over the meaning of Jesus' flesh and glory. These dual aspects of Jesus' being are then emphasized within the narrative, as the first edition seeks to draw the audience into believing that Jesus is indeed the Son of God; the later material emphasizes his fleshly humanity as a means of addressing docetizing concerns. Later church discussions of this material came to define things in terms of being and essence, but for the Evangelist and his audiences, things are more fluid and dynamic. From its origin to its delivery, the experiential character of John's dialectical tradition accounts for its human and divine presentation of Jesus as the Christ.

■ The Father-Son Relationship: Egalitarian, Subordinate, or Neither?

The Father-Son relationship in John is one of the most perplexing subjects in Christian theology, contributing especially to the trinitarian debates of the early church's third through fifth centuries. While modern scholars have wondered if John possesses multiple Christologies (one subordinate, the other egalitarian), these actually represent flip-sides of the same coin—a prophet-like-Moses agency schema rooted in Deuteronomy 18:15-22. The Son is equal to the Father in all ways precisely because he does solely what the Father instructs. Therefore, the primary origin of this theological tension is *the Mosaic agency schema*, which also appears to be misunderstood by the religious leaders in Jerusalem.[4] In answering the challenge regarding his healing on the Sabbath, Jesus speaks of his commissioning by the Father. The Jewish leaders, however, accuse him of "making himself equal to God" (5:17-18), and Jesus explains over the rest of the chapter that all of his authority is derived from the Father. Yet because he represents the Father, to honor the Son is to honor the Father who sent him, and to dishonor the Son is to also dishonor the same Father they claim to serve (5:23). Thus, the Fourth Evangelist presents Jesus as fulfilling this Mosaic agency schema, providing the central missional thrust of the narrative; he may even be representing the gist of actual challenges to Jesus' authority in doing so.

A second origin of the tension within the Father-Son relationship in the Fourth Gospel seems rooted in *the dialectical Johannine situation*. Before the religious leaders in Jerusalem Jesus is accused of being the presumptuous prophet of Deuteronomy 18:20, and the Pharisees of John 8:13 accuse Jesus of testifying about himself, thus disqualifying the validity of his witness.[5] While Jesus had already declared as much (5:31), he yokes a multiplicity of witnesses to the authenticity of his mission: the Father, the Spirit, and his words and works, and even Moses and the Scriptures attest to his being sent from the Father—to dispel all doubt (5:31-46; 8:14-19). Therefore, the Son glorifies the Father as his authentic agent, and the Father glorifies the Son as his verifying witness (17:1).

As Johannine Christians expressed their faith in Jesus and his messianic agency from the Father, they drew in other christological titles and typologies as part of their corporate confession. In addition to viewing his mission in the trajectory of the Mosaic Prophet, the Jesus of history likely referred to himself as the Son of Man, alluding either to the humble and obedient Son of Man of Ezekiel or the eschatological and glorious Son of Man of Daniel, or both. The Johannine Evangelist, however, came to associate the title with Jesus' paradoxical being lifted up on the cross (3:14; 8:28). The lifting-up motif also came to have a double meaning, in that Jesus' being "lifted up" and drawing all to himself both referred to witnessing to the cross as well as exalting him and his mission (12:32-36).

A third agency motif came to involve the *Logos* motif, which connected the agency mission of Jesus with the Word of God in Genesis and the divine *Logos* of Heraclitus of Ephesus and Philo of Alexandria.[6] For Heraclitus, the *Logos* of God is the source of reason, bringing order out of chaos; for Philo, the *Logos* of God is the source of creation and the redemptive bridge between God and the world. In translating Mosaic agency into more Hellenistic terms, including a preexistent Christology (like the hymns of Paul and Hebrews, Phil. 2:5-11; Col. 1:15-20; Heb. 1:1-4), Johannine Christianity's creative worship life thus created connections between Jesus' mission, its narration in the Gospel, and the experience of both Jewish and Gentile members of the community (1 John 1:1-3→John 1:1-18).

Rooted in the Mosaic Prophet typology, these agency motifs came to serve as a bridge between the Jewish setting of Jesus' original ministry and the later Hellenistic setting in which the Johannine tradition was finalized.

■ Signs Faith versus Blessed Faith?

The tension between signs faith and belief without having seen is a curious one in the Fourth Gospel. On one hand, Jesus' signs are featured with prominence in order that people might believe that Jesus is the Messiah/Christ. On the other hand, Jesus rebukes the seeking of signs, and those who believe without having seen are considered blessed. Rather than reflecting the Evangelist's dialogue with an alien source, however, John's signs and discourses appear to have had an integrated relationship within the formation of the Johannine tradition itself. Therefore, rather than see the theological tension here as external to the Evangelist's thinking (after all, if he really was adverse to signs faith, why did he include the signs from the start?), we probably have an intratraditional dialectic in which the Evangelist presented his own set of signs but also felt free to develop their theological significance.[7] Therefore, the primary source of this set of tensions is *the Evangelist's dialectical thinking*.

But how might he have come to think dialectically about Jesus' signs? Does his emphasis on the blessedness of those who have not seen and yet believe (20:29) reflect his *not* being a first-generation believer with firsthand acquaintance with Jesus' ministry, or might it reflect the *opposite*—a means of drawing in later audiences precisely because the head-turning miracles of Jesus are no longer as available for later generations? If we can take at face value the emphasis upon having "seen and heard" at least some of the ministry of Jesus "from the beginning" (1 John 1:1-3; Acts 4:19-20), the latter is arguably the case. Here we have a reflection of the Evangelist's cognitive crisis: perception and hope being followed by experience and disappointment. In that sense, the Johannine presentation of the wondrous reflects answering not only the question of why miracles happened, but more pressingly, why they did not happen, at least not as often as expected. The hope that Jesus' followers will do even greater works than he has done (14:12), while at the same time facing the problem of suffering and loss, is palpable. To echo both sisters of Lazarus, "Lord, if you had been here, my brother would not have died" (11:21, 32). The Johannine tradition thus accounts for the relative dearth of miracles in the life of the early church as not having been the main point of Jesus' ministry, but as an opportunity for faith that is even greater in its potency than signs faith, valued as it may be.

The Markan traditions also deal with the absence of miracles, but they do so differently. For the Synoptics, the primary reason miracles do not happen is the lack of human faith. In Jesus' hometown even he "could do no deed of power" (except, of course, that "he laid his hands on a few sick people and cured them," Mark 6:5). Therefore, the relative dearth of miracles is neither God's fault nor Jesus'; it is the fault of unbelieving humans. Did such a teaching, however, originate with Jesus or with the pre-Markan purveyors of tradition about Jesus? It involved at least the latter. If someone like Peter might have been a primary source of Mark's material, and if his presentation in Acts is at all representative of a powerful personality whose ministry may have been accompanied by power manifestations (psychologically induced or otherwise), one can imagine wonders and their significance being a part of the pre-Markan tradition.[8] Every sermon of Peter in Acts makes reference either to a wonder, a vision, or some divine action authorizing the apostle's message. Therefore, one can imagine Peter or leaders like him connecting faith with the enablement of miracles, while also blaming lack of faith for their dearth.

If John or someone like him had anything to do with the Johannine tradition and its development, it is noteworthy that Peter is presented as performing miracles in Acts, whereas John is not. Of course, it is impossible to know whether these two figures had anything to do with the Markan and Johannine traditions, despite clear second-century claims to that effect; such is not being argued here in particularity. What is interesting is that their presentation in Acts, corroborated by two individuated traditions, suggests a diversity of giftedness between plausible purveyors of traditions, whether apostolic or not. Cognitive and experiential factors would clearly make a difference in how different preachers narrated Jesus' ministry, so cognitive-critical analysis deserves to be included within Gospel-tradition analysis.[9] If the Fourth Evangelist believed that Jesus had performed wondrous signs, while at the same time facing experientially the relative dearth of signs, this would account for his holding them up as important, while also pointing to their signifying function as their primary value. One can also understand why the Fourth Evangelist might have challenged the predominant valuation of the feeding miracle in all five Synoptic renderings—they ate and were satisfied (6:26).[10] In a later setting where the poor are always present (12:8) and where hunger and thirst were not satisfied by wondrous feedings (6:35), the unseen food that Jesus has, gives, and is becomes nourishment for their souls (4:32; 6:27, 55), and the water he provides wells up like a fountain from within (4:13-15; 7:37-38). While human plight is often the result of human shortfalls (5:14), it is not necessarily so; ultimately it becomes an opportunity for the manifestation of God's work (9:1-3)—so the Evangelist theologizes reflectively.

A second factor in the tension between signs faith and blessed faith is *the Evangelist's literary designs* in constructing a compelling narrative. Because signs do lead people to believe in Jesus within the narrative, this sets a pattern for later audiences to follow. As Jesus fulfills the typologies of Moses and Elijah, the signs of the first edition of John are selected because they pose a distinctive complement to other renderings, such as Mark. At the same time, the Johannine Jesus is presented as resisting sensationalism—rebuking people for seeking signs (4:48; 6:26)—and this seems the equivalent of the Markan Jesus' insistence on secrecy after performing a miracle. In both traditions we have a presentation of a Jesus who resists nationalistic and sensationalistic acclaim, as his mission is not devoted to popularity but the furthering of an unseen kingdom: the reign of God.

The narrative also notes that some have seen but refuse to believe, and this is presented with some irony. In particular, the greater the audience's religious investment, the greater is their inability to glimpse the revelation and to see the significance of Jesus' words and works. Without embryonic faith—even a bit of openness to what God is presently doing, believing is elusive. This serves also to explain the fact that as the Johannine witness continues to be delivered, some believe, but others do not. Here the exhortation to believe, at least on the basis of the signs, that Jesus is sent from the Father gets one on the path to receiving further revelation as it might unfold. Indeed, the signs are presented climactically, with the words of the steward in John 2:10 coming true in the raising of Lazarus—you save the good wine until now [the end]! Of course, the greatest sign in John, as in the Synoptics, is the resurrection of Jesus and his appearances to his disciples. Jesus appears to his followers for the third time (21:14), and the Johannine record itself becomes a sign, welcoming hearers and readers across the confines of time and space into the community of postresurrection existence.

▮ The Way to Salvation in John: Particular or Universal?

So what do we do with John's apparent contradictions regarding the means of salvation? On one hand, John's soteriology (theology of salvation) is the most particular and exclusive anywhere in the Bible: Jesus declares, "I am the way, and the truth, and the life. No one comes to the Father except through me" (John 14:6). On the other hand, John is the most universalistic and inclusive of biblical texts: "The true light, which enlightens everyone, was coming into the world" (1:9). But if all have access to divine enlightenment, why is coming to the Father through Christ required? And if people could be redeemed by simply responding receptively to God's Light, why did Jesus need to come and die? The primary source of this tension is *the Evangelist's agency Christology*, and it has as much to do with anthropology (understanding what it means to be human) as with theology.

These verses, however, are often misunderstood. Jesus' being the singular means of access to the Father often gets wrongly interpreted as a divine regulation: "God has a rule, and unless that rule is followed, people forfeit salvation." But this is not what the text is saying. This text is also misconstrued as the privileging of one religion over another: "Only 'Christians' [as the reader defines them, of course] will be saved; the rest will be lost"—or so the well-meaning interpreter wrongly infers. If we ask *why* this text is true, the answer is a factor of the human condition rather than a divine requirement: no one has seen God at any time (1:18; 6:46)—only the Son, who is from God. Therefore, humans cannot attain knowledge of God's saving/revealing work except it be disclosed; "No one can come to me unless drawn by the Father who sent me; and I will raise that person up on the last day" (6:44, 65), declares the Johannine Jesus.

Note that Jesus does not say that no one *may* come, as a factor of God's permission; rather, it is a factor of human limitation and lack of potentiality—no one *can* come except being drawn by the Father. That is, the same God who has drawn humanity to divine love in many times and in many ways (see Heb. 1:1-4) has now spoken in God's Son Jesus Christ as the time-changing means of communicating divine love to the world (John 3:16-17). So the reason Jesus is the only effective way to the Father, far different from a "religious" means of grace, is precisely that it is *not* a religious answer to the human condition; it is a revelational answer to human blindness and deafness. Because God's saving/revealing agency has come in fullness in Christ Jesus, in continuity with other means of addressing the world before and after the incarnation, humanity is thus shown the way to the Father in ways that no other medium ever could. The incarnate expression of God's love is much fuller than a code, a text, a rite, a regulation, or even the finest of religious systems. The origin of such scaffolding is human initiative and ingenuity, but the only hope for humanity is *the divine initiative*—effected not by religious means, but by encounter.[11] This is precisely where John 1:9 comes into play.

The means by which God shares love and life with humanity is presented as *light*—available to all—made visible in the life and ministry of Jesus as the Light of the world (8:12; 9:5; 11:9). Like the *Logos* of Heraclitus, which brings order out of chaos and is available to all as a divine principle of reason, the Light of Christ is accessible to all, even though some reject it. This relates, then, to a common misconception about the Light and its universality. Despite being accessible to all, this does not mean that all will recognize the Light as such, nor that all who do so will be receptive and responsive. Indeed, the significance of the Light of Christ as the saving/revealing initiative of God is too easily missed for several reasons. First, it cannot be imagined; it must be revealed. Humans live by merit—by judgment—receiving what we deserve, which inevitably is death except for God's grace.[12] Again, this is why no one can have access to the Father except by being drawn by God, whose world-changing initiative Jesus as the Jewish Messiah was and is. God's saving grace is finally unmerited. Therefore, there is no hope without the revelation of God's undeserved love and saving grace. It is not that we loved God, but that God has first loved us; such is the heart of the evangel (1 John 4:10).

Another way we get things wrong is to project our needs and perceptions onto God's enlightening work, forcing revelation into human systems and contrivances looking more like our ways than God's. Therefore, humans too easily distort the Light and God's saving/revealing work, jamming it into our own time-bound understandings of how things "ought" to work. Such is idolatry; worse yet, it misses the authenticity of God's self-disclosure. Perhaps this is why God had to send his Son to live and die—humans cannot grasp the paradox of grace and undeserved love except it be revealed from beyond. This is parallel to Paul's view: just as Abraham was reckoned as righteousness through his faith (Rom. 4:9), so will the Gentiles be reconciled by their faith, not by religious contrivance (Gal. 3:8). Indeed, any who respond to the Light of Christ may receive the gift of salvation, even if they do not know particulars about Christianity; they might even come to the Father through the agency of Christ without knowing the outward story of Jesus. However, this is less likely precisely because humans tend to distort the Light, adding conditions and qualifications in ways that make it into a religious construct rather than the divine gift of grace. Further, humans tend too easily to craft it into something born of blood, or the will of the flesh, or the will of humanity instead of being born of God (John 1:13). Revelation is required for salvation precisely because no one has seen God at any time; yet when we receive revelation, we tend to reduce it into religion—thus making it something of human initiative rather than of the divine.

This points directly to a second reason the world needs the gospel, according to the Johannine witness. While some were open to Jesus and his works, others were closed to revelation—they loved darkness rather than light and refused to receive the Revealer lest he expose the insufficient character of their religious programs and platforms. Therefore, revelation presents a scandal to religious and political authorities, who love the praise of humans more than the glory of God (12:43); "all who do evil hate the light and do not come to the light, so that their deeds may not be exposed" (3:20). "Sin" in John thus refers not to debauchery, lawlessness, or moral failure; it is used to describe the closing of oneself to God's saving/revealing work because of religious certainty and conventional investments. Jesus is thus rejected in John as the liberating truth of God because people claim knowledge

(9:41; 15:22-24; 16:7-11). Ironically, religious leaders too easily miss the work of the Revealer precisely because receptivity demands a humble and open approach to truth, which itself is always liberating (8:32). This is as true for religious and non-religious people today as it was for religious leaders of the first century. Glimpsing the revelatory work of God hinges upon embryonic openness to God's unseen work in the world,[13] which often comes to us in unaccustomed packaging.

A secondary origin of John's tensions between universal and particular aspects of God's saving work involved *the delivery of the gospel to various audiences* within the Johannine situation. We have here a reflection on how the message was sometimes unevenly received. In seeking to account for why some responded favorably to Jesus as the saving/revealing agency of God's love while others did not, the Fourth Evangelist notes that some had been open to receiving new expressions of truth, but not all. Therefore, while the light shone in the darkness, the darkness has neither understood nor comprehended it. The Word came unto his own, but his own received him not; and yet, as many as received him received the power to become the children of God, as many as believed on his name (1:5, 11-12). As John's gospel message was received among Gentile audiences, sheep "not of this fold" were seen to be gathered by Christ (10:16). As the message was resisted, even among some religious leaders who surprisingly did not recognize their own Messiah, God's sending the divine Son that whosoever might believe in him would receive eternal life is presented as God's gift of love to the world (3:16; 20:31). The only way the Evangelist can imagine how Jesus could have come to his own people and how they could have rejected the Revealer (1:11) is to infer that they had been closed to revelation from the start (1:13; 3:19-21).

Therefore, John's soteriology is inclusive in its means, but it is humanity that requires a revelation to glimpse the undeserved love of the Father; such is what Jesus as the Christ conveys eschatologically. This also explains John's apparent tension between free will and determinism. While Jesus appears to know who will receive and reject him, ultimately the gift of salvation is available to any and all who receive it in faith. No one can come to Jesus without being drawn by the Father; the question is whether people will open themselves to the loving/drawing work of God, extended ultimately through the agency of the Son. Revelation creates a crisis, however. Will the individual open up to new understandings of truth, or will one slink back into the short-lived comfort of the conventional and the familiar? To seek to preserve one's life (and religious investments) is to lose it (them); the only way to find eternal life is to forfeit the securities of the world (12:25-26), especially conceptual ones. The Fourth Gospel is thus written that all might believe (20:31)—with a receptive response to the divine initiative.

■ Johannine Dualism: Jewish or Greek?

The Fourth Gospel's dualism is closely related to its soteriology and the question of free will and determinism. On one hand, the Father so loves the world that God's only begotten Son was sent into the world that humanity might believe and be saved. On the other hand, the uneven success of that salvific mission is explained on the basis of dualistic realities. Humans fail to respond to the Light because they prefer darkness and are threatened by the Light. In that sense, John's dualism accounts for two primary realities and motivates a third. First, it accounts for why God had to bridge the gaps between life and death, that which is from above and that which is from below, and the earthly and the heavenly. Second, it explains how some could have rejected the Son, even while claiming to adhere to the Father. The Evangelist surmises that they were not abiding in the truth of God to begin with; they had put stock in inauthentic existence rather than the liberating truth of God. Third, it motivates responsiveness to the gospel over lesser alternatives.

Until half a century ago, John's pervasive dualism led scholars to assume that its origin was Hellenistic, or even Gnostic. It was thought that Judaism of the day was monistic (that is, recognizing only one power in the heavens—God alone), so the Fourth Gospel was divorced from a Palestinian context and located within a Gentile setting. In 1947, however, the Dead Sea Scrolls were discovered at Qumran, and it quickly became apparent that the Judaism of Jesus' day was extensively dualistic, thus alerting scholars to this false dichotomy about dualism.[14] The *War Scroll* of Qumran sketches the warfare between the "children of light" and the "children of darkness," leading some scholars even to surmise that the Fourth Evangelist must have had some firsthand experience with Qumran and its religious ethos. John Ashton argues that Qumran cosmology is in the bones of the Evangelist, positing at least a period of residence within that community.[15] Especially the *Community Rule,* found in Cave 1, presents at least a dozen parallels between Qumran and Johannine dualism. Whether or not firsthand contact with the Essenes is demonstrable, it is at least clear that John's dualism is perfectly at home within contemporary Judaism. John may have been finalized in a Hellenistic setting, but its thought-world is thoroughly Jewish in its origin.

Box 8.3: Parallels between the Dualism of the Fourth Gospel and the Qumran Community Rule[16]

The Fourth Gospel	1QS 3:14—4:26
the Spirit of Truth (14:17; 15:26; 16:13)	Spirit of Truth (3:18-19; 4:21, 23)
the Holy Spirit (14:26; 20:22)	by the Spirit of Holiness (4:21)
sons of light (12:36)	sons of light (3:13, 24, 25)

eternal life (3:15, 16, 36; 5:24, *passim*)	in perpetual life (4:7)
the light of life (8:12)	in the light of life (3:7)
and he who walks in the darkness (12:35)	they . . . walk in the ways of darkness (3:21)
he will not walk in the darkness (8:12)	to walk in all the ways of darkness (4:11)
the wrath of God (3:36)	the furious wrath of God's vengeance (4:12)
the eyes of the blind (9:32; 10:21; 11:37)	blindness of eyes (4:11)
full of grace/fullness of grace (1:14, 16)	the fullness of grace/his grace (4:5, 4)
the works of God (6:28; 9:3)	the works of God (4:4)
their works (of men) were evil (3:19)	works of abomination/of a man (4:10, 20)

Other parallels also abound between the Johannine and Qumran dualisms and their function. First, they are both directed against the Jewish leadership in Jerusalem. The "children of darkness" are not the Romans or pagans but, rather, the religious leaders who should have known better (from the writers' perspectives) yet rejected the group's message. Second, the authors side with the Spirit of Truth, the Holy Spirit, the light of life, the truth, the fullness of grace, and the works of God over against the ways of darkness, blindness, and the works of humanity. The former will lead to eternal life, but the latter will provoke the wrath of God, leading to death. In that sense, Johannine and Qumranic dualisms seek to motivate others to choose the way of life over the way of death. Indeed, the rhetoric of eternal consequences involves strong language, and the goal is to convince wavering audiences, both internally and externally, of the merits of its convictions. Dualism here is thus highly rhetorical, planting its apologetic appeal squarely upon a cosmological stage.

This is where John's dualism finds impressive parallels with the dialogues of Plato, addressing the problem of his spurned teacher, Socrates. The leaders of Athens should have known better, but some rejected wisdom and even sentenced its master purveyor to drink the hemlock—which he did willingly. As a parallel attempt to account for the ironic death of the Jewish Messiah/Christ at the hands of the Judean and Roman leaders, the Fourth Evangelist presents his rejection as the willful choosing of darkness over light based on flawed conceptions of value and the truth. Like Plato's Allegory of the Cave (*The Republic* 8), those who have grown secure with darkness and the pride of being able to predict the movement of shadows on the wall are reluctant to welcome the "good news" that the shadows in front of them are not reality, but only shadows of reality. While John's dualism bears striking similarities to Qumran dualism, the defensive choosing of darkness rather than light would also have been recognized by any member of the Greco-Roman world who knew Plato's description of Socrates and his ironic presentation of those who preferred darkness rather than light. Consider these extensive parallels.

Box 8.4: Plato's Allegory of the Cave and Johannine Dualism

Plato tells an allegory of Socrates, who describes to Glaucon (Plato's brother) a group of men who have been living in a cave since childhood, chained at the neck and legs so that they cannot move. A fire behind them casts shadows on the wall in front of them, appearing to be reality.

The Johannine Evangelist tells the story of Jesus, who as the Light of the World is a threat to darkness. Religious leaders think they know Moses, the Scriptures, and the ways of God, but their understandings are from below, not from above. They know the things of the world, but not that which is of God.

These men had become quite good at guessing the movement of the forms in front of them, and they even derived pride and esteem from their predictions and appraisals of reality— though these were false.

Religious leaders in John claimed to "see" and loved the praise of men over the glory of God. To claim "we know" in John is ironically to proclaim one's ignorance.

Imagine one man breaking loose from the chains: feeling the eyestrain of seeing the sun, noting the condition of the prisoners, and coming back to declare that what they thought was reality was actually only shadows.

Jesus declares that no one has seen the Father except the Son; he has made the Father known to the world. He came to testify that the world's deeds are evil and that its religious scaffolding is of human origin, not divine.

Upon telling the prisoners about the light, however, the others had this person killed so that they could remain happily in darkness—holding on to the security of their false appraisals of reality rather than be liberated by the truth.

The Jewish leaders sought to kill Jesus, threatened by his claiming to speak the truth, ironically accusing him of being the presumptuous prophet of Deuteronomy 18:20 and thus deserving of death.

Plato uses this story on two levels: first, as a means of accounting for the ironic and tragic trial and death of Socrates; second, as a means of addressing his own audiences at a later time, hoping to convince them to be seekers of the truth and lovers of wisdom.

John likewise uses dualism on two levels: first, to account for the ironic rejection of Jesus by those who should have received him as the Messiah/Christ; second, as a means of confronting contemporary audiences, seeking to motivate their choosing light over darkness, and life over death.

John's dualism thus functions in a twofold way. First, it explains the inexplicable—how Jesus as the Jewish Messiah/Christ could have come to his own and not have been received by them. Explanation They loved darkness rather than light; they refused to come to the light lest it be exposed that their religious platforms and scaffoldings were of human origin rather than divine; they must not have known the Father, despite acting in his name; they are not of Jesus' fold, nor to they recognize the Shepherd's voice. Without openness to the truth and new understandings of it, one cannot be certain of one's convictions. Second, the dualistic presentation of the way of death versus the way of life is highly apologetic and motivational. Message: Walk in the light rather than darkness; you must be born from above lest you fail to see the kingdom of God; choose the life-producing food instead of death-producing alternatives; even the blind can have their eyes opened if they will but believe. Therefore, John's dualism fits both within Jewish and Greek contemporary forms, and it is not deterministic. Those who believe in Jesus shall know the truth, and the truth shall set them free (8:32); and all are invited to do so. The question is whether they will be open to the saving/revealing initiative of God and whether they will be receptive and responsive to the divine address.

■ The *Ioudaioi* in John: Pro-Semitism, Anti-Semitism, or Neither?

The presentation of "the Jews" in John has been one of the most problematic in the history of biblical interpretation. When combined with Matthew's presentation of the Jerusalem crowd crying out to Pilate, "His blood be on us and on our children!" (Matt. 27:25), the presentation of the Jerusalem crowd in John as emblematic of the unbelieving world makes it understandable how theological anti-Semitism has emerged within Christianity. That sentiment has contributed to the tragic suffering of Jewish people at the hands of Christians, and also at the hands of atheists or the nonreligious, who readily yoke religious sentiments to godless political causes. Matthew and John, however, are not anti-Semitic; these Gospels were written by Jewish authors advocating a Jewish Messiah to largely Jewish audiences, and their communities were experiencing both fellowship and conflict with other Jewish groups. They eventually lost those struggles, and Christian Jews became Jewish Christians. The particular problem with the Fourth Gospel is that the religious adversaries who sought to put Jesus to death and who turned him over to the Romans, insisting that a death sentence be carried out, are called the *Ioudaioi* in Greek, which can be translated "Jews" but is more accurately translated "Judeans."

The inadequacy of simplistically rendering *hoi Ioudaioi* in John as "the Jews" instead of "the Judeans" is clear. First, *everyone* in the narrative is Jewish except for the Romans, the royal official and his household, and possibly the Greeks that come seeking Jesus in John 12 (although they might have been Hellenistic Jews). *Everyone else* in the story is Jewish, including Jesus' disciples, their families, the Galileans, and the Judeans. Therefore, they are *all Semitic*. Further, *most* of the Semites in John believe in Jesus, which would include the Israelites, the Galileans, and the Samaritans; even some of the southern *Ioudaioi* believe in him (7:31; 8:30-31; 10:42; 11:45; 12:42). Therefore, to see Jewish people in general as the enemy of Jesus of Nazareth is thoroughly to misread the Fourth Gospel. This is not to excuse anti-Semitic interpretations of John; it is to say they are *wrong* and *have always been so*.

Second, Jesus is extolled as Israel's Messiah/Christ, who is prophesied by the Hebrew Scriptures, and who fulfills the Jewish typologies of Moses and Elijah. Further, all the I-am sayings in John fulfill particular aspects of the true Israel embodied in the man Jesus.

Box 8.5: The I-Am Sayings of Jesus: Typologies of Biblical Israel

One does not live by bread alone, but by every word that comes from the mouth of the Lord (Deut. 8:3).	Jesus is the Bread of life (John 6:35, 48) and the Word of God (1:1), giving life to the world through his word (6:31, 50-63).
God provided bread from heaven to eat (Exod. 16:4; Ps. 78:23-25).	Jesus is the living Bread that came down from heaven (6:51).
The people of Israel will be a light to the nations (Isa. 42:6; 49:6; 60:3).	Jesus is the light of the world (8:12; 9:5).
God will gather the remnant of Israel as sheep in a fold (Mic. 2:12).	Jesus is the gate of the sheepfold; he will also gather sheep outside the fold (10:7, 9, 16).
Israel's leaders are shepherds, called to nurture the flock, not themselves (Ps. 78:70-72; Jer. 23:2; Ezek. 34:2).	Jesus is the good and true shepherd who does not abandon the sheep amidst danger but lays down his life for the sheep (10:11-14).
Job knows his Redeemer lives and that he will indeed see God (Job 19:25-26).	Jesus is the resurrection and the life (11:25).
The way of Yahweh is to walk in his truth, leading to the way of life (Ps. 86:11; Jer. 21:8).	Jesus is the way, the truth, and the life (14:6).
Israel is the vineyard of the Lord (Isa. 5:7).	Jesus is the true vine (15:5).

As the fulfillment of Jewish ideals, the Fourth Gospel's presentation of Jesus as the Messiah must be considered pro-Jewish, not anti-Jewish. In the Fourth Gospel, revelation indeed challenges religion, but that challenge is not unique to Judaism as a religion: revelation also scandalizes Samaritan religion, Christian religion, Roman imperial religion, and even religious atheism. The Fourth Gospel thus is neither anti-Semitic nor anti-Jewish. It depicts the Revealer challenging religious and political authorities and conventions in the name of God's truth. That same challenge continues, however, in every generation and setting—confronting our own most beloved constructions as well. In so doing, revelation also purifies religion, restoring it to its highest values and most authentic expressions. As well as convicting, the truth is always liberating.

Third, (as discussed above) the most literal and accurate identity of *hoi Ioudaioi* is a sociological reference to "the Judeans"—religious leaders from the South representing the Jerusalem-centered establishment, which stood in opposition to Jesus' northern, rustic, and unofficial claims to authority.

This is why the *Judeans* (*not* "the Jews") came from Jerusalem (in Judea) challenging John the Baptist at the beginning of Jesus' ministry and why they eventually opposed Jesus. He did not meet their religious criteria for what the Messiah should be like. They were scandalized by Jesus' prophetic demonstration in the Temple, healings on the Sabbath, coming from Nazareth and Galilee instead of Bethlehem in Judea, calling God his Father and claiming to speak and act with divine authorization, and teaching about the direct accessibility of God—in the Temple of all places! They were further scandalized because some Judeans believed that he indeed was the Messiah, and the religious leaders are presented as being threatened by the likelihood that the "whole world" was going after Jesus (12:19). These factors being the case, the Judean leaders were threatened by Jesus because he challenged their place of religious privilege; his growing personal authority jeopardized their structural authority and capacity to hold sway societally.

Therefore, the primary origin of John's presentation of Jewish leaders and their opposition to Jesus is *the dialectical situation of Johannine Christianity.* The first crisis within the Johannine situation involved a set of North-South tensions, whereby the Judean religious leaders (*Ioudaioi* meaning "Judeans" in a Palestinian setting) not only rejected the northern prophet, but they also resisted his Galilean followers. Those religious tensions are still palpable within the later rendering of the Jesus story. When the Johannine leadership resettled in Asia Minor after the destruction of Jerusalem in 70 c.e., a new round of Jewish tensions emerged, and here members of the Jesus movement found themselves again at odds with other Jewish religious leaders now in a predominately Gentile setting. This led to a secondary source of John's *dialectical presentation of Jewish leaders in the narrative*—the rhetorical and apologetic interests of the Evangelist. At this stage, *Ioudaioi* came to mean "the

Jews," i.e. those other Jews, in a Diaspora setting. By showing some (not all) religious leaders failing to grasp the revelation, the narrator hopes to convince Jewish members of his audience that Jesus really was the Messiah/Christ. This apologetic thrust is especially characteristic of chapters 2–3, 5, and 7–12, which were part of the first edition of the Johannine Gospel. By the time later material was added (chaps. 6, 15–17, 21, and so on), the tensions with the *Ioudaioi* have apparently been calmed, and the emphasis is more upon abiding and remaining with Jesus and his community.

■ Conclusion

In the light of their origins and character, John's theological riddles can be understood and interpreted more adequately. Originating within the Evangelist's dialectical thinking, John's high-and-low Christology and tensive presentation of Jesus' signs reflect an intratraditional dialogue between perception and experience. Originating in a Mosaic agency schema, the Father-Son relationship and John's distinctive dualism reflect the divine-human dialogue whereby God's saving-revealing initiative is received variously in the world. To respond to the Agent is to respond likewise to the Sender, and thus the coming of the Revealer brings about the crisis of judgment in the world. John's presentation of Judaism is neither pro-Jewish nor anti-Jewish; it originated in the experience of the Galilean prophet's ambivalent reception in Judea, echoed also within an uneven reception in a later Hellenistic setting. Jesus is presented rhetorically as the Jewish Messiah in John—the one of whom Moses wrote—and ironically, it is some of the religious leaders who have the most difficulty with glimpsing the authenticity of his mission. While the enlightening work of God is available to all persons everywhere, no one has seen God at any time, and no one can come to God unless being drawn by the Father. Therefore, unless humans are receptive and responsive to the divine initiative—that which Jesus as the Messiah/Christ was and is—the flesh profits nothing. The Revealer is the Way, the Truth, and the Life, and a believing response to the truth is always liberating.

■ Questions to Consider

1. If all nine of the Johannine I-am metaphors and other absolute I-am sayings are present in the Synoptics, why are the distinctive Johannine I-am sayings different, and what might have been their likely origin and development?
2. If Jesus is the way, the truth, and the life—the singular means of access to the Father—how does this relate to the light that enlightens everyone universally, and why do some respond to the light, while others do not?

3. If *Ioudaioi* refers to "Judeans" in most cases in the Fourth Gospel, and if it was written by a Jew arguing that Jesus was the Jewish Messiah/Christ, why has this text been a source of religious and political anti-Semitism, and what is the best antidote to such distortions? Does Jesus as the Revealer also challenge Christian religious and theological constructs?

▣ Terms to Understand

- *anagnorisis*
- *Logos*
- dualism
- determinism

The Jesus of History in John

A Fourth Quest for Jesus?

A great irony of religious studies in the modern era is that the only Gospel claiming to convey tradition rooted in direct access to Jesus and his ministry is also the only Gospel that is programmatically expunged from studies of the historical Jesus. Reasons for this judgment, of course, are understandable. John is the most theological among the Gospels, and it is also the most different. Further, on many a score, one cannot have it both ways. One must choose either the Synoptics or John on many issues: the timing of the Temple incident (early or late?), the teachings of Jesus (extended revelatory discourses or short, pithy sayings?), the ministry of Jesus (exorcisms and healings of lepers or not?), and the dating of the Last Supper (before the Passover or on the Passover?), to name a few. With three Gospels posed against one, John seems to be the lone Gospel out and thus the historical loser.

Then again, as we have seen above, if Matthew and Luke built upon Mark, many of these issues are not matters of a three-against-one majority but of John versus Mark. Some exceptions might include short, pithy teachings on the kingdom of God in parables,[1] where the Synoptic traditions would indeed win the historicity contest, but not on all accounts. Some issues deserve consideration as a John-versus-Mark analysis, and if the Johannine Evangelist was familiar with Mark, some of John's differences may have been *intentional*—posing a knowingly different presentation. These are just a few of the reasons why we need a far more nuanced treatment of the issues involved.[2] John *is* highly theological and different, but that does not mean that all, or even the majority, of John's differences reflect the theologizing interests of the Evangelist.[3] The differences must be evaluated case by case.

"The theologizing interests of the Evangelist" may well be the most recklessly used and uncritically speculative basis for explaining John's distinctive material and presentation in biblical scholarship in recent years. While features of any text can be interpreted symbolically, the Johannine narrative is especially rife with such possibilities. On one hand, the Johannine Jesus does indeed speak in the Evangelist's language and thought-forms. Likewise, the I-am sayings of Jesus in John most likely represent the teaching ministry of the Beloved Disciple, paraphrasing Jesus in his own terms rather than representing the speech-forms of the historical Jesus' teachings. Furthermore, given that the raising of Lazarus and the wedding miracle would likely have been reported if known by any of the Synoptic writers, thoughtful scholars must consider sources for John's material other than the historical ministry of Jesus.

On the other hand, if (as argued above) we regard the first edition of John as having acknowledged Mark and appearing to augment it with non-duplicative material, the enumeration of the first two signs in John 2 and 4 reflects a filling out of the beginning of Jesus' ministry in Mark, and the other three signs (in chaps. 5, 9, and 11) fill out the southern ministry of Jesus, which is largely missing in Mark. Therefore, John is *different on purpose*. Further, as we shall see, many other aspects of John's presentation of Jesus and his ministry actually seem historically superior to presentations in the Synoptics. For this reason, seeking glimpses of Jesus through the Johannine lens is by no means a fruitless endeavor; the question is how to proceed.

▪ The Historical Realism of the Fourth Gospel

While the Fourth Gospel is highly theological, it contains an impressive amount of historical realism, which subverts attempts to discredit its contributions to Jesus research. Several points here deserve to be kept in mind. First, John is not alone in presenting history with theological interests in mind; so is Mark, and so are Q, Matthew, and Luke. For instance, the preaching that underlies Mark was crafted to meet the needs of the church, and Mark was also targeted to address the needs of Christians around the third or fourth decade of the Jesus movement.

Second, it cannot be said that the Gospel intention is theological only, because it makes a number of direct historical claims. It claims firsthand contact with Jesus, asserts particulars of chronology and topography, and declares firsthand testimony that water and blood flowed forth from Jesus' side. As well as being referred to as "the spiritual Gospel," John can also rightly be called "the mundane Gospel." Note that the eyewitness claim in 19:34-35 attests Jesus' fleshly humanity, not his divinity! Especially if the Prologue was added to a later edition of the Gospel, it should be taken as a window into the meaning and reception of the text, not as a window into the authorial process of composition or a diminishment of its historical character. Upon such an assumption many programs of interpretation have foundered.

Third, the fact of Johannine empiricism demands consideration historically.[4] Information is reported as a factor of all five senses in John: things are *seen* with ocular sight (1:14, 29, 32, 33, 34, 38, 39, 47, 48, 50; 2:23; 3:11, 32; 4:45; 5:6; 6:2, 5, 14, 19, 22, 24, 36; 9:1, 8, 37; 11:31, 32, 33, 45; 12:9, 21; 14:7, 9, 19; 15:24; 16:10, 16, 17, 19; 18:26; 19:6, 26, 33, 35; 20:1, 5, 6, 8, 12, 14, 18, 20, 25, 27, 29; 21:9, 20, 21), *heard* with auditory reception (1:37, 40; 3:32; 4:1, 42, 47; 6:60; 7:32, 40; 9:27, 35, 40; 11:4, 6, 20, 29; 12:12, 18, 29; 14:28; 18:21; 19:8, 13; 21:7), *touched* with fingers or hands (20:27), *tasted* (2:9; 19:29-30), and *smelled* (11:39; 12:3). This information could have been fabricated, of course, but how would that be known or judged? If some detail was added as an imitation of reality (called "mimesis" among literary theorists), how do we know that *all* of it was? While it is impossible to demonstrate that all of John comes from firsthand observation, it cannot be claimed that none of it did. John's citing of empirically derived impressions is an empirical fact; until it is falsified historically, can it be denied critically? Positivism must be applied to falsification as well as verification, if it is to be employed with critical adequacy—another oversight of modern critical scholarship.

Fourth, the realism of personal knowledge of pre-70 C.E. Palestine is confirmed by the details presented in John, especially knowledge of Jerusalem and its environs, which archaeological discoveries have largely corroborated. In addition, knowledge of relationships, towns that people come from, particular distances and measurements, weights and costs, languages and alternative names of places, topographical and geographical references, time measures and sequences, and seasons and temperatures are all mentioned as realistic aspects of the narrative. Most of these details are not developed symbolically, as if they served a rhetorical function. Rather, they seem to corroborate at least some degree of firsthand familiarity with the events and settings being described within the narrative, and hundreds of these details are a part of John's distinctive presentation of Jesus and his ministry. As mentioned above, while Matthew and Luke add units of tradition to Mark, they tend to omit or generalize details, including names and places. Therefore, the contention that all of John's details were added to enhance fictive realism appears itself to be a fiction. Some of them may have been added, but to claim they all were goes beyond critical argumentation to pure conjecture.

Fifth, John contains a good deal of what I call religious realism, which contributes to a fuller historical understanding of Jesus and his ministry. In other words, John conveys knowledge of Jewish customs, Jewish relations with Samaritans and

Romans, Jewish names of persons and places, and other Palestine-related details as though rendered for Gentile audiences far removed—say, in a setting such as Asia Minor. Further, North-South tensions between Galileans and Judeans are palpable within the narrative, and John contributes particularly valuable knowledge about these relationships in ways that enlighten socio-religious aspects of Jesus' ministry and its reception. John's religious realism also sheds light on the likelihood that Jewish leaders were acutely threatened by the popular attraction to Jesus' signs, teachings, and his challenging of religious institutions and status. John also portrays the crowd and the religious leaders as invested in maintaining lateral approval from their peers as a factor in their willingness to go along with those who sought to get rid of Jesus, which also seems a plausible inference.

Sixth, in addition to religious realism, John's political realism comes through lucidly within the narrative. Rather than the nearness of the Passover representing "the theological interests of the Evangelist" (2:13; 6:4; 11:55), the motif is better interpreted as alluding to political realities. In reflecting upon the Romans' having destroyed the Temple in 70 c.e., the reference to destroying "this temple" in John 2 would have brought knowing nods from later audiences. Likewise, the account of the feeding in the wilderness has nationalistic associations in John, which are echoed in Mark.[5] Many in the crowd are presented as seeing the event as a potential gathering of momentum toward marching to Jerusalem and dealing with the Romans. They abandoned Jesus when it became clear that he had no aspirations to be a triumphal prophet-king like Moses (6:14-15), and these were even described as some of Jesus' disciples (6:66).[6] That seems a realistic outcome rather than an imagined one. Further, Caiaphas is presented as fearing that the Romans would exact a backlash if much of a movement gathered around Jesus, so the politically motivated decision of the Jerusalem leaders to "sacrifice" him to the Romans (11:49-51) is highly realistic.[7] Even Pilate's failed attempts to release Jesus show the impotence of political power—a likely factor of experience and observation, not just rhetorical presentation on the part of the Evangelist.

Seventh, the realism of referentiality is an overall feature of the Johannine tradition that suggests more of a dramatized history than a historicized drama.[8] In general, when details are added to embellish a theme or plot development in a narrative, they tend to follow a point being made. In John, however, the sequence is often the reverse. An event happens, or a detail is mentioned in passing, and then comments serve to connect some meaning with the event or incident. Most notable here is the relation between the signs and the discourses in John. Christological meaning revolves around the signs, and one has the impression that signs and discourses enjoyed an extensive history of development together, as the latter shows reflection upon the former. Details are not always elaborated upon, however; sometimes, they are simply mentioned. This is often the case with references to time and space in John: the majority of mundane details in John are innocent of symbolization.

Time and Space in the Ministry of Jesus

Because scholars have wrongly taken John's theological interest to mean that the Evangelist's "head was among the stars,"[9] and that he had no interest in itineraries or mundane considerations, many of John's time and space references have either been overlooked or misinterpreted. If we do indeed have an alternative Jesus tradition designed as a complement to Mark, however, several things follow with regards to time and space in John. Regarding *time,* with relation to Mark's itinerary, the following inferences can be made. First, an explicit corrective to Mark 1:14 is implied by the narrator's stating that "John, of course, had not yet been thrown into prison" (John 3:24). That the Baptist and Jesus ministered simultaneously for some period of time is also a likely inference.

Second, if Mark's narrative were known to the Evangelist, the emphasis on the first two signs performed in Galilee suggests that the narrator intended to fill out the beginning of Jesus' ministry as a means of augmenting the narrative in Mark 1 with reports of the earlier ministry of Jesus (2:11; 4:54). Matthew corroborates this move independently, in that he also adds to Mark's narrative a good deal of material before the healing of Simon Peter's mother-in-law in Capernaum, and in particular, the healing of the centurion's servant from afar (Matt. 8:5-13, an event similar to John 4:46-54). Therefore, John's numeration of early signs should be taken not as a feature of a hypothetical signs source or speculative numerology, but as a knowing chronological augmentation of Mark. Eusebius mentions an early tradition stating that John included early reports of Jesus' ministry not included in the other Gospels (*Hist. Eccles.* 3.24); perhaps this is what he meant.

A third chronological difference from Mark is John's presentation of three Passovers instead of one (2:13; 6:4; 11:55). This would mean that Jesus ministered for more than just part of a year, as suggested by the Synoptics, and that his movement would have had more time to get going—and likewise, resistance to it. From that angle, John's rendering seems more realistic and plausible. Highly likely also is that Jesus would have gone to Jerusalem several times during his ministry, and John mentions other Jewish feasts that occasioned such visits—an unnamed feast (5:1), the festival of Booths (7:2), and the festival of Dedication (10:22). Granted, these could all have been wrapped into just over one year if either of the first two Passovers were to be harmonized into one, but even that scenario is more realistic than the presentation of the Synoptics. Is it likely, for instance, that after beginning his ministry Jesus attended only one festival—the Passover—and ignored all the other ones that year? On this score, John's presentation of three Passovers, and other feasts, seems the more historically plausible way to envision Jesus' ministry. This explains two things: why Jesus continued to threaten the Jerusalem religious authorities, and why the Romans did not arrest him when he first rode in on a donkey. They had seen him before and, as Paula Fredriksen has argued, that is why they viewed his entering the city as a harmless, familiar occurrence.[10]

A fourth chronological difference from Mark is John's early presentation of the Temple incident. While most scholars see Mark and the Synoptics as historically accurate and John as conjectural on this matter, a strong case can be made in the opposite direction. If Mark crafted his narrative so as to fit all the judgment teachings of Jesus, all the Jerusalem-related events, and all the apocalyptic material in Jesus' ministry into one culminative visit, such a presentation could have been made for conjectural and dramatizing reasons, thereby accounting for Mark's order rather than historical knowledge or interests. Conversely, trying to make John's early Jerusalem visit out to be motivated by solely "theological" interests overlooks the fact that the narrator makes reference to that first visit later as an eventful one. Many believed because of the Temple incident, seeing it as a prophetic "sign" he had performed in Jerusalem (2:23); Jesus spent some time in the Judean countryside after that Jerusalem visit (3:22) and "had to go through Samaria" on his way from Judea to Galilee (4:3-4); the Galileans welcomed Jesus when he arrived because they had seen what he had done at the Jerusalem festival (4:45); upon his second visit to Jerusalem, the religious leaders make plans to kill him already, implying an earlier offense, although the charge is still serious—healing someone on the Sabbath and then making God out to be his Father (5:18). It cannot be said that the Evangelist did not have a sequential conception of Jesus' first two visits to Jerusalem. He may have been wrong, but it cannot be said that "theology" was his singular intention in presenting an early Temple incident.

A further detail here corroborates John's early Temple incident: the incidental mention of forty-six years as the time it had taken to build this Temple (2:20). If Herod began the reconstruction of the Temple in 19 or 20 B.C.E. as suggested by Josephus, we should locate that comment around 26 or 27 C.E. If Jesus indeed had been born before Herod the Great died in 4 B.C.E. and had begun his ministry around his thirtieth year (Luke 3:23), we should locate the Temple incident at the beginning of Jesus' ministry rather than at the end—especially if he ministered for two or three years instead of only part of a year. Against the current inclination of most scholars, these factors privilege the Johannine rendering of an early Temple incident over and against the Markan account followed by Matthew and Luke.

A fifth chronological difference from Mark involves the dating of the Last Supper. The Synoptic Gospels present the occasion as a Jewish Passover meal (Matt. 26:17-19; Mark 14:12-16; Luke 22:7-13), but John locates the Last Supper on the day before the Passover, which was also purportedly a Sabbath that year (John

13:1; 19:14, 31). While Mark connects the day of Preparation with the killing of the paschal lambs (Mark 14:12;), John makes no explicit reference to the slaying of lambs, nor does John's Last Supper include much paschal symbolism at all. Therefore, the argument that the Fourth Evangelist has moved the supper a day earlier in order to conform Jesus' death to the slaughter of lambs (a Markan detail not mentioned in John) falls flat on the basis of evidence, unless one wants to argue that the "lamb of God" references in John 1 establish such a motive. The Synoptic accounts, however, take great pains to show that the Last Supper was amply laden with Passover imagery, and the event is thus rendered as a Jewish Passover meal serving as a pattern for emerging Christian eucharistic practices. That being the case, the "cultic innocence" of John's presentation, featuring the washing of dirty feet rather than the setting up of a symbolic meal of remembrance, seems far more plausible historically.

One further point deserves to be made, and it is posed in the form of a question. If the Last Supper really occurred on the evening of Passover, as presented by the Synoptics, why do *none* of the Gospels (including all three Synoptics!) present the crucifixion as taking place *on* the day of Passover? Therefore, Mark's rendering suffers an internal problem in that it presents the Last Supper as a Passover meal,[11] and yet it does not present the crucifixion as happening on the Passover (the same day, by Jewish reckoning—a detail unlikely to have been omitted if it were based in historical fact). Of course, it could be that Mark and John used different calendars; but the fact that churches early developed a Christian ritual of "remembrance" around the Jewish Passover meal makes it more likely that Mark's crafting of the Last Supper as a Passover meal was rooted in theological interests than in historical reminiscence. It also seems unlikely that Pilate would have offered to release Barabbas, a murderer (Mark 15:6-15), to appease the crowd *after* the Passover meal, when the whole point of such appeasement would have been to prevent disturbances *before* the festival reached its peak.

On these five chronological issues, John's rendering is historically preferable over the Synoptics, and at least the first four imply a knowing corrective to Mark's chronology on the part of the Evangelist. The fifth may or may not reflect such an interest, but it does prepare the way for a more historically plausible presentation of the Last Supper and subsequent events. John thus sheds light on the evolution of Christian sacramental practice, as Mark presents the meal as a Passover meal in order to address the emerging religious needs of his Christian audiences. While not all of John's chronological differences from Mark suggest knowing contrast, at least to some degree intentionality is likely.

Topography and spatial features of the Johannine narrative may also make their own claim to historicity, and this material should give pause to interpreters who naïvely assume that lofty spiritual insight displaces lowly mundane knowledge. In

John both are evident, and extensively so. Assuming Johannine familiarity with at least some of Mark, John's "grounded" presentation of Jesus includes the following features. First, the other three signs in John's first edition material all take place in Jerusalem or Bethany, and this suggests a geographical augmentation of the largely northern Markan itinerary. Note that even Matthew makes a general reference to Jesus' healing "the blind and the lame" in Jerusalem (Matt. 21:14) in the Temple area. Is Matthew familiar with the Jerusalem miracles performed by the Johannine Jesus? It also is reported in Mark that Jesus stayed in Bethany while attending the festival in Jerusalem (Mark 11:11; 14:3), so his ministering in Bethany is a likely inference. John's augmentation of the northern ministry of Jesus in the Synoptics is thus corroborated indirectly by related details in the Synoptics.

A second feature follows: John's firsthand knowledge of Jerusalem and its environs is entirely compelling from an archaeological and topographical standpoint. The pool of Bethzatha with five porticoes near the Sheep Gate (5:1-2) conforms to the discovery of two pools together (plausibly with five rows of columns, one on each side of each pool and a row between the two pools). Not far from the Temple, a second pool of Siloam (a large *miqveh* for ritual purification before entering the Temple) was discovered in 2004, explaining why Jesus commanded the formerly blind man to wash in the pool enabling his religious purification (9:7, 11). Moreover, Jesus and his disciples cross the Kidron brook and valley on the way to the garden (18:1); Pilate's praetorium is described (18:28, 33; 19:9), along with the stone pavement (*lithostrōtos*, 19:13) and the Aramaic term for the place on which the judgment seat is located (*Gabbatha*, 19:13); the Aramaic name for the place of the crucifixion is featured (*Golgotha*, 19:17) and translated into Greek ("place of the skull"); the location of the crucifixion is listed as outside the wall ("near the city," 19:20, comporting with Heb. 13:12); and the tomb was an unused one (John 19:41, corroborated by Luke 23:53). Urban von Wahlde notes over twenty topographical references in John, which are corroborated by literary and archaeological evidence combined.[12]

Box 9.1: Topographical and Archaeological References in John

- John did his baptizing work "across the Jordan" (1:28; 3:26; 10:40) and in Aenon near Salim ("where there is much water," 3:23)
- Bethsaida—where Philip, Andrew, and Peter were from (1:44; 12:21)
- Cana of Galilee with six stone water jars, where Nathanael was from (2:1, 6; 21:2)
- Capernaum (2:12; 4:46; 6:17, 24, 59), where Jesus performed a healing and a feeding and preached in the synagogue
- Familiarity with elevation—Jesus and others "went up" to Jerusalem (2:13; 5:1; 11:55; 12:20) and "went down to" Capernaum (2:12)

- Areas of the Temple are mentioned (the cleansing, 2:14-16; the formerly lame man, 5:14; where Jesus taught, 7:14, 28; 8:20; 18:20; its treasury, 8:20; Solomon's portico, 10:23; where they searched for Jesus, 11:56)
- Sychar—the site of Jacob's well (4:4-6)
- Mt. Gerizim—a Samaritan site of worship (4:20)
- The Sheep Gate in Jerusalem (5:2)
- The Pool of Bethzatha with five porticoes (5:2)
- The Sea of Galilee (also called "Tiberias," 6:1; 21:1)
- The Pool of Siloam is a purification pool (9:1-9)
- Bethany is near Jerusalem (the home of Lazarus and also his tomb, 11:1—12:11)
- Jesus visited Ephraim (11:54)
- The Kidron is a winter-flowing stream (18:1)
- The house and courtyard of the High Priest are described (18:13-15)
- The Praetorium of Pilate is mentioned (18:28, 33; 19:9)
- The stone pavement is described (in Hebrew called *Gabbatha*, meaning "ridge of the house," 19:13)
- *Golgotha* is the place of the crucifixion (meaning "place of the skull," 19:17)
- Jesus is buried in an unused garden tomb (19:41-42)

This leads to a third feature, which involves the fact that details of Jesus' ministry in the Temple are described with specificity instead of generally. Jesus teaches in the Temple (7:14, 28)—specifically in the Temple treasury (8:20); the Temple police are called in to arrest him but are taken back by his personal authority (7:32, 45-46); Jesus is stopped and interviewed by the religious authorities while walking through Solomon's Portico in the Temple (10:23); Jewish authorities awaited Jesus' return to the Temple in order to arrest him (11:56-57); and Jesus declares at his trial that he had been speaking openly in the synagogues and Temple (18:20). Further, whether early or not, the Johannine rendering of the Temple incident, including the declaration of Jesus, is corroborated by the other Gospels and even Acts. Note that Mark twice presents people who quote what Jesus had declared about the Temple regarding his raising it up in three days after its destruction (Mark 14:58; 15:29); interestingly, the *only* place Jesus is described as saying this is in John 2:19. Matthew follows Mark in both accounts (Matt. 26:61; 27:40), and even the allegations against Stephen in Acts by members of the "Synagogue of the Freedmen" reflect consternation over Jesus' having spoken publicly of destroying the Temple (Acts 6:14)—again, an event narrated only in John.[13] Thus the Synoptics and Acts indirectly corroborate the Johannine presentation of Jesus in the Temple.

A fourth feature involves the realism of such incidental topographical details as elevation and environs that are clearly known to the Johannine narrator. Jesus went "down to Capernaum" (2:12; see also 4:47, 49); the disciples went "down to the sea" (6:16); Jesus and others went "up to Jerusalem" (2:13; 5:1; 7:10; 11:55; 12:20); and Jesus went "up into the temple" (7:14). Also, the place where John was baptizing is "across the Jordan" (1:28; 3:26; 10:40), which Jesus is reported to have visited more than once (corroborated by Mark 10:1). The feeding was across the Sea of Galilee, so that the disciples had to come back to Capernaum, and when the Tiberias crowd came across the sea looking for him, they had to sail back to the Capernaum side to find him (6:17-24), as he had crossed back again. Aenon near Salim is a place where John baptized because there was much water there (3:23); Jesus withdrew to a town in Judea named Ephraim (11:54); Jacob's well is in Sychar (4:5-6); a place of Samaritan worship is located atop Mount Gerizim (4:20); Jesus preaches in the synagogue of Capernaum (6:59); and the stone jars used in the Cana wedding fit purification practices of the time (2:6). These incidental details suggest topographical familiarity with places being described. They could not have been invented by a non-Palestinian.

A fifth aspect of spatial knowledge in the Fourth Gospel involves the use of measurements and references to particular distances and weights within the narrative. Before the sea crossing, the boat was twenty-five or thirty *stadia* from the shore (three or four miles; 6:19); Bethany was fifteen *stadia* (just under two miles; 11:18) from Jerusalem; the boat at Jesus' postresurrection appearance was two hundred *pēchōn* from shore (a hundred yards; 21:8); the six water jars held two or three *metrētas* each (twenty or thirty gallons; 2:6). Likewise, the weight of the spices to embalm Jesus was one hundred pounds (19:39); the cost of the bread would be two hundred *denarii* (eight months of wages; 6:7); and the cost of the perfume at the anointing of Jesus would be three hundred *denarii* (a full year's wages; 12:5).

Of course, any of these time and space details in John could have been fabricated or added for rhetorical effect (although rhetorical features are largely absent), but claiming that all of them were fabricated is excessive. None of them are impossibly unrealistic, and they all could have originated in firsthand familiarity with Jesus and his ministry. The reason this is significant is that these mundane details must also be considered alongside more elevated and theological presentations of Jesus' ministry in John. Moving from the most certain to the most speculative features of Jesus' ministry, glimpses of his passion, works, and words through the Johannine lens may still be discerned if interpreted correctly.

■ The Passion of Jesus

Unlike the Synoptics, which set off the Passion events with a Passover meal of remembrance pointing to the sacrifice of Jesus over and against the slaughter of the paschal lambs, the Johannine Last Supper emphasizes the call to serve one another. As Jesus washed the feet of Peter and the others, so his disciples are to wash the feet of others—serving them—if they are truly to follow Jesus' example. The Johannine Evangelist is probably familiar with the double commandment of the Synoptics, reducing the Law of Moses to two commandments—the love of God and the love of neighbor (Mark 12:30-31), but what good are those injunctions if believers are having trouble getting along with one another in community? The Markan teaching that greatness hinges upon being the servant of others (Mark 10:43-44) and Luke's presenting Jesus as inviting his followers to take a lower seat at the table (Luke 14:10), coming as one who serves (22:26-27), are both rendered in a complementary way in John's presentation of a Jesus who actually performs such service and then gives a new commandment: "Love one another" (John 13:34-35). Seeing the unfolding Passion events, then, as the ultimate expression of Jesus' love for his own and his love for the world (15:12-13) adds an important perspective to understanding Jesus' mission. It was rooted in love, and it was intended to produce loving actions on behalf of his followers. Therefore, the washing of his disciples' feet—featured only in John—exemplifies the love commands and exhortations to serve others, which are central to Jesus' teachings in John and the Synoptics.

A second feature leading up to the Passion and contributing to an understanding of Jesus' mission is the way he is presented as understanding and even predicting his death at the hand of the Romans. Since the beginning of the quest for the historical Jesus in the nineteenth century and even earlier, scholars have argued that Jesus did not know he would die; descriptions of his fateful mission are later projections back onto Jesus in the telling of the story. But what if such speculations were wrong? Growing up in Nazareth, he certainly would have known of the Romans' having crucified two thousand Jewish people in Sepphoris around the time he was born; he would have known what happens when authorities were challenged. He also may have understood something about the paradoxical workings of God, bringing life out of death and hope out of despair. He may even have known what Martin Luther King Jr. recognized later—that violence, suffered unjustly, is always redemptive.

Whatever the case, Jesus is certainly presented in John as speaking about the sort of death he would die, and in Johannine perspective, these predictions often made reference to a Roman cross as the means of losing his life. In John 12:31-36, Jesus speaks of being lifted up and drawing all to himself, and the narrator connects this reference to the manner of death by which he would die—on a cross. This connection goes back to John 3:14, however, where Jesus compares his being lifted up to Moses' lifting up a bronze serpent on a pole (Num. 21:9). In John 18:31-32, the Judeans' turning Jesus over to the Romans anticipates the means by which Jesus would die—implying death on a cross. Of course, the suffering and death of the Son of Man is presented in the Synoptics as well (Mark 8:31-34), so John's content here is not unique. Distinctive, though, is John's presentation of Jesus' prediction regarding his death on a Roman cross—an image leading to the Evangelist's reflections upon paradox, not just his use of rhetorical irony.

A third feature of John's contribution to Jesus research is the particular set of insights related to Jewish dynamics in the arrest and trials of Jesus. Notice that Jewish police and Pharisees accompany Judas and a cohort of Roman soldiers, aided by Judas's knowledge (the one disciple from Judea, *Kerioth*; 6:71; 12:4; 13:2, 26) as to the place Jesus would meet with his disciples (18:2). This shows collaboration between the Jewish leaders and the Roman authorities, plausibly reflecting some religious and political give and take—finding a way to rid themselves of the Galilean prophet while also staving off a Roman backlash (11:46-57; 18:14). The Jewish council meeting referred to in John 11:47 seems more plausible than the Markan presentation of a full Sanhedrin in the middle of the night on Passover (Mark 14:55-65) and again on Passover morning (Mark 15:1). The Jewish trials of Jesus in John shows particular realism in that the guards take Jesus first to the former high priest, Annas, whose personal authority as a longstanding religious leader would have been unquestioned—followed by taking Jesus next to the "official" high priest that year, Caiaphas (identified correctly as Annas's son-in-law, John 18:13). It is unlikely that the Evangelist would have concocted a narrative that Jesus received two Jewish trials. However, a more formal council meeting, called by the chief priests and the Pharisees five days earlier (11:47), followed by an unofficial trial before Annas (perhaps still called "the high priest"?) in the middle of the night and a subsequent "official" confirmation of judgment before Caiaphas, has its own plausible integrity precisely because of the apparent interplay between official and unofficial authority.

A fourth feature of John's contribution to Jesus research relates to the Roman dynamics in the trial, sentencing, and crucifixion of Jesus. Here the presentation of Pilate as not wanting to get caught up in Jewish internal debates seems entirely plausible. Even his retorting question, "Am I a Jew?" thrusts the responsibility back on Jesus' people, although Pilate eventually gives in to their pressure (18:35). Here the topic of kingship arises; if Jesus were to claim being "the King of the Jews," he could be charged with political sedition. However, in his responding that he is a king, whose kingdom is not of this world but is one of truth, and that all who belong to the truth hear his voice, Jesus sums up a good deal of the Synoptic teaching on the kingdom of God in two verses (18:36-37). If the backdrop of the kingdom sayings of the Synoptic Jesus is the Roman Empire and Jewish approaches to dealing with it, it seems odd that the Synoptic Jesus makes no statements about the character of God's kingdom before Pilate; only the Johannine Jesus does so. Perhaps the entirety of Jesus' kingdom sayings should be read from the perspective of John 18:36-37—Jesus' kingdom is one of truth; it is not a worldly reign but a spiritual one. That is why he told his disciples not to fight—to put away the sword and to love their enemies: his kingdom cannot be furthered by violence, or force, but only by truth; all who are given to truth hear the voice of Christ. The irony of what follows is thick. Pilate confesses that he is a stranger to the truth; though he declares he has all power to set Jesus free or to crucify him, he fails in his begging the crowd to let him let Jesus go (exposing himself as the impotent potentate). The Jewish leaders accuse Jesus of blasphemy but commit blasphemy themselves, chanting, "We have no king but Caesar!" (19:15); yet Pilate declines their request to qualify the title over the cross, "he *claimed*, 'I am king of the Jews,'" declaring, "What I have written I have written!" (19:21-22). Historical contributions here relate to issues of power and truth in Jesus' sentencing and conviction. Indeed, truth threatens power, and the only authority is moral authority—in narrative and in real life.

A fifth historical contribution of the Johannine Passion narrative to understanding Jesus' mission relates to his crucifixion and burial. The realism of the details particular to the Johannine rendering is impressive, as only in John is "Jesus of Nazareth" added to the title posted to the cross, and only in John are its three languages described (19:19-20). Further, the detail that the crucifixion took place "near the city" is corroborated in Hebrews 13:12 (Jesus suffered outside the city gate), and this would have made sense as a warning to any coming into the city that this is the sort of thing that happens to insurrectionists. The Johannine depiction of the crucifixion as an intimidation to others and as a means of "keeping the peace" bears a good deal of political realism to it. While the use of spikes in crucifixions may have been expensive (some scholars argue that because John alone mentions nails in the crucifixion, Jesus must have been crucified with ropes—a cheaper and more common means), John alone describes the nail holes in Jesus' hands (20:25), Jesus' bones as unbroken (19:33), and a spear piercing his side (19:34). Of course, these details could have been fabricated, but based on the 1968 discovery of a spike through the heel bone of a crucifixion victim in Jerusalem, dating around 70 C.E., John's graphic details also ring true. Luke presents the resurrected Jesus as showing his disciples his hands and his feet, offering indirect corroboration of the nail wounds in John (Luke 24:39-40). Also particular to John is the presence of women at the cross, instead of observing at a distance as in Mark. Jesus' entrusting his mother to the care of the Beloved Disciple also reflects human concerns and familial care accompanying these devastating events (John 19:25-27). The preparation of Jesus for burial in John is distinctively graphic, as Nicodemus brings a hundred pounds of embalming materials (although that sounds like a lot!) as well as linens for the wrapping of the body (19:38-40). While other Gospels also connect Joseph of Arimathea with Jesus' burial, John mentions that the tomb was unused and that it was the day of Preparation (19:41-42), details followed by Luke (Luke 23:53-54).

In addition to these five larger themes, note also the graphic realism of the incidental details in John 18–19: lanterns and torches light the way to the garden site (18:3); Peter cuts off Malchus's right ear with a sword (18:10); Peter's admission to the courtyard of the high priest is explained (compare Mark 14:54)—the "other disciple" was known to the high priest and was thus able to secure Peter's entrance (18:15-16); because it was cold Peter and others were warming themselves around a charcoal fire (18:18); Annas sent Jesus bound to Caiaphas (18:24); Peter's third denial follows being questioned by a relative of Malchus, whose ear Peter had severed (18:26); and from Caiaphas Jesus was led to the Praetorium, but the Jews did not enter the house lest they be defiled and made unable to celebrate the Passover (18:28).

With Mark and other Gospels, John incorporates vivid details about Jesus' trial and sentencing, including his receiving a crown of thorns and a purple robe (Mark 15:17, 20; John 19:2, 5); the "Place of the Skull" being called by its Aramaic name, *Golgotha* (Mark 15:22; John 19:17); Pilate's posting a sign reading "King of the Jews" (Mark 15:26; John 19:19); and Joseph of Arimathea's being allowed by Pilate to bury Jesus' body (Mark 15:43; John 19:38).

As mentioned above, details particular to John include: it is early when Jesus arrives before Pilate (John 18:28); the name of the stone pavement (*lithostrōtos*) is called by its Aramaic name, *Gabbatha* (meaning "Ridge of the House"; 19:13); "Jesus of Nazareth" is the prefix to the title, "King of the Jews," written in Hebrew, Latin, and Greek (19:19-20); the crucifixion is outside (near) the city and visible to passersby (19:20); four soldiers divide his clothes among them but cast lots for his seamless tunic (19:22-23); a jar of sour wine is present, and a sponge is lifted to Jesus' mouth with a hyssop branch for him to drink (19:29); Jesus' side is pierced with a spear (19:34); Nicodemus comes bringing one hundred pounds of a mixture of myrrh and aloes for the preparation of Jesus' body for burial according to Jewish custom (19:39-40); and Jesus' body was buried in an unused tomb on the day of preparation (19:41-42). These corroborative and independent details simply bolster the autonomy of the Johannine memory, likely reflecting the memory of one(s) present at least at some of these events.

These distinctive details in the Johannine Passion narrative make it impossible to believe that all of this material was either constructed on the basis of Mark or invented out of thin air. Even Bultmann had to imagine a "Passion source" as the origin of John's Passion narrative, assuming as he did that the Evangelist could not have been an eyewitness.[14] There is too much independent and corroborative material in John to consider it unhistorical or dependent on any of the Synoptics. Therefore, the Passion narrative compellingly bolsters the view that the Johannine tradition is an autonomous one, and thus it contributes in several ways to a more textured and nuanced understanding of the final days of Jesus of Nazareth.

▓ The Works of Jesus

The works of Jesus as glimpsed through the Johannine lens provide an independent corroboration of the presentation of Jesus in the Synoptic Gospels, and like the

Passion narrative, the works of Jesus come across as quite coherent, even in bi-optic perspective. Jesus begins his ministry in connection with the ministry of John the Baptist, performs healings on the Sabbath, feeds a multitude, is connected with a sea rescue, challenges Jewish authorities (both cultic and legal), advances to Jerusalem, is anointed by a woman, is received with a triumphal welcome, and then the Passion events run their course. On these scores, the Johannine rendering provides an independent attestation of the main features of Jesus' ministry and bolsters the Synoptic accounts of Jesus' ministry precisely because it is both distinctive and corroborative. In asking what John might contribute further to Jesus research, noting John's distinctive material—both in content and slant—provides a place to begin. Assuming John's familiarity with Mark, John's unique contributions reflect the addition not only of early and southern material, but of several other features as well.

A first feature of the Johannine presentation of Jesus involves a more sustained history of engagement between his ministry and that of John the Baptist. Having explained that a history of engagement between Jesus and John preceded his being thrown into prison (reading John 3:24 as referring to Mark 1:14), the Fourth Gospel presents important information about the Baptist that elucidates his ministry and also that of Jesus. As the primary witness to Jesus, John denies being either Elijah or the Prophet (Moses) when asked if he were either (John 1:19-21); in the Synoptics he is associated with both. This detail represents the theology of the Fourth Evangelist, as he presents Jesus as fulfilling both the typologies of Moses and of Elijah in his being sent from the Father and his performing familiar signs. Might this also explain why the Fourth Evangelist omits the appearance of Moses and Elijah at the transfiguration? In addition to avoiding duplication with Mark, he clearly wants to show Jesus as fulfilling these typological roles. While this understanding of the Elijah/Moses issue does not argue for Johannine historicity over against the Synoptics (indeed, the opposite may be the case), it might explain why the transfiguration is omitted from the Fourth Gospel.

Another feature of the Baptist's ministry worth noting is that his followers leave him and follow Jesus, elucidating also the geographical scope of the ministries of Jesus and John. Archaeologists have discovered a historic baptismal site of John across the Jordan (called *Bethabara* or *Betharaba* in some texts, not the familiar Bethany added by later copyists in 1:28), and he also baptized at Aenon near Salim in Samaria (3:23), a detail not likely to have been fabricated. If John also baptized in the Jordan to the south and around the Sea of Galilee, as other traditions attest, this gives a much broader understanding of John's ministry than would otherwise be known. The fact that a Judean had engaged John's disciples about "purification" (3:25) is also telling. John's immersing people in free-flowing water, rather than officially designated pools for ritual purification (the *mikva'ot*), suggests something of his challenge to institutional Jewish religious practice.

Ultimately, though, John points to Jesus, who baptizes not with water, but with the Holy Spirit (1:33).

Another feature of the Johannine presentation of Jesus is the implication of an early Temple cleansing as an inaugural prophetic sign rather than a final "swan song." According to Mark, the Temple incident provides the final offense that seals Jesus' fate; in John, it is the witness of Lazarus, raised from the dead, that poses the last straw for the Jewish leaders. Thus, they plot to kill Lazarus as well (John 12:9-11). While it is impossible to demonstrate the superiority of the Johannine rendering of an early Temple cleansing, references in Mark (John 2:19 is alluded to by Mark 14:58; 15:29) suggest its authenticity. In other words, Mark (followed by Matthew 26:61; 27:40) includes two references to what Jesus had said *only in John* in the Johannine Temple prophecy—that is, that the Temple would be torn down and rebuilt. Of course, the prophecy of Jesus in John 2:19 could have been made during a later incident instead of an earlier one, but the Markan echoes of the Johannine presentation of the event suggest something of the authenticity of John's presentation. Two further things are significant about John's rendering of the Temple episode in chapter 2. First, if Jesus began his ministry with a prophetic demonstration in Jerusalem, a more programmatic concern is suggested. He came not only to challenge the legal use of Jewish Scripture with the heart of the law, that is, love; he came also to challenge the cultic role of the Temple by becoming a revelatory bridge between God and humanity—a gift of the Father's love to the world. Considering the fact that the Romans destroyed the Temple in 70 C.E., the references to the tearing down of "this temple" would have caused those hearing the Gospel after 70 to nod their heads with knowing familiarity; in view of the Johannine accounts of the appearances of the risen Christ in chapters 20 and 21, the reference in chapter 2 to the rebuilt "Temple" and dwelling place of God would similarly have sparked recognition among subsequent believers. That is, later audiences would have taken the (originally misunderstood) words of Jesus regarding the Temple as having been fulfilled—in more ways than one.[15]

Further, rather than seeing Jesus as running into trouble with religious authorities only at the end of his ministry, what if he intentionally challenged institutional authorities from the start? Two details in Mark corroborate this likelihood. (a) Scribes and Pharisees came from Jerusalem early on, seeking to evaluate Jesus' ministry (Mark 3:22; 7:1). They might have been intrigued if news of Jesus' miracles had reached Jerusalem, but following up on the Galilean prophet after an initial Temple disturbance (such as John reports) poses a more realistic explanation. (b) Mark distinctively presents the Temple clearing as an intentional deed, not as a loss of temper. In Mark 11, Jesus arrived at the Temple, looked around, and because it was late departed to return the next day, suggesting an intentional demonstration. That being the case, a Jesus who makes a whip and drives out the animals and the merchants at the beginning of his ministry follows well alongside this similar intentional understanding. If Jesus indeed came teaching new ways of thinking, doing, and being relative to the active leadership (kingdom) of God,[16] why not start with a challenge to the Temple and its systems?

Yet another feature of Jesus' works in John is the likelihood of a series of sustained engagements with Jerusalem authorities over the heart of God's desires for the world. In continuity with the disturbance at his inaugural visit to Jerusalem in John 2, his subsequent visits in John 5, 7, and 12 did not fare much better. Note that the healings in John 5 and 9 were both performed on the Sabbath, and as with such actions in the Synoptics, Jesus appears to break the Jewish law with intentionality.[17] This is not, of course, to say that either the Jewish populace or its leaders agreed on Sabbath observances or that Gospel presentations of religious leaders are straightforward and devoid of caricature. It *is* to say that the growing resistance of Jerusalem authorities to Jesus is more realistic over the four visits that John presents, in contrast to a single visit in the Synoptics. If Jesus preached in the treasury area of the Temple (8:20), Mark's featuring a parable about the value of the widow's contribution (Mark 12:41-44) corroborates the possibility that Jesus had visited that area of the Temple during his ministry, although such a visit is not mentioned in Mark. Further, Synoptic and Johannine traditions agree that Jesus had taught extensively and openly in the Temple ("Day after day I was with you in the Temple teaching," Matthew 26:55; Mark 14:49; Luke 22:53; "I have always taught in the synagogues and the Temple," John 18:20). Now, these could be references to an intensive last week of Jesus' Temple teaching in Jerusalem (Luke 21:37-38), with no visits before that, but that seems to be a Synoptic condensation of what must, more realistically, have been a larger history of Temple ministry as presented in John.

Two further points are noteworthy. First, questions of Jesus' authorization were central to these debates with Jerusalem authorities. Especially if Jesus claimed to speak on God's behalf as one having received divine instruction (Deut. 18:15-22), this would have raised more than a little consternation among those used to more conventional appeals to legitimation (John 7:15, 46; 8:28). Second, the southern prejudice against the northern prophet (7:40-52) lends valuable insight into the reception and rejection of Jesus, reflecting the predictable societal biases of institutional authorities at the religious center of Judaism against charismatic leaders from the periphery. John portrays these factors with greater clarity than any other Gospel, and hence we find insights not only into the history of Jesus' ministry, but also the character of first-century Palestinian Judaism. John is one of the best primary sources of that information.

Another aspect of the presentation of Jesus' ministry in John features his relational, informal, and experiential connectedness with people. Whereas the Synoptic Jesus often seems driven by a mission, calling for the willingness to hate one's family in supreme loyalty to the advance of the kingdom (Luke 14:26), John's presentation of Jesus is one that shows loving concern for family and others within one's community. Rather than a programmatic calling of twelve disciples, Jesus in John simply invites a handful of men to "come and see" (1:39, 46). Likewise, Jesus is invited to attend his friend's tomb with the same words (11:34). People are also described as experiencing something of an encounter with Jesus in a variety of ways, and this is intriguing as an experiential clue to the character and origin of John's distinctive presentation of Jesus' ministry. The ministry of Jesus is rendered in John from the perspective of ones who had known him closely, and this affects ways he is portrayed—from the perspective of relational connectedness. Jesus' first sign enhances the merriment of a wedding celebration; he comes to bring abundant life in the here and now, not just in the afterlife (2:1-11; 10:10). Jesus' final sign is introduced by the narrator's noting that Jesus loved Martha and her sister, and Lazarus, too (11:5); even the Judeans comment on how Jesus loved Lazarus, as expressed by his tears (11:36). The Last Supper is described as a demonstration of Jesus' love for his disciples (13:1), and Jesus loves his own with the same love that he has known with the Father (17:23-26). Finally, Jesus' concern for protecting his own comes through, as he prays that none of them would be lost and volunteers himself quickly in the garden—requesting that the others be released—that his desire for their protection would be fulfilled (17:12; 18:8-9).

The critical realism of the Johannine presentation of Jesus involves a less formal organization and a broader range of partnership in his mission. In two particular ways, the Johannine Jesus elucidates two organizational approaches that are more primitive than those presented elsewhere in the Gospels. First, we have a less formal set of cultic observances to be set up by Jesus' followers. While some of his disciples baptized, Jesus himself did not (4:2), making a point of historical clarification. As Christian practices of baptism clearly developed in the early church, sometimes creating divisions among believers (Acts 8:5-39; 18:24—19:7; 1 Cor. 1:13-18), it is easy to imagine how Jesus might have been associated with John's baptism quite closely. Or, perhaps it was simply a means of clarifying John 3:22 and 4:1—John's disciples baptized, but Jesus did not. The Gospel of John also shows a less formal approach to table fellowship, remembering the feeding of the multitude as a fellowship meal rather than instituting a rite of remembrance at the Last Supper. Perhaps, despite being finalized later, John omits the more cultic presentations in the Synoptics precisely because John's tradition is more primitive and closer to the Jesus of history than to the Jesus of the developing Christian movement.

Second, we also have a more primitive presentation of women in leadership—against the male-oriented depictions of leadership in the pastoral epistles and elsewhere in the second- and third-generation church. In John, the role of "the Twelve" is diminished, as is that of Peter. Rather, the focus is upon a broader range of partnering with Jesus, extending beyond "the Twelve" to include Israelites, Judeans, Samaritans, women, and even children.

The Jesus of history probably did not come challenging Jewish religious forms and structures, just to set up superior (read: "Christian") forms in their place. If Jesus of Nazareth did indeed offer a more fluid and relational approach to Jewish faith and practice, the Fourth Gospel lays out such a presentation more clearly and fully than any other text. The primitive quality of John's presentation here suggests its historicity.

■ The Words of Jesus

Glimpses of the words of Jesus through the Johannine lens come through in a variety of ways. First, we see a clear picture of Jesus' self-understanding of his mission related to his being sent by God as the Mosaic prophet of Deuteronomy 18:15-22. While it is wise to resist a view of Jesus that confuses his self-understanding with later christological developments, it is still important to ascertain how he thought about himself and his mission. That being the case, he probably thought of himself more as a prophet like Moses than a king like David, although he did enact the Davidic prophecy of Zechariah 9:9 in his entrance into Jerusalem on a donkey's colt. His spoken words, however, likely were delivered with a sense of divine commission, rooted squarely in Deuteronomy 18:15-22. The Father-Son relationship in John flows directly as a means of explaining his commission as being sent from the Father; that is why he declares only what the Father tells him to say, and that is why he and the Father are one. Some of this reflects a Johannine paraphrase of Jesus' defending the legitimacy of his mission; but even in the Synoptic parable of the vineyard (Mark 12:1-9; Matt. 21:33-41), the fact that the owner sends his beloved son to represent him shows that the Johannine rendering of the agency motif within the Father-Son relationship is not unique; it likely goes back in some form to Jesus' teaching and understanding of his own mission.

Given the bi-optic reports that Jesus refers to himself as a prophet (Mark 6:4); that the guards ridicule Jesus, commanding him to prophesy (Mark 14:65); that the Samaritan woman identifies him as a prophet (John 4:19); that the crowd desires to rush Jesus off to make him a prophet-king like Moses (John 6:14-15); that some in Jerusalem really take him to be "the prophet" (John 7:40); and that the formerly blind man declares him to be a prophet (John 9:17), the Johannine Jesus' presentation of himself as the prophet of whom Moses wrote seems likely historically, not just theologically.[18] He is certainly remembered as such in a multiplicity of traditions, but nowhere is the particular connection with Deuteronomy 18:15-22 as clear as it is in the Fourth Gospel.

Second, we derive distinctive insights into Jesus' teachings on the kingdom from the two Johannine passages that develop this theme. Despite the fact that John has only two passages on the kingdom, if we assume that the Johannine Evangelist sought to augment Mark, this would suggest that he sought not to be duplicative, but to contribute additional kingdom motifs. If we take John 3:1-21 seriously as a depiction of the kingdom of God, several important points follow. One cannot glimpse the active workings of God unless one is born from above (3:3); being born of the Spirit is essential for understanding the dynamic leadership of God. Neither physical birth nor water purification will suffice; one must be born of the Spirit, which is the baptism Jesus came to bring (1:33). The Revealer comes as a scandal because he exposes the character of one's existential foundations; rejecting the revelation brings judgment on oneself, but whoever is rooted in the truth will welcome the light and thereby be liberated (3:16-21). These are all kingdom themes, although the language is used only in verses 3 and 5. The second kingdom passage takes this point further. Jesus *is* a king, but his kingdom is one of truth; all who belong to the truth hear his voice. Jesus' kingdom is not of this world, therefore worldly means and force cannot advance it (18:36-37). Rather, God's reign proceeds as a factor of truth, light, and love, and being immersed in these realities is what it means to be born from above.

Third, the fact that John's presentation of Jesus' teachings is so different from that of the Synoptics might reflect possible correctives to a variety of Markan themes and presentations in ways that show another side of Jesus' teachings. In Mark 4:11-12, parables are given for outsiders, not insiders, and they are delivered as means of separating insiders from outsiders; in John 16:29-30, however, Jesus' abandonment of figurative speech allows his disciples finally to understand and believe. Did the Fourth Evangelist agree with the sentiment that parables were for outsiders? —The Markan Jesus calls for messianic secrecy with disturbing frequency (Mark 3:12; 5:43; 7:36; 8:30; 9:9), calls that Matthew and Luke soften. Does John counterbalance secrecy with messianic disclosure (John 8:24, 28, 58; 9:37; 10:36; 12:32; 18:5, 6, 8)? —The Markan Jesus speaks in short, pithy sayings; does the Johannine Evangelist seek to augment staccato speech with more extended and thought-evoking discourses? —The Markan Jesus reduces the commandments of Moses to the love of God and neighbor (Mark 12:30-31); does the Fourth Evangelist feel that such lofty ideals must start at home, within the community of faith, if they are to be a consistent witness in the world (John 13:34-35; 17:20-26)? If the Johannine community was facing the sort of divisions and strife reflected in the Johannine epistles, the love of God must be reflected in the love of one's brothers and sisters within the community for it to be legitimate at all (1 John 4:7-8). While none of these dialectical moves is entirely demonstrable, we should exercise caution before assuming that John's extensive differences from the teachings of Jesus in the Synoptics baldly implies ahistoricity. They could imply a set of alternative perspectives on the teachings of Jesus, reflecting alternative aspects of historical memory—especially as refracted through the teaching ministry of the Beloved Disciple.

Fourth, we find several Synoptic themes embellished and taken further in John in distinctively Johannine ways. As mentioned above, while the Synoptic Jesus does not speak in the I-am forms of the Johannine Jesus, all nine of the I-am metaphors in John are also found in the Synoptics. The I-am sayings probably developed as a Johannine paraphrase of themes from the ministry of Jesus, but they are not disconnected from his teaching ministry. Jesus of Nazareth was probably more self-effacing than his presentation in John suggests, so John's counterbalancing of Mark may have stretched things a bit. But even the theme of Moses and the burning bush is present in the assertions of Mark's Jesus, so one cannot say on the basis of the Synoptic record that Jesus never uttered the I-am motif.

A Markan theme that does come through clearly in John is an invitation to the way of the cross. Jesus declares that his bread is his flesh given (on the cross) for the life of the world, and that his disciples must ingest his flesh and blood (risking martyrdom if required by the truth) if they expect to be raised with him on the last day (John 6:51-58). Further, some of these sayings of Jesus in John are even presented in aphoristic form as short, pithy agrarian metaphors. These are similar to the most characteristic of Synoptic Jesus sayings while also being particular to John: "Unless a grain of wheat falls into the earth and dies, it remains just a single grain; but if it dies, it bears much fruit" (12:24). Another Markan theme coming out clearly in John is that of the seeds and the harvest. One sows, another reaps, but the fields are now ripe for harvest (4:35-38). Even Jesus' priestly prayer in John 17 can be seen to include and expand all the elements of the Synoptic Lord's Prayer (Matt. 6:9-13; Luke 11:2-4). The Johannine paraphrase of Jesus' teachings appears to have condensed some themes while expanding others. Or did the Synoptic traditions condense or expand John's rendering of Jesus words?

Fifth, if Jesus indeed came to inaugurate the age of the Spirit, John provides a more developed set of teachings on the directly mediated workings of the Holy Spirit in the lives of believers and the church. Again, while a Johannine embellishment of earlier material is likely here, it also casts valuable light on the Spirit-based teachings and ministry of the prophet from Galilee himself. Centrally, the Synoptic promise of Jesus, that in the hour of trial the Holy Spirit would effectively guide his followers (Matt. 10:16-20; Mark 13:11; Luke 12:11-12), is developed extensively in John 14–16. Here the Holy Spirit is promised as an advocate who will be with and in Jesus' followers forever (14:16-17), will teach and remind them of all that Jesus has said to them (14:26), will testify on Jesus' behalf during their times of trial (15:26), and will guide believers into all the truth and will declare the things that are to come (16:13). While these Spirit teachings developed later in the Johannine tradition, they carry forward a distinctive element in Jesus' teachings, reminiscent of an important part of his actual message. The implications of this content are significant. If Jesus of Nazareth really taught that God's inspiring and revealing work was to emerge as a result of his ministry, John's presentation of Jesus' teaching rings true in its own ways. Jesus cites Isaiah 54:13, "And they shall all be taught by God" (John 6:45); he declares that out of one's innermost being shall flow rivers of living water—a reference to the Spirit (7:38); and after the resurrection he breathes on his disciples and commands them to receive the Holy Spirit (20:22).

The distinctive sayings of Jesus in John present the greatest historical challenge because they differ in so many ways from those in the Synoptics. If we suppose that the Johannine Evangelist was familiar with Mark, however, and that he sought not to duplicate Mark but to present an alternative rendering of Jesus' ministry, including his teaching, some of these problems are eased. Historically minded scholars are too easily influenced by all three Synoptics, as though Matthew and Luke demonstrate the best way to accommodate Mark. If we had only one Synoptic Gospel, however, with which to compare John, would John's differences be as much of a historical problem? The fact of the threefold Synoptic witness has too often eclipsed the historical contribution that John independently presents. If the Johannine Evangelist condensed some teachings of Jesus while expanding others, and if this rendering of Jesus' teachings also counterbalanced Mark in several ways, John's distinctive presentations of Jesus' teaching ministry might be seen not so much as an affront to history but as an alternative presentation of it. Granted, the Johannine Jesus speaks with the Evangelist's words and thought-forms, but even a paraphrase may at times gets closer to the historical truth than a direct quotation.

Here is an illustration of the point from my own childhood. I was five years old, and our family was headed for Medellín, Colombia. My father had just been hired by the U.S. State Department to direct a bi-national cultural center and he was teaching us Spanish. At my grandmother's table, I reached for a bowl of green peas and nearly knocked over my glass of milk, upon which my father said, "*Cuidado, muchacho, con lo que tu haces*" (meaning, literally, "Watch out, boy, with what you're doing"). My grandmother asked, "He doesn't really understand you, does he?" My father replied, "Sure he does; Paul, what did I say?" I responded, "Dad said, 'Don't spill your milk.'" Not a single word of my response was the same, or even similar, to the more general statement my father had made. The particular content of the paraphrase, though, was a perfectly good rendering of what my father meant—and much more to the point in that specific situation. We still have a thing or two to learn about historicity and its representations; a child can understand that, and scholars can, too.

■ The Revelatory Prophet

As the Mosaic prophet typology does not appear in later christological hymns or confessions in the New Testament, this is not a feature likely to have evolved later within the early church. Rather, it seems more primitive in its origin—perhaps even rooted in the self-understanding of Jesus and his mission. If Jesus saw himself as sent by God, delivering God's message as God's agent, connections with Deuteronomy 18 are likely. His reference to himself also as the Son of Man provided another way of speaking of his divine agency as God's eschatological ambassador of judgment and redemption.

Several years ago, Marcus Borg offered a helpful survey of "portraits of Jesus" emerging from recent Jesus scholarship.[19] Leading recent portraits describe Jesus as a cynic-challenger of institutions, a wisdom-oriented sage, a non-eschatological prophet, and a holy person. What is interesting is that while all of these portraits were constructed with the intentional exclusion of John, each of them can be seen within the Fourth Gospel, presented in distinctive ways. As a *cynic-challenger of institutions*, Jesus begins his ministry in John with a Temple-cleansing prophetic sign, and he challenges both cultic and scriptural authorities within Judaism, as well as Roman imperialism, with rigor and verve. As a *wisdom-oriented sage*, Jesus is presented throughout John as the personification of the Word and Wisdom of God, baffling authorities with his knowledge and insight. As a *non-eschatological prophet*, Jesus in John is thoroughly presented as the prophet like Moses, who speaks nothing on his own initiative, but only what he has heard from the Father; his word invariably comes true. As a *holy person*, Jesus in John knows people's thoughts, evokes epiphanic spiritual encounters with those he meets, performs signs up close and from afar, and bestows the Holy Spirit upon his followers.

The most central portrait of Jesus in John, however, is that of the *revelatory prophet*. John presents Jesus as the prophet predicted by Moses in Deuteronomy 18:15-22, saying and doing only what the Father instructs as the divine agent. According to Jewish Merkabah mysticism, as Peder Borgen has argued, the agent is in all ways like the one who sent him.[20] Humanity will thus be held accountable for responding to God's agent as though responding to God. This is how people know if the one claiming to be sent is authentically from God: his word always comes true. Therefore, if a prophet speaks of himself or of other gods, or his word does not come true, this is not a true prophet, and he should be put to death (Deut. 18:20). One of the great ironies of the Fourth Gospel is that despite Jesus' word coming true time and again, and despite his performing signs after the patterns of Moses and Elijah, the religious leaders of Jerusalem still do not perceive him to be sent from God. Further, they interpret his claiming to represent the Father as blasphemy, and they endeavor to put him to death—the penalty for blasphemy and also for being the presumptuous prophet. As well as being sent from God with a message of God's love for humanity, however, the Johannine Jesus declares a world-changing message: God continues to speak, and God's revelatory Word is available to any who will be receptive and responsive to the divine initiative. Therefore, as the divine agent Jesus comes with a message of immediate access to the Father—available as grace and received by faith. This is the work of the Spirit, which carries forth the revelation of the Light, which Jesus declares and is. Sometimes confused with Gnostic religions in later settings, these themes are already present in Jewish Scripture, and just as the Revealer challenged the religious structures of his day, that challenge continues in every generation following.

Within the Johannine presentation of Jesus as the revelatory prophet, his mission is needed because no one has seen God at any time; only by the saving/revealing initiative of God can humanity be "drawn" to the Father. Therefore, Jesus comes to the world as the agent of God, revealing God's love and truth to the world. The world's reception of the Revealer is ambivalent, however. Some believe, but others do not. Those who know God reportedly receive the Revealer, but those who reject the authenticity of Jesus and his mission expose their spiritual condition. Jesus affirms his speaking and doing only what he has heard and seen from the Father, attested by his words and works. The world is therefore invited to respond believingly to the Father's agent as responding directly to God. Those who believe receive life and further light; those who reject the Revealer preserve the "comfort" of their darkness but remain therein. The goal of the Evangelist, however, is to present the story of Jesus' ministry and its reception in such a way as to lead the hearer/reader to believe that he is the Christ, the Son of God, and by believing to have life in his name (20:31). In so doing, he presents the Jesus of history *as* the Christ of faith.

■ Conclusion

In addition to being highly theological, the Johannine narrative makes considerable contributions to our understanding of the Jesus of history. Not only are chronological and geographical features of Jesus' ministry clarified by the Fourth Gospel, but John's religious and political realism adds valuable insights to a contextual understanding of Jesus' words and works. Cast in the role of a prophet like Moses, the Johannine Jesus not only teaches God's love for the world; he embodies it and calls for his followers to display the same in community and in the world. He brings a message that God's active leadership and direction are available here and now, for all people, inviting a response of faith to the workings of the Holy Spirit within and among authentic seekers of the truth. The spirituality of Jesus does not replace one set of Jewish forms with an endorsed set of Christian ones; it declares that God's presence and movements are above and beyond human-derived conventions. One can therefore understand why the Revealer was a scandal to religious and political authorities of his day; he continues to be the same within every worldly setting.

■ **Questions to Consider**

1. Note the different types of realism in the Fourth Gospel and consider what their origin(s) might have been if the Johannine tradition was not rooted in historical memory. Are alternative explanations compelling or weak? Either way, how so?

2. Consider chronological features of John's presentation of Jesus' ministry and comment on whether they seem to be presented as knowing alternatives to Markan presentations. If so or if not, what might the implications be?

3. Consider the various portraits of Jesus put forward by recent Jesus scholars and reflect upon John's distinctive contributions to each of these images of Jesus as the revelatory prophet.

■ **Terms to Understand**

- realism
- topography
- empiricism
- referentiality

The Life of the Church

Johannine Ecclesiology

Bolstering the life of the church is one of the central interests of the Fourth Gospel, and the Evangelist seeks to engage the life of believers with the presence of Christ as the risen Lord of the church. The other Gospels also share this interest, but John excels in its distinctive approaches to church vitality. John's is a theology of encounter. It rises from transformative encounter and seeks to engender the same in later audiences. Whether a wader or a swimmer, the reader is finally invited to jump into the water and see what happens experientially.

■ A Vision of Relational Connectedness to Jesus

At the outset, the reader is invited into fellowship with the community that composed the Prologue. This is why the Prologue (1:1-18) becomes such a powerful introduction to the earlier narrative. It betrays the community's response of faith to the story of Jesus as conveyed by the first edition of John, and it invites later hearers and readers into that same level of experience. Its poetic form and stanza-like structure invites others into a participatory mode, connecting with the first-person plural—"*we* have beheld his glory"; "from his fullness *we* have received grace upon grace" (1:14, 16). In so doing, third- and fourth-generation readers are invited into fellowship with those who have encountered Jesus in firsthand ways. By now it is a spiritual encounter alone that is available, but incarnational fellowship holds open the possibility that the love and ministry of Jesus will be experienced among his followers. This vision of relational connectedness to Jesus begins with community, but it also extends to the personal.

The Prologue pivotally extends the invitation for later audiences to become children of God, personally and meaningfully. However, the advent of the Light and *Logos* of God receives an uneven reception in the world. "He came to what was his own, and his own people did not accept him. But to all who received him, who believed in his name, he gave power to become children of God, who were born, not of blood or of the will of the flesh or of the will of man, but of God" (1:11-13). Alan Culpepper sees this as the pivotal fulcrum of the Prologue; while it begins and ends with God and the mission of God's Son, it centrally brings his mission home to the hearer/reader. Will she or he respond receptively in faith to the divine initiative, becoming a child of God? This *is* a deeply personal matter, and as the rest of the narrative unfolds, the scaffolding that props up humanity's approaches to life, God, and the world become challenged—even assaulted—by the inadequate responses to Jesus as sketched in the story.

Like Nicodemus, our "profound" religious wisdom is exposed as foolishness before the free-flowing ways of the Spirit. Like the woman at the well, we see that we have mistaken the source of true refreshment for something lesser. Like the crowds at the lakeside, we seek the crusts of bread when we really need the staple nourishment of life. Like Pilate, we are deluded into thinking that political power has clout, when truth alone is genuinely liberating.

Therefore, the hearer/reader is confronted existentially as to whether he or she will respond in faith to the divine initiative, for one cannot see the kingdom of God unless one is *born from above* (3:3). The paradox of the cross dashes all our conceptions of success and conventional wisdom. It is in the lifting up of the Son of Man and his political/religious "failure" that the saving love of God is revealed (3:14-16), and like the serpent of Moses lifted on a pole, all who embrace the paradoxical manifestation of God's grace on the cross are healed/saved.

A further point to be noted in the Gospel Prologue is its inclusive outreach. Whereas the earlier edition of the Gospel was especially crafted to convince Jewish family and friends that Jesus was indeed the Jewish Messiah, the Prologue extends the outreach to Gentile audiences of the broader Hellenistic world. Raymond Brown rightly points out the connections between the beginnings of the Johannine Prologue and the book of Genesis ("in the beginning," the agency of God's creative word, etc.); this message would also have been welcome among those who knew the works of Heraclitus of Ephesus.[1] Most interesting here is the way the Johannine leadership has reworked the agency motif in ways that speak to the existential lives of the audience. Just as the Greek philosopher argued that the force that holds things together and makes order out of flux is the *logos* of God, Christ as the Logos speaks order into the chaos of human lives. And, just as Philo of Alexandria connected the *Logos* of God with the creation and redemption of the cosmos, so Christ's creative-redeeming work is embraced existentially. In John's Prologue, the redemption availed through Jesus is presented in cosmic perspective. From the beginning, it was the source of God's creative work (Genesis 1–3); in the present, it continues to bring order out of chaos in the lives of individuals and communities that are receptive and responsive to God's redeeming and liberating work, full of grace and truth.

In these and other ways, the Fourth Gospel conveys a vision of relational connectedness to Jesus as the Christ, bridging past and present, individual and community, and Judaism and Hellenism. And that vision extends also from readers in the distant past to modern readers in the contemporary present. This engaging outreach is also furthered through John's images of the church.

■ Fluid and Dynamic Images of the Church

In contrast to more "petrified" models of the church built upon the "rock" of Peter, his confession, or the revelation he received (Matt. 16:16-19), the Johannine images of the church are fluid and dynamic. Dialogues between institution and charisma can be seen in all New Testament discussions of the church, and these dialogues took place within traditions and between them. In John the first image of the church is that of *the flock* of Jesus, accompanied by the images of the sheep and the shepherd. In caring for the sheep, Jesus calls his sheep by name (10:3), and his sheep recognize his voice (10:2, 4, 17). Within this relationship the intimacy of deep acquaintance is central. Jesus knows his sheep, they know his voice, and they follow him (10:27). As a result, the sheep are not only directed by the Shepherd, but their needs are also cared for as he guides them out to pasture and brings them back into the sheepfold for shelter and rest. Here the interactive quality of the relationship between Christ and the church is featured with prominence. The heart of church vitality is a dynamic relationship with its Lord, and this is the central feature of the Johannine imagery of the Shepherd and his flock.

As a community of faith, the flock is to be led by the Shepherd, Jesus, who is defined as "good" and is distinguished from the hireling, who runs in the face of danger (10:10-14). By contrast, the Good Shepherd lays down his life for his sheep, setting the pattern for others to follow. This courageous example of selfless leadership would have played on several levels. It would have been remembered by Jesus' actual followers, who saw him brave the opposition by Judean leaders and Roman authorities in Jerusalem, providing an example for them to follow as they faced danger in their own ministries. Somewhat later audiences might also have thought of such leaders as Judas the Galilean, Theudas, the Samaritan, and the Egyptian—described as false messiahs and pretenders by Josephus and by Gamaliel in Acts

5:36-37 (see also Acts 21:38). In the second and third periods of the Johannine situation, the courageous leadership of Jesus would have made a strong statement to emerging leaders among the mission churches of Asia Minor and beyond. Solidarity with Jesus and his community may exact a cost, but such is the leadership after the example of Jesus, and his true followers can do no less.

A third aspect of the imagery is important here—namely, the emphasis upon other sheep from other folds. These are also called "my sheep" by Jesus, and his desire to bring them into "one fold" under "one shepherd" displays a radically open view of fellowship. The basis for welcome inclusion is neither a set of religious criteria nor a litany of theological beliefs. Rather, simply discerning and responding to the voice of the Shepherd is the basis for being included in his sheepfold, whether or not they know his name. Indeed, Jesus desires to gather the scattered children of God from around the world (11:52), and this appears to actualize already in the coming of the Greeks to see Jesus (12:20-23). Before Pontius Pilate Jesus declares, "Everyone who belongs to the truth listens to my voice" (18:37), and the cross-cultural and trans-religious outreach of the Johannine message becomes apparent.

A second image for the church and believers in John is *the vine and the branches*. As Jesus' followers are described as "branches" (15:5-6), the important thing is connectedness to the Vine. The mutual abiding of the branch and the vine is not only the source of vitality; it is also the only way to fruitfulness. If the branch is cut off from the vine, it withers; it bears no fruit (15:4). Therefore, Jesus' disciples are exhorted to abide in him and he in them if they expect to be fruitful producers of the love he provides. On the other hand, fruitlessness is not only an outcome of disconnectedness from the vine; it is also a basis for removal. While such is simply described as a reality, it also implies something of a warning. If Jesus' disciples do not bear fruit, what is the Vinedresser to do? He will inevitably prune back the dead wood to make room for a more robust harvest in the future (15:2).

As Jesus' will is for his disciples to be fruitful and for their fruit to remain (15:16), such will finally be manifested in their love for one another in the world. To abide in Jesus is to abide in his love (15:9), and his commandment is for his followers to love one another (13:34-35; 15:12, 17). Here abiding in Christ finally manifests itself in being organically connected to knowing and doing his will as his partners in the world. Jesus calls his partners "friends" rather than slaves, because they know what his will is and are actively engaged in carrying it out (15:14-15). This relationship finally becomes a factor of expanded agency, whereby the Son's being sent by the Father is extended to believers' being sent by him into the world. This is what it means to share in the oneness that the Son has known with the Father since the beginning of time (17:18-26)—a factor of agency rather than being. As the Son carries out the mission of the Father, so believers carry out the mission of the Son and the Father in the world.

In both its shepherd/sheep and the vine/branches imagery, for believers the importance of connectedness to Christ is central in John. This relationship, then, has extensive implications for ministry, worship, sacraments, and the organizational life of the church.

■ Gospel Ministry: Compassionate, Empowered, Inclusive

Ministry in John is a matter of love and compassion rather than of position or a religious transaction. Several actions in the narrative make this clear. The pivotal example of ministry in John is that of washing the feet of others. Jesus here invites his disciples to serve one another in caring for their mundane and physical needs, taking on the role of a servant as the authentic marker of leadership. Peter's misunderstanding of Jesus' washing his feet is presented rhetorically. For all aspiring church leaders in the emerging situation, the willingness to serve and be served is emphasized with clarity. Mary's anointing of Jesus' feet in the previous chapter (12:1-8) provides the backdrop for Jesus' ministering to his disciples. Here the service-oriented leadership of women offers a pattern embraced by Jesus, which is to be followed by his disciples as well. The apostle is not greater than the one who has sent him, and servants are not greater than their masters (13:16). Yet, the character of ministry and service is compassionate and loving, and that quality transcends positions and structural roles of leadership on all accounts. Indeed, Jesus' *new commandment* in John 13:34-35 is for his followers to *love one another*, and by this will they be known as his disciples, just as Jesus has laid down his life in love for the world (1 John 3:16; John 15:12-13).

Authentic ministry is also rooted in spiritual empowerment, and Jesus promises the gift of the Spirit as the basis for personal transformation and effective ministry. Jesus baptizes with the Spirit (1:33), and he gives the Spirit without measure (3:34). From one's innermost being shall rivers of living water flow (4:10; 7:37-39), and after the resurrection the Johannine Pentecost is portrayed as Jesus' breathing on his disciples, inviting them to receive the Holy Spirit (20:22). Jesus must depart in order that the *Paraklētos* might be sent, convicting the world of sin, righteousness, and judgment (16:7-11). Jesus will not leave his followers as orphans but will empower them to do greater things than Jesus has done (14:12). The Advocate will be with Jesus' disciples forever (14:16). The Spirit of Truth will abide with them and in them (14:17); will teach them all things and remind them of Jesus' teachings as required by the situation (14:26); will testify on Jesus' behalf (15:26); will guide them into all truth; and will impart that which is from Jesus and disclose it directly to his followers (16:13-14). The flesh profits nothing, but the words of the Lord indeed are power and life (6:63).

Ministry in the Fourth Gospel is also inclusive in its scope. Christological confessions are made by those not numbered among the Twelve, such as Nathanael

(1:49), and even by women, such as the Samaritan woman (4:19, 29), Martha (11:27), and Mary Magdalene (20:16). Further, beyond being merely mentioned by name, Andrew, Philip, and Thomas play no individuated roles in the Synoptics, whereas in John they are presented as meaningfully engaged in Jesus' ministry. Andrew brings Peter to Jesus (1:41), introduces the boy with the loaves and fishes to Jesus (6:8), and tells Jesus of the Greeks who seek him (12:22). Likewise, Philip brings Nathanael to Jesus (1:45), is the one Jesus asks about procuring food for feeding the multitude (6:5-7), is the one who connects the Greeks with Andrew and Jesus (12:21-22), and requests Jesus show them the Father at the Last Supper (14:8). Finally, Thomas (the twin) plays the role of casting gloom (11:16), does not know the way the Lord is going (14:5), was not present when Jesus first appeared and thus refuses to believe until he sees and touches the flesh wounds of Jesus (20:24-25), but finally makes a climactic confession (20:28) as a powerful demonstration of moving from doubt to faith. When Jesus commissions his followers as apostles and priests in John, the scope is decidedly plural and inclusive in its emphasis (20:21-23); we see in John a multiplication of apostolic ministry rather than its hierarchical constriction to a few.

The priesthood of believers is more than a mere idea in the Fourth Gospel, as from the beginning of Jesus' ministry until the very end disciples bring people to the Lord, serving as bridges between others and Jesus. After John the Baptist points his disciples to Jesus as the Lamb of God (1:36), two of his disciples become followers of Jesus, who simply invites them to "come and see" (1:39). They in turn bring others to Jesus, also saying, "Come and see" (1:46). Andrew brings his brother Peter to Jesus, and Philip brings Nathanael to him. The Samaritan woman also says to her townspeople, "Come and see a man who told me everything I have ever done! He cannot be the Messiah, can he?" (4:29). She thus becomes an apostle to the Samaritans. After the death of their brother, Mary and Martha become bridges between Jesus and Lazarus as they say to the Lord, "Come and see" (11:34), whereupon Jesus weeps and then raises Lazarus from the tomb. In John 12:21, Greeks come to Philip saying, "Sir, we wish to see Jesus." Philip and Andrew then report their quest to Jesus, which signals the "hour" of his ministry. After the resurrection, Mary Magdalene becomes the apostle to the apostles, as she declares to the disciples that she has seen the Lord (20:18); the other disciples become a bridge between the Lord and Thomas, declaring that they too had seen the Lord (20:25). Finally, the Beloved Disciple points out the Lord to Peter in the boat (21:7), thereby becoming a personal bridge. Beyond the narrative in John, gospel ministry involves *being* the good news to others—typified by connecting others to the Lord.

Therefore, gospel ministry in the Fourth Gospel is compassionate in its character, inspired in its empowerment, and inclusive in its scope. Indeed, Martin

Luther's primary biblical basis for his doctrine of the priesthood of all believers is built squarely on John 20:21-23. And he got it right!

On Worshiping in Spirit and in Truth

Just as the Fourth Gospel lays out a theology of ministry, it also poses a clear theology of worship and in that sense is unique among the Gospels. As the source and direction of the wind is unknown, so it is with the life of the Spirit; one must set one's sail to the movement of the divine initiative, and being receptive and responsive to the Spirit's promptings is ever the way of faith (3:6-8). This is why authentic and transforming worship can never be confined to a particular place or form, whether it be in Jerusalem or on Mount Gerizim. While Jesus indeed declares that salvation is *of the Jews* (4:22), he also refuses to endorse a temple made with human hands as the exclusive locus of God's presence or the singular place in which the divine is encountered. He thus declares to the Samaritan woman:

> Woman, believe me, the hour is coming when you will worship the Father neither on this mountain nor in Jerusalem. You worship what you do not know; we worship what we know, for salvation is from the Jews. But the hour is coming, and is now here, when the true worshipers will worship the Father in spirit and truth, for the Father seeks such as these to worship him. God is spirit, and those who worship him must worship in spirit and truth. (4:21-24)

As C. K. Barrett reminds us, this passage paradoxically holds present and future together in ways that also transcend particular approaches to worship.[2] While the challenging of the Samaritan worship site is clear, we do not have in John the elevation of the Jewish center as though one religion and its holy place are superior to another—either Judean or Galilean. Sacred place and space in John are not topographical but incarnational. The Word became flesh and tabernacled among humanity neither in a cultic edifice nor at a historic site. Rather, God came to humanity in a human being, and in the fleshly humanity of Jesus is the *Shekinah*-glory of God revealed and encountered (1:14).[3] With the Markan Jesus and with Stephen in Acts, God does not dwell in temples made with human hands (Mark 14:58; Acts 7:48), and the temple to be raised up in three days after its destruction is the body of the Lord (John 2:21). Therein, that is, within an incarnational "temple," abides the saving/revealing presence of God.

Neither does authentic worship hinge upon the correct religious form, nor the aesthetics of liturgy—either Jewish or Christian—as pleasing as these may be. These may be valued by humans; they are never a requisite for God. Even while Scripture furthers the revelation of God, humans all too easily miss the central thrust of its revelatory power in failing to approach the text with spiritual sensitivity. It is a great irony, mused Ernst Käsemann, that the Fourth Gospel was included within a closed canon, when the Gospel of John teaches clearly that the Holy Spirit continues to speak and lead *beyond a closed canon*![4] Like the religious leaders in John 9, claiming "we see" may indeed blind one to the workings of the Revealer. In that sense, revelation is ever a scandal to religion; religion consists of human constructions of patterns and forms designed to further and replicate a spiritual value, ideal, or experience. Paradoxically, however, only as the worshiper releases oneself to unpredictable and uncontrolled winds of the Spirit can one actually encounter the presence of the divine. Our all-night toil counts for nothing; only as the Lord leads and directs do our nets come up full.

Lest it be felt, however, that the life of the Spirit is beyond human reach, Jesus emphasizes that God's initiative is actively on the move. It is precisely those who open themselves to God's loving presence and grace that the Father actively seeks to draw into transforming worship and encounter (4:23). Jesus' kingdom is one of truth, and all who belong to the truth hear his voice (18:37). This includes Samaritans and Judeans, as well as Galileans and Ephesians—and even members of premodern, modern, and postmodern societies. Encountering the truth is always liberating, and abiding in the Word of the Lord is the sustenance of true discipleship (8:31-32). It may involve places, forms, and words, but the divine address can never be delimited to them; it will ever be encountered in spirit and in truth.

■ An Incarnational Sacramentology

If the only New Testament book we had were the Gospel of John, there would be no biblical basis for the Christian rites of baptism and communion. As the only Gospel boasting claims to direct contact with the ministry of Jesus, this poses a striking problem for Christian sacramentology. In John, the standard terms for sacramental discussions do not apply.[5] As an *ordinance*, Jesus does not ordain rites of baptism or communion in John. As an *institution of the church*, Jesus' followers are not presented as establishing such rites. Sacraments as a means of *instrumentality*, transactions by which grace is received, conflict with salvation being received through faith in Christ alone.

While John's sacramental associations seem clear to some, the practice of water baptism itself seems in this narrative deemphasized. John is not portrayed as baptizing Jesus in the first chapter; the emphasis in John 3:5 is upon the second item rather than the first (water alone is insufficient; the new birth *must* involve the Spirit); and John 4:2 claims that Jesus himself never baptized—only his disciples did. Likewise, with reference to eucharistic forms, Jesus does not institute a meal of remembrance at the Last Supper in John—contrary to his presentation in the Synoptics and 1 Corinthians 11. Rather, the "bread" Jesus offers makes reference to the cross in John 6:51—calling his followers to costly discipleship rather than a cultic rite.[6] Finally, the meal on the shore of Galilee smacks more of a fellowship meal than a cultic one.

While some scholars assert that the Fourth Evangelist does indeed include a Eucharist—simply placing it in chapter 6 rather than in chapter 13—this assertion bears two major problems, making it untenable. First, if the Evangelist (or the editor) wanted to include a clear reference to a eucharistic rite, why not simply add it to the Last Supper? As he probably would have known the association with the Last Supper, the absence of a meal of remembrance from John 13 makes it seem that the Evangelist is anti-sacramental, or at least critical of emerging Christian formalism. Further, if the story of John's baptizing Jesus was omitted knowingly, might this imply an adverse stance toward emerging Christian sacramental forms?

A second problem with taking John 6:51-58 to be a eucharistic reference is that if neglecting to eat and drink the eucharistic elements means one has no life in oneself (6:53), this is like saying, "Take the Eucharist or be damned." If such is the case, Bultmann's judgment stands that this cannot be the voice of the Evangelist, for whom Jesus is the Way, the Truth, and the Life (14:6).[7] It must have been added by a second hand representing an alternative soteriology. However, verses 53-58 follow directly on verse 51, with the emphasis being on the way of the cross rather than a cultic rite. Therefore, the injunction is to be willing to ingest the flesh and blood of Jesus as an expression of one's willingness to suffer and die with him on the cross—if required by the truth. Akin to the moral exhortations of Mark and Paul (Mark 8:34-38; Rom. 6:1-23), if one is not willing to risk suffering and dying with Christ in the here and now, one cannot hope to be raised with him on the last day.

The emphasis here is upon solidarity with Jesus and his followers, even in the face of adversity, if one expects to receive eternal life. That view is perfectly consonant with the rest of the Evangelist's theology; the focus is not on a eucharistic rite, but on faithful discipleship—even if costly. Further, this martyrological thrust was likewise the earliest association with sharing Jesus' cup and baptism (Mark 10:38-39), implying that John's presentation of eating and drinking Jesus' flesh and blood is early, despite John 6 being added to the final edition. While Paul called for the community in Corinth to transition into a symbolic meal instead of a full fellowship meal (1 Corinthians 11:13-34), did *all* early Christian groups do so? Johannine Christianity evidently maintained a more primitive form of the fellowship meal, wherein the emphasis was upon faithfulness to Jesus and his community as a factor of costly discipleship. Therefore, celebrating table fellowship together in community, in memory of the Lord's ministry and sacrifice, is what is emphasized in John 6, 13, and 21, rather than a formalized rite. This is because the Evangelist's sacramentology was *incarnational* rather than cultic.

Clifford J. Wright describes the "sacramental principle" of the Fourth Gospel as the belief that the physical can be the vehicle for the spiritual. God's revealing work takes place through the signs of Jesus, through his signifying words, and ultimately through the incarnation itself. If a "sacrament" can be described as a physical and outward expression of a spiritual and inward reality,[8] a living, breathing *person* has greater capacity to convey the saving love and presence of God than inanimate means or objects—including rites, forms, and symbols. God's revealing work in John thus takes place most powerfully through *persons*—incarnated means of God's self-communication to the world. Because God so loved the world, the Father sent the Son (3:16); the Word became flesh, and in his incarnated agency is the Glory and Presence of the divine encountered (1:14). Through him the Holy Spirit comes in fullness so that spiritual baptism arises from the inward encounter of faith, whereby rivers of living and purifying water flow from one's innermost being. For the Fourth Evangelist, such is the essence of authentic baptism. It is not a hydraulic reality, but a pneumatic one, and this is the point conveyed by virtually all pairings of John's and Jesus' baptisms in the New Testament. John baptizes with water, but Jesus baptizes with the Holy Spirit (Mark 1:8; John 1:33; Acts 1:5; 11:16—"and with fire" in the Q tradition: Matt. 3:11; Luke 3:16). Thus, the true and outward evidence of spiritual transformation is the believer's character and life. By this will Jesus' authentic disciples be known: that they have love for one another (John 13:35)—an incarnational reality and measure.

Likewise, the essence of authentic communion is also experienced incarnationally in the Fourth Gospel. In continuity with the commensality of Jesus' ministry, communion is experienced where, in Matthean terms, two or three are gathered together in the name of Jesus (Matt. 18:18-20). Building on the Jewish understanding of God's being present at common meals (see Exod. 18:12; Deut. 12:7, 18; 14:23-26), even enemies are reconciled around table fellowship together (see Ps. 23:5). Note that Peter vacillated on eating with Gentiles (Gal. 2:12), fearing that this would imply reconciliation without the Gentiles' having become "clean" religiously. Just as the Synoptic Jesus challenged those codes and dined with "tax gatherers and sinners" as a declaration of God's grace and reconciling presence, the Johannine Jesus continues to extend that manner of table fellowship to his followers without a movement toward a symbolized meal or a cultic rite. For the Fourth Evangelist, such is the essence of authentic communion. It is a celebration of the real presence of the divine in community—independent of cultic forms: an incarnational reality.

As an outward and physical expression of an inward and spiritual reality, however, how does John's *incarnational sacramentology* find expression in the world? The true and outward evidence of divine presence and love, according to the Johannine Jesus, is the embodied expression of God's love in the world. It was so for Jesus; it will ever be so for his followers. By this will all recognize Jesus' authentic follow-ers—that they have love one for another—demonstrating the same love which the Father and the Son shared from the beginning of time until the present day (13:35; 17:26). Thus, the authentic measure of sacramental reality according to John is also incarnational. This being the case, the apparent disparaging of sacramental forms in John could be a factor of setting the record straight historically—Jesus did not come to challenge Jewish and Samaritan forms of worship just to set up new "Christian" ones in their place—and from a basic historical standpoint John may be right. On the other hand, the Evangelist may simply want to emphasize incar-national aspects of God's saving/revealing work as well as the locus of authentic Christian fellowship and outreach. Whatever the case, John's incarnational sacra-mentology deepens a biblical understanding of how God's love is encountered and conveyed in the world.

■ Peter, the Beloved Disciple, and the Ongoing Leadership of Christ through the Holy Spirit

The presentation of Peter and the Beloved Disciple in John poses an interesting contrast: the Beloved Disciple always gets it right, but Peter often gets it wrong. Of course, the disciples are presented as misunderstanding Jesus in all four Gospels, but in narrative, miscomprehension is always rhetorical; the question here is *why*? Reflected here is probably not a personal struggle between members of Jesus' band, although in John Jesus predicts the martyrdom of Peter (John 21:18-19) and in Mark he predicts the martyrdom of the sons of Zebedee (Mark 10:38-39). In those same passages a touch of jealous enmity is reported (Peter's toward the Beloved Disciple in John 21:20-23; of "the ten" toward James and John in Mark 10:41), and in both Gospels Jesus emphasizes following his example in serving others (Mark 10:43-45; John 13:13-17) and calling his disciples to "follow me!" (John 1:43; 12:26; 21:19, 22; Mark 1:17; 2:14; 8:34; 10:21). The main teaching point in this juxtaposition of two leaders in Jesus' band is to present the right way and the wrong way to think of Christian discipleship and leadership for later generations.

Because the Beloved Disciple always gets it right, he exemplifies the right way to think about discipleship for believers. While unnamed disciples are mentioned several times in John, the first mention of the Beloved Disciple is at the Last Supper, where he reclines against the breast of Jesus (13:23). Here the image of intimacy with the Lord characterizes what authentic discipleship is all about. The second presentation of the Beloved Disciple features him, alone among the Twelve, present at the cross (19:26-27). This exemplifies courage in the midst of danger and faithful-ness regardless of the circumstances. Note also that women are present at the cross (19:25), whereas in Mark they observe from a distance (Mark 15:40). In John, Jesus rewards the Beloved Disciple's faithfulness by entrusting his mother to his care. In contrast to his entrusting the instrumental keys to Peter in Matthew (Matt. 16:17-19), here the image of church leadership and authority is couched in relational and familial terms. The third presentation of the Beloved Disciple shows his faithful visiting of Jesus' tomb along with Peter; even though he arrives first, he stands aside and allows Peter to enter (John 20:1-9). Note the generosity of spirit here exemplified. Whereas charisma may outrun hierarchy, it also is called to be gracious and patient until others have seen and believed. The fourth appearance of the Beloved Disciple appears to account for his death, while also connecting him with the one who "wrote these things" and whose "testimony is true" (21:20-24). Therefore, he serves as the faithful witness, connecting later generations with the Lord authentically and effectively. In all these ways, the Beloved Disciple becomes a model of authentic discipleship—an ideal example of leadership for others to follow—all the more powerfully because he was a real person, not just a literary device.

While Peter still plays a prime role among the disciples (Matt. 10:2 adds the word *first* to the calling of Peter), he is also presented as miscomprehending. If the abrupt leadership of Diotrephes "who loves to be first" (3 John 1:9-10) reflects his endeavor to hold his church together with an assist from Petrine authority, he and his kin might well be a target of the Johannine corrective to rising institutionalism in the late-first-century situation. The first ambiguous presentation of Peter in John features his confession. As in the Synoptics, Peter makes the climactic confession after the feeding; here he declares, "Lord, to whom can we go? You [alone] have the words of eternal life. We have come to believe and know that you are the Holy One of God!" (John 6:68-69). On one hand, Peter affirms Jesus' sole authority, ostensibly returning the "keys" to Jesus (as contrasted with Jesus' words to Peter after his confession in Matthew 16:16-19). In that sense, Peter is presented as reversing institutionalizing approaches to the way Christ leads the church.[9]

Oddly, though, after Peter declares Jesus to be "the Holy One of God" (as does the demoniac in Mark 1:24), Jesus seems in John to reject the triumphalism of election ("I have *not* elected you, the Twelve . . ."), although the editor seems to clarify that he must have been referring to Judas—he couldn't have meant Peter (John 6:70-71). Just as the Markan Jesus rejects Peter's Son-of-Man triumphalism after his confession (Mark 8:29-33), the Johannine Jesus rejects Peter's wonder-working triumphalism after his confession in John 6. The call to discipleship involves the way of the cross in both Mark and John, although it is expressed in different ways (Mark 8:34-38; John 6:51-58). The disciples who abandoned Jesus and walked with him no longer (John 6:66) left not because they misunderstood Jesus; they were scandalized because they understood full well the cost of discipleship. Indeed, the invitation to seek not the food that perishes but that which leads to eternal life (6:27) is served on a platter formed in the shape of a cross.

The second ambiguous presentation of Peter shows him as the one whose feet Jesus offers to wash, but who misunderstands Jesus' act of servant leadership (13:1-17). When he does understand, he goes overboard by requesting that Jesus wash also his hands and head, prompting Jesus' final instructions: "Very truly, I tell you, the servant is not greater than his master, nor is the *apostle* greater than the one who sent him" (13:16, my translation). This is the only time the Greek word *apostolos* ("one who is sent") appears in John, and it may be a way of emphasizing that apostolic leadership (Petrine or otherwise) should not overshadow the ministry of the Lord. His work is that of a servant, and those who follow his example are truly blessed (13:17).

The third ambiguous presentation of Peter shows him striking Malchus with a sword and cutting off his ear. He has totally misunderstood the character and destiny of Jesus' mission, and Jesus rebukes him and commands him to put away his sword (18:10-11). Jesus *is* willing to drink the cup set before him, and those who shepherd his flock (in contrast to the hireling) should be willing to do the same (10:11-13). After all, Jesus' kingdom is not of this world, and that is why his disciples cannot further it by violence or by force (18:36).

The final ambiguous presentation of Peter in the Fourth Gospel plays a dual role. After denying the Lord three times around a charcoal fire, Peter is given a threefold chance to affirm his loyalty to Jesus—also around a charcoal fire (18:18; 21:9). On one hand, it appears that Peter is reinstated to a position of leadership among the disciples after his fall. On the other hand, Peter does not answer with the same word for "love" as Jesus asks of him. Twice Jesus asks if Peter loves him with *agapē* love, and twice Peter responds that he loves Jesus with *philia* love (21:15-16). The third time Jesus resorts to Peter's language and asks if he loves him with *philia* love, whereupon the narrator declares that Peter was hurt because the Lord asked him a third time if he loved him (21:17). Raymond Brown argues that these two terms for love are basically interchangeable in John, and he is correct. However, the fact that Peter's anguish over Jesus' third question is mentioned makes this something less than a simple affirmation. Peter is reformed, but it is an ambivalent reinstatement. We may infer that Petrine leadership will be as valid as the degree to which it cares for, nurtures, and feeds the sheep and the lambs of the Lord's flock; anything less is a forfeiture of the charge.

As models of discipleship in the Fourth Gospel, the Beloved Disciple and Peter exemplify both correct and corrected ways to envision leadership in the church and in the world. Nothing can replace personal connectedness and intimacy with the Lord; that is a must for all disciples. Authentic discipleship must be willing to undergo danger and self-sacrifice, always concerned with serving others as the true mark of apostolic leadership. While Christ continues to lead the church by means of the Holy Spirit, present within the community of faith, human leaders also play a role in feeding and nurturing the flock. Charisma and structure go hand in hand, and yet neither is the sole answer; true discipleship hinges upon knowing the Lord's will and following his lead in loving obedience. This is what transforms disciples into apostles and servants into friends as Jesus' partners in the world (15:14-15).

Ultimately, however, the juxtaposition of Peter and the Beloved Disciple in John is not a matter of charisma versus structure, or more primitive familial organization versus emerging hierarchical leadership; it is about pointing to the ongoing leadership of the risen Lord, who continues to teach and lead through the workings of the Holy Spirit. Just as Jesus himself was the first advocate, teacher, and guide for his followers (1 John 2:1), he promises to send another *Paraklētos*, who will be with and in his followers forever (John 14:16). As the one whom the Father and Son will send (14:26; 15:26), the Spirit of Truth (14:17; 15:26; 16:13; 1 John 4:6) will teach them all things, reminding them of Jesus' teachings and guiding them into the truth they need for the day (14:26; 16:13). For any first-generation believers within the Johannine tradition, this promise bolstered their recalling Jesus' teachings in timely ways, as needed. For later believers the promise still held relevance, as they felt connected by the Holy Spirit to that which they had heard from the beginning (1 John 1:1). Here the testimony of eyewitnesses and their interpreters is confirmed in its implications and meanings for later believers by the witness of the Holy Spirit (John 19:34-35; 1 John 5:6-8). Even in discerning right and wrong when faced with ambiguous moral issues, the Holy Spirit convicts of both sin and of righteousness (John 16:7-11). As the risen Lord breathed on his disciples, inviting them to receive the Holy Spirit (20:22), their inspiration continues as effected by the Present Teacher. Here both institution and charisma share the same calling: to facilitate the attending, discerning, and minding of God's leadership, as revealed through Christ and as directed through the Holy Spirit, sent as an advocate, helper, and guide.

■ Conclusion

While hearers and readers of the Fourth Gospel are called to existential responses of faith as individuals, its thrust is not finally individualistic but communal. To believe in Jesus is also to be called to abide with him and his community, following his example and direction in loving one another as he has loved his own. Believers are called into relationship, with God and with one another, and if they will but yield to divine direction, their service and ministry in the world will prosper. Authentic worship is neither determined by place nor form, and empowered ministry is not a function of gender or status; these are ordered by the spiritual workings of the Holy Spirit at work within and among the members of the fellowship. The incarnational sacramentology of the Fourth Gospel conveys a profound truth: in choosing to be revealed to the world, God chose neither a written text nor a cultic form; God spoke in the flesh-bound life of a person. If one asks where God is encountered in the world today, the Fourth Gospel suggests it will also be in the lives of persons seeking to follow the Master, and the true evidence of Christian belief is the love that persons display in the world—again, an incarnated measure. In Johannine perspective, authentic leadership is neither positional nor coercive; it has its roots in relationship, and it nurtures the flock in service and in truth. The goal of every believer, of course, is following Jesus—both by embracing his example and by discerning his leadings. If that happens, Jesus' followers will know the truth, and the truth will be liberating indeed!

▦ Questions to Consider

1. Describe the Johannine presentations of worship and ministry and explain how these visions might be relevant for authentic religious life today.
2. Describe John's incarnational sacramentality and explain how this vision might pose a challenge to religious developments within Christianity as well as facilitating authentic spirituality.
3. Describe the juxtaposition of Peter and the Beloved Disciple in the Fourth Gospel and explain how it might reflect a challenge to rising institutionalism in the late-first-century situation, with implications for effective leadership in later generations.

▦ Terms to Understand

- *Shekinah*
- incarnational
- instrumental
- familial

Summation of Part 3

Having outlined and addressed the riddles of the Fourth Gospel, their interpretation follows readily. Given John's dialogical autonomy, understanding it as an individuated tradition developing parallel to, but not dependent upon, the Synoptics, allows the Fourth Gospel to retain its own voice. Rather than being a nuisance or a scandal, John's literary perplexities provide keys to understanding the composition and design of this distinctive narrative. Furthermore, considering the multiplicity of dialogical factors in the tradition's development and understanding the character and origin of John's theological tensions allows one to appreciate more adequately their meaning. Likewise, John's historical conundrums are eased in noting the way the Gospel's distinctive rendering of Jesus' ministry poses an alternative to Mark, while at the same time contributing modestly to the development of other traditions. Therefore, the Fourth Gospel can be seen as the key to interpreting the other Gospels instead of a scandal to them.

Finally, both the Christ of faith and the Jesus of history are elucidated in the Fourth Gospel, and John may yet contribute to the quest for the historical Jesus. This, of course, may require a *fourth quest* for Jesus. As the Fourth Gospel calls hearers and readers into relationship with God and with one another, the spiritual and ecclesial dimensions of its message are also enduring. One can understand why the Gospels of Matthew and John were favorites in the second century c.e. and beyond. They both emphasize learning about and from Jesus—a call to redemptive partnership with the Galilean Master in the world.

Conclusion

Navigating the Living Waters
of the Gospel of John

Nicodemus came to Jesus "by night" making bold claims about what he "knew" as a religious leader, while ironically revealing his ignorance of the ways of the Spirit in the ensuing discussion. Did he come around or did he remain in the dark? Notice that he stood up for Jesus in John 7 and was present at the cross, helping to bury the body of Jesus (19:39). Likewise, while the woman at the well initially misunderstood the offer Jesus was making, she came to see him as the Messiah. Not only did she believe, but she became an apostle to the Samaritans, bringing many to faith because of her witness. If Nicodemus and the Samaritan woman came around, maybe there's hope for today's readers, as well! Despite initial misunderstandings, or partial comprehensions of the Johannine message, fuller perspectives may yet emerge. Then again, as with every subject, the more we learn, the more questions we may have. Therefore, if this book even partially succeeds in its purpose, not only will readers have some questions addressed, but more questions will also be raised as we humbly realize how much we still do not know.

In navigating the living waters of the Fourth Gospel, though, how do we appreciate its theology, while at the same time not falling into the dogmatism of religious certainty that the Revealer seems to challenge? Put otherwise, how does one exercise a response of faith, like the formerly blind man in John 9, without claiming that "we see"—the flaw of the spiritually blind religious authorities? The way forward, in

Johannine terms, involves holding both poles of the Johannine witness together, in tension. In addition to appreciating the Son's faithful subordination to the Father, this is what makes him equal to the Father in terms of representation. While the glory of God is displayed in the advent of the *Logos*, that encounter is conveyed in the fleshly humanity of Jesus as the Christ. While Jesus as the revelational way, the truth, and the life provides singular access to the Father, the saving Light of Christ enlightens all humanity, at least potentially—according to the Johannine text.

To deprive the Johannine witness of its theological tension is to make it other than itself. Many of the classic theological discussions in the first half-millennium of the Christian movement found their resolution in restoring Johannine dialogical tension over against more monological doctrinal approaches, and the same would be true in later discussions. Appreciating at least something of the origin and character of John's theological tensions, as well as its historical and literary perplexities, will also facilitate a more adequate understanding of the content's meaning. Establishing such a base has central implications for taking the Fourth Gospel seriously, both personally and intellectually.

■ Feeling Included without Becoming Exclusive

Taking the Fourth Gospel personally allows one to receive the gift of divine love experientially as one welcomed into the family of God, while at the same time acknowledging the underserved character of that gift. It is not that we have loved God, but that God has first loved us that counts. This is the gift of divine grace that transforms the world, a gift at the heart of Hebrew Scripture, and it *must* be revealed because it is contrary to the conventional ways of the world. In the world people live by merit—deservedness. Deservedness, however, brings judgment, which finally produces death. Therefore, the revelation of God's undeserved love is essential for the redemption of humanity, not because God requires it, but because humans cannot conceive of it on their own. No one has seen God at any time, and no one can come to the Father except by being drawn by God, which is what God's saving-revealing work does.

This also explains why revelation is ever an affront to religious and political systems. These operate transactionally, motivating particular behaviors and beliefs with instrumental systems of rewards and punishments. The divine initiative, however, operates transformingly—as a factor of truth and its liberating power; to receive grace is to be born from above. The revelation of God's undeserved love comes to humanity as a gift to be received, and, as Bultmann would say, humanity is faced with an existential choice: whether to respond for or against the Revealer.[1] Such is the crisis of faith, personally and existentially.

As an unmerited gift, though, grace is thus a humbling reality. One cannot take personal pride in receiving what is undeserved; one can only be grateful, and humbly so. Authentically to become a member in the family of God therefore leads not to exclusivity but to inclusivity. If one is mindful of one's insufficiency apart from grace, extending grace to others becomes a new and the only conceivable way of being. By their love for others will Jesus' authentic followers be known, and such will ever be the truest measure of discipleship. As the Johannine Jesus reminded his followers that he has sheep "not of this fold" who hear his voice and follow him, he likewise confronts later readers with the reminder that the love of God is an inclusive reality, not an exclusive one. Therefore, the character and conduct of believers should respond to friends and strangers alike as though they were members of the family of God—either actually or potentially. Again, our religious and political means of setting markers of inclusion effectively become boundaries for exclusion. On the other hand, if we raise up as the center of faith and practice God's transforming love and redemptive initiative, all are welcomed, and we serve one another in facilitating connectedness to the divine Center.

Therefore, in terms of personal encounters with God's gift of love, humans are invited to respond in faith to the divine initiative, which of course challenges all that is of human initiative. Is this not the heart also of the gospel, even in Synoptic and Pauline terms? Receiving grace creates a sense of humble gratitude and loving openness. In being welcomed into the family of God, authentic believers celebrate the gift of inclusion rather than becoming exclusive. For "such was ever love's way," as Robert Browning says in his timeless poem about the apostle John's reflections in his later years: "to rise, it stoops."[2] In leading, one must serve; in receiving life, one must be willing to release it; in knowing, one must acknowledge ignorance. In addition to personal responses of faith, appreciating the character and origin of the Johannine riddles facilitates one's intellectual engagements of faith with seriousness, without becoming dogmatic.

■ Responding in Faith without Becoming Dogmatic

Just as the best antidote to Johannine exclusivism is a stark confrontation with Johannine inclusivism, the best antidote to Johannine dogmatism is Johannine dialogism. To take the Johannine witness seriously is to be confronted not only with the dialectical presentation of its content, but also the dialogical character of its origin and development. Indeed, inferring the literal meaning of a text implies a proper appreciation of its literary form and context. Therefore, the dialectical character of John's theological, historical, and literary riddles deserves consideration before one can claim a particular meaning of a text, and several dialectical realities are at work on each of these levels.[3]

Theologically, the Johannine narrative is a product of *the Evangelist's dialectical thinking*, looking at a subject from one side and then another. His approach is a conjunctive one, operating in both-and ways instead of either-or dichotomies. Therefore, multiple sides of topics and themes should be considered in discerning an understanding of any aspect of John's theological content. Central to the narrative, however, is the *Mosaic agency schema*, wherein Jesus fulfills the prophecy of Deuteronomy 18:15-22, inviting a response to the agent as though responding to the one who sent him. While some characters in the story are scandalized by the Son's claims to represent the Father, that Jesus' word comes true shows that he fulfills the scriptural measure of authenticity. Finally, the *divine-human dialogue* represents the Johannine Gospel's larger theological framework, within which the mundane story of Jesus offers a time-changing gift to the world. As God has spoken at many times and in many ways, the flesh-becoming Word calls for humans to respond either for or against the Revealer. This happens within the story of Jesus and his ministry, but it is not limited to it. The Light that enlightens all humanity engages the divinely beloved world before, during, and after the ministry of Jesus—inviting a response of faith across the confines of time, space, culture, and even religion—or the lack thereof. In the Evangelist's view, to say yes to the saving/ revealing initiative of God is to receive the Father's gift of life and love through the operation of Christ, whether one knows the outward story of Jesus or not. And yet, the outward story is also important. In hearing it, the authentic believer's recognition of the gospel is confirmed and clarified; for others, an invitation to life-producing faith is thereby extended.

Historically, the Johannine tradition also shows evidence of several dialectical features that have influenced its development and presentation. The first involves John's *intratraditional dialogism*—reflection within John's tradition over earlier and later inferences of meaning and significance. This feature shows growth and development of perception and memory, as modified by experience and fuller understanding. A second feature of John's historical dialogism involves *intertraditional dialogism*—engagements with other traditions, either in complementary or in corrective ways. Especially clear is the way the first edition of John augments Mark, setting the record straight a bit here and there as well. Some mutual influence is discernible in the oral stages of the early Markan and Johannine traditions, as well as the later Johannine and Matthean traditions. A third level involves *the narrator's addressing the Johannine dialectical situation* as the narrative develops, crafting presentations of Jesus and his audiences within the text in ways that would engage later audiences beyond the text. Here, the narrative can be seen to address acute issues in the emerging Johannine situation, and this accounts for several features of John's theological content and rhetorical thrust.

Literarily, John's narrative declares its apologetic purpose with clarity, although with regard to earlier and later editions, we should use the plural, *purposes*. As the calling to believe in Jesus as the Christ, the Son of God, and believing to have life in his name represents a call to faith as the original purpose of the Johannine Gospel, the later material associates believing with abiding in Christ and his community. In that sense, the Johannine narrative invites both initial and continuing responses of faith, and the narrative thus functions on both evangelistic and pastoral levels. A second literary feature of the Johannine narrative is the way it invites the hearer/reader into community *experientially*, as a welcomed member of the divine family. Jesus' sheep recognize his voice individually, but they are invited into a flock corporately, wherein they are exhorted to love one another with the same measure of love they have received. A third dialogical feature of the Johannine narrative involves the constructed dialogues with Jesus, whereby the Revealer challenges conventional notions of later audiences and their miscomprehension in the story becomes a *corrective challenge* to still later audiences. Stupidity in a narrative, according to Mikhail Bakhtin, is always rhetorical. It rips off the masks of high and lofty authorities in the story, thereby challenging later audiences in their approaches to the truth.[4] In that sense, the reader is drawn into an imaginary dialogue with the protagonist, Jesus, and thereby drawn closer to the *truth*, which alone is liberating.

In these and other ways the dialogical origin and development of the Johannine tradition poses the most effective antidote to dogmatism. When the dialogical character of the Johannine witness is considered intellectually, monological readings of the text often fall by the wayside on their own. This is not to say, however, that the Fourth Gospel does not speak with a clear voice on particular issues. What it does affirm is that the full truth on any given matter usually transcends particular statements about it.[5] Therefore, the multidimensional character of truth deserves consideration within any approach to it. In that sense, the time-changing revelation of God's love comes to us not in the form of a doctrinal missive, but as the Incarnate Word, expressed not as an inanimate form or lifeless concept, but as a living, breathing, speaking, acting, feeling, thinking *person*. The only way to comprehend this subject is from the perspective of encounter—to behold the glory of the flesh-becoming Word, full of grace and truth (1:14). When that happens, the reader is moved from the Johannine riddles into mystery, where a new set of riddles emerges.

Notes

Preface and Acknowledgments

1. While I shall argue a cluster of new paradigms and theories in this book, length will not allow a full treatment of proposals argued elsewhere. Nor will extensive treatments of scholarly discussions be included in this book. Therefore, readers interested in fuller treatments of issues should consult the works referenced in the annotated bibliography and the bibliographic appendix.

2. The Chart of the Johannine-Synoptic relations (p. 151) was first published in Anderson 2006, 126.

Introduction

1. Attributed both to Augustine and Pope Gregory the Great, who describe Scripture as "a stream in which the elephant may swim and the lamb may wade," a recent application of this imagery to the Gospel of John is made by Paul F. Brackman, who said "Someone has described the remarkable character of this Gospel by saying that it is a book in which a child can wade and an elephant can swim" ("The Gospel according to John," *Interpretation* 6, 1952, 63). I develop some of these themes further in my Pendle Hill Pamphlet, Anderson 2000.

2. See Tenney 1948; Beasley-Murray 1991; Kirvan 2006.

3. See Kysar 2007; Eisler 1938; Wiles 1960.

4. This may be one of the most exhaustive outlines of John's problems and riddles, since the four *"Aporien im vierten Evangelium"* essays by Eduard Schwartz in the *Nachrichten von der Königlichen Gesellschaft der Wissenschaften zu Göttin-*

gen (1907-1908) over a century ago. Facing John's perplexities may be key to its meaningful interpretation.

5. Exceptions will be noted; the reader is encouraged to use any good translation, and even more than one, side by side, if serviceable.

Chapter 1

1. This term is used by Raymond Brown in his commentary as a means of dividing chapters 1-12 and chapters 13-20, which he calls "the Book of Glory" (1966, cxxxviii–cxliv). Most commentators since then have followed his lead with the same designation.

2. See essays on women in the Fourth Gospel in Brown, 1979, 183–98; Kysar 2007, 177–85; Schneiders 2003, 3–14.

3. Käsemann 1968.

4. William Loader 1981.

5. Borgen 1997.

6. Bultmann 1971, 60–63; Ernst Käsemann, "The Structure and Purpose of the Fourth Gospel," in his *New Testament Questions of Today* (London: SCM, 1969), 160–61.

7. Culpepper 1998, 116.

Chapter 2

1. C. K. Barrett, "Christocentric or Theocentric? Observation on the Theological Method of the Fourth Gospel," in his *Essays on John* (1982, 1–18).

2. Kysar 2007, 118–26.

3. Bultmann 1971, 218–19.

Chapter 3

1. I discuss six "planks" in each of these platforms in Anderson 2006, 43-99.

2. Anderson 2006, 8–37.

3. Now in its tenth year, the John, Jesus, and History Project is an international enterprise of scholars working on these issues. Its three volumes so far address "critical appraisals of critical views" (Anderson *et al.*, eds., 2007), "aspects of historicity in the Fourth Gospel" (Anderson *et al.*, eds., 2009), and "glimpses of Jesus through the Johannine lens" (Anderson *et al.*, eds., scheduled for 2011).

4. Cited by Eusebius, *Ecclesiastical History* 6.14, around 325 C.E.

5. This mistranslation was made by Arthur Cushman McGiffert in 1890, in his translation of Eusebius in the Philip Schaff and Henry Wace edition of the Nicene and Ante-Nicene Fathers library, Vol. 1 (Buffalo, NY: Christian Literature Publishing Co.), and it has wrongly become part of the standard scholarly appraisal of John in the English-speaking world for over a century.

6. In 2004, a second pool of Siloam was discovered, just south of the pool that has been called the Pool of Siloam for over a century now; see Urban von Wahlde, "The Pool of Siloam: The Importance of the New Discoveries for our Understanding of Ritual Immersion in Late Second Temple Judaism and in the Gospel of John," Anderson *et al.*, eds., 2009, 155–73.

7. Four gradations of symbolization are laid out in Anderson 2006a: non-symbolic, possibly symbolic, implicitly symbolic, explicitly symbolic.

8. Paula Fredriksen, "The Historical Jesus, the Scene in the Temple, and the Gospel of John," Anderson *et al.*, eds., 2007, 249–76.

9. Martyn 2003 (first published in 1968).

Chapter 5

1. Translated from the Latin in *New Testament Apocrypha, Vol. 1*, rev. ed., Wilhelm Schneemelcher, English trans. R. McL. Wilson (Cambridge/Louisville: James Clarke & Co. Ltd./Westminster/John Knox, 1991), 34–35.

2. Westcott 1886, v–xxxii.

3. Hengel 1989.

4. Richard Bauckham has argued this thesis with verve in *Jesus and the Eyewitnesses: The Gospels as Eyewitness Testimony* (Grand Rapids: Eerdmans, 2006).

5. Charlesworth 1995.

6. Brown 1979, 33; Schnackenburg Vol. 3, 1990, 375–88.

7. Ben Witherington III, "What's in a Name? Rethinking the Historical Figure of the Beloved Disciple in the Fourth Gospel," in Anderson et al., eds., 2009, 203–12.

8. On Simon the leper, see Kevin O'Brien, *But the Gates Were Shut: Operation of Jerusalem's Perimeter Gates within New Evidence and a New Methodology for Dating and Locating the Last Supper and Identifying the Beloved Disciple in John 13:25* (Bethesda: International Scholars, 1996); on John Mark of Alexandria, see Herman C. Waetjen, *The Gospel of the Beloved Disciple: A Work in Two Editions* (New York: T&T Clark, 2005); on a woman as possibility, see Robert T. Fortna, *The Fourth Gospel and Its Predecessor: From Narrative Source to Present Gospel* (Philadelphia: Fortress, 1988), xi; Thomas Butler identifies the Beloved Disciple with Mary of Bethany in *Let Her Keep It!* (Tracy, CA: Quantum Leap, 1998); Sandra Schneiders connects the Samaritan woman with the Johannine witness, 2003, 233–54. On the apostle Paul, see Michael Goulder, "An Old Friend *Incognito*," *Scottish Journal of Theology* 45, 1992, 487–513.

9. Haenchen 1984, Vol. 1, 24.

10. Friedrich Schleiermacher investigates the ministry and teaching Jesus using the Gospel of John in *The Life of Jesus*, trans. S. Maclean Gilmore (Philadelphia:

Fortress, 1975). His work was refuted by David Friedrich Strauss, *The Christ of Faith and the Jesus of History; A Critique of Schleiermacher's The Life of Jesus,* trans. Leander Keck (Philadelphia: Fortress, 1977); quotation from p. 41.

11. Haenchen 1984 1:34; see Anderson 2008a.

12. Fortna 1970.

13. When all features of Bultmann's stylistic evidence for disparate sources underlying the Fourth Gospel are applied to John 6 as a case study (there we should be finding four of his five major sources: signs material, sayings material, the Evangelist's work, and the redactor's additions), not only is the distribution inconclusive; it is nonindicative (Anderson 1996, 72–89). The style of the Prologue is distinctive, but the rest of John is largely unitive in its style.

14. Interestingly, while Bultmann describes modern theologians as operating dialectically, he fails to regard the Fourth Evangelist as a dialectical thinker. Here the cognitive-critical methodologies of James Loder (transformational knowing) and James Fowler (faith development) offer ways forward in understanding how early Christian leaders thought and taught about their experiences and understandings of the Jesus of history and the Christ of faith (Anderson 1996, 137–93; 2004).

15. Fortna includes the Passion narrative with the signs material and comes up with a self-standing (non-Johannine and Mark-like) text. However, to de-Johannify and re-Markanize a text does not a signs source establish (Fortna 1970; Anderson 1996, 90–109).

16. Barrett 1978, 42–66.

17. Barrett 1972.

18. Neirynck 1977; Brodie 1993.

19. Barrett 1978, 44–45.

20. Bauckham 1998.

21. In my comparison of John 6 with Mark 6 and 8, I find forty-five similarities between John 6 and Mark 6 and 8 alone, but no identical ones; John's literary dependence on Mark is implausible (Anderson 1996, 98–102).

22. In his new introduction Brown calls this feature "cross-influence" (Brown 2003, 102–4); I prefer "interfluentiality" to "intertextuality" (a term used by recent literary critics to denote the fluency of themes and ideas between traditions) in some cases, as the oral tradition was not yet a text.

23. Dunn 1991; also see Walter J. Ong, *Orality and Literacy; The Technologizing of the Word* (London: Methuen & Co. Ltd., 1982).

24. In John 6, for instance, at least three levels of dialogue are apparent in John's presentation of the feeding, sea crossing, discussions, and Peter's confession: an internal traditional dialogue between earlier and later impressions, dialogues with other traditions, and dialogues with audiences over several decades (Anderson 1996, 167–251).

25. Anderson 2006a, 2006b.

26. Such inferences often cite Erich Auerbach, *Mimesis: The Representation of Reality in Western Literature,* trans. Willard R. Trask (Princeton: Princeton University Press, 1953).

27. This is the approach of Bultmann (1971, 118–21) and history-of-religions scholars.

28. Look again at Box 3.10.

29. Anderson 1996, 187–92.

30. Anderson 2006b.

31. Anderson 2006a.

32. Gardner-Smith 1938; Smith 2001.

33. Brown 2003, 62–78.

34. Barnabas Lindars (1972, 50–51) refers to the later material as "supplementary" in that it could have been added over more than a single editing. While his view that the Lazarus material displaced the Johannine Temple incident is not compelling, his argument that John's later material included 1:1-18, Beloved Disciple and "eyewitness" passages, and chaps. 6, 15–17 and 21 offers the simplest and most efficient accounting for John's major aporias.

35. Ashton 1991, 82–101.

36. Ashton 1997, 12–13.

37. See also Barrett 1986.

38. See especially Smith 1984 and 2008.

39. Anderson 1996, 221–51; 1997; 2007a; 2007b; 2007d.

40. Therefore, it is not as sectarian as recent scholars have argued.

41. Anderson 2008.

42. Paul Duke wrote the first book-length treatment of irony in the Fourth Gospel (1985), Gail O'Day showed how John's theological claim was couched in narrative mode (1986), and Jeff Staley applied reader-response criticism to the text of the Fourth Gospel (1988). Mark Stibbe then explored the artistry of John's author as a storyteller (1992), Charles Talbert developed an approach to reading the Johannine Gospel and epistles in literary and theological perspective (1992), and Fernando Segovia edited a two-volume collection of new literary treatments of John presented at the national Society of Biblical Literature meetings in the early 1990s.

43. Richard Burridge, *What Are the Gospels? A Comparison with Graeco-Roman Biography,* 2nd edn. (Grand Rapids: Eerdmans, 2004).

44. Robinson 1985.

45. See the essays by Hofrichter, Berger, and Charlesworth in *Für und Wider die Priorität des Johannesevangeliums,* ed. Peter Hofrichter; Theologische Texte und Studien 9 (Hildesheim/Zürich/New York: Georg Olms Verlag, 2002).

46. Dunn 1983.

Chapter 6

1. Anderson 1996, 137–66; 2004.

2. Anderson 1996, 187–92.

3. Anderson 1996, 183–87; 2001; 2002; 2007c; 2008; 2010d.

4. With Bauckham 1998; Anderson 2006, 101–26.

5. See Barrett 1972, 49-50 (Barrett uses Jewett's translation of Plato—the soul's dialogue with *herself*).

6. On more about the origin and character of the numinous in religious experience, see Rudolf Otto, *The Idea of the Holy*, 2nd ed., trans. John W. Harvey (Oxford: Oxford University Press, 1958).

7. Anderson 2008, 2008b.

8. See Kysar's momentous change of opinion on evidence for *any* sources underlying John in *Review of Biblical Literature* 1, 2001, 38–42.

9. Anderson 1996, 252–71.

10. Anderson 1996, 137–66; 2004.

11. Anderson 1999.

12. Anderson 1999; 2008b; 2009b.

13. Meeks 1997.

14. Suetonius, *The Life of Domitian* 13; Cassidy 1991; Carter 2008.

15. Anderson 1996, 221–51; 1997; 2007b; 2007d; 2009a.

16. See Rensberger 1988. A fuller history of the competition between Ephesus and other sites for Roman imperial favors is developed by Stephen J. Friesen, *Twice Neokoros: Ephesus, Asia and the Cult of the Flavian Imperial Family* (Leiden: E. J. Brill, 1993).

17. In addition to hardship suffered from those "who claim to be Jews but are not" (Rev. 2:9; 3:9) and the problem of emperor worship, see also the host of moral issues faced by the churches of Asia Minor around this time as addressed by Revelation 2–3. Those claiming falsely to be apostles are scrutinized (2:2)—in particular the licentious Nicolaitans (2:6, 15); Antipas had been martyred in Pergamum, where "Satan has his throne," and the teachings of "Balaam" and "Jezebel" led to eating food sacrificed to idols and fornication (2:13-14, 20). Claiming to be "without sin" in 1 John 1:8 is not a factor of Gnostic perfectionism but a denial of certain practices being "sinful" by Gentile Christians, who had not yet left behind the immoral ways of the world (1 John 5:16-21) in the view of Jewish Christians. Anderson 2007b; 2009a.

18. Anderson 2007d.

19. Anderson 1997.

20. Anderson 1996, 226–49; 2007c.

21. Graham Stanton notes that the Gospels of Matthew and John are found coupled together in several second-century collections of the Gospels, suggesting

they both served didactic functions in the early church. *Review of Biblical Literature* 1, 1999, 53–56.

22. See esp. Anderson 2007b.

23. Anderson 1996, 194–224; 2007b.

24. This thesis is also developed in Anderson 1996, 274–77; 2010a.

25. Culpepper, 1994, 131. Polycarp also attests to having been a disciple of John the apostle in Asia Minor, and several Johannine themes can be found within his letter to the Philippians (doing God's will and walking in his commandments, 2.2; 4.1; to refuse to confess Jesus' coming in the flesh is to be the antichrist, 7.1).

26. Given Luke's extensive departures from Mark in Johannine directions, this associative connection is also bolstered by literary evidence. See Cribbs 1973; Matson 2001; Anderson 2002; 2007c; 2010a.

Chapter 7

1. Anderson 2008b.
2. Anderson 1996, 260–63.
3. Anderson 2007e; 2007f.
4. Anderson 2004.
5. Anderson 1996, 137–83.
6. Anderson 1996, 202–9.
7. Anderson 1996, 110–36.
8. Anderson 1996, 52–69; 1997, 17–24.
9. Anderson 2001; 2006, 101–54.
10. Anderson 2006, 154–73.
11. Anderson 2010b; 2010c; 2010d.
12. Anderson 2006, 175–92; 2006b.
13. Anderson 2008b.
14. Anderson 2007a.

Chapter 8

1. Oscar Cullmann, *The Christology of the New Testament,* rev. edn., trans. Shirley C. Guthrie and Charles A. M. Hall (Philadelphia: Westminster, 1959), 1–3.

2. See Alan Culpepper's treatment, 1998, 71–83.

3. Presentations similar to Boxes 8.1 and 8.2 were first published in Anderson, 2006, 57–58.

4. Anderson 1996, 174–76; 1999, 36–44; 2008b, 331–33.

5. Anderson 1996, 260–64; 1997, 32–40; 1999, 44–51.

6. Anderson 2008b; 2009b.

7. Anderson 1996, 167–93.

8. Anderson 2004.

9. Anderson 1996, 137–65; 2004a.

10. Anderson 1997, 28–32.

11. Abraham Heschel describes the work of the Hebrew prophets as facilitating the dialectic of Divine-Human encounter; that is precisely what the Johannine Jesus is presented as effecting. Abraham Joshua Heschel, *The Prophets* (New York: HarperCollins, 1962), 624–25.

12. Anderson 2007e.

13. Kysar 2007, 93–113.

14. Anderson 2010.

15. Although he has softened his view a bit since, according to Ashton, the Fourth Evangelist had Qumranic dualism "in his bones." *Understanding the Fourth Gospel* (Oxford: Clarendon, 1991), 237.

16. James Charlesworth's outlines of the parallels between Johannine dualism and that of *1QS* 3:14—4:26 (originally published in *New Testament Studies* 15 [1968–69]: 389–418) are slightly modified here.

Chapter 9

1. If the Q tradition (material common to Matthew and Luke, but not in Mark) is considered as well as the three Synoptic Gospels, the terse kingdom sayings of Jesus would be a four-to-one majority over the longer discourses of the Johannine Jesus. I appreciate Stephen Harris pointing this out, Anderson 2010d.

2. We may even need to reconsider the meaning of "history"—drawing critical theory on the subject into biblical studies, which ironically has been largely missing from historical-critical biblical studies. Anderson 2006, 175–92.

3. Appealing to "the theologizing interests of the Evangelist" often amounts to "theologizing speculation gone awry" when seeking to account for John's mundane and historical-seeming material. Anderson 2006a.

4. Anderson 2006b.

5. Anderson 1996, 170–93.

6. Anderson 1996, 194–220.

7. See Helen K. Bond, "At the Court of the High Priest: History and Theology in John 18:13-24," in Anderson, et al. 2009, 2:313–24.

8. See Derek M. H. Tovey, "On Not Unbinding the Lazarus Story: The Nexus of History and Theology in John 11:1-44," in Anderson *et al.*, eds., 2009, 213–23.

9. Articulating this misconception, Edgar J. Goodspeed, *An Introduction to the New Testament* (Chicago: University of Chicago Press, 1937), 310, declares:

> It must be remembered that topography and chronology were among the least of the author's concerns. His head was among the stars. He was seeking to determine the place of Jesus in the spiritual universe and his relations to the eternal realities. These were the matters that interested and absorbed him, not

itineraries and time tables, so that practical mundane considerations that might apply to Mark, Matthew, or Luke have little significance for his work.

10. Paula Fredriksen, op. cit., Anderson et al., eds., 2007, 249–76.

11. With the Jewish day beginning at sundown, this would mean that the crucifixion was less than fifteen hours later, *on* the Passover, as Mark's crucifixion was at 9:00 a.m. (the third hour, Mark 15:25). The Babylonian Talmud (*Sanhedrin* 43a) also asserts that Jesus was killed the day before the Passover, corroborating the Johannine rendering.

12. Urban von Wahlde, "Archaeology and John's Gospel," *Jesus and Archaeology*, ed. James H. Charlesworth (Grand Rapids: Eerdmans, 2006), 523–86. See also Albright 1956; Anderson 2006b.

13. In Mark 13:2, Jesus tells his disciples privately that not one stone of the Temple will be left upon another, but the public declaration of the Temple's destruction and its rebuilding is mentioned only in John.

14. Smith 1965, 44–51.

15. Coloe 2001.

16. This is Mark Allan Powell's thesis in response to Fredriksen's essay, "On Deal Breakers and Disturbances," in Anderson et al., eds., 2007, 277–82.

17. Based on the criterion of dissimilarity, Jesus' healing on the Sabbath is not a likely feature to have been invented; based on multiple attestation, it is confirmed independently in all four canonical Gospel accounts.

18. Ferdinand Hahn makes this point in his treatment of Jesus' self-conception as the eschatological prophet, *The Titles of Jesus in Christology* (London: James Clark & Co., Ltd., 1969), 352–406.

19. Marcus Borg, *Jesus in Contemporary Scholarship* (Valley Forge, Pa.: Trinity Press International, 1994); see Anderson 2006, 92–97.

20. Borgen 1997.

Chapter 10

1. Brown Vol. 1, 518–24.

2. Barrett 1982, 111–13.

3. The word for "dwelt" among us in Greek is *eskēnōsen,* evoking echoes of God's glory and presence in the tabernacle in the wilderness (Exodus 40:34-35; Leviticus 9:23; Numbers 20:6). See Coloe 2001.

4. Käsemann 1968, 76.

5. Anderson 1996, 112–14.

6. Anderson 1996, 110–36; 207–220.

7. Bultmann 1971, 218–37, 604–8.

8. Wright 1950, 81–82.

9. Anderson 1996, 221–51; 1997, 50–57; 2007a.

Conclusion

1. Bultmann's appraisal of John 6:35, where Jesus first claims to be the Bread of Life, is as follows (1971, 227):

> The whole paradox of the revelation is contained in this reply. Whoever wants something from him must know that he has to receive Jesus *himself.* Whoever approaches him with the desire for the gift of life must learn that Jesus is *himself* the gift he really wants. Jesus *gives* the bread of life in that he *is* the bread of life. . . . Whoever wishes to receive life from him must therefore believe in him—or, as it is figuratively expressed must "come to him."

2. Robert Browning, "A Death in the Desert," in his collection of poems, *Dramatis Personae* (London: Chapman and Hall, 1864), line 134.

3. In contrast to what Mikhail Bakhtin refers to as intellectual "monologism," dialogical narratives must be read dialogically lest they be miscomprehended. Anderson 2007b; 2008; Mikhail Bakhtin, *The Dialogic Imagination,* ed. Michael Holquist (London/Austin: University of Texas Press, 1981).

4. Bakhtin, ibid., 403.

5. With Rudolf Bultmann, "The Significance of Dialectical Theology for the Scientific Study of the New Testament," in his *Faith and Understanding,* ed. Robert Funk, trans. L. P. Smith (London: SCM, 1969), 146. The best of theological *and* historical operation bears in mind that few realities can be adequately described within a single statement or perspective.

Glossary

agency schema—the agency schema underlying the Fourth Gospel shows the Son's being sent by the Father as a representative agent.

anagnorisis—meaning "recognition" or "discovery" in Greek, this term refers to pivotal moments in Greek drama when the truth is encountered and a character comes to know something in ways significant.

aphorism—meaning a short, pithy saying that articulates a larger truth in a memorable way, likely the sort of speech used by Jesus as represented in the Synoptics and somewhat in John.

apologetic—a defense of an argument, often with a theological purpose in mind.

aporia—meaning "without passage" in Greek, this term is used especially to refer to literary perplexities that pose an impasse for interpreters. Rough transitions, problems with sequence, and other contextual problems affect one's views of how the Fourth Gospel was composed.

Bi-Optic Hypothesis—seeing John and Mark as "the Bi-Optic Gospels," each having its own distinctive set of impressions of Jesus' ministry from the earliest to the latest stages of their traditions; while Matthew and Luke built *upon* Mark, the first edition of John built *around* Mark.

Birkat ha-Minim—literally, "the blessing against the heretics," this term refers to the adding of a curse against the "Nazarenes" (that is, followers of Jesus of Nazareth) to the twelfth of eighteen benedictions recited in Jewish synagogue worship after the fall of Jerusalem in 70 C.E.

chiastic—a literary structure, wherein a pattern (ABC . . .) is repeated, often inversely (. . . CBA), as a means of showing both the symmetry of a unit and its emphasis—the pivotal fulcrum as its central turning point.

Christology—pertaining to theology about Jesus as the Christ.

cognitive-critical biblical analysis—the study of the roles human perception and experience play in the formation of biblical content and material, including explanations for different first impressions and histories of perceptual developments within traditions.

dehistoricization of John—the inclination to see the Fourth Gospel's literary and theological features as displacing nearly everything historical in its tradition.

de-Johannification of Jesus—the programmatic exclusion of the Johannine tradition from Jesus research, assuming its ahistoricity.

determinism—a doctrine inferring that humans have no choice as to their responses to God; those have been determined beforehand.

diachronic/synchronic—literary material that came together at different times and from different sources is called "diachronic" in contrast to a "synchronic" development, involving a similar time and origin of the text.

dialectical/dialogical—both terms are based on the word *dialogue*, but "dialectic" implies either a cognitive, sociological, or theological dialogue, while "dialogism" connotes more of a literary dialogue.

dialogical autonomy of the Fourth Gospel—the view that the Johannine tradition represents an autonomous and independent tradition, which develops in several dialogical ways—cognitively, theologically, historically, and literarily.

Docetism—from the Greek *dokein*, "to seem"; some Gentile Christians argued Jesus did not suffer or die, he just "seemed" to—that is, he was divine, not human.

dualism—the presentation of dual opposites within texts, either used rhetorically to motivate positive choices over negative ones, or reflectively to explain valued or disappointing developments or outcomes.

ecclesiology—the theology of the church (*ekklēsia*).

empiricism—the view that reality is determined and known by that which is ascertainable by the five senses.

eschatology—the study of last (*eschatos* means "last") things, assuming God acts with finality in human history.

familial—having to do with family-oriented organization and leadership and informal authority.

historicized drama/dramatized history—the first approach assumes historical detail has been added for the sake of verisimilitude; the second sees John as a historical narrative with rhetorical features added.

I-Am sayings (absolute; with the predicate nominative)—absolute I-Am sayings involve self-standing sayings; predicate nominative I-Am sayings involve a metaphorical reference.

incarnational—referring to the fleshly humanity of Jesus, as well as God's manifestation through human means.

instrumental—the affecting of an outcome contingent upon having a required action.

interfluence/interfluentiality—the phenomenon of influence in more than one direction between Gospel traditions, especially during their oral forms of development.

intertraditional dialogue/intratraditional dialogue—dialogical reflection likely happened within traditions (intratraditional) or between traditions (intertraditional).

Ioudaioi—literally meaning "Judeans," this term also means "Jews"—some of whom accepted or rejected Jesus as the Messiah in the Johannine narrative.

Logos—meaning "word," "principle," "thought," "reason," and "act"—this term is used as a Johannine reference to the means by which God communicates God's saving/revealing love, life, and truth to humanity.

Paraklētos—meaning "one called alongside (to help)," this term is used with reference to Jesus in 1 John and the Holy Spirit in the Fourth Gospel—an advocate, comforter, and legal counselor.

realism—an emphasis on plausible actuality versus theoretical possibility, based on either cause-and-effect inferences or verifiable aspects of a report.

referentiality—a means of assessing whether a report may be historical in its character on the basis of its being referred to as a known event or reality.

rhetorical—furthering a particular argument with the intention of convincing an audience of a particular assertion.

Shekinah—a reference to the glory and presence of God in Hebrew Scripture.

soteriology—the doctrine of salvation.

subordinationism/egalitarianism—raising the question of the Son's relation to the Father, as to whether it is on an inferior or an equal status.

theophany—the appearance of God, most directly associated with God's appearance to Moses via the burning bush in Exodus 3.

topography—having to do with spatial features and the lay of the land.

typological—following a pattern or "type" of a notable figure or example.

Annotated Bibliography

While the views of leading scholars are discussed tersely in the text above, the reader is encouraged to delve deeper into the leading treatments of John. The following list is *not* exhaustive, but should be considered a bare-minimum list of valuable texts to be considered for interpreting meaningfully the Fourth Gospel. A descriptive sentence has been added to each reference as a means of building an understanding of what the perceived value of each of these works is for the introductory reader; a list for scholars, of course, would include many more texts than these.

Leading Commentaries on John:

Barclay, William. 2001. *The Gospel of John.* 2 vols. Revised and updated. Louisville: Westminster John Knox. While not intended to be scholarly, Barclay's commentary on John is one of the most lucid analyses of the Greek text available, with thoughtful analyses of relevant ancient sources.

Barrett, C. K. 1978. *The Gospel according to St. John: An Introduction with Commentary and Notes on the Greek Text.* 2nd ed. London: SPCK; Philadelphia: Westminster. One of the finest exegetical commentaries available; with a keen sensitivity to theological issues, Barrett calls for interpreting the Fourth Gospel as a unity and argues for John's dependence on Mark and the Synoptics.

Beasley-Murray, George R. 1999. *John.* 2nd ed. Word Biblical Commentary 36. Nashville: Thomas Nelson. A thoughtful analysis of the text with helpful analyses of the secondary literature, this commentary is scholarly yet accessible.

Brown, Raymond E. 1966–70. *The Gospel according to John.* 2 vols. Anchor Bible Commentary 29–29A. Garden City, N.Y.: Doubleday. For over forty years now, this continues to be the strongest overall commentary on the Fourth Gospel—a first-rate set of introductory essays, excellent treatments of passages, and thoughtful treatments of secondary literature: a must for serious readers of John.

Bultmann, Rudolf. 1970. *The Gospel of John: A Commentary.* Translated from the revised German edition (1962) by G. R. Beasley-Murray, R. W. N. Hoare, and J. K. Riches. Louisville: Westminster John Knox. One of the most significant New Testament books in the twentieth century, this masterpiece of diachronic studies argues for sources underlying the Gospel of John, an extensive rearrangement of the text, and the editor's adding of disparate material as a means of addressing the Johannine riddles.

Carson, D. A. 1991. *The Gospel according to John.* Leicester: Inter-Varsity; Grand Rapids: Eerdmans. This is one of the best conservative commentaries in the last two decades, with keen analyses of the Greek text.

Ellis, Peter F. 1984. *The Genius of John: A Composition-Critical Commentary on the Fourth Gospel.* Collegeville, Minn.: Liturgical. This book poses a chiastic reading of the entire Gospel of John, breaking it down into sections with similar beginnings and endings and a pivotal theme in the middle.

Haenchen, Ernst. 1984. *John: A Commentary on the Gospel of John.* 2 vols. Ed. Robert W. Funk and Ulrich Busse; transl. Robert W. Funk. Hermeneia. Philadelphia: Fortress Press. An excellent diachronic commentary, made invaluable by its insightful introductory essays and expansive bibliographies.

Hoskyns, Edwyn C. 1947. *The Fourth Gospel.* Ed. Francis Noel Davey. London: Faber and Faber Limited. One of the most insightful British commentaries on John; its treatment of John's theological tensions and the relation between history and theology in the Fourth Gospel is especially valuable.

Keener, Craig S. 2003. *The Gospel of John: A Commentary.* 2 vols. Peabody, Mass.: Hendrickson. This excellent commentary provides the fullest treatment available of ancient sources—both Jewish and Hellenistic—in connection with their relevance to the Fourth Gospel.

Koestenberger, Andreas. 2004. *John.* Baker Exegetical Commentary on the New Testament. Grand Rapids: Baker. A first-rate Evangelical commentary on the Greek text of John, it also takes into account the Johannine situation illuminated by the Johannine Epistles.

Lincoln, Andrew T. 2006. *The Gospel according to St. John.* Black's New Testament Commentary 4. London: Continuum; Peabody, Mass.: Hendrickson. An excellent commentary with thoughtful analyses of literary, theological, and historical issues, this is one of the best British commentaries on John within the last decade or so.

Lindars, Barnabas. 1972. *The Gospel of John*. New Century Bible. London/Grand Rapids: Marshall, Morgan & Scott/Eerdmans. One of the best single-volume commentaries, its highly plausible two-edition theory of composition addresses most of John's literary aporias efficiently and simply.

Moloney, Francis J. 1993. *Belief in the Word: Reading John 1–4*;

———. 1996. *Signs and Wonders: Reading John 5–12*;

———. 1998. *Glory Not Dishonor: Reading John 13–21*. Minneapolis: Fortress Press. These three volumes provide an excellent literary interpretation of the Fourth Gospel by a leading Catholic scholar. This commentary moves effectively from the author's intentionality to meaningful interpretation by today's audiences.

Morris, Leon. 1995. *The Gospel according to John*. New International Commentary on the New Testament, revised edition. Grand Rapids: Eerdmans. A leading conservative commentary for four decades, this commentary argues John's apostolic authorship and independent tradition.

O'Day, Gail. 1995. *The Gospel of John*. New Interpreter's Bible, vol. 9. Nashville: Abingdon. An excellent commentary for interpreters of the text, this text is written lucidly with special sensitivity to theological and literary issues.

Ridderbos, Herman. *The Gospel according to John: A Theological Commentary*. Transl. John Vriend. Grand Rapids: Eerdmans, 1997. Arguing that the Evangelist was himself the "tradent" underlying the Johannine tradition, this commentary expands upon how the facts of the Jesus story are engaged theologically as impacted by the ongoing witness of the Spirit.

Schnackenburg, Rudolf. 1968, 1980, 1982. *The Gospel according to St. John*. 3 vols. Transl. Kevin Smith. Herders Theological Commentary on the New Testament. London/New York: Herder & Herder/Seabury. This major commentary rivals those of Brown and Barrett for being the best of commentaries in the last several decades.

Smith, D. Moody. 1999. *John*. Abingdon New Testament Commentary. Nashville: Abingdon. A measured and thoughtful commentary by the current leading Johannine scholar in the United States, this commentary interprets John's independent tradition helpfully within its social and religious setting.

Talbert, Charles H. 1992. *Reading John: A Literary and Theological Commentary on the Fourth Gospel and the Johannine Epistles*. New York: Crossroad. A leading literary interpretation of John, this commentary also yields excellent theological insights.

Temple, Stephen. 1947. *Readings in St. John's Gospel*. London: Macmillan. An insightful set of essays interpreting the Fourth Gospel, this book has been a favorite among readers of John, technical and otherwise.

Tenney, Merrill. 1948. *John: The Gospel of Belief*. Grand Rapids: Eerdmans. In addition to an analytical treatment of the text, this book includes valuable essays on John's distinctive features.

von Wahlde, Urban C. 2010. *The Gospel and Letters of John* (3 Vols.). Grand Rapids: Eerdmans. This major treatment of the Johannine writings argues for three literary strata of the Gospel with the letters written before its finalization.

Westcott, Brooke Foss. 1886. *The Gospel according to St. John*. London: Murray. A leading British commentary at the end of the nineteenth century, this commentary defends the traditional view of John's authorship.

Witherington, Ben III. 1995. *John's Wisdom: A Commentary on the Fourth Gospel*. Louisville: Westminster John Knox. This lucid commentary develops the wisdom-oriented features of the Johannine tradition in both Jewish and Hellenistic perspective.

Important Works on John:

Anderson, Paul N. 1996. *The Christology of the Fourth Gospel: Its Unity and Disunity in the Light of John 6*. WUNT 2/78. Tübingen: Mohr Siebeck. Third printing with a new introduction, outlines, and epilogue. Eugene: Cascade, 2010. This book seeks to identify the origins of John's christological tensions, introducing cognitive-critical methodologies to the investigation of Gospel traditions.

————. 1997. "The *Sitz im Leben* of the Johannine Bread of Life Discourse and Its Evolving Context." Pages 1–59 in *Critical Readings of John 6*, ed. R. Alan Culpepper. BIS 22. Leiden: Brill. This essay identifies four crises in the Johannine situation as viewed through the lens of John 6 and corroborated by the Johannine and Ignatian epistles.

————. 1999. "The Having-Sent-Me Father—Aspects of Irony, Agency, and Encounter in the Johannine Father-Son Relationship." *Semeia* 85, pp. 33–57. Two dozen points of contact are identified between the Prophet-like-Moses typology of Deuteronomy 18:15-22 and the Johannine Father-Son relationship.

————. 2004. "The Cognitive Origins of John's Christological Unity and Disunity." Pages 127–49 in *Psychology and the Bible: A New Way to Read the Scriptures,* vol. 3, ed. J. Harold Ellens and Wayne Rollins. Westport and London: Praeger Publishers. First published in *Horizons in Biblical Theology* 17, 1995, pp. 1–24. This study applies the cognitive-critical methodologies of James Loder and James Fowler to the analysis of Gospel traditions.

———. 2006. *The Fourth Gospel and the Quest for Jesus: Modern Foundations Reconsidered.* LNTS 321. London: T. & T. Clark. paperback 2007. A full-length treatment of the historical Jesus within the Gospel of John, including larger discussions of the issues; this work also outlines a fuller theory of inter-fluentiality among Gospels.

Anderson, Paul N., with Felix Just, S. J., and Tom Thatcher, co-editors. 2007. *John, Jesus, and History, Volume 1: Critical Appraisals of Critical Views.* Symposium Series 44/Early Christianity and Its Literature 1. Atlanta/Leiden: SBL Press/E. J. Brill. This collection features major reviews, methodological essays, a major case study, and an assessment of why this study is needed and why it is needed now.

———. 2009. *John, Jesus, and History, Volume 2: Aspects of Historicity in the Fourth Gospel.* Early Christianity and Its Literature 2. Atlanta/Leiden: SBL Press/E. J. Brill. This collection highlights many historical features in the Johannine narrative.

Ashton, John, ed. 1997. *The Interpretation of John.* 2nd ed. London: T. & T. Clark. The most valuable single collection of leading Johannine essays. The revised edition includes an excellent introduction to Johannine studies and recent essays on the new literary criticism.

———. 2009. *Understanding the Fourth Gospel.* 2nd ed. Oxford/New York: Clarendon/Oxford University Press. A major treatment of key issues, including John's composition, theology, and religious background, this book makes connections with Johannine and Qumranic dualism.

Barrett, C. K. 1972. "The Dialectical Theology of St John." Pages 49–69 in idem, *New Testament Essays.* London: SCM. This seminal essay explores the character of the Evangelist's dialectical thought processes.

———. 1982. *Essays on John.* Louisville: Westminster John Knox. This is a valuable collection of essays, especially helpful on John's history and theology.

———. 1986. *The Gospel of John and Judaism.* London: SPCK. This short book shows John to be the most Jewish of the Gospels.

Bauckham, Richard. 1998. "John for Readers of Mark." Pages 147–71 in Richard Bauckham, ed., *The Gospel for All Christians: Rethinking the Gospel Audiences.* Grand Rapids: Eerdmans. This essay argues that John was written for audiences that would have been familiar with Mark, thereby accounting for some of the particular contact between these two traditions.

———. 2007. *The Testimony of the Beloved Disciple.* Grand Rapids: Baker. While seeing the Beloved Disciple as an ideal figure, this book nonetheless argues for an independent eyewitness source of the Johannine tradition.

Borgen, Peder. 1997. "God's Agent in the Fourth Gospel." Pages 83–96 in *The Interpretation of John,* 2nd ed. by John Ashton. Edinburgh: T. & T. Clark. First published in Jacob Neusner, ed., *Religions in Antiquity,* Leiden: E. J. Brill, 1968, pp. 137–48. This important essay shows how the agent is in all ways like the one who sent him in Jewish Merkabah mysticism and also in John.

Brodie, Thomas L. 1993. *The Quest for the Origin of John's Gospel: A Source-Oriented Approach.* Oxford: Oxford University Press. Assuming that John was the last Gospel to be finalized, this book assumes Johannine dependence on other traditions, especially the Synoptics.

Brown, Raymond, E. 1965. *New Testament Essays.* Garden City: Image. This collection of essays contains several important works on such Johannine topics as historicity, relations to the Synoptics, and the sacraments.

———. 1979. *The Community of the Beloved Disciple.* New York: Paulist. The single most important text outlining a plausible history of the Johannine situation, this book outlines Brown's larger theory as developed in his Anchor Bible commentaries on the Johannine Gospel and Epistles.

———. 2003. *An Introduction to the Gospel of John: Edited, Updated, Introduced, and Concluded by Francis J. Moloney.* ABRL. New York: Doubleday. This new introduction to John, finalized by Frank Moloney after Brown's untimely death in 1998, reformulates his five-stage composition theory within three stages.

Burge, Gary. 1987. *The Anointed Community: The Holy Spirit in the Johannine Tradition.* Grand Rapids: Eerdmans. The leading treatment of John's pneumatology shows how Johannine theology reflects the experience of believers.

Carter, Warren. 2006. *John: Storyteller, Interpreter, Evangelist.* Peabody, Mass.: Hendrickson. This is an excellent introduction to John, interpreted in the light of its situation, literary features, and theological interests.

———. 2008. *John and Empire: Initial Explorations.* London: T. & T. Clark. Situating Johannine Christianity in Ephesus, this book explores the dialectical tensions between Johannine leaders and the imperial Roman presence in the late first-century C.E.

Charlesworth, James H. 1995. *The Beloved Disciple: Whose Witness Validates the Gospel of John?* Valley Forge, Pa.: Trinity Press International. In what is the most extensive treatment of the Beloved Disciple in the English language, Charlesworth argues that the best explanation for the independent Johannine tradition is a leading apostolic figure, whom he identifies as Thomas.

————. 2010. "The Historical Jesus in the Fourth Gospel: A Paradigm Shift?" *Journal for the Study of the Historical Jesus* 8: 3–46. In this important essay, Charlesworth calls for a change in Jesus studies—away from ignoring John to including John—acknowledging that the shift has already begun.

————, ed. 2006. *Jesus and Archaeology.* Grand Rapids: Eerdmans. This collection draws together over three dozen essays by leading archaeologists around the world, elucidating the ministry of Jesus as informed by recent archaeological research; three fifths of the gospel text references are to John.

Cribbs, Lamar. 1973. "A Study of the Contacts that Exist Between St Luke and St John." Pages 1-93 in *SBL 1973 Seminar Papers,* ed. G. MacRae. Missoula, Mont.: Scholars Press. In this significant analysis, Cribbs shows that Luke apparently depended on the Gospel of John as a literary source.

Culpepper, R. Alan. 1975. *The Johannine School: An Evaluation of the Johannine-School Hypothesis Based on an Investigation of the Nature of Ancient Schools.* SBLDS 26. Missoula, Mont.: Scholars. In outlining parallel communities and schools in the Greco-Roman world, this book sketches a plausible construction of what the Johannine "school" may have been like.

————. 1983. *Anatomy of the Fourth Gospel: A Study in Literary Design.* Philadelphia: Fortress Press. Arguably the most important book in Johannine studies over the last quarter century, this book offers fresh literary tools for analyzing the plot, characters, sequence and literary design of the Johannine gospel narrative.

————. 1994. *John, the Son of Zebedee: The Life of a Legend.* Columbia: University of South Carolina Press. This book traces the presentation of the son of Zebedee over several centuries, including both historical memory and heroic legend.

Dodd, C. H. 1953. *The Interpretation of the Fourth Gospel.* Cambridge: Cambridge University Press. In addition to a brief commentary section and excellent treatments of a dozen leading ideas, this book offers one of the best English treatments of the religious background of the Fourth Gospel.

————. 1963. *Historical Tradition in the Fourth Gospel.* Cambridge: Cambridge University Press. Focusing on the independent tradition underlying John's treatment of the Passion, works, and words of Jesus, this book offers arguably the most sustained and thorough investigations into the historical character of the Johannine tradition in the last half century.

Dunn, James D. G. 1983. "Let John be John." Pages 309–39 in *Das Evangelium und die Evangelien,* ed. Peter Stuhlmacher. WUNT 28. Tübingen: J. C. B. Mohr. In this important essay, Dunn argues for allowing Johannine individuality to stand without holding it to Synoptic standards in comparison.

Eisler, Robert. 1938. *The Enigma of the Fourth Gospel: Its Author and Its Writer.* London: Methuen. Noting the idiosyncrasies of John, this book argues for Lazarus as the Beloved Disciple.

Fortna, Robert T. 1970. *The Gospel of Signs.* Cambridge: Cambridge University Press. This book seeks to identify an underlying source within the Fourth Gospel involving the distinctive miracles and passion of Jesus.

Gardner-Smith, Percival. 1938. *Saint John and the Synoptic Gospels.* Cambridge: Cambridge University Press. Noting departures from the Synoptics at every point of contact, this book argues for the thoroughgoing independence of John.

Goodenough, Edwin R. 1945. "John: A Primitive Gospel." *Journal of Biblical Literature* 64:145–82. This important essay features the primitive material in the Fourth Gospel.

Hengel, Martin. 1989. *The Johannine Question.* Philadelphia: Trinity Press International. This book and its longer German presentation connects Johannine authorship with John the Elder, as an individuated firsthand memory of Jesus' ministry.

Hill, Charles E. 2004. *The Johannine Corpus in the Early Church.* Oxford: Oxford University Press. This extensive treatment of second-century treatments of the Johannine literature shows that the Gospel of John was neither a favorite of Gnostics nor disparaged by the orthodox.

Käsemann, Ernst. 1968. *The Testament of Jesus: A Study of the Gospel of John in the Light of Chapter 17.* Trans. G. Krodel. Philadelphia: Fortress Press. This important book sees John 17 as a last will and testament of Jesus for the church, seeing Johannine Christianity as being closer to the center of the Christian movement than the periphery.

Katz, Steven T. 1984. "Issues in the Separation of Judaism and Christianity after 70 C.E.: A Reconsideration." *JBL* 103:43–76. This essay challenges the Martyn hypothesis, arguing that Christians and Jews of the late-first-century situation enjoyed a good deal of fellowship and interaction.

Kimmelmann, Reuven. 1981. "*Birkat Ha-Minim* and the Lack of Evidence for an Anti-Christian Prayer in Late Antiquity." Pages 226–44 in *Jewish and Christian Self-Definition, Vol. 2: Aspects of Judaism in the Greco-Roman World*. Ed. by E. P. Sanders et al. Philadelphia: Fortress Press. This essay questions the view that a post-70 c.e. curse against Christians to be used within synagogues was either organized or effective.

Koestenberger, Andreas. 2002. *Encountering John: The Gospel in Historical, Literary, and Theological Perspective*. Grand Rapids: Baker Academic. An excellent introduction to the Fourth Gospel, including its riddles, this book offers a thoughtful and concise treatment of the text with many helpful study aids.

Koester, Craig, 2003. *Symbolism in the Fourth Gospel: Meaning, Mystery, Community*. 2nd ed. Minneapolis: Fortress Press. This is the best book available on Johannine symbolism, elucidating its character and functions.

———. 2008. *The Word of Life: A Theology of John's Gospel*. Grand Rapids: Eerdmans. This book offers one of the best recent treatments of John's theology by a seasoned interpreter of John.

Kysar, Robert. 2006. *Voyages with John: Charting the Fourth Gospel*. Waco: Baylor University Press. A leading expert on the Johannine secondary literature, Kysar here updates his earlier reviews of the Johannine literature and brings Johannine interpretation into the post-modern era.

———. 2007. *John, the Maverick Gospel*. 3rd ed. Louisville: Westminster John Knox. In its third edition, this is the leading introduction to the Fourth Gospel—dealing with the main literary, theological, and literary issues in readable ways.

Lincoln, Andrew T. 2000. *Truth on Trial: The Lawsuit Motif in the Fourth Gospel*. Peabody, Mass.: Hendrickson. The best of recent books on truth, testimony, and juridical presentation in the Johannine tradition, this book develops the lawsuit motif in John in ways that lead the reader to consider its argument in contemporary settings.

Loader, William R. G. 1981. "The Central Structure of John's Christology." *New Testament Studies* 30: 188–216. In Loader's analysis, John 3:31-36 can be seen as the central structure of John's Christology.

Martyn, J. Louis. 2003. *History and Theology in the Fourth Gospel*. 3rd edition. Louisville: Westminster John Knox. One of the most significant Johannine works in the last half century, this book sketches the history of the Jewish-Christian dialogues behind the Johannine text.

Matson, Mark A. 2001. *In Dialogue with Another Gospel.* SBLDS 178. Atlanta: Scholars. In its analysis of the Johannine-Lukan relationship, this book argues that Luke employed at least the Johannine Passion narrative as one of his sources.

McGrath, James F. 2001. *John's Apologetic Christology: Legitimation and Development in Johannine Christology.* SNTSMS 111. Cambridge: Cambridge University Press. John's apologetic thrust is analyzed in the context of its Jewish audience and its presentation of Jesus as the Christ.

Meeks, Wayne A. 1967. *The Prophet-King: Moses Traditions and the Johannine Christology.* Leiden: Brill. John's Christology in its Palestinian setting shows Jesus to have more than fulfilled the prophetic and kingly roles of Moses, inviting disciples of Moses to become disciples of Jesus.

O'Day, Gail R. 1986. *Revelation in the Fourth Gospel: Narrative Mode and Theological Claim.* Philadelphia: Fortress Press. John's narrative is analyzed in the light of its theological claims, yielding valuable insights into the rhetorical features of the Johannine narrative.

Painter, John. 2006. *The Quest for the Messiah: The History, Literature and Theology of the Johannine Community.* 2nd ed., revised and enlarged. London: T. & T. Clark. This book explores the quest narratives in John in the light of the community's situation history in both Jewish and Hellenistic settings.

Reinhartz, Adele. 2002. *Befriending the Beloved Disciple: A Jewish Reading of the Gospel of John.* London: Continuum. A sympathetic yet critical analysis of Jewish-Christian relationships as envisioned through the Johannine text.

Rensberger, David. 1988. *Johannine Faith and Liberating Community.* Philadelphia: Westminster. This book explores the social and political implications of the sectarian theology of the Johannine community in dialogue with Judaism and the larger world.

Robinson, John A. T. 1985. *The Priority of John.* Ed. J. F. Coakley. London: SCM. On the basis of the primitivity and autonomy of the Johannine tradition, this monograph challenges the assumed posteriority of John, arguing its priority as the first among the Gospel narratives to be written.

Schnelle, Udo. 1992. *Antidocetic Christology in the Gospel of John: An Investigation of the Place of the Fourth Gospel in the Johannine School.* Transl. Linda A. Maloney. Minneapolis: Fortress Press. This book illuminates the human and suffering features of John's Christology, seeing it as a challenge to Docetism in the early church.

Segovia, Fernando. 1996, 1998. *What is John?* 2 vols. Atlanta: Society of Biblical Literature. This is a landmark collection of essays gathering together new literary approaches to John.

Smalley, Stephen. 1979. *John, Witness and Theologian.* Rev. ed. London: SPCK. This book highlights distinctive features of the Johannine narrative, including treatments of John's development and theological thrust.

Smith, D. Moody. 1964. *The Composition and Order of the Fourth Gospel.* New Haven: Yale University Press. This monograph outlines the diachronic composition theory of Rudolf Bultmann and poses a constructive critique of the theory's tenability.

———. 1984. *Johannine Christianity: Essays on Its Setting, Sources, and Theology.* Columbia: University of South Carolina Press. In addition to dealing with the Johannine situation, this book challenges various views inferring Johannine dependence on alien sources or the Synoptics.

———. 1995. *The Theology of the Gospel of John.* Cambridge: Cambridge University Press. This book interprets John's theology in the light of its origin and situation.

———. 2001. *John among the Gospels: The Relationship in Twentieth-Century Research.* 2nd ed. Columbia: University of South Carolina Press. This book is the leading analysis of theories regarding John's relation to the other traditions, maintaining Johannine independence but not isolation.

———. 2008. *The Fourth Gospel in Four Dimensions: Judaism and Jesus, the Gospels and Scripture.* Columbia: University of South Carolina Press. Smith here develops John's relationship to Judaism, the historical Jesus, the other Gospels, and later readers.

Staley, Jeffrey. 1988. *The Print's First Kiss: A Rhetorical Investigation of the Implied Reader in the Fourth Gospel.* Atlanta: Society of Biblical Literature. This creative analysis of the rhetorical thrust of the Fourth Gospel introduces reader-response criticism to Johannine studies.

Thatcher, Tom. 2006. *Jesus the Riddler: The Power of Ambiguity in the Gospels.* Louisville: Westminster John Knox. This book develops the thesis that Jesus used riddles and ambiguity in his words and deeds as a means of transporting his audiences to higher levels of understanding.

———. 2006a. *Why John Wrote a Gospel: Jesus—Memory—History.* Louisville: Westminster John Knox. This book traces the development of the Johannine tradition from its oral stages of development to its written delivery—engaging friends and foes alike in the larger situation.

———. 2008. *Greater than Caesar: Christology and Empire in the Fourth Gospel.* Minneapolis: Fortress Press. The bold Christology of the Fourth Gospel must be seen in its defiance to its imperial Roman context; Christ has overcome the ruler of this world.

Thompson, Marianne Meye. 1988. *The Humanity of Jesus in the Fourth Gospel.* Philadelphia: Fortress Press. This book develops a clear incarnational picture of Jesus in John; he was not only a divine figure.

———. 2001. *The God of the Gospel of John.* Grand Rapids: Eerdmans. This book shows how the Father's authority to give life was entrusted to the Son—a theocentric presentation of Jesus as the Christ.

Van der Watt, Jan. 2008. *An Introduction to the Johannine Gospel and Letters.* London: T. & T. Clark. Catching the reader up on the best of recent Johannine scholarship, this text interprets the Johannine writings in their literary and historical contexts.

Wead, David. 1970. *The Literary Devices of John's Gospel.* Basel: Friedrich Reinhardt Kommissionsverlag. One of the first book-length treatments of its literary devices, this book features Johannine irony, double entendre, and other important rhetorical features of John.

Bibliographic Appendix

While my overall views on John's riddles and how to address and interpret them are laid out in this book, the discussions above are not as detailed as my fuller treatments of themes elsewhere. Therefore, in addition to pointing the reader to other publications in the notes, this bibliographic appendix provides a guide to other places where I have addressed these issues more fully—both in terms of engaging the secondary literature and providing fuller discussions of Johannine texts. The additional bibliography below augments the select annotated bibliography above, pointing the interested reader to other published sources where these theories are developed in further detail. For fuller treatments of important subjects, see the following works:

Engagements with scholarship:

Literature reviews of John's Christology and composition are found in *Christology* (Anderson 1996, pp. 1–69); literature reviews of historicity and John are found in *Quest* (Anderson 2006, pp. 1–37). An overall review of Johannine scholarship in the last several decades was published in *Expository Times* (Anderson 2008a).

Engagements with reviews of *Christology* were published in *Review of Biblical Literature* (Anderson 1999a), a reception report on the cognitive-critical analysis of Gospel traditions was responded to by James Fowler (Anderson 2004a), a response to reviews of *Quest* was published in *The Journal of Greco-Roman Christianity and Judaism* (Anderson 2009b), and responses to other reviews of *Christology* were included in the epilogue of its third printing in Anderson 1996 (third printing, 2010, pp. 330-58).

A review of literature on Qumran and the Fourth Gospel was published in a collection of essays on that theme (Anderson 2011).

Theological treatments:

John's theological issues, the flesh/glory of Jesus, the Father's relation to the Son, tensive relations between signs and faith, present and future eschatology, John's sacramentology and ecclesiology, etc., are covered extensively in Anderson 1996, and the epistemological origins of John's christological tensions are explored further in the Bauckham/Mosser collection (Anderson 2008b).

Cognitive-critical approaches to Gospel traditions are first laid out in Anderson 1996 pp. 137–69, and are taken further in the *Psychology and the Bible* collection (Anderson 2004; 2004a; 2004b).

John's Mosaic Agency Christology is developed most fully in the *Semeia* issue on the Father in the Fourth Gospel (Anderson 1999).

The Johannine Prologue and its theology are treated in further detail in the NIDB essay on "Word" (Anderson 2009b; see also 2008b).

Historical treatments:

Analyses of the Johannine community and situation are treated in a variety of sources: Anderson 1996, pp. 119–27 and 194–251; 1997; 1999; 2005; 2007a; 2007b; 2007d; 2008; 2008b; 2009a; 2010.

Aspects of Johannine historicity are treated in the essay in the Charlesworth collection (Anderson 2006b), Anderson 2006, pp. 43–99, and extensively in the *John, Jesus, and History* volumes (Anderson 2007; 2009; see also 2010a).

The historical Jesus in the Fourth Gospel is treated in the *Quaker Religious Thought* essays (Anderson 2000a; 2002a), the *Psychology and the Bible* collection (Anderson 2004b), Anderson 2006, pp. 127–73, and the *Bible and Interpretation* essays (Anderson 2010c; 2010d).

Literary treatments:

Source, redaction, and composition theories are covered most extensively in Anderson 1996, pp. 1–166.

The dialogical autonomy of the Fourth Gospel is introduced in Anderson 2006, pp. 37–41, and developed further in Anderson 2008.

A Bi-Optic Hypothesis and a *theory of interfluentiality* (mutual influence among Gospels) are developed in a variety of places: Anderson 2001; 2002; 2006a; 2007c; 2009b; 2010b; 2010d.

Rhetorical features of the Johannine narrative, drawing in the work of Mikhail Bakhtin, are developed in several places: Anderson 1996, pp. 194–97; 1997, pp. 17-24; 2007b.

The purpose of the Fourth Gospel is addressed most comprehensively in Anderson 1999.

Interpretive treatments:

Interpretive essays include treatments of faith (Anderson 2007e), truth and power (Anderson 2007f), and leadership and church unity (Anderson 2005).

A dialogical reading of the Fourth Gospel is developed in Anderson 2008.

Additional Works by Paul N. Anderson

2011. "John and Qumran: Discovery and Interpretation over 60 Years." Pages 15–50 in Mary Coloe and Tom Thatcher, eds., *The Fourth Gospel and the Dead Sea Scrolls.* Atlanta: SBL.

2010a. "Acts 4:19-20—An Overlooked First-Century Clue to Johannine Authorship and Luke's Dependence upon the Johannine Tradition." *Bible and Interpretation,* September 2010. online: http://www.bibleinterp.com/opeds/acts357920.shtml.

2010b. "From Mainz to Marburg—A Diachronic Exchange with the Master of Diachronicity and a Bi-Optic Hypothesis." *Bible and Interpretation,* August 2010. Online: http://www.bibleinterp.com/opeds/mainz357911.shtml.

2010c. "A Fourth Quest for Jesus . . . So What, and How So?" *Bible and Interpretation,* July 2010. Online: http://www.bibleinterp.com/opeds/fourth357921.shtml.

2010d. "The John, Jesus, and History Project—New Glimpses of Jesus and a Bi-Optic Hypothesis." online: http://www.bibleinterp.com/articles/john1357917.shtml. First published as "Das 'John, Jesus, and History' Projekt: Neue Beobachtungen zu Jesus und eine Bi-optische Hypothese." *Zeitschrift für Neues Testament* 23, 2009, pp. 12–26. Longer online version in English: http://www.znt-online.de/anderson.pdf.

2009a. "Revelation 17:1–14." *Interpretation* 63:1. Revelation as a Critique of Empire. January, pp. 60–61.

2009b. "Honest to John! A Response to the Reviews of *The Fourth Gospel and the Quest for Jesus.*" Pages 151–64 in *The Journal of Greco-Roman Christianity and*

Judaism 5. A response to four reviews of *The Fourth Gospel and the Quest for Jesus*, "John *Versus* Jesus?" by Jeff Staley, Matthew Lowe, Anne Moore, and Michael Pahl appears on pages 125–64. Online: http://www.jgrchj.net/volume5/JGRChJ5-7_Anderson.pdf.

2009c. "The Word." Pages 893–98 in *The New Interpreter's Dictionary of the Bible*, Vol. 5, edited by Katherine Doob Sakenfeld. Nashville: Abingdon.

2008. "From One Dialogue to Another—Johannine Polyvalence from Origins to Receptions." Pages 93–119 in *Anatomies of Narrative Criticism: The Past, Present, and Future of the Fourth Gospel as Literature*, edited by Stephen Moore and Tom Thatcher. Resources in Biblical Studies 55. Atlanta: SBL; Leiden: E. J. Brill.

2008a. "Beyond the Shade of the Oak Tree: Recent Growth in Johannine Studies." *Expository Times* 119:8, pp. 365–73.

2008b. "On Guessing Points and Naming Stars: The Epistemological Origins of John's Christological Tensions." Pages 311–45 in *The Gospel of St. John and Christian Theology*, ed. Richard Bauckham and Carl Mosser. Grand Rapids: Eerdmans.

2007a. "'*You* Have the Words of Eternal Life!' Is Peter Presented as *Returning* the Keys of the Kingdom to Jesus in John 6:68?" *Neotestamentica* 41:1, pp. 6–41.

2007b. "Bakhtin's Dialogism and the Corrective Rhetoric of the Johannine Misunderstanding Dialogue: Exposing Seven Crises in the Johannine Situation." Pages 133–59 in *Bakhtin and Genre Theory in Biblical Studies*, ed. Roland Boer. Semeia Studies 63. Atlanta: SBL Press.

2007c. "Aspects of Interfluentiality between John and the Synoptics: John 18–19 as a Case Study." Pages 711–28 in *The Death of Jesus in the Fourth Gospel*, ed. Gilbert van Belle. Colloquium Biblicum Lovaniense LIV, 2005. Leuven: University Press/Peeters.

2007d. "Antichristic Errors—Flawed Interpretations Regarding the Johannine Antichrists," and "Antichristic Crises: Proselytization Back into Jewish Religious Certainty—The Threat of Schismatic Abandonment." Pages 196–216 and 217–40 in *Text and Community: Essays in Commemoration of Bruce M. Metzger*, vol. 1, ed. J. Harold Ellens. Sheffield: Sheffield Phoenix Press.

2007e. "The Johannine Conception of Authentic Faith as a *Response* to the Divine Initiative." Response to John Painter's essay. Pages 257–60 in *What We Have Heard from the Beginning: The Past, Present and Future of Johannine Studies*, ed. Tom Thatcher. Waco: Baylor University Press.

2007f. "Power, Truth, and Christ," in *Quaker Religious Thought* #108, pp. 30–33.

2006a. "Gradations of Symbolization in the Johannine Passion Narrative: Control Measures for Theologizing Speculation Gone Awry." Pages 157–94 in *Imagery in the Gospel of John*, ed. Jörg Frey, Jan G. Van der Watt, and Ruben Zimmermann. WUNT II 200. Tübingen: Mohr Siebeck.

2006b. "Aspects of Historicity in John: Implications for Archaeological and Jesus Studies." Pages 587–618 in *Jesus and Archaeology*, ed. James C. Charlesworth. Grand Rapids: Eerdmans.

2005. "Petrine Ministry and Christocracy: A Response to *Ut unum sint.*" *One in Christ* 40:1, pp. 3–39. Online: http://www.georgefox.edu/discernment/petrine.pdf.

2004a. With J. Harold Ellens and James Fowler. "A Way Forward in the Scientific Investigation of Gospel Traditions: Cognitive-Critical Analysis." Pages 246–76 in *Psychology and the Bible: A New Way to Read the Scriptures,* vol. 4, ed. J. Harold Ellens and Wayne Rollins. Westport and London: Praeger Publishers.

2004b. "Jesus and Transformation." Pages 305–28 in *Psychology and the Bible: A New Way to Read the Scriptures,* vol. 4, ed. J. Harold Ellens and Wayne Rollins. Westport and London: Praeger Publishers.

2002. "Interfluential, Formative, and Dialectical—A Theory of John's Relation to the Synoptics." Pages 19–58 in *Für und Wider die Priorität des Johannesevangeliums,* ed. Peter Hofrichter. Theologische Texte und Studien 9; Hildesheim/Zürich/New York: Georg Olms Verlag.

2002a. "Jesus Matters: A Response to Professors Borg, Powell, and Kinkel." *Quaker Religious Thought* #98, pp. 43–54.

2001. "John and Mark—the Bi-Optic Gospels." Pages 175–88 in *Jesus in Johannine Tradition*, ed. Robert Fortna and Tom Thatcher. Louisville: Westminster/John Knox Press.

2000. *Navigating the Living Waters of the Gospel of John—On Wading with Children and Swimming with Elephants.* Pendle Hill Pamphlet #352. Wallingford, Pa.: Pendle Hill.

2000a. "On Jesus: Quests for Historicity, and the History of Recent Quests." *Quaker Religious Thought* #94, pp. 5–39.

1999a. Response to five reviews (by Robert Kysar, Sandra Schneiders, Alan Culpepper, Graham Stanton and Alan Padgett) of *The Christology of the Fourth Gospel: Its Unity and Disunity in the Light of John 6. Review of Biblical Literature* 1, pp. 62–72.

Subject Index

Name Index

Anderson, Paul N., xi, 151, 245–54, 262–63, 271–73, 275–77
Ashton, John, ix, 117, 187, 249, 252, 263–64
Auerbach, Erich, 249

Bakhtin, Mikhail, 152, 243, 254, 273–74
Barclay, William, 259
Barrett, C. K., ix, 27, 111, 123, 227, 246, 248–50, 253, 259, 261, 263
Bauckham, Richard, 118, 247–48, 250, 263, 272, 274
Beasley-Murray, George R., 245, 259, 260
Berger, Klaus, 122, 249
Bond, Helen K., 252
Borg, Marcus, 217, 253, 275
Borgen, Peder, 20, 118, 217, 246, 253, 264
Brackman, Paul F., 245
Brodie, Thomas L., 111, 248, 264
Brown, Raymond, E., ix, 10, 102, 115–19, 123, 169, 222, 233, 246–49, 253–54, 260–61, 264
Browning, Robert, 241, 254
Bultmann, Rudolf, ix–x, 22, 26, 34, 40–42, 106–12, 117, 123, 131, 141, 168–69, 208, 229, 240, 246, 248–49, 253–54, 260, 269
Burge, Gary, 264
Burridge, Richard, 120, 249

Carson, D. A., 97, 260
Carter, Warren, 118, 250, 264
Charlesworth, James H., 101–2, 122, 247, 249, 252–53, 265, 272, 275
Coloe, Mary, x, 253, 273
Cribbs, Lamar, 251, 265
Cullmann, Oscar, 251
Culpepper, R. Alan, ix–x, 22, 119–21, 123, 154, 222, 246, 251, 262, 265, 275

Dodd, C. H., 115, 265
Duke, Paul, 249
Dunn, James D. G., 122, 248–49, 266

Eisler, Robert, 245, 266
Ellis, Peter F., 260
Eusebius, 97, 99, 105, 145, 199, 246–47

Fortna, Robert T., 103, 108, 111, 141, 168, 247–48, 266, 275

Biblical Index

CPSIA information can be obtained at www.ICGtesting.com
Printed in the USA
268695BV00005B/5/P